Lanowce: Memorial Book of the Martyrs of Lanowce Who Perished During the Holocaust

(Lanivtsi, Ukraine)

Translation of
Lanovits: sefer zikaron le-kedoshei lanovits she-nispu be-shoat ha-natsim

Original Book Edited by: H. Rabin

Originally published by Association of former residents of Lanowce, 1970

A Publication of JewishGen
Edmond J. Safra Plaza, 36 Battery Place, New York, NY 10280
646.494.2972 | info@JewishGen.org | www.jewishgen.org

©JewishGen 2025. All Rights Reserved.
JewishGen is the Genealogical Research Division of the
Museum of Jewish Heritage – A Living Memorial to the Holocaust

Lanowce: Memorial Book of the Martyrs of Lanowce Who Perished During the Holocaust (Lanivtsi, Ukraine)
Translation of *Lanovits: sefer zikaron le-kedoshei lanovits she-nispu be-shoat ha-natsim*

Copyright © 2025 by JewishGen. All rights reserved.
First Printing: October 2025, Tishrei, 5786
Original Yizkor Book Edited By: H. Rabin
Project Coordinator: Sol Sylvan z"l
Cover Design: Rachel Kolokoff Hopper
Layout and formatting: Jonathan Wind
Indexing: Stefanie Holzman

This book may not be reproduced, in whole or in part, including illustrations in any form (beyond that copying permitted by Sections 107 and 108 of the U.S. Copyright Law and except by reviewers for public press), without written permission from the publisher.

JewishGen Press is not responsible for inaccuracies or omissions in the original work and makes no representations regarding the accuracy of this translation. Digital images of the original book's contents can be seen online at the New York Public Library website or the Yiddish Book Center website.

Library of Congress Control Number (LCCN): 2025937570

ISBN: 978-1-962054-30-0 (hard cover: 346 pages, alk. paper)

About JewishGen.org

JewishGen, is a Genealogical Research Division of the Museum of Jewish Heritage - A Living Memorial to the Holocaust, serves as the global home for Jewish genealogy.

Featuring unparalleled access to 30+ million records, it offers unique search tools, along with opportunities for researchers to connect with others who share similar interests. Award winning resources such as the Family Finder, Discussion Groups, and ViewMate, are relied upon by thousands each day.

In addition, JewishGen's extensive informational, educational and historical offerings, such as the Jewish Communities Database, Yizkor Book translations, InfoFiles, Family Tree of the Jewish People, and KehilaLinks, provide critical insights, first-hand accounts, and context about Jewish communal and familial life throughout the world.

Offered as a free resource, JewishGen.org has facilitated thousands of family connections and success stories, and is currently engaged in an intensive expansion effort that will bring many more records, tools, and resources to its collections.

Please visit https://www.jewishgen.org/ to learn more.

Director of JewishGen: Dr. Paul Radensky

About the JewishGen Yizkor Book Project

Yizkor Books (Memorial Books) were traditionally written to memorialize the names of departed family and martyrs during holiday services in the synagogue (a practice that still exists in many synagogues today).

Over the centuries, as a result of countless persecutions and horrific atrocities committed against the Jews, Yizkor Books (Sefer Zikaron in Hebrew) were expanded to include more historical information, such as biographical sketches of famous personalities and descriptions of daily town life.

Following the Holocaust, the idea of remembrance and learning took on an urgent and crucial importance. Survivors of the Holocaust sought out other surviving residents of their former towns to memorialize and document the names and way of life of those who were ruthlessly murdered by the Nazis. These remembrances were documented in Yizkor Books, hundreds of which were published in the first decades after the Holocaust.

Most of these books were published privately, or through *Landsmanshaftn* (social organizations comprised of members originating from the same European town or region) that still existed, and were often distributed free of charge. The languages used to document these crucial histories and links to our past were mostly Yiddish and Hebrew. JewishGen has undertaken the sacred responsibility of translating these books into English so that the culture and way of life of these communities will be preserved and transmitted to future generations.

In 1986, a group of farsighted JewishGenners started a project to pool their efforts together in groups based upon their ancestors' towns and donate funds to translate the Yizkor books of their ancestral towns into English. As the translated material became available, it was made accessible for free at https://www.JewishGen.org/Yizkor . Hardcover copies can be purchased by visiting https://www.jewishgen.org/Yizkor/ybip.html (see section below).

It is our hope that the translation of these books into English (and other languages) will assist the countless Jewish family researchers who are so desperately seeking to forge a connection with their heritage.

Director of JewishGen Yizkor Book Project: Lance Ackerfeld

About JewishGen Press

JewishGen Press (formerly the Yizkor Books-in-Print Project) is the publishing division of JewishGen.org, and provides a venue for the publication of non-fiction books pertaining to Jewish genealogy, history, culture, and heritage.

In addition to the Yizkor Book category, publications in the Other Non-Fiction category include Shoah memoirs and research, genealogical research, collections of genealogical and historical materials, biographies, diaries and letters, studies of Jewish experience and cultural life in the past, academic theses, and other books of interest to the Jewish community.

Please visit https://www.jewishgen.org/Yizkor/ybip.html to learn more.

Director of JewishGen Press: Joel Alpert
Publications Manager - Susan Rosin
Managing Editor – Peter Harris

Notes to the Reader

The images in the original book were reproduced from photographs from the time of the first edition. These reproductions were already of poor quality, most being pre-war and others at least 60 or more years old. As a result, the images in the book are the best achievable.
A reader can view the original scans of the book on the websites listed below.

The original book can be seen online at the Yiddish Book Center website:

https://www.yiddishbookcenter.org/collections/yizkor-books/yzk-nybc313849/rabin-chaim-lanovits-sefer-zikaron-li-kedoshe-lanovits-she-nispu-be-shoat

OR

at the New York Public Library Digital Collections website:

https://digitalcollections.nypl.org/items/c2f2d660-096e-0133-2fe8-58d385a7b928?canvasIndex=0

To obtain a list of Shoah victims from **Lanivtsi, Ukraine**, the reader should access the Yad Vashem web site listed below; one can also search for specific family names using family name option. These lists are continually updated by Yad Vashem, so it is worthwhile to periodically search them.

There is more valuable information (including the Pages of Testimony, etc.) available on this website: https://yvng.yadvashem.org/

A list of all books available from JewishGen Press along with prices is available at:
https://www.jewishgen.org/Yizkor/ybip.html

Additional Resources: https://kehilalinks.jewishgen.org/lanovtsy/lanovtsy.html

Sol Sylvan z"l (1993 – 2023) obituary:
https://www.legacy.com/us/obituaries/tricityherald/name/solomon-sylvan-obituary?id=52008557

Cover Photo Credits

Cover Design: Rachel Kolokoff Hopper

Front and Back Cover:

Color and texture by Rachel Kolokoff Hopper

Front and Back Cover:

Photo collage by Rachel Kolokoff Hopper. (Photos public domain).

Poem on Back Cover: *In memory of martyrs* by Rivka Perla (the granddaughter of Yitzhak Melamed). [Page 100].

Geopolitical Information

Map of Ukraine showing the location of **Lanivtsi**

Lanivtsi

Lanivtsi, Ukraine is located at 49°52' N 26°05' E 200 miles WSW of Kyyiv

	Town	District	Province	Country
Before WWI (c. 1900):	Lanovtsy	Kremenets	Volhynia	Russian Empire
Between the wars (c. 1930):	Łanowce	Krzemieniec	Wołyń	Poland
After WWII (c. 1950):	Lanovtsy			Soviet Union
Today (c. 2000):	Lanivtsi			Ukraine

Alternate Names for the Town:

Lanivtsi [Ukr], Łanowce [Pol], Lanovits [Yid], Lanovtsy [Rus], Lanowitz [Ger], Łanowice, Lanovitz, Lanovtse, Lanavtse, Lanivtsy

Nearby Jewish Communities:

Belozërka 8 miles SSE
Vyshhorodok 9 miles SW
Yampil 10 miles NE
Katerynivka 13 miles NW
Vishnevets 15 miles W
Teofipol 15 miles E
Shums'k 17 miles N
Bilohirya 17 miles ENE
Ozhyhivtsi 17 miles SSE
Podlesnoye 18 miles NW
Rakhmanov 18 miles N
Zbarazh 19 miles SW
Bazaliya 20 miles ESE
Stryyivka 22 miles SSW
Kam'yanky 22 miles S
Kremenets 23 miles NW
Pidvolochys'k 23 miles S
Volochysk 23 miles S
Kornytsya 24 miles ENE
Novyy Oleksinets 26 miles W
Bilohorodka 26 miles ENE
Velikiye Berezhtsy 26 miles NW
Kupil 27 miles SE
Pochayev 29 miles WNW
Kuniv 29 miles NNE
Skalat 30 mil

Jewish Population in 1900: 1,174

Table of Contents

Editorial Comment		2

Chapter 1:   **Lanovits, History and Experiences**

H. Rabin	Historiography	4
Shalom Avital	Lanovits at the Beginning and at the End	10
Motke Roichman	Man and his Environment	12
Eliezer Zinberg	Our Home in the Lanovits	25
Beiril Goldberg	Memories of My Family	27
Bluma Miller	My Shtetl and My Family	30
Bonia Stein-Spitzer	About Your Lanovits and my Aunt Elka Wolf Koifsitz	32
Shlomo Pacht	This Event Happened	33

Chapter 2:   **Lanovits-Holocaust and its Aftermath**

Moshe Rosenberg	In the Lanovits Ghetto, from the Beginning until its Liquidation	37
Meir Beker	The Lanovits Ghetto and my Escape from it	49
Issac Landau	Horror Journal	54
Shlomo Pacht	Lanovits-Majdanek, 1944	66
Shalom Segal	How my Daughter was Saved	69
Moshe Rosenberg	About Idis' Daughter	71
Byya Goldberg	Horror Details	72
Rivka Perla	In memory of martyrs	73
E. Rabin	Memorial candle	73
E. Rabin	I want to live	74
	Reply to a grandson	74

Chapter 3:   **In the Soviet Diaspora**

Feiril Melamed	Remembering Lanovits in My Wanderings	77
Aryeh Ginzburg	From Lanovits to the Soviet Union	79
Batya (Melamed) Taitel	This is How We Lived in Russia	84
Shlomo Taitel	An Addendum to Batya's Report	88
Joseph Weiner	My Experience Under the Soviet Regime	89
Mendel Brimmer	Difficult Separations	92
Zvi Meil	I Was in Lanovits After the Holocaust	97
Editors	Yosef Marder, Caretaker of Our Mass Graves	100
Mendel Brimmer	Moishe Marder	104

Chapter 4:	**In the Thicket of Redemption**	
Moni	Each Generation and its Zionists	106
Israel Glazer	First Hehalutz Branch in Lanovits	110
Zvi Brimmer	Hehalutz Hatza'ir in Lanovits	114
Sonia Shar (Shifman)	My Pioneering Days in Lanovits	117
Sarah Kitikisher	Beitar Hakhsharah in Lanovits	120
Etil Adler Spiler	Redemption that Ended Poorly	121
Moni	Dramatics in Lanovits	121
Josef Buchstein	Changes in Class Standing in Lanovits	124
Shalom Avital	Youth and Its Yearning	127
Cherna Rabin	In Memory of Those Friends that Perished	129
Chapter 5:	**Significant Persons and Dr. Zinberg**	
Hayim Rabin	The Legacy of Lanovits in the Writings of Dr. Y. Zinberg	134
David K'na'any	The Author and his Project	138
Eliezer Zinberg	In Memory of Yisroel Zinberg	141
D.A.	Zinberg's Heritage and Posterity	145
Ozer Lerner	Our Late Rabbi Motel Speizman	148
Rabbi Aharon Wertheim	Rav Aharon Rabin, Our Last Town Rabbi	151
	The Late Reb Yisroel (Srulikol) Rabin	153
Lola Friedman Katilansky	The late Zeyda Katilansky	154
Editor	About Shaiky and Zuni (Rabin)	156
Lola Katilansky	Yosef Ozer Shprit	159
Rabbi Y. Opatovsky	Lanovits and its Notables	161
Ch. Livne	Feiga, the Bath Attendant	163
B. Harin	Leizer "The Greener"	164
Yeheskel Shmukler	Arenda Holders	167
Chapter 6:	**Lanovits in Legends**	
Ch. Rabin	Lanovits Legends	171
Editor	The Original Barons of Our Town	174
Yisrael Glazer	Experiences We Do Not Forget	176
Yizhak Meir Weitzman	Calling Up 4th to the Torah	177
Ch. Rabin	Yizkor for Lanovits's Martyrs	181
Chapter 7:	**Our Losses in Our Homeland**	
Ch. Rabin	Feiga Roichman (Nechtelman)	184
Yisrael Glazer	Our First Halutzah, Feril Yishpe-Gilboa z"l	187

H.M. Ran	The Late Zvi Rabin (1913 – 1946)	189
B. Y. Haran	The Late Shoshana (Rozhya) Stein-Koitel	190
Moni	Fotsi - Yizhak Gluzstein	192
Ya'acov Valaizi	The Late Avraham Roichman	193
Y. Glazer	The Late Y. Zingel	195
Y. Glazer	The Late Yizhak Kirshon	197
R. Hadar	The Late Hava (Mirochnik) Taichman	198
Editor	Hayya Fuchs	200
Ya'acov Fialkov	The Late Hayya Feiga Fleishman	201
Editor	Rav Glazer	202
Ch. Rabin	Yizhak Shemesh	203

Chapter 8: **Yiddish Section - Lanovits, History, People & Memories**

Ch. Rabin	Lanovits History and Memories	207
Yosef Warrach	Lanovits, a Spiritual Concept	210
Avraham Teichman	Lanovits, Types and Pages	214
Yosef Warrach	A Visit to Lanovits	224
Byya Goldenberg	A Few Family Remembrances	226

Chapter 9: **Death and Horrors**

Moshe Rosenberg	In the Lanovits Ghetto- From the Beginning until its Liquidation	232
Meir Becker	My Escape from the Lanovits Ghetto	232
Byya Goldenberg	How Our Rabbis Perished	232
Ya'acov Kagan	In Our Shtetl and Far Away	233
Aryeh Ginzburg	From Lanovits to the Soviet Union	236
Batya (Melamed) Taitel	This is How We Lived in Russia	236
Shlomo Taitel (Tamari)	An Addendum to Batya's Report	236
Joseph Weiner	My Experience Under the Soviet Regime	236
Yitzhak Weinstein	It pulled me…	237

Chapter 10: **Dr. Yisroel Zinberg**

Hillel Alexandrov	Zinberg Pages [and his archive]	244
H. A.	Zinberg's Archives	249
Avraham Belov	The Rich Archives of Y. Zinberg in Leningrad	251

Chapter 11: **People and Types**

Muni	Dina Kavkes	255
Muni	Uziel Chaim Mordche's	256
Sarah Fiks	Shalom Weisman	257

Shalom Kwaitel (Avital)	My Three Sisters	259
Yitzchak Weinstein	Regarding Zunye (Azriel) Rabin	260
Muni	Elazar (Luzer) Meil	262
Z. Katz (Rabin)	My Grandfather Akivah	264
Moshe Zak (Mexico)	My Family	265
Yechezkel Shmukler (Beit Yitzchak)	Farmers	266
Ch. R.	Shmuel Fisher, of blessed memory	270
	Alphabetical List of those Who Perished	273
	List of Homeowners of Houses Shown on Lanovits City Sketch	311
	Name Index for the English Edition	323

Lanowce: Memorial Book of the Martyrs of Lanowce Who Perished During the Holocaust
(Lanivtsi, Ukraine)

49°52' / 26°05'

Translation of
Lanovits: sefer zikaron le-kedoshei lanovits she-nispu be-shoat ha-natsim

Edited by H. Rabin

Published by Association of former residents of Lanowce

Acknowledgments

Project Coordinator:

Sol Sylvan z"l

This is a translation from *Lanovits: sefer zikaron le-kedoshei lanovits she-nispu be-shoat ha-natsim*,

(Lanowce: memorial book of the martyrs of Lanowce who perished during the Holocaust); editor H. Rabin; Association of former residents of Lanowce; Tel Aviv, Israel, 1970

This material is made available by JewishGen, Inc. and the Yizkor Book Project for the purpose of fulfilling our mission of disseminating information about the Holocaust and destroyed Jewish communities.
This material may not be copied, sold or bartered without JewishGen, Inc.'s permission. Rights may be reserved by the copyright holder.

JewishGen, Inc. makes no representations regarding the accuracy of the translation. The reader may wish to refer to the original material for verification.
JewishGen is not responsible for inaccuracies or omissions in the original work and cannot rewrite or edit the text to correct inaccuracies and/or omissions.
Our mission is to produce a translation of the original work and we cannot verify the accuracy of statements or alter facts cited.

[Page 5]

Editorial Comment

As we publish the Lanovits book we basically let the remnants of our community commit to print their deepest memories. These memories are part of their reality. Their story is the story of townsmen who thought they were contributing to the Ukrainian economy. They stole neither their neighbors' fields nor their assets. They practiced the crafts known to them, without pushing out anyone else.

These Jews wanted to live in a quiet place, untouched by history, where they could develop their culture, and practice their religion. It was there they planned to await their redeemer to lead them to the Promised Land. As they managed through their thrift to reach a reasonable standard of living, their Gentile friends destroyed them.

This was a town of good, thoughtful and interesting people. Its youths dreamt of a better future, while sensing the fermentation within the Russian administration. The town had its creative people and its Hasidim who left their mark on its citizens.

The generations who follow us need to know that our parents were people of faith. They believed in the goodness of men and were let down. Gentiles not only disappointed us, they disappointed themselves.

Lanovits is no longer. Its residents were killed in a most cruel manner by members of one of the most enlightened nations of this century.

[Page 6]

Those who survived this tragedy are in a position to describe its details with accuracy and candor. Their stories are testimony to the animal spirit in man. The rulers of the world need to realize that a safe place for Jews (in Israel) contributes to world peace.

We endeavored in our book to provide an accurate description of our town's culture; of a community fenced-in by its religious faith, but also subject to nationalist aspirations and international hopes (socialism).

The culture of Lanovits is described in order to emphasize all that was lost with its demise. It is a reminder to small nations what can happen to them when they remain undefended. The individual stories serve to illustrate the spirit of our town.

Let the testimony of each of our survivors be a warning to all of us as to what can happen.

[Page 7]

This book describes the Lanovits community as it was. As such, it can serve as a research tool to social scientists who wish to better understand the source of strength that made it possible to maintain a successful autonomous community for hundreds of years. The book can also serve as a source of documentation to the government of Israel should it in future wish to demand compensation from Germany and the USSR.

Above all, the book is to serve as a fitting testimony by which to commemorate all those of our community who perished in the Holocaust. Let their memory never fade.

[Page 8] [Blank] [Page 9]

Chapter 1:

Lanovits, History and Experiences

[Page 10] [Blank] [Page 11]

Historiography

By H. Rabin

Lanovits in the sources and "Lanovits Journal"
(Historiographical review)

It is difficult to establish accurately when Lanovits was founded. There are only a few sources and their authenticity is doubtful. In our research, we tried to weigh the scientific evidence as to when the town was founded. This evidence contradicts the local legends that had developed over time. Let us instead quote from the notes of our beloved historian, the late Shmuel Auerbuch, who dedicated his last years in the United States to record the history of his town in his journal. His work shows the influence on him of his first twenty years growing up in Lanovits. According to his research, the town was founded in 1625. However, Lanovits is already mentioned in the list of towns composed by the Council of Four Lands [Active from the middle of the 16th century to 1764-Ed]. According to these notes Lanovits was listed as being in the province of Vohlyn as an organized legal community.

From other historical sources such as census and tax records, we learn that the town was given to Pashkov Yalowicki [Ref.: Illostrovi Pashwadni po Vohlyn] in 1444, and to the Kozminska family in 1545.

In all the geographical encyclopedias, Lanovits appears to be a Jewish town, separated by 12 km. from the Ukrainian village of Laniwitz.

[Page 12]

The town of Burchiwky, between the two, appears to have been the district town. According to these sources, it is reasonable to assume that Lanovits existed since the 15th century.

According to the (Polish) "Slovnik Georgraphichny" published in 1902, a publication noted for its anti-Semitic bias, Yalowicki collected taxes (in Lanovits) from 15 garden plots, 15 smoke-stacks and 2 grinding mills. The dearth of garden plots indicates few farms, while the 15 smoke-stacks, to differentiate from chimneys, suggests that Lanovits was already industrialized. This is another indication that the town was likely Jewish because in that historical period, Jews were the primary contributors to Russian industrialization.

The above mentioned period precedes the Jewish exodus from Spain. Who knows how Jews got to settle in Lanovits.

The Town's Residents and Their Occupations

We have better data starting in the first half of the 19th century and its second half. Yet some contradictions surface even in these periods. Slovnik Geographichny lists the town's inhabitants as 623, of whom 46% are Jews, i.e., 274 persons. Encyclopedia Evreyiska on the other hand lists 523 Jews based on the 1847 census.

The Slovnik data has over the years shown a tendency to minimize the minority population numbers. If we consider that the Slovnik data is based on taxpayer records, whereas Encyclopedia Eevreiska is based on census records, we can accept the latter data as the more accurate of the two sources. This data is further confirmed by the 1897 census showing the town's Jewish population to have risen to 1,174. It is reasonable to expect a two-fold increase in the population in 50 years, not a four-fold increase, as implied by the Slovnik data that was published 13 years after the 1897 census. We shall therefore accept the Encyclopedia Evreyiska as the more accurate data.

[Page 13]

According to the notes published by the late Mr. Auerbuch, Pani Laniwitz, the governor of Lanovits, published a flyer and sent messengers in the late 19th century to other parts of Vohlyn and Podolia to recruit settlers. In his flyer he cited the merits of settling on his land Jews responded to this publicity and came. They liked the jobs that were promised dealing with estate management and the sale of its food products.

In addition, Lanovits was blessed with sources of mineral water, a fact mentioned in the flyers and in Auerbuch's notes. This must be a reference to the seven springs that in our days were used to operate medical spas. It is assumed that the flyer's mention of mineral water sources was meant to attract persons wishing to develop them.

We arrive at the conclusion that Lanovits Jews based their economic future on trade in produce, truck farming, lumber, warehousing, management of public baths, the production of liquor, beer and charcoal, and flour milling. In summary, Jewish light industry existed since 1583 in Lanovits on a continuous basis.

Disturbances and Continuity of the Settlement

When studying the history of Lanovits, we cannot pass over the Khemelintsky revolt of 1648 without wondering why the town is not mentioned in any sources dealing with this period. The villages of Kozachak and Nadovka, near Lanovits, are mentioned in Sankiewicz's books as the launching pads for attacks against the Polish Counts. These historical sources provide accurate information about the fate of nearby towns such as Vishnivits, Vishugrod, Shumsk, Dubna, Kremenec and others. These sources detail that Tartars ruined one town, that another was destroyed by the Swedes or the Ukrainians. Inasmuch as Lanovits is not mentioned in any of these historical accounts, suggests that its continuity was left undisturbed by these wars. The question is why.

The best explanation available is that Lanovits belonged to the Russian Lord Yalowicki. Local Jews were protected by him, thus saved from attacks by local insurgents. By contrast, nearby towns such as Vishnivits, Kremenec, Dubna and Jampoli belonged to Polish Counts. These towns were targeted by insurgents and its Jews decimated. The Jews of Vishnivits were attacked twice, once by Ukrainians, and later by Poles who accused them of conspiring with the insurgents. Lanovits was saved this fate, thanks to the (political) efforts of the Yalowicki family. This family was a "black sheep" among the Russian nobility due to the liberal tendencies of its members. In the political struggles that followed,

[Page 14]

their non-conformist stand and support of proposed reforms helped them survive politically. The family supported all minorities regardless of nationality or religion, hence their support of the (Polish) Kosciuski revolt, their encouragement of Jews to settle on their land, and their protection of these settlers.

Lanovits apparently did not suffer internal community disputes under early Polish rule. The records of the Council of 4 Lands, that had the authority from the Polish king to adjudicate all Jewish internal disputes, show no judicial activity in Lanovits.

For several centuries, Lanovits was under a liberal administration that promoted development and public harmony. Under these conditions the town Jews lived undisturbed until the beginning of the 20th century. In this century, European nations in general and the Russian empire in particular were badly shaken. That was also the fate of Lanovits's Jews. In the 20th century Lanovits experienced the 1905-06 pogroms when the Russian Romanoff rulers tried to deflect the national anger at their defeat in the Russian-Japanese war onto "guilty Jews." Small pogroms occurred when Cheka bands robbed and beat up local Jews.

Lanovits also experienced the Petlura-Machno turbulence of 1916-1918 and the destruction caused by the soldiers of Polish General Heller. The resultant killing and destruction were not unique to Lanovits; they were experienced by the Jews of the entire region.

The Town As Described in "The Lanovits Journal" by Auerbuch

One need look at this journal as a recording of events in our community. Our editors reviewed its emotional content comparing it with facts that were independently gathered. To this end, the journal serves as a record of recent history of our town. It describes the public and social happenings of the community in the first half of the 20th century. From it we can learn the ethno-historic image of Jewish Lanovits.

According to the accounts in this journal, Lanovits was a bustling town. Its inhabitants were well established in the town and had strong commercial connections with the peasants of the surrounding area. In the beginning of the 20th century and in the 1920ies some of the youths of the town reached the conclusion that the town's future is bleak. They severed family and social connections and emigrated. The emigration was not for the purpose of redemption.

[Page 15]

They immigrated to America, to Argentina, and a portion crossed the (Austrian/Russian) border illegally and settled in Austria, the land of the liberal monarchy, one tolerant to Jews. The cause of emigration were the Polish residents who instigated friction between Ukrainian and Jews before they came to power. They oppressed the Jews after they became the rulers of the province (in 1920). Living among an incited Ukrainian population raised doubts about the future whenever political turbulence occurred.

In the 1920's, the Lanovits youths did not emigrate to Palestine. They did not view Palestine as a place of safe refuge or as a refuge at all.

The Lanovits community was then under the delusion that Hasidism promised: "to keep the Sabbath in full and wait for the redeemer." The leaders of the community did not seek solutions to Judaism's basic problems nor look for solutions. The thought was that adequate livelihoods will remain available because of the availability of Ukrainian peasant customers; that one could somehow always deal with the Poles. If one has to lower one's head under certain circumstances, there were historical precedents for such cases in our Musar books. The prevailing attitude was to thank God for one's livelihood and not seek more.

During the 1920ies, when a Yeshiva was established under the leadership of Rabbi Motel Speizman, a noted pedagogue, the secular schools attracted most of our youths. The maintenance of this Yeshiva with all its splendor became an example of the futility of return to biblical sources. The youths that attended the Yeshiva came away disappointed. The school provided neither general learning nor a livelihood. This group of students provided the source of ferment for a Zionist solution as a practical solution for the future.

It was then that Zionism as a solution began to be accepted. We have the first organized departure to Palestine (Israel Glazer, Yizhak Kirshon, David Gurewitch, Meir Rosental). A carpenter that was disliked in the community leaves for Palestine because they need carpenters. We suddenly find that Palestine solves both personal and global problems. The community's youths now started to make life decisions, disregarding its parent's or village wise men's opinions, whereas the town's community was still wrestling with routine issues that engaged it for generations.

Lanovits was noted for its learned men and capable businessmen. The latter were instrumental in having the railroad line built to connect Lanovits to larger towns. A Hassidic Rabbi's visit to the town was both a stormy attraction and a spiritual uplifting.

None of the happenings in Lanovits affected communities outside its area. The public was periodically concerned with issues affecting the selection of Rabbis. There were usually two camps, but both behaved with decorum.

[Page 16]

Most members of the community remained indifferent to these quarrels.

Two personal stories need to be mentioned that became significant beyond the confines of our town and the time they occurred.

The first is the arrival of Itzi Shrulis in Lanovits. His story includes a tragic element. We would not mention it, where it not for its social lessons. Itzi Shrulis, who married a young lady from Lanovits, and lived there, was unusually talented in art, music, philosophy and Jewish commentary. Yet he was only employed as a local teacher of young married students. The students loved and revered him. However, he was not offered a position of Rabbi in our town.

The reluctance of the community to employ him as a local Rabbi was on the surface because his brother, equally brilliant, was involved in cases of theft and robbery in the local area. Our leaders did not want to risk nominating him as their Rabbi if the next day the police would request that he appear as a witness for an inquiry into the deeds of his brother. In truth, the reasons for their reluctance to accept him were different. This episode sheds a light on the social image of the Lanovits community.

It appears that the Lanovits community could not deal with a person whose knowledge exceeded that of its best scholars, nor did it want to risk its reputation by hiring a Rabbi that dabbles in philosophy, sculpture and art. Even his students, who admired him, had reservation about his candidacy.

This person, who loved his adopted town, had to look elsewhere for a rabbinical position. He became the Chief Rabbi of Bessarabia. His fame reached Lanovits. The community could have regretted their decision, however, its leaders remained wedded to the wisdom of their decision against hiring him. The episode illustrated the small-mindedness of our community.

Dr. Israel Zinberg was saved from a fate similar to his predecessor, mentioned above, because his great talents were recognized by a much wider reading audience.

Dr. Zinberg, who had studied the Talmud, Zohar, & Halakhah sources and the accumulated Jewish literature saw danger signs that the latter may be lost. He was aware of the challenge that Hellenistic literature posed to Jewish literature in its day.

[Page 17]

He feared that Jewish literature that accumulated over the ages, since Talmud time, may, one day, be pushed into a corner and not be accessible to researchers who wish to study it. He made it his life goal to save its record. By composing a listing of this literature and its history, he was able to catalog it, and explain its significance to his readers [in his book "History of Jewish Literature" – Ed].

Israel Zinberg saw Lanovits history as a prototype of Jewish history. Its historical record raised danger flags for the (Jewish) nation's future. In the fixed ideas of its learned men, and the negative reactions to historical events, Zinberg identified a rhythmic pattern in Jewish life (periodic pogroms) that prevents the Jewish nation from advancing.

For Dr. Zinberg, Lanovits was a laboratory of ideas. For us who are the recorders of its history, Dr. Zinberg's perspective is an important addition to our records. Lanovits was able to give birth to a giant thinker and doer, but it could not adapt his ideas.

The town attitude remained unchanged. Its leading citizens believed that their humility, periodic ducking under pressure, pride in their heavenliness on one hand, and materialism on the other, will enable them to survive all those who want to harm them in the future.

Lanovits was known for its high cultural level. Its youths were familiar with world problems, and skeptical regarding their proposed solutions. However, the community leadership was too certain that past solutions to problems will work again. When the Holocaust hit Poland, it ended the life of a 500-600 year old community. Its long life was partly due to its having no evil intentions against others. As an experiment in peaceful living, it was an interesting challenge to war planners.

The evil hand that ended the Lanovits community terminated an interesting social experiment the world needs. A peaceful and creative world was lost. When towns such as Lanovits disappeared, Europe lost islands of good intentions and good people. Our loss is greater, but mankind lost institutions that had the ability to control international crime.

[Page 18]

Bibliography

Slovnik Geographichny
Published 1884
Editors: Phillip Solimersky, Bronislav Chalibowsky, Wadislaw Wolbesky

Lanovits

"…. A town on the Zhirek river that flows into the Moryn river. In 1970 (?) 201 houses were registered inhabited by 623 residents of whom 46% were Israelites. (The town includes) a Polish, Russian church, a Jewish Synagogue, 5 stores and 40 workshops. …. The town scheduled 3 market days per week.

The Cherkva was built by the landowner Yalowicki in 1857.

The Catholic Church was built in 1860 by Bishop Borowsky. The town was known for its curative mineral waters.

Slovnik Geographichny
Published 1902, addendum to 1884 Edition.

Lanovtse

A town located on the confluence of the Boha-Lovka and Zhirek rivers. Kremenec district, Bielzurka County; mail station Jampoli, 40km from Kremenec. 319 houses; 2376 inhabitants. …..In 1545 Lanovtse belonged to the Kominasky Count. It was later transferred to Count Yalowicki.

In 1583, Saveh Yalowicki collected taxes from 15 orchards, 15 businesses and 2 grinding wheels (owners).

Vohlyn Resources
Published 1919
Volhyn antiquities – Dr. Zygmund Morwitz. Art & Antiquities – Dr. Zygmund Pioterkowsky. First edited 1913. Published 1919.

…. Lanowtse, a small town given as a present by King Casimir to Pashkov Yalowicki. From then until 1863, the town remained in the hands of the Yalowicki family. That year, Lanowtse was sold at an auction as punishment for the support Yalowicki provided the Koscieuszko uprising.

[Page 19]

Since the 15C, Lanovits had a palace whose content is described in a document housed in the Polish National Museum.

…. Several large lakes are located near the town. One, named Borsokowitz, is located 10km west of the town, and created by the Horyn River, 5km long and 2km wide. The lake was emptied every 5 years to catch its fish. The catch brought in 100,000 Polish gold pieces to its owner every 3 years.

Sources: Ilustrovni Poshynadnik. Po Vohlyn – Dr. Michislav Orlowitz.

Lutsk. 1929

…. In Lanowtse existed a large fortress built by Pashkov Yalowicki. It remained in the possession of the family (until 1863) when it was sold by the Russian government at an auction. The town includes an Imperial Kasziul that was built in 1857 by Theodor Yalowicki after the former palace burned down. In the distant past, Lanovtse was the centre of the feudal land that included six villages encompassing an area of 80sq.km.

Pinkas of The Council of Four Lands
by Halperin

Lanovits – a Jewish settlement in the province of Vohlyn. (From) page 530 of Evereiska Encyclopedia, published 1908, edited by Dr. Y. Katnelson and Dr. A. Harkavy.

Lanovtse – a town in the province of Vohlyn, Kremenec district. According to the 1847 census, the Jewish community of Lanovtse consisted of 523 persons. According to the 189 census, Lanovtse had 2525 inhabitants of whom 1174 were Jews.

[Page 20]

Lanovits, Its beginning and End

by Shalom Avital (Kwaitel)

Lanovits was a typical Jewish *shtetl* [small town], located on the Horyn river between Yampol and Vyshynivets in the district of Volynia, Poland. These latter towns were also located on the Horyn river. This shtetl was not known for either famous people or historical events. Its charm stemmed from its residents, all warm-hearted Volynian Jews. These residents were hard-working people who maintained an orthodox way of life. Among them were tradesmen and professionals, Maskilim [free thinkers] and Zionists.

I am not familiar with when the *shtetl* [small town] was founded or with its history. Instead I shall cite my understanding, based on stories I have heard from community elders. The legend I heard was: The town was founded at the beginning of the 18th century. The surrounding land, where the town is located, was owned by a Polish nobleman (unnamed). He owned thousands of acres of local territory. On one occasion the nobleman went in his carriage to inspect his property. At the town's location his carriage sank in the local mud to its axles. The nobleman remarked that this location was only suitable for grazing. In Polish he called the area "Lan oviatz" [grazing land]. It is interesting that the residents of Lanovits called the village entrance area "Die Blote" [a floodplain]. These same residents waded through the mud of their local streets for years before these were paved, yet they singled out their entrance. The nobleman's prediction as to the area's attributes was accurate. The land surrounding the town included large areas suitable only for grazing, and some agriculture.

Lanovits's Jewish residents came originally from the surrounding villages and from Russia's interior. The Jewish population increased significantly over the decades. According to official census data, 523 Jew resided in the town in 1847. In 1897 it had 1774 Jews out of a total population of 2525. Before the Holocaust Lanovits had over 2000 Jewish residents.

The town's appearance was similar to that of neighboring towns. The great synagogue, located on a hillside, was its distinguishing feature. It was taller than its neighboring buildings, hence could be seen from afar.

[Page 21]

To a visitor approaching the town, it was a prominent landmark. In addition to the great synagogue there was a Beyth Midrash [prayer & study house], a Kloiz [a small synagogue for artisans], several Steebles [small Hasidic houses of prayer] and its main street named "Der Markt" [the market]. These were the landmarks defining the Jewish part of Lanovits.

Jewish life in Lanovits proceeded like a steady stream. For generations some Jewish families worked as artisans, as retailers or manning market stalls. The market took place once a week and drew to it hundreds of peasants from neighboring villages. This weekly market supported the livelihood of most of the Jewish residents.

In the Beyth Midrash the day's events, including politics, were discussed by the locals between the afternoon prayer and evening prayer. Public issues were, for example, the coming election of a Rabbi or gabbai [synagogue treasurer]. Similar discussions were held in the public bathhouse. Additional topics were local quarrels and slights concerning in what order a person was honored at the synagogue [the order of calling a congregant to the Torah reading]. These were the primary issues that concerned the local residents for generations until a new generation arose that was also interested in secular issues. New ideas regarding education and literature, Zionism and the settling of Palestine slowly penetrated the dark alleys (and homes) of Lanovits Jewry.

These new ideas were brought up by occasional visitors and itinerant tutors who came to Lanovits from afar. The orthodox fathers naturally fought against these new ideas of the younger generation. They called these youths *Sheketzim* [heretics, a term usually applied to Gentiles]. The local youth fought their elders stubbornly. The youths suggested that time had come to consider new ideas and discard the old. These arguments, which formerly took place in the Beyth Midrash, now, gravitated to within the local youth groups. They argued over the nature of the future, over physical culture, spirituality, literature, Jewish renaissance, the reclaiming of Zion, and so on.

The older generation was determined to preserve the old order, as if their survival depended on it. When the author's grandfather returned to Lanovits from America in the 1920s, he went to pray in his accustomed Beyth Midrash. He felt like an old-timer returning to his inn. Before his return to Lanovits my grandfather managed to absorb some of the new concepts of the bigger world. Consequently, he could not acquiesce to local sanitary conditions that had existed for generations. Before the Passover holiday, he, on his own initiative, performed a daring act. He hired a woman to wash the Beyth Midrash floor in honor of the coming holiday. The act caused a storm in town. For generation there existed a tradition of sweeping the facility floor with a broom made of reeds, claimed the head of the orthodox faction Reb Yankel, a learned Jew, and here comes an "American" Jew and introduces *Goyish* [Gentile] standards.

* * *

What cannot be achieved by wisdom is sometimes facilitated by the passing of time. The general developments (i.e. cultural and political) in the life of the community also affected the older generation, especially after the 1917 Balfour declaration [statement by the then British foreign minister, stating that the Britain favors the establishment of a Jewish homeland in Palestine]. As the idea of redemption (return to Zion) became more real, the attitude of the older generation toward Zionism changed with it. Whereas hospitality to all visitors was an important value heretofore, now the needs of Zion became the locals' chief concern. Rich and poor contributed to the national [Zionist, e.g. KKL] charities. To them it became a holy objective that they revered.

This period was the Golden Age of the younger generation. New ideas emerged into daylight. Young men were no longer regarded as heretics by their parents. Teachers were no longer persecuted for their national activities. Zionist youth movements, which once functioned secretly,

[Page 22]

now sought actively to implement the Zionist ideals. A "Tarbut school" was founded where boys and girls received an education in the Hebrew language. The school had a Zionist orientation, instilling in the students a love for Hebrew literature. The school's library was one of the largest in the area. Zionist organizations, primarily *Hehalutz*, became rooted in the town, drawing to them the youth of the community.

While the attitude of the parents became more sympathetic towards Palestine, they remained ambivalent concerning the *aliyah* [immigration to Palestine] of their sons and daughters. The struggle between the generations was re-kindled. The parents wanted proud enjoyment from their offspring, that they should marry locally, and establish a family. The youth, on the other hand, absorbed the nationalist ideas to escape the Shtetl, to emigrate to Palestine, establish a home there, and have their parents join them later in their new home. Unfortunately, the Holocaust prevented a large portion of the youth from leaving the shtetl in time. In August 1942 most Lanovits Jews perished. Only a few who escaped into Russia survived.

Lanovits, as it looks now

[Page 23]

Man and His Environment in Lanovits

[His image in his Synagogue]

by Motke Roichman

Three synagogues existed in Lanovits. They were near one another on a side street. These were obscure buildings, unlike the churches of the Gentiles. The synagogues were built as if their inner light was to be hidden from strangers. They stood on a local hillside. The main synagogue was the dominant building. It was solid and beautiful architecturally, built with reddish bricks, decorated with purple curtains. Its exterior design was thoughtful, and its interior design was exotic. The building was well aired, having dozens of windows. Light and air filled the interior. The women's section was ten meters above the men's section. It appeared hung in mid-air on the base of carved wooden posts. Its design was a work of art.

This synagogue did not serve the community's elite. It congregants were the local proletariat: the tailors, shoemakers, carpenters, etc. These artisans enjoyed the beauty of their synagogue on the Sabbath and on holidays, as compensation for the dreary life during the week.

Reb [Mr.] Simcha, the tailor, had a prominent seat at the Eastern wall. He was a tall man with an eagle nose and a white beard spread over his broad chest. Known as "Der Damske Shneider" [a women's tailor] he was a learned man who knew his *Mishna* [Bible commentary], and *Ein Ya'acov* [a collection of legends from the Talmud]. In his professional work he handled the cloth cutting, leaving the fitting to his daughters. It was his way of insulating himself from the attractiveness of his women clients.

Next to him sat Reb Yosef Shneider in his permanent seat. He was short. His eyes were often red from tears he shed while reading the Psalms. He kept this book near him day and night, not parting with it while he fitted the slacks of his customers. In the same row sat Reb Reuven Shneider. He was of medium height, with a black beard including a few silver colored strands. He liked to quote a saying from *Pirkey Avot* [Ethics of the Fathers]: "Today's world is only a pathway to the world to come."

[Page 24]

One has to prepare oneself to enter the latter. To this end he requested of his sons, in his testament, that his gravestone be constructed of wood, using his heavy tailoring table. It was meant to be a testimonial that he, Reb Reuven, never benefited from the alms of strangers.

Next to the aforementioned sat Reb Selig, the tailor. His beard was thin, and his face lined as a result of his many worries. He mourned his bitter fate continuously. His only consolation in this world was his pride in his only son Abraham. The latter was nicknamed "Abraham the teacher." The son was short, modest and spoke softly. In his youth he befriended the sons of the local wealthy families. When he matured, and started to help support his family, his friendship with them dissolved. He tutored many of the town's children, sharing his knowledge with them. He taught them good handwriting and the basic four algebra operations. Like his father, he dreamed of a better world order as described by revolutionary writers in their brochures.

Reb Ber Avraham Moishehes sat, together with his sons, on the other side of a pillar, next to the same Eastern wall. Ber Furman (his nickname) was a horse dealer, also one who frightened those who met him. He was tall, muscular and broad shouldered. His arms could bear-hug anyone in his midst; his looks could kill. Horror stories circulated about him. One such story concerned an ambush he set for thieves who came to steal horses from his barn. He ambushed these thieves armed with an ax. The bodies of two Ukrainian terrorists ended at the bottom of the local river. After that he slept better at night.

The authorities ignored the above act, fearing Reb Ber's wrath. Another story concerned a violent Cossack who was in the habit of sleeping in Reb Ber's barn with his horse and load. When time came to pay for the service, he disregarded his financial obligation. This Cossack paid with his life. No one knows where he is buried. It was said of Reb Ber that whoever bothers him plays with fire. I remember an episode several days before his passing. He was already old, resting on his thick cane. Reb Ber was suffering from damaged lungs that made breathing difficult. His eyes protruded from their sockets. Realizing his terminal condition he insisted on going out to see his beautiful surroundings for the last time. He wanted to see the world that in the past had bent to his wishes, how it looked at the end of his life. He walked with difficulty. The town's children, watching him walk, laughed at his infirmity. These "town Lilliputians" angered their "Gulliver". He reacted to their taunts by striking the ground with his cane with such force that it broke into many pieces. He meant to tell them: I am still strong and able; you children better take heed of this fact.

Next to Reb Ber sat his eldest son, David Hirsh. David inherited his father's steel demeanor. He was a small copy of his giant father, but just as tough. His gaze projected authority. When he was angry he stammered. His second son Yerukham was more restrained. He had an athletic body and a short mustache decorating his lips when he smiled. He socialized with the town's elite, careful not to demonstrate his physical strength.

[Page 25]

He used his strength only rarely, but when he did, his victims suffered.

Once, in the 1920s, he demonstrated his strength in an altercation with Gentiles. That day a rumor spread in town that Gentiles were fencing the area known as *Die Blote* [a floodplain between two parallel rivers] to use it as grazing area for their cattle. This meadow had a thick green cover. Die Blote was bordered by two rivers that defined the space between the Jewish part of town and a nearby Gentile settlement. Lanovits Jews took advantage of this no-man's-land, regarding it as a gift for their children. Their children wandered the meadow, or played there after *Heder* [primary religious school] study hours. The Gentiles wanted to use the meadow to graze their animals. The peasants of the murderous village of Novosilky were certain that it would be possible to scare the Lanovits Jews so that they would give up use of Die Blote. The village of Novosilky had a number of murderers. One of them murdered my friend Monish, on the road between Vyshhorodok and Lanovits. He ambushed Monish, pretending to be his friend and murdered him in cold blood. The man was acquitted for lack of evidence. I trailed him for years, once striking up a conversation with him while he was drunk. He almost admitted his crime, but in the last moment bolted and escaped. During the 1942 liquidation of Lanovits Ghetto Jews, the Novosilky peasants participated in their murders. Let their cursed name be remembered for eternity.

I have many fond memories of playing in Die Blote. At the time we attended Heder, after school hours we children sometimes entered the gardens of Novosilky homes, picked their tobacco leaves and rolled ourselves "cigarettes." As scouts we once lined up on the meadow's sport field, each group under its flag, to welcome the local Polish bishop who was to arrive in Lanovits from his seat in Kremenets. We waited for him all day. He arrived late that night, ignoring both us and our town elders, who welcomed him with the traditional bread and salt.

On moonlit nights we walked in the meadow, singing songs about the beauty of Canaan. Die Blote was our heritage. The Gentiles wanted to block access to it. We were determined to defend it by all means. Of all the participants in this altercation I remember Avraham Weitzman, a short but muscular youth. With a wooden board in his hand, he smashed the heads of several young Gentiles. I especially remember the aforementioned Ber's Yerukham wandering through the melee unobtrusively, his knuckles in his pockets.

[Page 26]

He hit those Gentiles where it hurts, their rib and kidney areas. He leveled scores of them with his fist. The Gentiles retreated from the fight. Since then no attempt was made to fence off Die Blote.

After some time passed, the Gentile shoemaker Merker complained to me that since that fight he had been spitting blood. He cursed all the Russian Orthodox people for involving him in this fight. Merker grew up in the home of Leiser, the Jewish shoemaker, learned his trade there, spoke Yiddish and was familiar with Jewish customs. He felt as if Satan had lured him to participate in this fight. Someone hit his left rib. Since then, life had not been worth living.

The Great Synagogue

[Page 27]

My grandfather, Reb Zalman, had a permanent seat at the synagogue's eastern wall, though he rarely occupied his seat. Instead he prayed at the *Kloiz* [a small synagogue frequented by artisans] of Rabbi Ahareli. Reb Zalman was born in Shumsk (northeast of Lanovits). His parents were grain and flax traders. After he settled in Lanovits he opened a butcher shop to support his family. He used a saying that originated with Reb Mordechai Shumsker [after whom I was named] to explain his trade choice: "This way I can enjoy the weekly market without depending on its customers". My grandfather was an admirer of Rabbi Ahareli. He told us children of his great feats. One story concerned one of his daughters who suffered from strange belching attacks. Various doctors were consulted, including the specialist Andreyewsky from Yampol. None were able to help her. Only the Rabbi, through his prayers, brought about her recuperation. Since that event, Reb Zalman adored the Rabbi, stayed at his home, and shared the Sabbath meal with him.

My grandfather, Reb Zalman Shumsker, was a tall man. He had broad, sturdy, calloused hands. He was well built and had a blemish on his lower cheek that was hidden by his beard. His wife Khaya was, in contrast to him, a small woman, with light skin and a delicate face. She rose with him each morning. On winter mornings she rose before him to light the furnace. Each morning she prepared his favorite breakfast: breadcrumbs dipped in salted boiling water. After finishing his morning prayer he would wash his hands and sit at a cloth covered table. While eating he lamented the past that is no longer: when his breadcrumbs were dipped in liqueur, and his bowl full. After he said his blessings he would put on his sheep-skin coat, fasten his belt, and go on his way. At times he returned in the early morning hours from a nearby village. One time he carried a thin animal, which could not navigate the deep snow, on his shoulders. He wore heavy boots supported by horse-shoe-like plates. He was 70 at the time.

I loved him dearly. It was he who taught me how to ride a horse, and how to hold the reins when driving a wagon. Chaos spread through the town after World War I broke out. Children no longer attended their school. That summer I traveled with my grandfather to visit nearby villages. I would hold the horse's reins, while my grandfather sat next to me dozing off from time to time. He remarked how beautiful God's world is. "It is bad people who are spoiling it by killing one another".

I remember a bad experience on one of our excursions. We landed at an inn that also served as a dormitory for workers who laid new rail lines. These opened our area to the world at large. The Russian Czar assembled these work teams from various nationalities, allowing their transports and families to be near the work site. The work crews included Cossack, Tartar and Kirgis men. The men wore wide burlap slacks. Some had Taras-Bulba [Ukrainian nationalist] like mustaches, and a large ring in one ear. They usually chewed strong tobacco that they occasionally spit out. These men accosted my grandfather, plucking his beard.

[Page 28]

In his anger he fetched a wooden board and beat up his assailants. I, a little boy, bit one of them. On the return journey, while I was still angry and in tears, seeing my grandfather's face-scratches, he patted me on the head and said, "Do not worry my child. In each generation men try to liquidate us [as in the Passover passage], yet we survive while our enemies rot in their graves." My grandfather was a simple man, one who loved to quote from the Psalms.

Some of the water-carriers sat along the western wall, behind the *Bimah* [pulpit]. One of them, Avraham Iser, was a short man with a wispy beard that reached to his shoulders. His shoulders were indented, the result of wearing a yoke to support two water buckets for years. On weekdays he used the main synagogue's well, to earn his living. Supplying clean cold water to the community was his livelihood. He came to this well rain or shine. In the summer the well water was cold and clear. In the winter, on the other hand, one could observe a warm mist rising from its depth. Avraham-Iser maintained this well. He regularly oiled its chain and greased its wheel. This well-formed part of his existence. Even his deep voice resembled a sound emanating from a well. The well was his life. It fired his imagination and sustained him. He tended to drift into deep thoughts about matters from another world.

One story of his musing dealt with an episode that allegedly occurred on a snowy winter night. As Avraham-Iser filled his buckets at dawn one day, he felt as if someone was licking his ear. Fearful, he closed his eyes, thought of the unknown and said to himself: I knew that this would happen someday. Then he saw images: dead persons, wrapped in white cloth, floating downwards from the synagogue's women's section towards his back.

Another story concerned Gedalya, his son-in-law, given to stammering and of limited intelligence. Gedalya collected the small change he earned inside a dirty rag, then gave it to his wife. She was of small stature, yet prolific. In this manner she accumulated 50 rubles. Gedalya felt that something had to be done with so much money. The couple put on their holiday attire and went to the house of Mendel, the village headman. They asked Mendel to keep the money for them and give them a receipt. Gedalya told Mendel that he understood this custodial service was not gratis. He promised to pay for the service by delivering water to him without charge.

Opposite the eastern wall along *Die Spiegel Wand* [the mirror wall] sat Reb Michel the blacksmith, a short heavyset man. He suffered from a chronic kidney ailment, yet his hands were powerful. He tamed and shoed wild horses with ease, was good hearted, and had a ready smile. His two daughters from his second wife, Zisel and Odil,

[Page 29]

received a Hebrew education and were members of a Zionist youth movement. The parents were proud of their two daughters. The latter were readily accepted in the youth movement by daughters of more prominent families.

Along Die Spiegel Wand, next to Michel the blacksmith sat Reb Yisrael Racheles, the tailor. He resembled a tree trunk, had no hips. His gaze was hard, somewhat frightening. His house was located next to the Russian Orthodox Church. The rowdy Gentiles that congregated near the church feared him. The church was surrounded by birch trees and a stone wall. His misfortune was to live next door and regularly see its Jew-hating parishioners going in to pray. Inside the church one could smell the congregant's sweat as they kneeled in front of their Lord. The church's bells, spire, and cross were gold plated, giving prominence to this edifice. We children would whisper naughty words as we passed the church, spitting three times. Living next to the church bothered Reb Yisrael constantly.

Reb Yisrael was, by nature, a quiet person. Praying in the synagogue, he occasionally uttered a demand for silence, accompanied by a pounding of his *shtender* [a compartment in front of his seat that served to hold prayer books and a prayer shawl]. His voice had an aura of authority. Teenagers, accustomed to playing pranks on each other, feared him, hence sought a place to hide when they heard his pounding.

Reb Hayim-Yisrael, the *krupedernik* [barley miller] provided this service to Gentiles of the surrounding area. The mill was built entirely of wood. When it turned, it shrieked, sounding like an old tree that refused to split apart. The mill was turned by a mare wearing blinders. This mare had to exert a pull that sometimes exceeded her ability. She did her task while wading through her own excrement, working from dawn until dusk. Sometimes the mare tired, lowered her head and stood in place. Reb Hayim-Yisrael would utter a curdling shout. The mare would awaken and start her rounds anew. She applied her remaining strength to provide Reb Hayim-Yisrael's livelihood. On one occasion his shouts failed him. It happened in 1918. Ukrainian bandits led by Batko, a leading anti-Semite, shelled the town for unknown reasons from their position at the railway station.

[Page 30]

The first shell hit Reb Hayim-Yisrael's house, killing his mare.

While covered with flour on weekdays, Reb Hayim-Yisrael's appearance was radically different on the Sabbath. Washed and combed, with his black beard and humped nose his image was typically Jewish. He too insisted on complete silence during prayers. More than once during the repetition of the *Amidah* [silent prayer] or the Torah reading, chatter was heard from the women's section. They would discuss family matters, exchange recipes, what spices to use. On such occasions Reb Hayim-Yisrael would raise his head and shout: "Quiet down, you ducks." He was addressing our dear mothers, grandmothers and aunts. Their attendance in the synagogue was for them a relaxation, an opportunity to chat with one another. They yearned for the holidays, to see others and be seen. The women dressed in their finery, their heads covered with a colorful silk scarf. These scarves were of superior quality. They were passed down from one generation to the next, representing a great tradition. Carefully wrapped and placed in a chest, these scarves were passed on from mother to daughter or daughter-in-law. We children sensed the humiliation our mothers felt, being insulted in this way by Reb Hayim-Yisrael.

Most of the women attended only on holidays; hence their familiarity with the content and sequence of prayers was limited. They listened attentively to a *Zagerin* [woman prayer announcer] who guided them through the prayers. Familiar with the prayer book's content and prayer sequence, the Zagerin brought tears to the eyes of the women with her low-voice *nigun* [sing-song].

Among these listeners was my late mother. Our daughter is named after her. My mother was a city girl. She grew up in Kishinev [capital of Moldova], where she witnessed its pogrom. This experience influenced her mood for many years. She was a loner, keeping a secret that none around her would understand. I recall winter Friday nights. Our town was dark, suggesting it was rest-time. No traffic or noise was heard outside. Our oil lamp extinguished itself a while ago. At such times I would sit by my mother, next to the house stove, listening to her recollection of the Kishinev pogrom [April 1903]. That week, she recalled, Russian Orthodox priests organized a religious procession. Leading the procession were young men dressed in white, shaking their bells repeatedly. Behind them marched the long-bearded priests. They wore high hats and walked holding copper-clad staffs. These staffs were topped with silver ornaments to impress the viewing crowd. The priests lined up by rank, in a manner similar to how a cannibal tribe procession is described in children's books. Icons and crosses were carried by men following the priests.

[Page 31]

Behind them followed an ignorant mob. Each person carried a candle. The smell of incense filled the air. Church bells rang, reminding one of the auto-da-fee [Spanish inquisition]. In the procession's aftermath were Jewish dead and wounded and burned homes. The pogrom was carried out in the name of the messiah who is reputed to have counseled forgiveness. To this day no one knows who crucified him. Because of him, much Jewish blood has been shed for generations. These processions sowed fear in hearts of local Jews.

My mother was one of several daughters born to my grandfather Reb David. He was a learned man, and his clothing was always spotless. He usually wore a "Kotolok" [type of hat], a white shirt and bow-tie. He was the *Starosta* [village headman] of Bialorotky, a village near Shiputovky. Subsequently, he was called upon to manage the Jewish welfare organization of Kishinev, where he was employed for many years. In his later years he moved to Lanovits to be with his daughter, my mother. His resting place is in Lanovits.

My mother was a modest, quiet person, careful in her relations with others not to bring out their weaknesses. This she learned from the events leading to the Kishinev pogrom. My mother, a frail person, maintained her fine facial features in her old age. It was said she was a beauty in her earlier years. She was proud of her hair, the color of honey. Days before her passing, she combed and stroked it, as if to reminisce a pleasant past.

Next to my mother sat my aunt Feige, the wife of Reb Hirsh Roichman. She was from the village of Merinik, near Shumsk. One day we traveled to her village in a carriage drawn by four horses. With us was a bridegroom about to wed a girl from her village. The event occurred when I was a small child, yet the lively wedding celebration remains engraved in my memory because it differed from ones customary among Jews. The villagers received us with dancing and music. Young villagers, including the bride's brother, competed in a horse race and other sports. It was their way of demonstrating their beauty and skill to the bride and her guests.

[Page 32]

The bride, Feige's sister, radiated charm, health and energy, yet was restrained in her behavior. Her solid chin and bright, laughing eyes suggested a person who enjoyed life, and was able to meet its challenges. Her sons inherited her image and qualities. The family lived in this village for generations. They earned their living from agriculture, orchards and cattle trading. The father, Reb Yeheskiel Meriniker, was a tall, handsome man. He was the village's unofficial judge. He dealt with all manner of local Gentile conflicts, such as land border disputes, theft of goods or animals. His decisions in these cases were locally accepted as if they were "the law". He was assertive with locals and they respected him. His sons dealt with their neighbors similarly. On the wedding evening, when their young sister Sonia wed Yankel Perchis, the brothers scared the villagers when they shot a few bullets skyward from their pistols.

My aunt Feige was the main breadwinner of the family. My uncle and aunt were a perfect couple. Their relation was devoid of friction or arguments. Their life had its ups and downs, including hunger and suffering. Yet they shared a mutual understanding and affection throughout their lives. She was always generous to the downtrodden and needy. My aunt was able to immigrate to Palestine with her sons, settling in the town of Hadera (between Haifa and Tel Aviv). She found Hadera to be a blend between her original village and Lanovits, where she lived while married. Her new home in Hadera was always open to guests, especially those from Lanovits. She was like a mother to them. I remember how delighted she was to visit us in Jerusalem. After all, she would say: In the synagogue we always prayed to be in Jerusalem one day.

Her happiness came to an abrupt end. One tragedy followed another. Her husband, Reb Hirsh was murdered. Shortly thereafter her eldest son died as a result of a road accident. He was a talented businessman who could have made a career in Poland, yet the pull to immigrate to Zion was strong. Arriving in Palestine shortly before World War II, he applied his customary energy and became the family's bread-winner, while consoling his widowed mother. When he died shortly before his scheduled wedding day, she lost all hope, and died shortly thereafter.

Among the women who sat near the Zagerin was my aunt Hannah, my father's sister. She was known as *Die Kropnitsky*, the wheat miller. Hannah was a heavy-set woman with a serious appearance. Widowed for several decades, she developed a masculine-like character. She managed her household with determination, raised her children, Ephrayim, Michael and daughter Miriam, to respect work and show good manners. Due to her guidance, all her children became hard and honest workers.

[Page 33]

They worked hard at the mill, starting as children, helping their mother with the sale of flour to the town's women. The latter were accustomed to doing their own baking. Aunt Hannah had a good-heart but was quick to anger. When provoked she did not hesitate to use her fists aimed at the stupid faces of her Gentile customers.

The women who attended services every Sabbath, the "regulars", sat on the side facing east. These women were familiar with the order of prayer and its rituals. Each one sat in a permanent seat with a *shtender* [shelf] in front of her, holding the "Korban Minchah" prayer book. It was a thick, leather-bound book. Attached to the book's binding was a copper clasp to keep it closed. These "regulars" were not content with reading the Sabbath order of prayers. While other women followed the prayer ritual, the "regulars" busied themselves with additional readings from the Torah and other Bible sources.

My mother-in-law, Elka Yishpa, was among those who attended this synagogue. She was tall, tanned, her eyes brown. Her face radiated happiness. She smiled when with friends or with strangers, hiding the tragedy of her fate. She experienced only three happy years while married to Reb Khanoch Henich, a *yeshivah* [seminary] student from the town of Potshayiv. He was the son of a famous butcher family. After their wedding the couple mapped out their future. They decided that the husband should travel to America, save some money and establish his academic standing, then return one day to Lanovits to be a leader in preserving Jewish traditions locally. He never made it back. He was killed in road accident. His wife, widowed with two small children, was left with memories of a short, happy, life.

Sometimes she would reminisce about that short past, while tears filled her brown eyes. She would recall how much he loved his eldest daughter, Rachel. This sweet child had the same brown eyes. He would call her "my angel" and she reciprocated showing her love for her father. This daughter, my wife, can no longer recall her father's features, nor how he looked. Elka's son, Ozer, never got to see his father. The latter ironed man's slacks in a New York shop at the time of his son's birth. Elka, a slim woman, would walk miles to the village of Kiskivits, where she was born. She knew everyone, and all knew her, enabling her to make a living trading with the villagers. Elka worked from dawn until dusk to support herself and her children on weekdays. Friday and Saturday were her holy days. Her small house was spotless by Friday noon. The delicious aroma of the food filled the home. On Friday evening her five year old son recited the blessing over the wine. She would lower her head while tears of joy rolled down her cheeks. After the meal the family walked over to uncle Yudel's home. His home was joyful due to his many children and learned guests. Elka would put on an apron,

[Page 34]

serve food to the attending guests at his table, thereby sharing the beautiful and holy atmosphere of uncle Yudel's home.

Elka's father, Reb Yisael-Asher was a learned man. He left his village shortly after his marriage. His academic interests clashed with the simple lifestyle of his village. He moved to Lanovits, supporting himself teaching *Gemarah* [Bible commentary]. Many of the town's students were tutored by him. He shared his daughter's sorrow and felt empathy for her plight, but in the end he parted from her. As a widow, her father's departure only increased her loneliness.

Her father lost his wife when shrapnel from a Ukrainian bomb killed her. He emigrated to America, taking on the task of educating his grandchildren, the children of his son Yosef, who died at an early age. He taught them our Bible and instilled in them a love for Judaism. One of his grandsons, Ozer Halperin, is prominent in Los Angeles. An orthodox person, he is active in the affairs of the Jewish community. His wife Sarah shares in his activism. She also speaks and writes Hebrew fluently. A whole generation of observant and dedicated Jews exists in California, due to the teaching activities of Reb Yisrael-Asher, a valued Lanovitser. My mother-in-law, his daughter, did not make it to Palestine. She perished with the other locals in the Holocaust.

The entrance to the synagogue included a large lobby. It was called "Der Polish". At the right of the lobby was a small prayer hall called "Das Shulechel". Horse traders, tanners and waggoners prayed in this hall. These men were a tribe of unique characters who developed their own behavioral standards and social environment. Each one had a nickname. These men were a mixed racial lot. Some were as blond as their Gentile neighbors; others were of dark complexion like the Gypsies. Their prayer book was printed in large letters. Their ability to read small print was limited. One noticed their black fingernails and tanned hands as they turned the book's pages. These men were a muscular and tough lot. They were hot-tempered and hard to control. The only one who exercised control over these congregants was the synagogue's *Gabbai,* Reb Hertsi the blacksmith. He was a tall, red-bearded man, with a pale complexion, a high brow, and huge blackened hands. It was his task to honor members of this special group of congregants periodically with an "Aliyah LaTorah" [being called up to participate in the Torah reading]. When necessary he hit those who refused, forcing them to accept the offered honor.

On high holidays the small prayer hall was empty. Its congregants found space in the main sanctuary, in order to hear the singing of Reb Yankel the cantor. Reb Yankel was a tall, masculine looking man, but as quiet as a baby. Aside from his cantorial job, he worked as a *sofer* [writer of Mezusoth parchment and Torah scrolls]. He was poor but known for his honesty. Many stories circulated about his honesty, leading to a strong feeling of sympathy for the cantor. One story dealt with Itzi Zabarer, a horse dealer. Itzi purchased a pair of *Tefilin* [phylacteries] at a New York estate market. Upon his return he asked Reb Yankel to inspect them, to assure their Kashruth [that the parchment writing and form were in accordance with the law].

[Page 35]

Reb Yankel returned the Tefilin to Itzi together with $2000. It turned out that someone had hidden his savings within the Tefilin parchment. These Tefilin ended up in the estate market. When Reb Yankel found the money, he returned it to Itzi the horse dealer to let him benefit from the unclaimed find.

Reb Yankel had a rich bass voice, reminiscent of the singer Chaliapin. He emphasized parts of the prayer dealing with "God speaking to us" with his powerful voice. When he reached the prayer "..with trumpets and shofar voice," the cantor switched to a florid coloratura singing of these phrases. Fear of Judgment and awe of the heavens filled the sanctuary. The congregants, who normally feared nothing, were in awe of the coming Judgment. When Reb Yankel reached *ne'ilah*, [the closing prayer], they all feared God's decision. Their souls had been pounded by the cantor's dramatic rendition of the *netaney tokef* prayer earlier in the day.

No one wore a hat in the main synagogue. All wore typical Volynian caps. These caps, called "hastelka," were round with a thin steel rod inside, to shape them, and a visor. The congregants wore these caps all year long. Before the holiday they brushed their hats with water to renew their looks. The congregants wore high boots made of leather, which they sealed using resin. The only special attire was that worn by Rabbi Ahareli. He had his own synagogue, but he honored the community by presiding over the services of the main synagogue on high holidays, and calling the shofar blowing sequences. He had an established claim on this honored function. In honor of the high holidays the Rabbi wore a heavy silk coat and a *streimel* [fur hat] of high quality. He walked into the sanctuary in small, measured, steps, as if he was gliding over the sinful people of this world. He took his honored place while the congregants looked on with deep respect for their spiritual leader.

These were the customs on Sabbath and holidays. On weekdays the main synagogue served as an assembly hall for the community. Khupah [canopy for a Jewish wedding] poles were kept in the entrance hall. Weddings had been celebrated here for generations. A festive atmosphere permeated the synagogue and surrounding houses on the eve of a wedding. The synagogue's extra-bright lamps were lit. Candles were placed on its window sills. A klezmer band from a neighboring village would play in the hall. Elazar Bass played a wind instrument and Shiky the fiddler, wearing a bow-tie, plucked on his violin, while winking at unmarried female guests.

[Page 36]

Those female guests were yearning for the day they would stand under the wedding canopy. Meanwhile they would giggle, shoving each other as they moved about. The last of the players was the drummer, Berl, a short, thin man whose hat covered a birthmark. The wedding-pair's parents each held a candle, their faces radiating happiness. The entire community came out to the festivity. The daring among them would climb the hall's wall brackets to get a better view of the newly-weds. The following day they would gossip about the merits of the newly-weds. Outside the hall, altercations between uninvited guests occurred at times. It was sometimes an act of retribution for wrongs done to them in the past. These altercations happened among horse-traders and waggoners who held grudges and were quick to raise their fists. On such occasions the wedding-couple's parents would come over, beseeching the warring parties not to spoil the happy occasion for which they had yearned for years. When calm was restored, the ceremony continued and a feeling of peace returned to the young couple and their guests.

The main synagogue sanctuary also served as an auditorium for our Zionist movement. The Balfour Declaration of 1917 was read from its pulpit by Mr. Brick, a resident of Rovno and son-in-law of Reb Yankel Alters, the owner of a fabric store. "Jews," declared the speaker, "this is our time of redemption. The messiah will come later."

In 1925, in this same sanctuary, our community celebrated the consecration of the Hebrew University on Jerusalem's Mount Scopus, thousands of miles from Lanovits. One of the speakers on that occasion declared, "The people of the book gave the world a great gift, the Bible. We were paid back for this gift with persecutions and murders. Now we will prove to the world that Torah will emanate from Zion again." Wild dancing, by both common folks and the town's prominent members, followed the speeches. In the same sanctuary we conducted an annual memorial service for the founder of the Zionist movement, Dr. Theodore Herzl. Young and old participated in this service.

We, the young generation, were recruited to organize this annual memorial event under the leadership of two men, both named Itzik. The first, Itzik Buchstein, was a short, stocky man who always smiled. He was the son of Reb Pinny Buchstein, a warm-hearted Jew. The second, Itzik Zingel, was of average height, with a black birthmark on his face. He was brought up and educated by his grandfather, Reb Aharon Michlis. Attracted to Zionism, he became very active in its promotion. It was he who founded the library for the local youth. He sold *shekalim* which entitled buyers to vote in the election of delegates to forthcoming Zionist Congress. He also distributed Jewish National Fund "Blue boxes," to be mounted on the wall of one's home, and organized exhibits illustrating the Zionist redemption process.

[Page 37]

He was an activist despite his poor health. These two men named Itzik were the Zionist veterans in the eyes of our community. On the evening of the aforementioned service, while the blue and white flag fluttered above, scores of candles were lit to commemorate the founder's anniversary. Our speakers spoke with fervor, describing the greatness of the author of "Der Judenstaat," Dr. Theodore Herzl.

The first speaker, Shlomo Berman, was the "Hercules" of Lanovits. His head was small compared to his 2 meter height. His private life was complex, consisting of occasional crises, yet his strong spirit masked these events. This tall man lifted the hearts of his listeners with his engaging words when he spoke. The next speaker was his brother-in-law Pesach (Pessy) Buchstein. This family has lived in Lanovits for generations. They owned retail stores selling various products. Pessy was the sole child of Shmuel Buchstein, owner of a metals store. He was nicknamed Pessiniu. His mother, Tzipy, was always unwell, afflicted with various strange diseases. His father, Reb Shmuel, was a man of solid appearance, with a smear of iron-rust on his nose. Pessy was fat, with thick lips. His expressive lips were able to readily reflect his various moods. He dressed in a sloppy manner and never wore a tie. His buttoned, short coat was of a style worn at the turn of the century. He wore boots both in summer and in winter. Pessy stored in his mind a rich collection of Jewish folklore. He had jokes for all occasions. These were mainly a way of laughing at himself. One story dealt with the medicines his mother gave him to cure him of various imagined diseases. Another concerned a Ukrainian soldier whom he had to carry on his shoulders during his military training. The story endings were always funny and entertaining. Despite his outward sloppy appearance, he was well connected with the local authorities. He used these contacts to help members of the community, rather than to his own advantage. Anyone with a local problem would seek Pessy's advice. An ardent Zionist, he was a member of the General Zionist organizations, a party that eschewed class distinctions. While on the speakers' platform during a memorial service, he sometimes expressed doubt with his lip movements during speeches by members of the Labor party. The last speaker was Uziel Reichman. The only child of his parents, he was of average height with a short convex nose. Uziel typically started his speech in a low voice.

[Page 38]

He slowly built up his delivery to a crescendo, weaving into his speech polished Greek and Latin phrases that his audience was generally not acquainted with. This was his way of explaining to us Hertzl's solution to the Jewish problem.

A stirring debate took place in the main synagogue between two Zionist factions named "on guard' and "time to build." The issue under debate was who should be the builders of Zion. Should immigration be limited to pioneers, an elite that would create something akin to a priestly kingdom, or is now the time to build the country quickly, eliminate selection, and thereby bring over as many Jews as possible? The entire community was stirred by this issue. Many participated personally in the debate or alternatively joined circles debating related issues. It was the primary issue of the day.

One summer evening the main synagogue was lit up, unusual for a weekday. Jews left their work places that day to participate in the afternoon prayer. That evening a battle of words took place. The two Zionist factions engaged their best speakers for this debate. The "on guard" faction recruited a "heavy cannon," a famous speaker from the nearby town of Kremenets. This trick angered the "time to build" faction, increasing the tension felt within the sanctuary. The synagogue was packed, its lamps illuminating the large audience. The debates continued for hours, with the guest speaker arriving at midnight. Neither side budged from their ideological positions, while the debate continued until dawn.

One Sabbath one of our friends, a young man our age, spoke to the congregants. It was an event we all remembered for a long time. It was the young man's first public speech, given at a time when the synagogue's podium was dominated by its elders. The speaker, Shaike Rabin, of the Rabinowitch family, was our soul mate and friend. His father, Reb Uziel, was a solidly built man with green eyes and a beard similar to that of Czar Nicholas III. He was ambitious and his life had its ups and downs. One day he was the owner of large properties, the next day he lost them. He behaved like an engine running at top speed. In his religious beliefs he was, however, steadfast. Almost fanatical in his admiration for Rabbi Mordechai Shumsker, the descendant of Rabbi Michaeli of Zlochow, he became a key supporter of Rabbi Ahareli of Lanovits. The Rabbi's followers were primarily simple Jews, hence Reb Uziel stood out among them.

I was interested in Reb Uziel because of his stature among our town's residents. One day I had the opportunity to meet with him, and a bond formed between us. The meeting occurred several months before my immigration to Palestine. Both of us were idle; I, while waiting for my *certificat* [entry visa], and he because of his financial crisis.

[Page 39]

We would often meet at the Beyth Midrash at noon time, sometimes alone. We discussed many issues. I found him to be well informed and a man of lofty qualities. He loved his children and expected a great deal from them. His oldest daughter, Manya, had her father's features and charm. As an adult she was the leading lady in several plays we put on. His youngest son, Zony [Ozriel], was a sweet boy. His middle son, Mony [Hayim], had a sharp mind. Mony rebelled against conventional ideas, often able to disprove them and defend his point of view. He would dissect ideas and analyze them. It was hard to fool him. His utterances were a mixture of sarcasm and sentimentality. With his curly hair and dark skin he resembled his mother, Dina.

Dina was born in Shumsk, the daughter of Reb Kupka, of a prominent local family. Well proportioned, with shapely legs, Dina walked the local wooden sidewalks proudly, like a matron. Her household was run based on her progressive ideas. She was considerate and friendly to all. Her son Shaike was a wonderful, intelligent young man whose knowledge of the world resembled that of a city youngster. He was the center of our social circle. Like his younger brother, Shaike was able to think analytically but was less temperamental. That Sabbath day Shaike stood at the synagogue podium, dressed in a light well-cut suit and red tie, wearing spectacles. He looked distinguished. The audience longed to hear his maiden speech. At first, nervous and sweaty, Shaike could not utter a word. Slowly he recovered, delivering a well-crafted speech in polished Yiddish. When he finished his delivery, we carried him out on our shoulders; proud of his accomplishment we kissed him.

We, his friends, all received the same education. As children we studied in a Heder, as youngsters we studied with Rabbi Motil, the brilliant student of the great Rabbi from Poltava. We had the opportunity to meet the great Rabbi once when he visited his student in Lanovits. He was short, with a big head typical of famous men. Because of his frailty he leaned on the shoulders of two of our students, gazing with pride at the new generation. We were astounded at the frailty of this great man, yet we revered him. Our yeshiva was established accidentally, but once in place it was our reality. Its creation was due to the efforts of its dean, Reb Motel Speizman, a man we all remember fondly.

[Page 40]

One day Reb Aharon Mashiles, our kloiz gabbai [treasurer], visited another yeshiva. At the recommendation of its dean, the gabbai returned with Rabbi Motil. The latter was an unusual teacher, quite different from the normal Lanovits teachers we studied with. Each student received individual attention. We were captivated by Rabbi Motil's personality. He was the first to show us how to wade into the sea of Talmud and study its plain meaning logically. When we students bade our good-bye to him, prior to our immigration to Palestine, he begged us not to forget him and to help him follow us. He was childless. None of his students continued in his footsteps to teach Torah. They were all swept away by the revolutionary spirit of those times.

In parallel with our yeshiva attendance we also studied in a Hebrew school, headed by Mr. Sfarim, the son of teachers in the town of Shumsk who taught Hebrew locally since the turn of the century. Raphael Sfarim was a short man with blond hair. He dedicated his life to study, preserve, and teach our ancient language. Living in the west, his heart was in the east. He passed on to us his values, telling us "your place is not in Lanovits, it is in Israel where almond trees bloom."

It is understandable that we, who received a combined Hebrew and traditional education, viewed the main synagogue as an auditorium, a forum that permitted us to express our reality and our feelings. Our synagogue will be inscribed in golden letters in the history book of Jewish Volynia.

[Page 41]

Our Home in Lanovits

By Eliezer Zinberg [Nir David, Israel]

Dr. Yosef Zinberg

I am looking at a memorial headstone for the Lanovits victims that were murdered by the Nazis. The memorial is the only thing left of our town; the rest is gone.

Twenty-seven years have passed since our town was destroyed. To this day it is difficult for me to reconcile myself to the thought that a town that was full of life, where I had relatives and friends that I would meet daily, is no more. I can recall the town's image, how it looked when I departed 30 years ago. In my mind I see the town's narrow alleys, wooden sidewalks, and its main street leading to the river. I also recall the hayfields surrounding the town, and the meadow where our youth would often meet.

Several large homes were located in the town's center. These were the dwellings of the large Holender family. My grandfather, Eliezer Zinberg lived in one of these houses. I was fortunate to live in the house of my grandmother Feige for several years. I remember her as a pleasant and quiet woman, who, at her old age, reminisced sometimes about the many wonderful accomplishments of her family. Having grown up in her home, I remember its appearance. It was similar to the other homes in our town.

My grandfather was primarily occupied with matters concerning his livelihood. However he was known in the community as a wise man, one having wide horizons and progressive views. He gave good advice, and was forthcoming to all who sought his help or advice. Jews and Gentiles sought him out.

Grandfather saw to it that his three sons and daughter (who died at a young age) received both a Jewish and secular education. He was duly proud of their accomplishments. His son Yisrael became a chemical engineer. He was one of the top students in his University class. During the Czarist regime he was accepted to a position in a weapons factory, Potilov, in St. Petersburg. It was not easy for a Jew to be accepted at such a work-place. He was recognized as a talented employee,

[Page 42]

and proved himself in this factory. In his after-hours, he devoted to research of Jewish literature published in past centuries. The result of his monumental effort was the publication of a 9 volume "History of Jewish Literature"; publish in Vilna in the Yiddish language. Three of his volumes were translated to Hebrew after his death. Yisrael Zinberg died in Vladivostok, USSR, in January 1939.

The second son, Shimon, was a pharmacist, well educated in both Jewish and secular subjects. He left Lanovits after his wife died, to join his only son in Leningrad. He died there subsequently. The third son, Joseph, my father, became a physician. He was known as a warm-hearted Jew and an active Zionist. Dedicated to his profession, he would visit the sick day or night. He provided medical care to both Jews and Gentiles, including farmers of the area. He served his patients regardless of the weather. The needs of the sick were his priority.

I remember an episode that happened in our home. My grandmother was terminally ill. We knew that her days were numbered, so the family stayed at her bedside. On one of those days a farmer came to my father, seeking urgent help for a sick man in a distant village. Father was pondering whether he could leave his mother temporarily in her present terminal state. Somehow, grandmother heard of the dilemma and demanded that my father fulfill his obligation to visit the sick farmer, and drive to him as soon as possible. My father went to see the sick man, spending many hours on this journey. When he returned he found his mother in the last hours of her life. Such episodes, such responses to need were typical of attitude of people in our town.

* * *

I was always drawn to Lanovits, even though I did not live there for many years. It was the town of my ancestors, the source of my spiritual guidance. While a small town, it had a rich cultural life. It included an amateur theatre and a significant public library. Periodic social gatherings were held to celebrate important events in Palestine. I still remember fondly my first Hebrew teacher, the late Mr. Siret.

Political organizations were active in our town, especially Zionist organizations. Most of our youth belonged to either "Hechalutz" [pioneers] or the "Zionist youth" movement. I acquired my first Zionist consciousness as a member of the Zionist youth movement.

Lanovits Jews were noted for their Zionist orientation. Donations to Zionist funds were made regularly. Political activity and fund raising was in high gear prior to a Zionist Congress. My mother, Gitel, was actively involved in these fund raising efforts.

Following my joining the youth movement I attended *Hachsharah* [agricultural training] prior to my immigration to Palestine. My parents blessed my plans to immigrate. My heart grieves to this day that only I, out of my entire family, emigrated from Lanovits and survived.

[Page 43]

My parents' house was a meeting place for many Jews, a pattern similar to what took place in my grandfather's house. Those who came did not appear to be connected socially. My parents were the ones to connect them. These visitors would congregate in our house regularly, especially during the long winter evenings, enjoying the warm cultural atmosphere. I still recall the faces of some of these visitors. They devoted many hours in our house to further the Zionist cause. These men and women are no longer with us.

Jews and Gentiles came to visit my parents, to seek advice, seek help when needed, or just exchange thoughts. My parents were available to all that came to our house.

After practicing for several years in Lanovits, my father was appointed director of the hospital in Vyshnivits. We moved to this larger town but did not sever our ties to Lanovits. Every summer we returned to our hometown to vacation there. My father needed this respite from his heavy responsibilities at the hospital. Here in Lanovits he relaxed, caring for the fruit trees on our property. As a child I sensed his deep love for agricultural work and plants, and inherited this disposition. My father felt creative when he attended to the fruit trees and the bees, on the land he inherited from his father. In his enthusiasm for these tasks he showed his yearning for a more rooted life for Jews in Zion. It is likely that his example was that which pulled me towards agricultural training and eventually to life on a Kibbutz.

My father was murdered on the first day the Nazis occupied the town of Vyshnivits, and my mother was murdered shortly thereafter. Both were murdered by Ukrainians to whom my father often provided medical care.

[Page 44]

Memories of My Family

By Beiril [Byya] Goldberg

My father was a registered resident of Pankowitz [a town on the Soviet side of the Polish/Soviet border of 1922 -1939]. Because of this fact, our family was denied Polish citizenship. Instead of an identity card, we were issued a *Karta Pobito* [residency permit], and were always regarded by the Polish authorities as suspect.

Pankowitz was a large village that changed hands several times in 1920s while the exact border location was being negotiated. In the final negotiations, the border was relocated from the Zbruch to the Horyn river. Pankowitz, with all its natural wealth, remained on the Soviet side of the border. The village was well known to a whole generation of Lanovits residents.

The Pankowitz area was famous for its river, its many fish and its water-driven mill. David Berman owned the mill and expected to benefit from its output for the next generation. When the mill remained on the other side of the border he lost his property. His memoranda to the Polish president, and his petitions to a local politician, Graf Zamoiski, to regain the mill, were fruitless.

For us the village was a source of family pride, a subject for discussion around the hearth, but also the source of our troubles with the local authorities. My father left the village as a child. Nonetheless, on the birth certificate of each child born to my father was written: "To (my father), a farmer from the village of Pankowitz, a son/daughter was born whose name is …"

Our family legend explained the matter with the following story: Czar Alexander II was accustomed to dressing as a commoner and visiting the corners of his land occasionally, to learn what people were saying about his regime. When he came to Pankowitz, a village of several thousand residents, second only to nearby Sbiatetz, he learned from locals that a single Jewish family lived in this village. Surprised to hear that a family so isolated from its co-religionists kept its faith, he wanted to meet them. He desired to assess the attitude of this Jewish family to its neighbors in view of the prevailing opinion among the authorities that Jews have no regard for other citizens.

[Page 45]

According to my grandfather, the Czar came alone to our house, knocked on the door, and asked if he could obtain a meal. He claimed to have come from afar, and to have no more funds with which to buy bread. Grandmother, who had just finished preparing her "gefilte fish" for the Sabbath, fed him this delicious dish and warmed his heart with Russian tea until he was satiated.

When he finished his meal he said to her, "Dear grandma, what would you like to receive from me so you will remember me forever?" Surprised, she asked him, "Who are you that you can offer such promises?" The Czar identified himself. Her request to him was: that her sons and grandsons not be obligated to serve in his army, thereby forced to eat non-kosher food. He replied that he could not honor such a request, that army rules are what they are. Having her initial request turned down, she asked instead that he provide her with a document stating that she, and her descendants thereafter, are permitted to legally reside in her village. In those days Jews were not permitted to reside in villages. The Czar promised to fulfill her request, thanked her for hosting him, and left. After a week, official surveyors came to the village, made measurements and departed. Sometime later, the Czar's emissary brought grandmother a deed for 24 acres of agricultural land and 18 acres of grazing land, including a farmer's residency permit in this village forever. The residency permit was a large document, with golden letters and the Czar's seal at the top. This document gave the family an uplifting legend, but also never-ending troubles.

* * *

As mentioned above, our family was not relieved of army service. When my brother Shlomo's turn came to serve in the Czar's army, he decided to cross the nearby border at Zbaraz, to Austria-Hungary, and emigrate to America. He and five other young men from the town went to a certain village to see a Wagoner known as an experienced border smuggler. The six men negotiated a fee with the smuggler, and left to meet him again the following night. That night, under the cover of darkness, the smuggler led the group to a deep valley. All was quiet until the smuggler shouted, "Halt" in Russian. One of the group members remarked to their leader that it is not customary to shout when crossing a border illegally. He was puzzled that an experienced smuggler would behave in this manner.

[Page 46]

The group realized too late that they were trapped by robbers.

In the confusion that followed, my brother Shlomo hid in nearby bushes, while Mosheki, the son of the Lanovits bathhouse owner, escaped. The rest, four youngsters, were caught by the robbers that surrounded them. The robbers searched the area for the two who escaped but did not find them. Shlomo heard one of the robbers express his fear that the escape of the two youngsters would lead to the discovery of their deed. As Shlomo tried to distance himself from the robbers, his movement was overheard. One of the robbers threw an iron bar into the thicket, injuring Shlomo's ankle. As he groaned in pain, the robber located him, grabbed his slacks and tore them off as Shlomo ran away. The money my parents had given to Shlomo for his journey was sewn into those slacks. When the robber felt the money as he held the torn slacks, he lost interest in pursuing him and let Shlomo escape.

Injured and in-pain, Shlomo ran to the only lit-up house in the nearby village of Vizeshrodok. It happened to be the home of a Jewish family. When he opened the door, the owner was at first shocked by Shlomo's appearance. However, after he heard Shlomo's tale in Yiddish, the owner let him into his house and decided to help him return to his family in Lanovits. The second escapee, Mosheki, hailed the local sheriff in the meantime in an attempt to find the robbers and rescue his friends.

* * *

Shlomo was my half-brother. His mother died at childbirth. My father married his late wife's sister, my mother, subsequently. The night of the above-mentioned event my mother awoke from a frightful dream, shaking and crying. In her dream she saw her sister arise from her grave to tell her, "My son is in danger, encircled by robbers who want to kill him. You do not care about him because you have other children, so I will go to rescue him for he is my only son." Father, skeptical of the veracity of her story, tried to calm his wife, and then fell asleep again. Mother remained restless and awakened my father a second time. Angry, he dismissed her dream as meaningless and asked her to let him sleep. My mother persisted, however, telling my father, "My sister appeared in my dream again, repeating her story.

[Page 47]

This time, however, she told me that her son has been saved, urging me to bring him home." In her dream her sister said, "To prove to you that this is no mere dream, I shall stop the ticking of your grandfather clock." To disprove her dream father lit a lamp, looked at their clock and was astounded to see that it had indeed stopped.

Shaken and sweating, father got dressed and asked his farmer friend, Dusi, to drive him quickly to Lanovits in order to consult his Rabbi and other wisemen as to what to do. The day was Wednesday, market day in Lanovits. Arriving early in the morning, my father entered a local tavern to await a more appropriate hour at which to visit the Rabbi. A Jew from Vizeshrodok, sitting next to him in this tavern, told my father that a young man came to their local sheriff informing him of six young men who tried to cross the border illegally, etc. This young man ended his story telling the sheriff that four of the six were caught by the robbers, that he escaped and the smallest youngster vanished. My father fainted, realizing that his wife's dream was confirmed. When father recovered, he asked Itsik-Shmuel to drive him to Vizeshrodok. There he found his son and brought him home.

* * *

During the court proceedings against these robbers, the following details came out:

Mosheki alerted the local sheriff. The police team was led to the site of the crime. At the site they found Shlomo's torn slacks and the iron bar used to injure him. The police team went to the village looking for Vladimir, who was known locally as a "killer for hire." Arriving at Vladimir's house, the sheriff found a five-year-old boy and an old woman sleeping on the hearth. The sheriff rested the iron bar on the hearth and asked the child, "Where is your father?" The child answered that his father had returned in the early morning hours, had awakened the household, placed a pile of money on the table and shouted, "We are rich." Mother, angry, had demanded that he leave the house with other people's money. Father had left, intending to hide the loot outside, because of mother's anger. As the old woman got up from her resting place on the hearth, the sheriff pointed to the iron bar, as if he had just noticed it. He asked to borrow the iron bar, to use it to fix his broken wagon. The old woman was shaken by this request, replying that she could not agree lest her son, Vladimir, would kill her if his iron bar was found missing.

In the end, the iron bar and the torn slacks served as evidence to convict the robbers. They were sentenced to years of hard labor in Siberia.

[Page 48]

My Shtetl and my Family

By Bluma Miller

I don't' know whether to write about Jewish Lanovits, its traditional lifestyle, its wonderful social relations and beautiful youth. All were eliminated in a barbaric fashion, in a manner that defies expression. They were all slaughtered. Shall I write about a generation that failed us? I am at a loss for words to describe the tragedy that befell our town. Perhaps my family's saga will exemplify what life in Lanovits was like.

My father was a learned man who saw value in secular studies. He was one of few men in town with progressive ideas, who saw value in secular learning in a changing society. My father, who taught Smulik der Rebizines and Shlomo Berman, recognized their study talents and thirst for knowledge. He urged them to continue their studies in larger towns. From his sons, my father demanded not only mechanical knowledge of a subject, but also a thorough understanding of the concepts involved.

My father was one of the few men in Lanovits who saw the Russian revolution as the wave of the future. Actually, I remember little about him personally. My memories of my father are based on what I absorbed from what was said about him at home.

My brother Eli was 17 when my father died. His dream was to become a writer, but with father's passing, he was needed to help support the family. He became a shokhet's apprentice.

In later discussions, my brother confided in me his inner struggle between his obligation to his mother and his desire to escape from home and study instead. He opted to support the family. He married, and had 5 children. Both he and my father died a natural death. However his wife, children and my mother were not so lucky.

My mother was a sensitive woman who suffered a great deal as a result of the loss of her husband. With the limited means at her disposal, she not only raised her children; she also supported several families of lesser means. Every Friday she would send me to several families, to deliver Chalah and meat items. (To be honest I did not make these deliveries willingly). Mother delivered food to several families herself to assure that we children remained ignorant of their identity.

I remember mother's loneliness as her children moved out, and I left the house to immigrate to Palestine. I recall our conversations. She did not dwell on her loneliness, asking instead if I had any idea of what it would be like to do menial labor in Palestine.

She wondered whether I could live under such conditions, hence preferred that I wait for an opportunity to work at a forthcoming trade fair to be held in Palestine.

[Page 49]

She was able to raise the funds for this project, ignoring her own financial needs. Her primary concerns were the welfare of her children.

I can recall with pleasure our celebration of holidays, the Sabbath, and Passover. One day, the Rabbi from Trisk came to our house, while I was still a child. I remember my father's joy when he met this famous Rabbi. I can still feel our inner satisfaction and pleasure, walking together as a family to the synagogue. I am at a loss for words to describe those feelings.

It was not accidental that our community and its institutions raised a generation of young men that sought a new path to perpetuate our existence as a people. Towns such as Lanovits provided the Zionist movement their best sons and daughters. These young men and women immigrated to Palestine, joined Kibbutzim, and, in general, helped prepare an infrastructure that was later was able to absorb Holocaust survivors. This same generation of dedicated Jews was the source of heroic mothers that chose to send their sons to the army to protect our homeland, so that we shall never again be slaughtered like cattle.

Our land brought forth heroic young men whose contribution to our future was greater than the contribution of the Maccabees. Our community's contribution to the defense of our country was not insignificant.

Lalit Deborah Shpieler (first from the right), Hana Miller (center), the late Z. Rabin (third from the left)

[Page 50]

About Your Lanovits and My Aunt Elka Wolf Koifsitz

By Bonia Stein Spitzer

Landscapes of Lanovits

The town was very picturesque. To reach the town it was necessary to climb from any one of the directions one came. The town's many trees gave it a green appearance, surrounded lakes and rivers. The town had a special charm. I do not know why I was so drawn to it. To this day I feel its beauty.

I came to Lanovits to live with my aunt Elka Wolf Koifsitz, to help her overcome the sadness of her terrible fate. She had lost all her children, one after another; only she survived. Her financial condition was satisfactory, but she worked hard to maintain it. She baked bread for local residents and specially braided challahs for Gentile weddings. She was well known in the area for her skill in baking this specialty item. I was truly impressed with her courage and determination to carry on her economic struggle despite her past tragedies. I believe I discovered what inspired her.

[Page 51]

It was the social atmosphere she found in Lanovits, its good-natured people. They were the ones that provided the impetus and gave her the inner strength to carry on. I came to this observation when I became better acquainted with its residents.

I visited Lanovits numerous times. Each time, when I returned home, I yearned to return to Lanovits. I enjoyed the company of its people, fell in love with its youth, and thrived in its atmosphere. Lanovits offered all of these attributes. For me the town was like a garden in which wonderful people grew. The residents interacted like members of a large family. They cared for each other and participated in celebrating one's joyous moments. I visited various towns, and each one was different. To this day I feel a deep attachment to your home town. It seems to me that I only need to be among you Lanovitsers, to again experience the uplifting I felt while being in your midst. Unfortunately, Lanovits is no more and all the attributes that characterized its residents are lost forever.

[Page 52]

This Event Happened in Lanovits

By Shlomo Pacht

I met both girls at the local "Hechalutz" clubhouse. Their names were Havaziah and Reisele. I fell in love with both the moment I saw them. I was stunned by the realization that I got to know two of the best choices among the girls of our town. Reisele was beautiful and sensual, while Havaziah was smart and pleasant. One day Reisele came to my house carrying a bag of cherries. I felt hot, blushing I thanked her. We exchanged a few words, and then she left. My father came over to me after she departed and said, "What is Reisele doing in our house? Remember you are a son of a tailor. Find your friends within your class. Do not push yourself into the elite circles. They will ridicule you and destroy you. Be careful when dealing with members of the elite." His admonition drove us underground. Our meetings were secretive and glowing; our love bloomed. Sometimes I would meet each of them separately, other times I met both together. Both girls wanted to run away from their parents' homes, to escape to a world that had no lineage rules nor strong parental will.

In the "Hechalutz" clubhouse our meetings were quasi-legal. There we were not alone. However, in our feelings we were detached from the other youths of the club. One evening Asher [Reisele's father] came to the club, pulled Reisele by her hair, beat her, called her disgraceful names and dragged her home. Ziporah [Havaziah's mother] reacted in a similar manner.

A year passed, and we continued to take walks in secret locations. We read a little and dreamed a lot; we tried to mature and find our freedom. The pressure from our parents did not deter us; going underground increased our resolve to continue to develop our relationship until we were redeemed.

On a glorious Sabbath morning, Havaziah and I sat alone near the seven springs, far from town. Life felt full of content, and we were at its epicenter. Suddenly an image appeared on the horizon. My heart raced, though I did not know who it was. Havaziah recognized the image, left me and ran toward her mother. Ziporah pulled her daughter's hair, beat her and shouted, "Better to fall into the arms of a Gentile boy than into the arms of a tailor." The next day Havaziah told me that she received additional beatings at home.

[Page 53]

* * *

This episode was the talk of the town the next day. My father reminded me again that a tailor needs to socialize within his class. I replied that I started to lease land parcels, and to trade in a manner similar to what Shmuel Bachtel had done successfully. My father went to Shmuel Nuskiss, Havaziah's grandfather, asking him to admonish me for my desire to betray my class. Shmuel responded to my father's request in a manner of an objective person dealing with an issue unfamiliar to him, for which he only had a general opinion, "Remain a cobbler and stick to your last." He said, "You are not the type to be a rich trader. Do not strive high, and be happy with your lot."

The above advice did not help me. I felt comfortable among my good friends Zuniah Rabin and Motil Buchstein. They respected me. While I socialized outside my class, I respected and loved those of my class, especially my hard-working and honest father.

* * *

The two girls decided to escape from their homes. Reisel told me that in a wardrobe of their home were three jars full of gold, paper-money and jewels. She wanted to steal them and run away. I did not let her do this. Instead I advised her to take along only a sum of money needed for her initial expenses.

The two girls left by train for Lvov on the first day of the month of Av [August]. In the letters they left for their parents they stated, "We have no ill feelings towards you. We want to learn a trade. Leave us be and think well of us." The next day both parents came to my father's house in search of the bandit [me]. They asked my father, "What does he want from our daughters?" My father distanced himself from the affair, claiming that he had no interest in seeing his son marry above his station; he begged them to leave him alone.

The girls studied in a girls' school located on Olovek Street 14, Lvov. I used to visit them every Sabbath. The school happened to be located next to the large house of Asher Scheinberg, a doctor from our town. This doctor was a specialist for kidney diseases, who later died in the house next to the sanatorium of Chanah Kesselman, to whom he referred his patients.

Ziporah appeared one Sabbath at her daughter's room for the first time. I have no idea how Ziporah discovered her daughter's address. Both girls and I froze in our place when we saw her. There was a moment of silence, and I left the room. Ziporah attacked her daughter in the presence of her friend, shouting, "My father knows his grandfather, a tailor the son of tailors. How shameful. I prefer to see you marry a convert, but not him."

[Page 54]

* * *

Reisel returned to her home and married.

Havaziah and I continued our relationship for another two years. At the end of that period, as Havaziah was about to finish her trade-school studies, we decided to reveal all to her mother. There was plenty to reveal.

Yoske Guberman, our good friend, provided cover for our correspondence. Havaziah addressed all her letters to me "Dear Yosele." All her needs were arranged by Yoske. Havaziah's mother relented and started to send her money and the items she needed. It was agreed between us to send her mother a letter, in which we informed her that we intended to get married. We further stated that if she did not approve of our decision, we intended to travel to Warsaw, join a *Hachsharah* {pioneer training] and immigrate to Palestine. In the letter we explained that Havaziah's letters to Yoske were meant for me. It was Yoske's task to wait for the postman to deliver this letter to Ziporah and slowly explain to her the entire complication.

Ziporah reconsidered the situation. She suddenly remembered that she herself married a man against the wishes of her parents; that she was against dividing society into more and less fortunate classes. She agreed to our match. We were about to wed when I was called up to serve in the Russian army. As the first recruit from Lanovits, called to serve in far and dangerous areas, I was accompanied to the railroad station by the entire community including Ziporah. She cried, kissed me like a mother and said, "I like you, I wanted to test you. Do not forget Havaziah. She will not be able to live without the assurance that you remember her."

[Page 55]

Chapter 2:

Lanovits-Holocaust and its Aftermath

[Page 56] [Blank] [Page 57] [Yiddish pages 313-328]

In the Lanovits Ghetto, From the Beginning until its Liquidation

By Moshe Rosenberg

In June 1941 the Russians authorities packed their bags and returned to Russia. The Soviet garrison that remained held the town for a few days, and then retreated eastward. During their retreat the soldiers lost their way and returned to our town from the direction of Bielozurka. The German army encircled the garrison. Lanovits became a battleground. The shooting continued for many hours with the residents in immediate danger. Thereafter the garrison surrendered and peace returned to the town.

This is How the Germans Arrived

A group of 3 German tanks arrived at first. The tanks climbed to the hilltop where the Pravoslavic Church is located. They positioned themselves opposite Glinik's house. The Ukrainian residents came out to see the new conquerors. Children and old men came to see the newcomers. This is the first time this crowd had seen a tank, it was sensational. There was also another factor: these people felt instinctively that it is desirable to develop friendly relations with the German platoon. To this end someone went to Zelig's house, where a Russian cooperative was located, took out a gramophone and started to play music in the middle of the street. The gramophone was placed on one of the tanks, playing popular music.

[Page 58]

Mechanized troops and cavalry followed the tanks. At the beginning the troops marched through the streets, thereafter they decamped to the "Blote" meadow. The next morning the soldiers spread through the town in search of food for their platoon and their horses. The soldiers entered all of the Jewish houses, removing from them sacks of grains, vegetables, flour and barley, items that saved in these homes for a "rainy day". There were instances where soldiers forced Jews to bring to their encampment these food items. It was not the food confiscation itself, but the manner in which it was carried out that introduced Nazi mentality to us.

The soldiers asked politely for butter, porkchops and poultry. This state of affairs continued for a week, accompanied by tension and uncertainty. Confiscation of food for the soldiers and their horses re-occurred daily. The rhythm of life as we knew it heretofore came to a standstill. After a week the army departed. High ranking Nazi officials arrived in private cars and left again. A small number of German officials remained to organize the local government. It is worth noting that at the beginning these officials did not maltreat local Jews. Here and there a bearded Jew was accosted and his beard cut off. The first victim was Michel the blacksmith. His beard was shorn by a soldier's bayonet. Otherwise the German officials confined themselves to uttering slogans such as "Russian kaput", "Jews kaput", "Poles are kaput" but Ukrainians are "good".

Our Neighbors Rule Us

Local administrative power was given to the Ukrainians. During the previous Soviet rule key local administrative positions were given to Jews, this time only Ukrainians were selected for these positions. With Ukrainians having local power, our troubles started. The Ukrainian officials visited Jewish homes to take their men to work. and to kill them. It was clear that these officials first dealt with Jews with whom they wanted to settle personal scores. Yisrael Katz, Mitzi Shpieler, Naphtali and Eliezer Weiner were their night casualties. These men were killed near the house of Lieber Bronstein and buried there. With Berchik the officials dealt differently, breaking his arm and beating him, then releasing him. He was murdered later, but after the first night, but he was indeed released after his beating the first night.

Sixty men were murdered during the first night of terror. After these killings, the Ukrainian murderers came to Alik Zap and Joseph Kleinman, gave them shovels and forced them to bury the dead. These two Jews also disappeared. Our impression was that the Ukrainian authorities were gradually perfecting their killing methods.

The Ukrainian officials also maltreated Jewish girls. They either killed them or released them after raping them. In general, judging by the men and women they selected for mistreatments, these Ukrainians were settling old personal scores.

[Page 59]

For example, Buriah Margalit was dragged from his home to the police station. His parents cried for help from anyone. Next they sought the help of the local German governor, whose office was located next to the railroad station. The governor mocked his parent telling them "Your son is not being killed, do not bother me. Buriah's parents returned home, helpless. Buriah disappeared. It later came out that Buriah's kidnapping was an act of revenge by a Ukrainian for injury that Buriah inflicted to the man's son.

While all these criminal activities were proceeding, the German authorities stood aside, permitting the locals to do whatever harm to individual Jews as they desired to carry out. The German authorities were content to let the local Ukrainians do the dirty work against the Jews for them.

Forced Labor and Hostage Taking

The second phase of Ghetto incarceration started in August 1941. The Ukrainian authorities started to draft men for public works. Local Jews volunteered for this work at first because of its economic benefits. The Jews worked at loading freight cars at the local railroad station. The workers would secretly bring clothing and kitchen implements with them for sale to Ukrainian farmers from nearby villages. The villagers waited for them at the freight yard. They traded food for these items. It is to be noted that the hunger in these Jewish homes commenced already during Soviet rule, due to the termination of capitalist trade. Under German-Ukrainian rule starting in July 1941, all commerce between Jews and Gentiles ceased. In this period Jews were primarily concerned to feed their families; they dreamt of food. However, when these Jews got a taste of the conditions attached to forced labor, i.e. the mistreatment on the way to and from the workplace, they started to avoid these assignments. The walk to the job assignment was accompanied by abuse on the part of Ukrainian guards. Young Ukrainians would throw stones at the marching workers. The workers had no one to complain to. Woe to him who complained about being mistreated.

The men who volunteered for work previously would hide in town to avoid being taken to work Women on the other hand were not mistreated. When workers were needed for an assignment, local gendarmes would come into Jewish homes to look for men. They even searched for them between houses. Sometimes they would enter a synagogue and kidnap all the men from young to old. Those who were qualified for work they would send to the workstation and the older men would be held hostage in an improvised jail. The shop of Yitzhak Burstein was fortified, and converted to house jail inmates.

Among those jailed were: Uziel Rabin, Yithak Melamed, Motil Speizman, Moshe Tepper, Moshe Kirschner. To these town notables a few outsiders were added, those that happen to be in the synagogue's Beis Midrash [small prayer room] to warm themselves during that winter month. We never got to see the above mentioned hostages again. We could only guess their bitter fate. These hostages did not have the opportunity to join us in the Ghetto.

German Authorities Prohibit Conception of Additional Jewish Children

After a while, Yacub Sotsky, the town's Soltis [elected village head], read a proclamation in the town square to the effect that effective that day, Jews are forbidden to conceive additional children. He added that the punishment for the ordinance's transgression is castration for men and the sterilization of the woman. The ordinance was read in Ukrainian. Yisraelik reb Aharulis was responsible for its public translation into Yiddish and Polish. This Jew did not understand many of the pertinent Ukrainian phrases. He thus failed to translate the ordinance properly. His incompetence landed him in jail where the rest of the hostages were held. Later, Yerukham Froman and Uziel Reichman were added to those already in jail. Their fate was the same as that of the remaining hostages. In addition to those persons already mentioned to have been jailed, several other previous civil servants active under the Polish regime were also arrested and jailed in the Burstein house.

[Page 60]

The jail was filled to capacity.

The improvised jail had no toilettes. Its inmates had to "do their thing" inside the jail in the very room where they ate and slept. During the first weeks after the arrest, the inmate's families were permitted to bring them food once per day. Later this service was forbidden. The inmates were left to starve, to suffer a slow death. To this day no one knows what happened to them at the end. According to accounts related by Ukrainians after the war, the inmates were driven to walk towards Bielozurka. Those who saw them on this death march noticed that they looked emaciated, some also wounded. Some locals alleged that they were murdered on the entrance road to Bielozurka, and buried in a nearby mass grave.

A Ghetto is erected Within Lanovits

After the 1941 High Holidays a rumor circulated in Lanovits that the German authorities will be erecting a Ghetto for the local Jews. The first house to be torn down according to this plan was the home of Asher Fogel. In this case the authorities left the old house standing but demolished the new part that was added to it subsequently. The new addition was attached onto the old house, as was customarily done in Lanovits.

Jewish workers started the ghettoization project by erecting a 3-4 meter high fence around the planned premises. The raw material for the fence came from Jewish houses that its inhabitants abandoned when they fled the town together with their Soviet employers. With the fence erected, the Ghetto's dimension took shape. At the beginning of the month of Adar [February 1942], a city ordinance was read that ordered all Jewish residents to transfer to within the defined Ghetto within 2-3 days. Locals who lived outside the Ghetto started to negotiate with landlords within the Ghetto for lodging. The Ukrainian Soltis [mayor] ordered the families within the Ghetto to "double up", i.e. shrink their house usage to accommodate their refugee brethren. This was generally done. The "insiders" accepted the "outsiders" in an orderly manner, sharing the new restriction and Ghetto living fate. Aside from Lanovits residents, the Ghetto also accommodated the Jews of Bielozurka and those of Katburg, small hamlets located nearby, as well as refugees from German-occupied Poland that ended up in the Lanovits area.

The Ghetto premises covered the area starting from the home of Ya'acov Gochman [the matzoh baker], then along the main street leading to the main synagogue all the way to the home of Simkhah Schneider. At the Schneider house the fence turned right in the direction of the home of Michael Golender. From there it continued to the home of Zalman Pines, and Shaindel Haikeles, then the home of Hayim Hersh Geller, where it joined the house of the aforementioned Ya'acov Gochman. All houses that were outside the fence were declared Hefker [abandoned property]. These remained empty of residents. The main synagogue now served as a granary [used for grain storage], half faced the free area and half was accessible from the Ghetto. The synagogue's main door faced the free area of the outside world. The synagogue, by virtue of its present usage was no longer under the control of the Jewish community. It's Beis Midrash [small sanctuary, used for weekday prayer sessions] was entirely within the Ghetto. It was used exclusively to house the destitute members of the community who were unable for some reason to arrange private housing within the Ghetto.

The Concentration of Lanovits Jews in its Ghetto

Two days before Purim 1942 all of the Jews of Lanovits were herded into its Ghetto. The Ghetto gates were closed, and were guarded by Ukrainian policemen. The latter were forbidden to enter the Ghetto, and its Jews were forbidden to leave it without permission.

[Page 61]

The Jews' entire existence and social contact was confined to within the Ghetto's small territory.

Before our family entered the Ghetto, we transferred our furniture to our Gentile neighbors. Our idea was to receive periodic food from them in return. We were forbidden to take furniture into the Ghetto, except for small items, for clothing bundles and beds. This restriction was not onerous because with the population density created by the Ghetto's dimension, we would not have been able to accommodate our furniture in the space allocated to us by our new landlord. There was no space for more furniture in the homes located inside the Ghetto, now that its residents had to "double-up". We saw therefore no reason to keep our furniture. When we met our Gentile neighbors thereafter, they acted as if they had no obligation towards us. They rejected our demand for food, and essentially dissolved their relationship our family.

* * *

Many instances of robberies of Jews occurred during the period prior to the establishment of the Ghetto. German officials devised methods through ransom of relieving well-to-do Jews of silver and gold items. This was done officially, through the arrest, then release of a person against a fine. A sort of modus vivendi around this procedure was established.

Dealing with robberies by Ukrainians was more difficult. These robbers went into town weekly. They knew their Jewish victims through prior relationships. The Ukrainian would hide near the rear of the house, enter it after darkness and take whatever he desired, for he knew that his victim had no recourse to the law. German officials or police would do likewise. Unlike the Ukrainians, who knew their victims status and resources well, Germans would enter into homes that were essentially empty of goods. They were attracted to jewelry and other items of value [Ukrainians sought more practical items for their kitchen, living room or barn-Ed.]

I remember a particular evening prior to our move into the Ghetto [their house was outside the Ghetto perimeter- Ed.]. That evening my father decided to take a sack of tobacco leaves to our new abode in the Ghetto. His plan was to use the leaves to hand-roll cigarettes and smoke them to relieve the forthcoming depression he expected to be part of Ghetto life. Our house door opened suddenly, and a German came into our home unannounced. He looked around, took the bag of tobacco leaves and a few other things, and then departed. We had to suffer this robbery in silence, for there was no recourse to the law. The latter did not exist when it pertained to Jews. On another occasion several Germans entered our house [the author does not state whether they were soldiers, policemen or officials-Ed.], took our stored sacks of grain and other items, then left. Unlike the official extortions, which we learned to handle, these random private robberies were particularly painful, for they took our last valuable food item which we relied on to survive the war years.

For a few days after the establishment of our Ghetto Dr. Lutwack was still allowed to live outside our Ghetto in the [former] Polish community center. One morning he received an order from the authorities to move into the Ghetto. He appealed this order to the German commander, H. Richter, asking for permission to move into the Kremenec [the district capital] Ghetto instead. In his petition he cited his superior intellectual training, suggesting that he would fit better socially into the Kremenec Jewish community, as compared to the proletariat Lanovits community. It was said that Dr. Lutwack also had friends in the Kremenec Jewish community. Herr Richter, the local commander agreed to Dr. Lutwack's request, furthermore suggested that Dr. Lutwack hire a number of carriage owners to carry all the belongings he wishes to move to the Kremenec Ghetto. Dr. Lutwack was delighted with Herr Richter's courteous attitude towards whim [Still in the pre-war mode of hierarchical thinking, where a Jewish doctor is treated with respect-Ed.] His hopes for a more pleasant future in the Kremenec Ghetto lifted his spirit. The carriages were filled with expensive items, including modern furniture. Once the carriages were all loaded, Herr Richter ordered the carriage owners to deliver Dr. Lutwack's goods to his house, and unloaded there. He told the unhappy doctor that he will not need these items in the Kremenec Ghetto.

[This is a stark illustration of the incredulity of some Lanovits Jews, and the connivance of the Nazi governor. The latter was going to demonstrate to Dr. Lutwack an aspect of the new National Socialist (NS) order, that no Jew is privileged any longer-Ed.]

I witnessed this episode. The previous day I had to run an errand in the village of Katzenberg. On my return from Katzenberg I met the downcast Dr. Lutwack and wife, on their way to the Kremenec Ghetto.

This sadistic act on the part of Herr Richter opened our eyes to what is in-store for us, the remainder of the Jewish community of Lanovits.

[Page 62]

Organization of Lanovits Ghetto Residents

Having completed the transfer of all local Jews into the Ghetto, the Community leaders sensed the need to organize many aspects of our lives that heretofore were strictly private or family affairs. We needed to develop:

1. Means of equitable distribution of food to needy Ghetto inhabitants.

2. Substitute for municipal services heretofore provided by the town administration such as garbage collection, daily water distribution, settling disputes, performing legal weddings, keeping birth, death and marriage records, etc.

Herr Richter was of like opinion. He appointed a JUDENRAT [city council], and a Jewish police force reporting to the Ukrainian chief-of-police. Both bodies were told that their main task is to carry out Herr Richter's orders in a faithful and orderly manner,

We were fortunate in Lanovits that the selected councilors and policemen had the community's interest in mind and served us faithfully with minor exceptions [which are detailed subsequently].

[The reader is to be aware that this report by Mr. Rosenberg was written at a time after WWII, when sordid (yet true) stories circulated among survivors of the mean and criminal behavior of Jewish policemen in the Warsaw Ghetto, of arbitrary behavior of Judenrat leaders in the Lodz Ghetto and in other Ghettos]

The Judenrat chief was a refugee German Jew [who understood the mentality of Herr Richter, and was respected by him in turn]. Judenrat [council] members were:

Benik Grawitz, Mordechai Akerman (the husband of Susia), Bunim Brimmer, and two additional men whose names I no longer remember.

The Jewish police was commanded by Raphael Krepman. Its members were:

Mendel Kishkeh, Azriel Brodsky (son of Zelman), Yekheskel Weitzman, Avraham Karper (of the Mates family), Leibkeh Weiss, Leiser Rosenberg (my nephew from the town of Tarkih) and others. The Jewish Ghetto police behaved honorably except for one man who failed us tragically due to his stupidity.

The first task tackled by the Judenrat was to organize a "soup kitchen" for the needy. The "kitchen brigade" was tasked to obtain food from various sources, legal and illegal. The Soup kitchen was located in the home of Mr. Wadas. The German authorities provided essential food stuffs, and our kitchen brigade added the rest. In this way we prolonged the life of the residents to some extent, many of whom were starving. The task of the kitchen brigade was not an easy one. An extra day of life was an extra day of hope that one will outlive the war period, and life will return to normal as we knew it. In the first month there was sufficient food for our people using the food reserves accumulated prior to the occupation. In addition, food was obtained from the nearby peasants through barter.

Residents would bring items of clothing to the synagogue. We of the kitchen brigade would take these items to the Ukrainian militiamen that guarded the local grain elevator. With their help we traded the clothing articles for potatoes, bread, legumes, and other items as required for the preparation of basic food that week. The aforementioned synagogue was part of the Ghetto wall, half within, half outside the Ghetto. Its main door faces the outside world. The Gentile peasants would bring their offerings to the door, and we our barter items inside the Shull. This trade continued for a while until we ran out of items to barter.

Hunger and Death in the Ghetto

At the beginning of our incarceration in this Ghetto the barter terms were: one suit = 100 kg sacks of potatoes. As our barter supply diminished, the value of a suit decreased. The peasants sensed our poor bargaining position, so they started to offer us valueless item to barter. As time went on many Ghetto residents went hungry, some dying of starvation. The task of the Judenrat in providing for its residents became more difficult by the week.

The Judenrat was also obligated to provide manpower for specified public-work projects demanded by the German authorities. We were fortunate in the Lanovits Ghetto insofar as these projects were either in our neighborhood, or in the city of Rovno, but no further. Those who were assigned to a work brigade were given a loaf of bread, an important enticement to volunteer for such an assignment. However as the food supply diminished, the Judenrat had to reduce the size of the food incentive. One needs to recognize that this Ghetto held approximately 2000 residents. Besides the Lanovits Jews, it housed Jews of Bielozurka, Katerburg, of outlying villages and lastly refugees from other Polish towns who tried to cross the old USSR/Poland border nearby but were unable to do so, hence remained in Lanovits, a border town. Such refugees were to be found in other border towns such as Tarnopol and Ostrog. Even after the annexation of Volyn in 1940/41 to the Ukraine the old border remained sealed.

[Page 63]

Hunger hung over the Ghetto. Children's bodies became bloated. Children died in the presence of their parents. The widespread hunger created an atmosphere of hopelessness.

The German and Ukrainian authorities denied permission to bury our dead in the Jewish cemetery located outside the Ghetto walls. We had to therefore bury our dead somewhere within the Ghetto. Whoever speaks of mass graves that resulted from subsequent liquidation action in the various towns in the Western Ukraine, and elsewhere, forgets that we were forced to create additional mass graves within the Ghetto as a result of the above mentioned refusal and the on-going starvation. Every day we would collect the dead by hand, doing away with the ritual cleaning procedures previously performed by the Chevrah Kadishah [Jewish burial society]. We would bury the dead in mini mass-graves somewhere inside the Ghetto. Once in a while permission was granted to bury a person in our cemetery. In such cases we did not have the strength to carry the body the full distance to our cemetery. Instead we loaded the body, or bodies on the only cart we had inside the Ghetto. This cart was pulled by a poor, hungry horse. The cart-driver was Michael Metusis, our traditional burial society driver. Michael transported the privileged dead body to our cemetery to be buried ritually. Some Ghetto residents envied the families whose deceased received such permission.

I do not remember seeing the bereaved crying during these burial procedures. The source of our tears had by then dried-up. We were apathetic, hungry, wishing to live no-longer.

I recall significant crying at only one funeral. It was the funeral of the son of Aharon Mehlman and Raisel Weisman [not clear why the names of the mother and father are in this case different- Ed.] who drowned in Rabbi Ahareli's pool. [What was the function of this pool insides the Ghetto? –Ed.] The child was 12 years old. He and other children were playing in Rabbi Ahareli's yard. The child's hat fell into the pool. [The Hebrew word used applies to a pool, not a well!-Ed] The child bent over to retrieve his hat and in the process fell into the pool and drowned. We all cried at the funeral to indicate this useless death was from a cause other than the inevitable starvation or disease. What else could we have offered to our living children in the case of this needless tragedy other than to cry our hearts out?

Zelig, the Doctor saves me from Death

As an experienced farmer I was privileged to travel in and out of the Ghetto in my function as procurer of food and other products for the for the kitchen brigade. The items I purchased were approved by the Judenrat and the Ukrainian authorities. On one occasion the Junderat was requested to supply the German authorities ½ ton of potatoes. We had to bring these from the town of Shumsk. To accomplish this procurement and delivery task I went to see my former business partner, the Gentile Andrusha. I asked him to lend me his horses and cart. [While the author does not state this in this article, my hunch is that this previous relationship with a Goy that lasted in this case, helped him survive-Ed] I proceeded to Shumsk with his transport. On the way to Shumsk I purchased a few products in addition to those ordered for the

Ghetto kitchen, to bring to my in-laws in the Shumsk Ghetto, and a few for my family living in the Lanovits Ghetto. I purchased green onions, beets, carrots and more.

Upon my return I found the Ghetto gate closed. It is normally open, guarded by a Ukrainian and Jewish pair of policemen, whose task is to search the persons and goods being brought into the Ghetto. This time I saw only Ukrainian policemen. My sixth sense told me this is a bad situation. I got off my cart and let him search me and the cart. The Ukrainian policeman found the few vegetables I was attempting to smuggle into the Ghetto. Having discovered my contraband, he closed the Ghetto Gate, preventing me from driving the cart into the Ghetto. Instead, I was taken to the Ukrainian militia's office, located in the former house of Michael Goldner. On the way to the office several my Gentile acquaintances followed us. They took the opportunity to beat me up. My ribs hurt, I was bleeding and my head felt faint. I threw up. When my acquaintances saw me puke, they were shaken by the consequences of their deed. As soon as the captain of the Jewish police, Raphael Krepman entered the office, these acquaintances left the scene.

[Page 64]

I ran towards the Ghetto gate, trying to save myself. When I reached Zelman Parnas' house, two Ukrainian militiamen came towards me, and beat me again. I arrived at my home in the Ghetto bleeding, with swollen limbs, and black & blue marks all over my body. For the moment I was totally confused by the beating experience. When the fog in my head lifted slightly I remembered that Andrusha's horses need be returned. I asked my sister Sarah-Yenta, who knew her way with horses, for help. She fulfilled my request and returned the two horses to Andrusha for me.

The Ghetto lasted for ½ year. In this period we starved and lost all hope for the future.

I arrived at my home in the Ghetto bleeding, with swollen limbs, and black and blue marks all over my body. Zelig Weiss took care of me. He remained with me until I recovered completely. For the moment I was totally confused…
…two horses to Andrushka for me.

* * *

The Ghetto lasted for ½ year. In this period we starved, and in the process we lost all hope for the future. The Jews I came in contact with behaved like prisoners who were awaiting their death sentences. Our neighbors sat on stoops of the tenement houses, more often silently than speaking. They lost the will to discuss matters, to hope for a better tomorrow. They seem to be afraid to speak lest they reveal the emptiness in their hearts. They seem to sense the oncoming of death and inevitability. They were not afraid of death, but they feared the process of waiting for it.

The worst aspect of this feeling of depression was the loss of faith. Orthodox Jews who in the past were known for their strong faith stopped praying, at least in public. Only a few continued to pray in the privacy of their homes. An additional few continued to hold prayer meetings at the home of Rabbi Ahareli. The Rabbi himself did not pray. Expressions normally used in the past such as "God have mercy on you" and "With the help of God" were no longer heard. Their former users appeared to have lost faith in their God. In that emotional state, the Ghetto Jews lacked the source from which to draw inner strength.

Children, Youth and Companions in the Ghetto

Our hearts went out to the children who previously believed in the power of mother and father to right wrongs, and to feed and clothe them. Now parents were as powerless as their children. They could do nothing to still their children's hunger. The children could not understand why their parents were helpless in this tragic situation. For days there was nothing for these children to do. Their days were empty, devoid of games, of a smile, of being either spoiled or criticized. Under these conditions children lost their emotional contact with their parents. They were instead left to roam the streets. They were essentially left to their own devices. The street scene stripped them of any protection that their parent represented under normal conditions. They lost all delusions that they may have had about life and their future.

At the beginning Ya'acov Margalit collected the children to work with them. With his brother-in-law Shmuel-Moshe Zafes he taught them whatever came to his head. Later he stopped his teaching activity as daily a child became ill and died of hunger. From one day to the next children gradually became phlegmatic, passive to all stimulate outside of food. The plight of our children caused us a level of depression that cannot be fathomed. We prayed for a quick end to our pathetic lives.

[Page 65]

Our youth assembled in various Ghetto corners. I do not know what these boys and girls talked about. They understood that their hopes for the future were cut-short. They seem to move in their own shadow. A boy was no longer drawn to a girl, nor vis-versa because they had neither the energy nor the hope of a future together. Only seldom did I see a pair walking together hand-in-hand looking forward to a life together. Instead these young men and women, after seeing each other briefly, hurried back to their respective families. When a boy was attracted to a girl, he visited with her, then returned to his family to make sure they were still intact. The same was when a girl went to see her boyfriend. The fear that a person dear to us would either disappear or die was ever-present in our minds.

The tragedy of our people became obvious when one noticed the absence of gossip. No one dared speak badly about a neighbor. One's heart did not permit one to joke about another person, when all were doomed.

At the beginning of our internment in the Ghetto people still mentioned the great love of Bienik Kopitz for Gitel Kagan, and that between Isaac and Bienblatt's daughter. It was said that Bienik Gurwitz loves to visit with the Berchick widow. These discussions were conducted with a heavy heart, as if these stories were bright spots that were slowly fading.

Policeman Rapha'el Krafman who failed Us

On one occasion I brought flour to the Ghetto secretly. It was a miracle that I was able to pass through the Ghetto gate to bring the flour home. Raphael Krafman noticed my deed after the fact, and came to me to demand "quiet money". When I refused, he complained about my behavior to one of his Ukrainian colleagues. These took me to the Militia station, beat me up, then abandoned me in the station. I felt faint, unable to help myself. I feared to stay at the station lest other militiamen will come and renew the beating. Fortunately for me, Brendele, the daughter of Yidel Buchstein worked in their office. She and Gitel Brimmer treated my wounds, and when I could walk again, accompanied me to the Ghetto, and my house, where I recovered. I later found out that Raphael did not mean to harm me. He merely mentioned my poor attitude towards him, a Jewish policeman, to his Ukrainian colleague. The latter took it upon himself to teach me a lesson in behavior towards a policeman, as a means of showing Rapha'el his collegiality viz. his Jewish friend.

Ghetto Liquidation

On the Saturday prior to the 1st of the month of Elul 1942 [ca. September] we suddenly noticed a large movement of Ukrainian policemen and many German policemen with fierce dogs. Their dogs were scary, constantly pulling on their leash intending to attack their targets. We feared the worst. We waited for the next command from the German authorities. A ring of these policemen, patrolling the perimeter day and night, was hermetically sealing the Ghetto. We knew this was our end. For the last 5 days we heard reports of Ukrainian workers digging large pits.

[Page 66]

Rumors reached us regarding the diggings by other Ukrainians who were in the past glad to be bearers of bad news. We did not know the depth of the dug pits. We could only estimate the depth based on reports that men dug the trenches and pair of horses were used to remove the dug Earth with steel rakes. We were told that hundreds of men were employed in this task, and many pairs of horses. We were informed of these details on the second day of the digging activity. Three terrible days passed. Our men and women were suddenly disturbed by the tension that the event created. Neighbors who lived with one another peacefully for the past six months started to quarrel with one another. The psychological tension was unbearable. People ran to and fro without any purpose. They wanted to escape, yet knew that escape was impossible, that their world was a closed one. The German authorities stopped paying attention to us. The Ukrainian militiamen looked upon us as bodies that no longer had any life, whose movements were a mere annoyance to them. They wanted us to not bother them in their forthcoming important task, that of ridding themselves of their fellow Jews.

Perhaps because I was strong as a lad, and the desire to live remained with me, I did not settle with my fate. Instead I decided to attempt to escape. to save myself. I too ran to-and-fro. I could explain my plan to no one. Somehow I succeeded to escape to Burshchiska. This was a stroke of luck. The authorities knew that as an authorized agricultural buyer I was permitted to travel in and out of the Ghetto. On a regular day I escaped.

[These statements are disingenuous. It is clear from his other tales that he was a privileged person to the end, and had to his credit, cultivated good relations with key Gentiles living in the neighborhood. In his previous accounts he shows clearly how much freedom of movement he had by virtue of his job as buyer for the Judenrat. Perhaps he tells it this way because of his guilt-feelings regarding his failure save his family at a time when it was still possible to do so- Ed]

* * *

My sister Miriam was sent to work, prior to the Ghetto closure, in Polwark, outside Lanovits. When the Ghetto was closed, she too did not return to the Ghetto. Instead she found out my whereabouts and came to me in Burshchivska. Later, the other girls working outside the Ghetto were collected in one place with the intent to kill them in place. Sarah-Yenta, who worked in the militia office, forewarned the girl of the impending roundup plans. My sister Miriam, forewarned, escaped to the forest near Polwark, where she knew of a Russian POW in hiding there, who worked occasionally for local Ukrainian farmers. The POW being lonely, asked Miriam to join him in escaping to the Russian interior. The two walked eastward hundreds of kilometers, slept in abandoned train coaches and ate food left over in the fields. In this manner she saved herself.

Sarah-Yenta could not escape with the other girls. She had to work in the militia office until the last day of the Ghetto's existence. A good-looking militiaman fell in love with her, though he was married. She was beautiful. He decided to save her, risking his own life, by hiding her in a village near Bielozurka. His wife suspected his infidelity, and threatened to report him to the authorities.

[Page 67]

However, she realized that by doing so she risked losing her husband, a fate she did not want. The militiaman placed Sara-Yenta with his sister in a nearby village, and arranged Aryan papers for her. For two months she was free to roam the nearby villages with other girls her age. She spoke the local dialect, so her past was not noticeable. One day when she went to grind grain for her patron, a Lanovits policeman saw her. At first he did not believe his eyes, then forced her to admit her identity. He took her to Bielozurka. On a hill overlooking the village, he murdered her.

I Visited the Ghetto After it was liquidated

I spent my first day in Burshchivka. I immediately contemplated how to save my family. At nightfall I left for Lanovits to try and find a way. I entered the Ghetto, and went home. My wife was shocked to see me [This bears-out that at least his wife knew of his plans to escape-Ed] fearing that I was returned to the Ghetto forcibly and perhaps beaten as well. We sat all night, discussing how to save ourselves. We decided that I should leave again immediately, and take along the special buttons my wife prepared for her last dress, buttons that covered several gold coins. They were to be used to entice a Gentile person to save the family. I left the Ghetto that night, headed to the village of Gribova, to the house of Mr. Andrushka, (my former partner). It rained all night. I traveled over the famous island in the local river known to us as "Das Zayde's Stickel" [Grandpa's field]. Due to the heavy rain the river was at high tide, so in crossing it I became thoroughly wet. When I arrived at Andrushka's farm I hid in the chicken coop. Andrushka discovered me the next morning. He gave me fresh clothes to wear.

I urged him to find a way to save my family. He promised to go to Lanovits, to find out what is happening, and explore ways to save my family. On Thursday Andrushka returned from Lanovits, and informed me that all Ghetto residents had been murdered already. I cried, I could not believe that the killing had already happened. I wanted to assure myself of this fact, so I left for the Ghetto after nightfall. I found the Ghetto empty quiet, and partly destroyed. There was complete silence. I next entered the home of one of our former neighbors outside the Ghetto, a Mrs. Lutzky. She verified Andrushka's account. All were taken out to the new cemetery under heavy guard of militia and dogs. All were led to the cemetery wagon-parking lot. There they were required to undress. The Ghetto residents were segregated according to sex and age. Men women and children in turn stood in front of the large pits and were shot at close range.

After this terrible night 40 Jews remained alive, saved by farmer Mantuk, also known as the bearded forest robber. He was a good friend of Reb Uziel Rabin. He hid these Jews despite great danger to himself. Among the hidden Jews were Ya'acov Sambirer, Avraham Kreper, Hayim Kreper, Michael Kreper and others whose name I no longer remember. The son of Hana-Reuven Teichman also survived the Ghetto's liquidation. His father gave him all his money and gold that he had. He sent his son to his friend in Gribova. These friends robbed the son and returned him to the Ghetto, where he was murdered.

[Page 68]

Someone reported on Mantuk to the authorities, that he was hiding Jews. The latter pulled the Jew out of their hiding places, brought them back to the Ghetto where they were killed. Moshe Kerner hid at Mr. Czerny's place and paid him well. The latter chased him away after a while, and Kerner was murdered by roving Banderovstsy. They threw him alive into a Feces well.

These tales scared me. Mrs. Lutsky confirmed that none of my family survived. I left her place at midnight and headed to Krasnolik, to Mitiah, a friend of my father. He was hiding my sister Idis, the wife of Shalom Segal, and the husband of Golda Mehlman. Mitiah told me that my father left a number of items with him. The local Banderovstsy learned of this fact and demanded to share in the loot. He claimed to have given them all that he had gotten from my father, but they did not believe him and wanted more. To this end, Mitiah said, they are likely to conduct a house-search and kill him if they discovered that he hid me and my sister. He urged us to leave, keeping only Golda's husband, whom he wanted for one of his daughters. Later Mitiah reputedly killed this young Jew.

Azriel Grawitz hid in the area for 18 months, first in Izkowitz, later in Rinkowitz. On his way to Rinkowitz one day, Bandera militiamen met him and murdered him. I myself left Mitiah and arrived at the house of a Stundist [a protestant sect prevalent in Wolyn, named after their custom to study for one hour in German] I confided in him, telling him that I wish to stay alive, and am in dire need of help. I also told him what Mitiah did to us. The Stundist was not surprised to hear the story he knew Mitiah's reputation, and the danger this man represents in my situation. The Stundist asked for time to consult on a suitable plan with his Stundist congregants. I was shaken by the consequent delay in deciding my fate, but believed in his judgment. I had previous good experience with Stundists, and was familiar with their custom to consult when making important decisions.

The Stundist called a meeting of his congregants in his house. I heard none of the discussion that took place for I was hidden in his house away from the meeting room. During their meeting they prayed as usual, each person creating his own version of the prayer. After the meeting ended, and each person went his way, the host called me out of my hiding place, and told me I am to stay with his neighbor, who is also his best friend.

That night the Stundist heard steps behind his window. He looked out after the person left, and saw no one. He knew that Mitiah is stalking him. The Stundist got scared of Mitiah's visit. I stayed with the neighbor for an additional three nights, then left. I wandered the area until I came upon a religious Gentile who knew me from before the war. I met him 8 months after the Ghetto's liquidation. While the local militia persisted in hunting escaped Jews, this farmer hid me in a hole that he dug on my behalf. This farmer was also a Stundist, and a person I had known and done business with for years., named Kalim. I stayed with him for 11 months, by which time the Red Army freed our area. During that long period he took care of all me needs, bringing me food and drink daily. I knew that his economic circumstances were modest so I sought and found work among the local farmers being paid with food and lodging. I typically worked for a farmer for 1-2 weeks at a time when he needed extra help.

After liberation I was drafted into the Red Army. I left my friend and savior, Kalim with a broken heart. He did more for me than anyone could expect.

[Page 69] [Yiddish pages 329-338]

The Lanovits Ghetto and My Escape From It
(The Story of a Child)

By Meir Beker

I was 13 when the Germans entered our village. The town was reeling, both economically and culturally, under Soviet domination. On one hand, our parents were depressed, fearful of what the future might bring. We children, on the other hand, enjoyed the parties and dances, the culture centers that were opened, and the symphony that was created under Soviet leadership. After the Germans marched in, these activities ceased.

With the departure of the Russian authorities, the town lost its active youth. Old people and children remained; at least that was my impression of those days. At first, the Jews hoped that the Germans would allow the community to again operate autonomously in the area of religious practice. They almost blessed the departure of the Soviets. In a few days the local Jews realized their mistake. Among the German authorities was a person by the name of Richter. He was a sadist, who took pleasure in the suffering of others. He would wander the streets of Lanovits and beat up any Jew that came his way. Richter was the one who made it clear to us that we were powerless from here on.

On the first Sabbath following their arrival in Lanovits, the German authorities arrested ten Jews. They were placed in the local prison that was created out of Piny Burstein's store. The prisoners were placed in its basement. They were killed a few days later. Among the ten Jews were Motel "Melamed" Speizman, Ozer (son of Yidel) Kiskiwitzer, Yizhak Melamed, Moshe Kofets, Uziel Rabin, and others. These were among the cream of Lanovits jews. Their arrest depressed the rest of the community greatly.

[Page 70]

The Erection of the Ghetto

On 28 February 1942, our Ghetto was erected. It was built by our own Jews. I remember how they carried the boards through the streets. I do not remember where they got the materials for its walls. In a few days a wall, 2-4 meters high, was erected around the ghetto, and all Jews had to move into it. Beside the Lanovits Jews, the Ghetto also housed the Jews from Bielozurka and Katerburg, even a few from Kremenec, and a few from other parts of Poland that came to Lanovits in the hope of avoiding the German occupiers.

The Ghetto included Targowa Street (the house of Raphael Krepman and Benjamin Yishpa-Gilboa). From there, it included the house of Reuven Teichman, Joseph Twerman, Yeshayahu Witelstein, Ogrodovoa Street, and the street that continued from the house of Moshe Steinberg (who walked poorly), to the house of Michael Goldener. The Jewish police were housed in the old Polish school. The number of rooms within the Ghetto was limited, so approximately 5 families had to live together in one house.

The Jews were allowed to bring into the Ghetto only that which they were able to carry on their back. A situation was created that whole families had no items to sleep on. The food they were able to take with them hardly lasted for 2 weeks. The Jews felt hunger from the first day of their arrival in the Ghetto. There were daily deaths, with no chance to change their fate.

According to the commands announced daily, Jews were forbidden to leave the Ghetto, except for departure to forced labor destinations and return. After a few weeks, an order was announced that forbade movement within the Ghetto at night.

The only entertainment available within the Ghetto was to wander the streets, to see other faces, and to hear small talk. With this restriction, life became more difficult. The Ukrainian guards watched us from a tower, to assure that this order was fulfilled.

The Judenrat and the Jewish Police

With the creation of the Ghetto, Germans took Jews out for public work outside of town. Daily, scores of men and women were taken to work. They were beaten often, while not receiving any bread [This is contrary to other reports in this book, probably unreliable information because he was so young. He probably heard it from others – Ed.]

The Germans organized a Judenrat for their convenience. The active members of the Judenrat I remember were Yerukham Forman (the son of Ben Avraham Mash'hes), Abramow, a refugee from Katowitz, a German Jew whose name I never knew (for they always called him, the Jew from Germany) who lived in the house of Leibel Zelkes. The Judenrat's task was to provide workers for the Germans. Their fate was most unfortunate.

[Page 71]

The Germans also established a Jewish police whose task was to assure that Jews went to work, and to carry out periodic forced-monetary contributions.

One time the German authorities requested a set of "young and beautiful women." Our parents knew the consequences of this demand, hence offered a significant sum as a financial alternative. The task of the Jewish police in these cases was a difficult and shameful one. Among the policemen were Raphael Karepman, Hershkey Chaikes (Lashek), Azriel Brodsky, Motil Kreper, Yeheskel Weitzman and others.

As a 13 year old, I was also taken to work. We were asked to load sugar beet roots in season. The work was difficult, and was carried out under supervision of armed Ukrainian guards. These would beat us when they noticed us slackening off at work. We would secretly bite off a piece of root to still our hunger. We worked at Bureskowitz. We typically left on Monday, and returned on Saturday. Others who worked in town returned home nightly. In the evening, the police would search them for any bread they may have smuggled on their body. In Bureskowitz, there were several Jews that earned a living from the large mill and from fishing. In general, Bureskowitz was a rich village. When we arrived, we found out that all of the village Jews were killed by the Ukrainians.

To Rovno and Back to the Ghetto

Each time I was sent to Bureskowitz, I was scared that the local Ukrainians would kill me, without trial. Yet, I had no choice but to go. Once the Judenrat was asked to send young boys to work in Rovno. I volunteered and was sent with 20 others. I wanted to distance myself from my unfortunate town, in the hopes of a better life.

On the first day of arrival, the Rovno Jews were called to the center of town to receive injections against an alleged epidemic. Eighteen thousand Jews were collected in this matter. None came back. They were all killed that day.

We worked for a "Folksdeutsche" family that lived in Rovno before the war, or came there recently. These men were managing local plants. During the first days of my work in Rovno, my uncle Ya'acov Beker, who lived on Voliya Street, Rovno, came to visit me. Later he disappeared. From other local Jews I found out that he and his household were murdered one day during a local action.

The Germans did not consider returning us to our homes. The yearning to see my parents overpowered me. At night I would cry, wishing to escape to Lanovits no matter what.

[Page 72]

The task was punishable by death. I felt I could not resist the desire to see my parents. What finally made me escape was the news that the Jews of the Rovno region were being killed. I arrived in Lanovits without a hitch. No one snitched on me. The poverty in the Ghetto was widespread, and the atmosphere depressing. Several people I knew had been killed. Two days after my return, the brothers Naphtali & El'azar Weiner were killed.

Several of the Ghetto residents were sick with no doctors to treat them. Dr. Lutwack, our Polish-speaking physician, had previously transferred to the Kremenec Ghetto, where he was shot. I, however, was relatively fortunate to be back with my parents.

Yellow Star

In the meantime, an order was promulgated that each Jew must wear a yellow star on one's back, and on the left-front, over one's heart. In Those days, I was in the Ghetto illegally, so each time persons were taken to outside work, I was told to go into hiding. The people in the Ghetto were resigned to their fate. They did not quarrel anymore. They had no energy for such matters. The Rabbis wandered about like shadows; they were superfluous. Jews no longer prayed, nor did they feel a need to pray. There was a case early-on when the Ghetto was established, ten Jews were arrested during a prayer session and killed on the spot.

Children and Youth in the Ghetto

The Ghetto children were bored and depressed. Some played quiet games underground. The children were warned by their parents of the danger of playing underground. The children were looking for something to do that would distract them from the constant feeling of hunger. They adopted an exaggerated carelessness and lack of interest in anything. Like old people, they too suffered disappointments and hurt.

The pain of our youth was great. Young men were drawn to young women, but something blunted the attraction, because they saw no future, and the attraction waned.

My own situation became most difficult. I wanted to live and save myself, yet I did not find the courage to escape the Ghetto.

[Page 73]

I knew of cases where Ukrainians, good neighbors of yesterday, caught their Jewish neighbors and turned them over to the German authorities. Among the Ukrainians, only Somolatski hid and saved Yisrael Brodsky. He was one of very few. There was a second Ukrainian, Mentach, who hid a number of Jews. However, when his neighbors noticed them, they reported him to the Gestapo. All those Jews were pulled out of their hiding place and killed. [The author does not say what happened to Mr. Mentach – Ed.]

Among the most famous Ukrainian murderers were: the son of Bantenko, and Mishkeh, the middle son of the Blacksmith Herutz [or Herotz]. These two created their own "Jewish Cemetery" near the "Seven Brooks." After the war, a mass grave was found there in addition to the mass grave the Germans created.

I was afraid to leave the Ghetto. I looked for ways to save myself, fearing to sink into an "I-don't-care" attitude. We had no bunkers inside the Ghetto [At least he knew of none -Ed]. Aharon Milman created a hiding place in his father-in-law Shalom Wiesman's house. The bunker filled up with water, and Milman's infant son drowned in it. This contributed to the death of Shalom Wiesman, who so loved his grandchild. I had no information regarding the goings-on outside the Ghetto. The neighboring Ghettos were separated from us so we had no information about their fate. I continued in this manner, to seek a way to save myself, until August, 1942.

Ghetto Closure

That day the Ghetto gates were closed. No one could leave. We were under a curfew for four days, without knowledge of what will be. We heard periodic shooting. Each shooting probably killed a Jew. I decided to save myself. At 8:00 a.m., on the first day of Elul, we were ordered to move, under heavy guard to the Jewish cemetery. Two large pits had been prepared previously. Several men, dressed in white-smocks were completing the second dig. I knew none of the diggers. On the way to the cemetery, one of the guards shot Reb Ahareli Rabin. I did not see the act myself, but was told about it.

The Final Liquidation of Lanovits Jews

The Ukrainian guards placed the men next to the first pit, and the women and children next to the second pit. The men had to undress in sight of their wives and children. When they were naked, they were ordered to face the pit. Following a command, the Ukrainians and Germans fired at them, and they fell into the pit.

[Page 74]

Next they did the same to the women and children. While this took place, I sneaked into the high wheat field nearby [This sequence seems unreasonable; how did he remain dressed? Perhaps the real story is somewhat different – Ed.] The guard did not notice my escape. The wheat field hid my low profile. I escaped, hearing shots behind me.

My Escape

I ran from certain death. I covered 35 kilometers through wheat fields in an unknown direction. I reached the village of Koshlek [=Koshlaki in Ukr.], on the old Soviet border. When I arrived, a man and his wife were harvesting their wheat. When they saw me, they took pity on me. They put a scythe in my hand, and asked no questions. I crossed the border with them from their field to their home [He apparently escaped dressed – Ed.] The farmer did not let me sleep in their house. Instead, I slept on a bed of straw. I cried all night. My hands were cut from the wheat sheaves. I cried because of my pain. I was also in shock. I knew in the morning that I must leave the village.

I continued my way, reaching Medyn. It was once a Polish village. Its Jews used to come to Lanovits to purchase cows. A Jewish family I knew from the past put me up for the night, but asked me to leave the next day. It was Saturday. They directed me to Podvolochisk, a nearby town. As I left the village of Medyn, a strong rain came down. I was wet to my bones, so I returned to Medyn. The aforementioned family took pity on me and let me stay for several months. The family hid me in the attic, and fed me regularly.

One day the Germans came and evacuated the Jews of the village to a nearby Ghetto. I found this out when I no longer received food. I was hungry so I escaped to Podvolochisk. There I found Laiser Klemchik, the son of Hannah Shachnes. He was already informed on the liquidation of Lanovits Jews. The Jews of Podvolochisk were already imprisoned, so I hid in the prayer house and later escaped to Zbarazh.

In Zbarazh a strange situation existed. Its local Ghetto was unfenced. The Jews lived in one section of town, and the Judenrat provided daily workers to the German authorities. The Judenrat police caught me and supplied me as a worker. On the way to work, I found out that we are all being shipped to Auschwitz [Very doubtful that the Jews knew the intended destination – Ed.] I escaped to the local bath house, and hid in its boiler room. When the local situation settled, I escaped to Tarnopil,

[Page 75]

from there to Leiserne [=Jezierna in Polish], to Bobricka to Khodoriv. I traveled at night. In Khodoriv, the local Jews were housed near the train station. The trains brought sugar beets to a local processing plant. Because the trains were needed for beet shipment, none were available to take the local Jews to Auschwitz [How did he know this? – Ed.] From Khodoriv I escaped to Skole, then to Lawachina on the Hungarian border. There I met another escaping Jew. Together, we hid in railcars that took us to Munkatch. When we emerged from our railcar hiding place, Hungarian police caught us. They wanted to return us to Poland. In this place many Jews were assembled for shipment to Poland. Some cut their wrists, in desperation. From there, I escaped to Budapest [No details given as to how he got from Munkatch to Budapest – Ed.] The local Jewish community placed us in a camp for refugees inside the town. In 1944, I left Hungary for Romania. I reached a village near Grosswardein [=Oradea, Rumania], but did not know how to cross the border. I was told of Hungarian farmers who smuggle persons across the border for a fee, but I had no funds.

I visited one smuggler, who told me to see a particular woman regarding my fee. This Jewish woman, a Mrs. Teicher, was from Krakow. She was with three children and needed help carrying them across the border. I volunteered for the task. She paid the smuggler my fee and her fee. Unfortunately, as we crossed the border one of her children started to cry, so we were caught by the Rumanian border guards. We were brought to their commander in Belnish, who transferred us to Arad.

The local Jewish Community paid a ransom to the guards to free us. From Arad, we traveled to Bucharest, where Zionist functionaries were actively recruiting Jews to volunteer to travel illegally to Palestine. Three ships left Constanza to Israel: Mfakra, Marina and Bulbul. The Rumanian Navy escorted the ships to the high seas. In the high sea, the ship Bulbul was attacked by Germans and sank. Only five survived. We collected them at sea. This way we arrived in Israel.

I left Israel after I fought in the Israeli Army. My friend, Mrs. Teicher, stayed in Israel. Her two sons are already married.

[Page 76]

Horror Journal

Years 1940 – 1945

Issac Landau

Editorial comment

The author of the "Horror Journal" in front of us, brought a unique collection of records. The interesting thing about all these lists is that out of multiple horrific experiences, he recorded only the ones before us, and a thread of truth and a special character of their author is inherent in them. We therefore found it appropriate to give at the beginning of the diary an excerpt of the author's own experience and memory, which reveal traits in his personality, which shed light on the value of the diary and the selection of the records recorded in it.

We tried to write the things according to the spirit of the author. He has a special privilege in this book also because he is the only ka-chat man in our town.

H. R.

I was born in Lanovits on 19 December 1913. I was educated by the teachers: Asher Leib, Itzik Melamed, David Melamed and Avraham Eliezer Havis, (all deceased). Thereafter I was tutored by the Hebrew teacher Mr. Sfarim. My late brother Joseph was tutored at all times by Hebrew teacher Sfarim, and was a steady friend of Shalom Kwaitel, Zvi Brimmer, the late Lieber Blank, the late Eliezer Azriel and the late Aba Kofets. These friends later joined the local Hehalutz (=Zionist Pioneer) branch.

During our Hanukkah festival, all of us got together to play with dreidels inside one of the houses. On a clear day, one of them would bring a sled; and we would slide down from the hill on which the priest's house is located. This hill was completely covered with snow. On such occasions, the boys would include me, despite being younger than them. The boys did not include me in other common adventures because I was younger than them.

[Page 77]

When I turned 18, in 1933, I attended together with other Hehalutz club members a memorial service for Dr. Binyamin Ze'ev Herzl in our main synagogue.

Bund (=Socialist party) club members: Byah, the late Michael Yithak Shmiel, the late Nahum Leib, and others met nearby. They had scheduled a play on the same day in the barn of the late Moshe Helban, hence claimed that the memorial service will interfere with their performance. [The main synagogue was near Mr. Helban's house and barn.] The Bund members entered the synagogue and busted the meeting, chasing all comers out of its hall. The last one to leave the hall was Joseph Buchstein, who fought them regarding their crazy act.

In 1934, when Bluma Miller left to immigrate to Palestine, a go-away party was given in her honor. At its conclusion, we sang our National Anthem, "Hatiqva". The kibbutznicks among us did not rise during its singing. The head of this group was Sander from Brestezka. Shlomo Berman, who headed the local Keren Kayemet (JNF-Jewish National Fund) had sharp words with Sander regarding his refusal to join in singing Hatiqva.

12 May 1935

When Polish President Piłsudski died, a procession was planned locally to provide him last honors. Shlomo Berman suggested the procession be led by the youth group "Hanoar Hatzair", and that the "Hehalutz" alumni should follow in their foot-steps. Aryeh Ginzburg (The red-head) disapproved. As a result, his group marched separately. Shlomo Berman succeeded once again to have a local fight, this time with Aryeh (Ginzburg).

In 1936 I was inducted into the (Polish) Army. I served in its infantry division near Krakow, in "Unit No. 20". I completed my army service in 1937.

12 August 1939

The late Asher, who was the chairman of the local Jewish Community became ill, and did not recover. He died that same evening. His funeral took place the next day. The Hesped (= funeral oration) was given in our main Synagogue, in the presence of the entire community. A Hesped in the synagogue hall is not in the Jewish tradition. In this case the community wanted to give him this special honor. After the oration, the entire community walked to the cemetery.

13 August 1939

That night, after I returned from Mr. Brilant's funeral, it was 2 AM. The town's Soltas (Mayor) Yeruham Berezh, brought me that night an army call-up notice. I asked him who else got a call-up. He replied that the late Shimshon Melenow, and Avraham Fitterman received notices. On my return from the funeral, I immediately left, accompanied by my brother, Joseph, and my mother, for the train station, Avraham Fitterman, who lived near me, left with me. None of his family accompanied him to the train station, because his wife was pregnant at the time.

[Page 78]

He expressed anger that his two brothers-in-law, Simcha and Meir did not accompany him. The train took us to Dubno, to Division No. 43. Avraham and I were in the same unit. I did not get to see Shimshon Melenow since we took the train to Dubno.

Avraham and I were given two wagons laden with military hardware that we were ordered to move to Shlonsk (=name of the border province that includes Katowitz, near the Polish/German border). When war with Germany broke out on 01 Sept. 1939, our unit No. 43 was relocated to a near-border position by rail. On the way, our train was attacked by German aircraft. Fortunately their bombs missed our train. However, we were ordered to jump off the train, unload the horses and wagons (that were apparently on the train) and escape with them into a nearby forest. At that point, Avraham and I parted company. After 3 days, we passed another unit, which included Avraham Fitterman. He recognized some of our soldiers, and asked about my whereabouts. They told him that I am lying in the forest nearby. He crawled on all fours and shouted "Isaac", until he found me. He fell on me and cried, "Who will remember if we perish?" After one hour, the Germans started to fire into the forest. The forest started to burn. We all ran in different directions, and Avraham and I become separated.

* * *

From this moment, my wanderings start. I am all alone, bereft of friends, but I have resolved to stay alive, to tell my next generation what happened to me.

19 September 1939

I was taken prisoner in Pelnitz. The Germans transferred me with other POWs to "Stalag 1A" near Koenigsberg. We received one loaf of bread for 10 persons. The next morning, we were sorted according to religion. In two barracks were housed 2,000 Jewish POWs. The Polish prisoners hit us, and took from us our good clothing.

4 January 1940

The Germans ordered us to go out and remove the snow covering (from a road). We cleared 12 km per day. My legs froze and I fell into the snow. A German guard hit me, and two buddies carried me back to our camp. The guard hit them too, because they chose to carry me. They brought me back and put me into the camp's mortuary, because they thought I died.

[Page 79]

The next morning, a Polish doctor noticed me and transferred me to the camp hospital where I remained for 5 months while I recovered.

15 October 1940

I was transferred to a Jewish POW camp near Biala-Podlaska (near Brest). We were guarded by German SS and Ukrainian guards. There we found out that a train loaded with Jews stood on the siding for several days, after which they were all killed. When we were left alone for several days, I thought our fate was also sealed. However, I was wrong. The Germans needed our labor to build an airfield. We were housed in a separate POW camp; however, we ate in the local Ghetto. Our meals were brought into the Ghetto daily. [How about that!– Ed]

The road from our camp to the airfield was a long one. Our Ukrainian guards would order us to run, hit us, and torture us. We would arrive at the airfield crying, and in pain. When the German commander heard our crying they asked what happened. We told them. The commander admonished the guards telling them, "They are productive workers who add to our military capability. We must maintain their ability to work. From now on our men will fetch and return them to their camp."

In the meantime, the commander found out how little our meal portions were. He ordered to feed us extra from his mess hall. When the Ghetto Judenrat heard about it, they reduced our food allocation. We forced an appeal, and our original allocation was re-instated.

15 April 1941

We were transferred to Konskowola (near Pulawy). We were shipped in freight cars with a German guard. On the way, three POWs jumped from the train and escaped. When the guards found out about the missing men, they beat us, the remaining POWs. In Konskowola, we worked at road paving. A German guard threw a stone at my head, causing a hole in my scalp.

We received only a 200 gram slice of bread and one liter of watery soup. One day, the German SS demanded workers from the local Judenrat. The latter refused to send local Jews because we actually worked while the Ghetto Jews that were sent were mainly being tortured, rather than worked.

A person from the Judenrat bribed the POW camp commander to send POWs to the SS instead of Ghetto Jews. We arrived to the workplace in military order. Our leader reported to the work camp commander: "I brought 200 POWs for work. The commander upbraided him, saying, "I need Jews, not POWs." We were returned to our camp.

[Page 80]

18 April 1941

Until the war between Germany & USSR broke out (June 1941), we got periodic food parcels from home. One day we returned from our workplace and were told that a POW from Tarnopol received a package of Matzoh. This was two days prior to Passover. We planned to conduct a Seder in our tradition. The next day, while in town (Konskowola) at work, we purchased 300 potatoes, and two onions. We bought enough potatoes for each of the POWs, but could not get more onions. The potatoes were sold to us by a Pole "under-the-table", who feared for his life. We smuggled the potatoes into the Ghetto. We cooked them in the Ghetto kitchen and each one of smuggled in his pocket a cooked potato into our camp. It was a dangerous act.

Monik Moldowan, a lad from Shumsk, who was in camp with me the entire period, helped us in the smuggling of the potatoes and onions. He functioned as a "ring joiner" and was a privileged POW in our camp. After we returned to our camp, we washed our hands. We ate our bread portion, and the watery soup, and our eyes all focused on the potatoes to signify the Seder plate. We sat on our beds, placed the potato into our mess kit, and conducted our Seder. We took a few matzohs out of the parcel that arrived, placed it on an upside-down box in the middle and broke up both matzohs so each of us got a portion. On separate beds, we placed small bottles with water, to replace the traditional wine.

Strangely enough, someone saw to it to get a "Haggadah". We started the Haggadah reading and blessed the "wine". When we got to "Hamotzih", we gave out the matzoh pieces. Each of us was able to bless the matzoh and eat it. Now came the holiest moment, when we pealed the potatoes, and ate them as our first course. We only looked at the onion, <u>for our lot was bitter</u> without eating them. We were fortunate that none of the German guards visited the hall, so the entire Seder went off without a hitch.

As we reached the end of the "Haggadah" to the sentence, "The next year we shall be free," we took the matzoh box, and carried it like a "Sefer Torah" around the room. We hugged and kissed one another as we yelled out the last sentence again and again during the walk around the room.

The next day, the local Folksdeutsche, and Ukrainians yelled towards us, as we marched to work, "Where are your matzohs? No more use of our blood for your crazy customs?" We were tempted to reply that we had matzohs nonetheless, but we thought better of it. To do so was dangerous, so we remained silent.

8 May 1942

After Passover, we were brought into town (Konskowola), and were ordered to tear down several wealthy Jewish homes because of a rumor that these Jews placed valuables inside their walls, and in other hiding places. We POWs erected the scaffolding, and the Ghetto Jews carried out the teardown.

[Page 81]

It was a terrible sight. The Jews, who were skeletons, tore down the walls brick by brick. Sometimes a brick would fall and injure a person below. German guards would remove the dead to the mortuary. We POWs tied ourselves to wagons and dragged these bodies to the cemetery. Some would beg us, "Jews, don't bury us, we are still alive".

We hoped, in vain, that the rumors are false, that nothing would be found. Unfortunately, the rumors were correct. Valuable items were found. In one house gold coins, silver items and holy books were found. In another, gold plated cutlery was found, placed in the order of usage, as was customary in that household. Cups, with Passover or Shavuoth symbols were found elsewhere. The most surprising find was a Sefer Torah together with money – the owner's two most important possessions.

In one place they pulled out a Gemmarah volume. As they held the book, out fell several dollar bills. We were sorely embarrassed at the sight. The German supervisors took the valuables, and threw the holy books into a bonfire.

6 September 1942

We were sent to work in Pulawy, 3 km. from Konskowola. We were brought to the Vistula riverbank to dig a parallel canal. When we opened the bypass canal, we were flooded with thousands of fish of all kinds. We were delighted but did not know what to do. Our Polish work master noticed the happening. He called us to his workroom, where he kept our work tools and said, "Take as many fish as you wish as long as I get some of them". We fulfilled his wishes, caught several hundred kilograms of fish and bartered these in a neighboring village for potatoes and barley. We were joyful to have the extra food, but a problem arose. A young soldier from Stuchin decided it was imperative to barter all the fish as soon as possible for other items before the fish spoil. He went back to the village and bartered the fish for bread, apples and barley. As he left the village, a Pole chased him, robbed him of his goods and wounded him with his knife all over his body. The soldier returned to our base, barely alive. We were frightened. Our luck was that our work master heard about what happened, and called a Doctor friend to treat him. The latter treated him with injections, and dressed his wounds. He left the soldier ointment and dressings for subsequent treatment. This episode left a deep impression on us, and added to our sorrow because the deed was done by a Pole, a group that is also being persecuted by the Germans.

[Page 82]

15 October 1942

Today, the last transport of Pulawy Jews left for Auschwitz. *[I doubt he knew the destination. – Ed.]* We were curfewed in our work camp. We could hear their cries, and we knew they were being sent to their death.

Wagner, the German work master, stood far from the railroad station, silently watching the proceeding. He, more than once, took risks to save Jews from death. We did not know his motivation. Some Jews suspected that he was secretly a Jew, for otherwise they could not fathom his willingness to save Jews. Even today, he has great conniptions about what is happening, but, like us, is powerless to intervene. I suddenly saw a blond Jewish child that was thrown out of the train wagon, walking instinctively back to the empty Ghetto. She sidled up to the Ukrainian that stood next to Wagner, like a little cub next to his mother, seeking protection. The Ukrainian lifted his foot and kicked the infant away from him. Wagner noticed the deed. He moved, took out his revolver. I was sure Wagner will kill the sadistic Ukrainian, and thereby will reveal his Jewish image. I was afraid for him, because I, too, knew him as a man who was good to Jews. To our surprise, he went over to the child, grabbed her hair with his left hand, and with his right hand shot her in the head. He tossed her on the floor like a chicken that had just been slaughtered, and kicked her with his foot. Wagner remained an enigma to me. The episode does, however, illustrate to me his German character.

Afterwards we transferred to Budzyn (See Ency. Judaica), near Krasnik. There I worked in a factory that made aircraft parts. In the factory I met POWs that came to the factory from Lublin. They told me that there is a concentration camp nearby where Avraham Fitterman, Yaacov Terlo and Yunek Farber are held. (He was probably referring to Majdanek, where the three perished.)

13 November 1942

Eight work foremen, all Jewish men, disappeared. The camp was stood on its head. The search was detailed, accompanied by beatings. Feigess (camp commander) himself supervised the search, but in vain. The search lasted three days. Those three days were hell for us. We knew the next day that the eight joined partisans in a nearby forest.

02 December 1942

Feigess' (camp commander) attitude softened when he noticed the many sick that resulted from the hard winter conditions. He constructed a hospital for us. We started to believe in miracles. After 3 days, when the sick were assembled in one place, he killed all of them, one after another. As they yelled and groaned, he changed bullets in his pistol in a quiet manner.

[Page 83]

13 December 1942

A new SS chief arrived at our camp. We wondered about his nature. Will he be our savior, i.e. a mench, or a wild animal? He wandered about the camp for two days, looked around, learned the goings-on. He looked sad, something seems to be bothering him. His deep thought did not fit the stereotype Nazi. We wondered about him. On the 3rd day Feigess hanged him publicly. It turned out he was a German Jew.

16 December 1942

A search was made in the barrack next to ours. They found money in the mattress of a 14 year old inmate that his parents probably left him before they were deported. Feigess rebuked him over a serious violation of camp rules, pulled out his pistol and killed him in the middle of the rebuke.

19 December 1942

We were all transferred to the Jew's camp. We are no longer POWs, but instead, Jews subject to slaughter. To illustrate the change in our status, Feigess took out 100 of us and killed them inside the camp.

21 December 1942

A week ago, a performance took place in our camp. A group of Jewish performers, headed by singer Slutsky, prepared a skit, per Feigess' request for his enjoyment. Goldstein, from Lodz, was outstanding; however, Slutsky treated us to a wonderful songfest. He is a superior singer. Feigess was so impressed by Slutsky's singing, he gave him a near-new coat. In the cold winter that we experienced, the coat was a significant present, a gift that preserves life. Slutsky was pleased with the present he received, yet after five days, he bartered it for food. Feigess met him later without his coat and asked him to explain. When he heard the answer, Feigess took him outside the camp and ordered him to dig his own grave. When the grave was finished, he ordered him to lie in it so Feigess could kill him while he lay there. Slutsky started to stammer. Suddenly Stockman, his Jewish superior, raised his whip and told him to sing. After a few hits, Slutsky started to sing. This helped. Feigess was again charmed by his singing, and retracted the punishment. Goldstein and Slutsky were freed later with me and survived.

07 January 1943

The Jew, Zoberman, was named deputy to Stockman. He was ugly, always bitter over what nature has wrought him.

[Page 84]

He took out his frustration on his fellow Jews. When we approached him for winter clothing from his stock-room full of clothes, he would hit us. We just avoided him, preferring to suffer the cold air.

Today, Zoberman behaved strangely. He became envious of Stockman, whom everyone, including the Germans, like. He noticed that no one is interested in his favors and he must have felt it. There is no other way to fathom his behavior. Today, he called us over, to receive clothing. To ensure we are not afraid of him, he threw the clothes to us from a distance. We came and took them.

When the stock room emptied, a box full of gold and jewelry was found. The Germans suspected Stockman that he collected and stored them, so he was arrested immediately. We were all worried about Stockman's welfare for we loved the man. Jews prayed for his deliverance. At the same time, Zoberman came out of his stock room and admitted to Feigess that he was the culprit, that Stockman is innocent. He asked that Stockman be freed. After two hours, we saw him dig a grave, surrounded by Ukrainians. When he finished digging, they lowered him into the grave and covered him so his head stuck out. We saw his body above ground. So ended the Zoberman affair.

18 June 1943

Remnants from the Warsaw Ghetto uprising were brought to our camp. The group was of ca. 300 men. Before they were assigned bunks in our camp Feigess took 15 of them and killed them. Afterwards he ordered the newcomers, who had survived several hells, to give him their valuables. I could not believe my eyes. They still had gold among their possessions. Among those that gave up his gold was an old man, named Pines, from a famous Warsaw family. I befriended him.

29 June 1943

Among the Warsaw Ghetto survivors was a blacksmith who constructed his own food bowl, a wastyn. Feigess approached him as he stood in line for his food in the kitchen and asked to be shown this wastyn. We felt that something is happening here. The wastyn had a double bottom, inside of which were gold coins. Feigess weighed the article in his hand, and asked what is inside. The blacksmith admitted his "crime". We suspected that he was reported by someone. After we finished our meal, we were called to report to the camp center. In the middle stood the blacksmith with a horse-chain around his neck. Feigess gave a signal, and the Ukrainians started to drag him around the parade ground. When they finished a round, they stood him on his feet, poured water over his head and swung him again, until he died while being dragged.

[Page 85]

04 July 1943

A 12 year old boy came to the camp and went straight to the kommandatura office. The Ukrainian guards taunted him. "Polish boy, go away, otherwise we will cut you in pieces." When he explained to them that he is a Jew, they laughed. "You better scram, otherwise we will kill you." The boy insisted on speaking to the German commander after which they can kill him. The Ukrainians brought him to the OberLieutenant

[=first lieutenant]. The boy told him the following: He and his family hid in a village with a Polish family. He was one of seven children with grandfather and grandmother. The parents had been murdered long ago. Grandfather used to pay the Polish host once a week with a valuable. After a while, the grandmother died and grandfather told his host that he has no more funds. The Pole demanded that they leave his house immediately. The family left for the forest. There grandpa took out his last asset that he hid in a place only known to him. It was a pot full of gold Dinars. He divided them among his grandchildren and told them to part, each going in a different direction. He then blessed each one. The Pole ambushed them; he apparently listened in to their conversation. He ran home, brought a pistol, robbed and killed all but one child. The 12 year old boy remained, for he hid in one of the trees. When the Pole returned home, the boy saw that he opened a door in the house floor where they used to hide and hid his pistol there. According to the boy's story, the Pole is a member of the Armia Krajowa (= Home Army), that he stores weapons in his home, that these will be used against the Germans at the appropriate moment.

The Oberlieutenant believed the boy. He took a group of soldiers to the village and went to the Pole's home. The family consisted of a wife and 10 children. The husband was absent, apparently hiding. The Oberlieutenant forced the family to find the murderer. He was brought to the forest. The family dug a grave, and the Oberlieutenant killed him personally in the family's presence. Various weapons were found in the hideaway. The boy's family name was Pinto. When he returned to our camp, the Germans gave him warm clothing and food. To the end of the war, Pintele, as he was called, was loved by us, and cared for by the Germans.

16 July 1943

Feigess became mad. He ordered to have all six camp children that remained brought in front of him. Among the children was one girl, whose mother was in the camp with her.

[Page 86]

When Feigess caught the girl, the mother would not release her. Feigess, angry, shot the mother. He left the girl alone. There were two brothers, the youngest of the two aged six, who was employed as a shepherd, tending Feigess' ducks. When Feigess passed him, the boy saluted him and reported: "One mother duck, and five little ones." Feigess loved the boy. He would return the boy's salute. He killed the rest of the children including the older brother of the shepherd. When the shepherd saw the killing of his brother, he ran into a wheat field and hid inside the field. After an hour, the boy came into the camp's kitchen located at the end of our camp. We were, at the time, slicing cabbage to be made into sauerkraut. A set of turned over beer vats served as chairs and tables. The boy approached the cook and asked him to hide him under one of the vats. The cook did so. Feigess entered the kitchen at that moment, angry, demanding that we reveal the child's hiding place. He claimed that he was told that the child ran into the kitchen. The cook withstood Feigess' threat and did not reveal the boy's hiding place. The next day, the child came to eat, however Feigess' anger had passed by then and the boy remained alive. He survived to this day.

9 August 1943

The rumors of German reversals multiplies. There is talk about the Red army nearing Budzyn where we are located. We felt that something need be done. The Ukrainian guards, who heretofore did the dirty work for the Germans, began to be concerned about saving their hide. Now they discovered another way to save themselves. Twenty

Ukrainians conspired to escape from the camp. They got in touch with our Jewish blacksmiths, tailors, and carpenters, to plan the mass breakout, and escape to the forest. The needed the cooperation with the camp Jews, as an alibi, that the breakout was meant to save the Jews, when the Soviets arrive.

The leader of the underground organization was a Ukrainian captain, one of the POWs named Shabtchenko. According to the prepared plan, we were to disconnect power to all the camp's lights. The Ukrainians were to open the weapon's storeroom, to distribute these weapons to the insurgents, to attack the guards and then escape. At the appointed hour, all lights went out, and the men ran to their posts. However, the chief of the Ukrainian police, who was in on the plan, went to his superior Feigess, and told him that something strange is taking place within the camp. Feigess and his 300 deputies, among them Ukrainians, caught the insurgents. The plan failed. Nineteen Ukrainian inmates managed to escape with their weapons in hand. One of them, together with 6 Jews was shot the next day by Feigess. The shot Jews whose names I remember are: Pomerantz, Mogilnick, Yekultiel and Gonser.

[Page 87]

15 October 1943

When the German army was defeated at Stalingrad, the German authorities sent German youths to the eastern front. Hitler stated that if German youths get used to killing, that is to see what killing is about by killing Jews, they would be more successful in front-duty. These young men were sent on a trial basis to concentration camps in the Lublin area, where 90,000 Jews were located. *[I have searched but have not been able to confirm the major parts of this story in other publications. It is something that the author appears to have gotten second hand – Ed].* German soldiers surrounded the camp, and German Youths were sent into the camp to become indoctrinated [*to kill Jews*]. The camp included 800 Jews who decided not to become "sheep ready for slaughter." Among them was Avraham Fitterman, Ya'acov Taitel, and Yunek Farber (all deceased).

Ya'acov Taitel

Instead, they took matches and started fires near the German officer barracks, and the hospital. Many of the Germans died in the fire. However, the authorities brought reinforcements who fell on the insurgents and took their weapons from them. Some of the inmates jumped into the fire. Among those who committed suicide were A. Fisherman and Ya'acov Terlo. We were told about the death of the Jewish POWs based on information that local partisans brought to us the next day *[apparently via contact men amongst the guards. Partisans did not visit the camp – Ed.]*

As we were crying, having heard of the death of other Jewish POWs, a German officer entered and was surprised that we were informed of the episode. He could not hide his astonishment, saying, "Look at these Jews. They have no newspapers, no telephones, no radio, yet they know all the news!"

[Page 88]

18 October 1943

The news of the insurgency in the Lublin camp spread to other camps. On the day of the revolt in the Lublin camp, ten Jews, who worked in a bakery in a village near Budzyn tried to escape to a nearby forest. The guards caught them and brought them to our camp. Feigess ordered that they be publicly hanged in our camp. They were so positioned that their heads hung down, to increase their torture prior to their death. Among those hanged was a person by the name of Aharonowitz from Lutsk and Mamot from Rovno.

November 1943

Thirty Jews were brought to our camp from a nearby forest where they hid after escaping from transports to death camps. Most of the Jews were women. The women were murdered by Scharfuerer (= SS rank) Feigess publicly. He left the men unharmed. One of the men was a primitive sort, with limited intelligence. He was illiterate who used to work as a cobbler. He was caught with his six-year old son. Feigess saw an opportunity to "correct" himself, i.e., not to shoot the child. He replaced his pistol in its holster, went back to the camp's store-room, and returned with an axe. He ordered the poor illiterate father to chop off the head of his son. The father lost his mind. Feigess killed him personally after a few days.

9 March 1944

A German Major came to the camp with his staff of automobile repair technicians from the Eastern front. He brought with him transport vehicles that needed repair. The major worked on these repairs together with his technicians. He asked Feigess to provide him with a Jewess that would clean his lodging while he worked. While the woman was in the major's room, Feigess came in to inspect her work. He found her drinking a cup of tea. He immediately ordered her to the camp's gate, made her crawl on all fours, lifted her skirt and prepared to give her 25 lashes. After 15 lashes, when she was about to faint, he ordered her to rise, and stand at the gate for the rest of the day.

8 September 1944

Several German cars with SS men in new uniforms arrived at the camp's depot. Their leader was a woman in SS uniform. She presented documents to receive a set of weapons from the camp's depot. The Oberlieutenant responsible for the arms depot countersigned these orders and we loaded the requested weapons and bullets onto their vehicles.

When they left, it turned out that the group was actually partisans, dressed in SS uniforms. Their leader was a woman, from Pintele's (little Pinto) village. She recognized him and signaled to him to remain quiet, to act as if he does not know her, and to disappear. He was a wise boy, unlike his age. Only after the group left did he tell us his findings. Thus we knew of the feat before the Germans realized they had been fooled.

[Page 89]

After a short while, our camp was surrounded. The SS wanted to liquidate the camp's Jews. However, one of the camp's officers was able to convince the SS group commander to spare us because we were needed for current military tasks. He persuaded them that liquidation can be carried out anytime in the future. The next day, we were transferred to Willizka to dig salt underground.

10 October 1944

We were transferred from Willizka to Flossenburg, where we stayed for two weeks.

October 1944

An order was received to transfer us to Leitmeritz (= Litomerice in CZ) in the Sudeten, part of Czechoslovakia. We again had to rid ourselves of lice, this time in a thorough manner. In the past, we did so outside the camp by searching for lice in the folds of our garments. This time, we were taken outside the camp, stripped naked, next taken to washrooms where German guards sprayed us with a hot water shower. We received new clothes and wooden shoes. When we saw the new clothes, we concluded that we are being taken to gas chambers. We said goodbye to each other and cried. The guards saw our mood but said nothing. It turned out that we were scheduled to work in Leitmeritz. Here I worked in a gravel pit. In the camps I was an inmate in the past, and we received 200g bread and one liter of soup. With such nourishment, we were expected to do physical labor.

06 December 1944

The Germans brought hundreds of Poles, remnants of the Warsaw uprising, to our camp in Leitmeritz. They were placed in the death camp. Every day, scores of this group were killed. Among them were two Warsaw Jews. They came to us and asked us to save them. When we related their request to Wittman, our work leader, a Berlin Jew, he went into action immediately. The two received our work clothes, joined us and thereby remained with us until we were liberated.

25 April 1945

We were transferred from Leitmeritz to Teresienstadt, 7 km from Leitmeritz. We stayed in the camp until 8 May 1945, when the Red army came and liberated us. After the end of the war, I was transferred to a Leitmeritz hospital for medical treatment. I recovered after 6 months and was discharged.

I traveled to Lanovits in the hopes of finding family members that survived. In Lanovits, I lodged in Didik's house. In the morning I left his house to see the destruction of my town. It is hard to describe the wide destruction and the empty lots. Only 8 houses survived intact. In Lanovits, I met Lyova Gluzstein, the brother of Fuzi. He was one of the POWs that survived. The late Zvi Kerper, the son of Benny, the deaf, also visited Lanovits. He had secured an important political position in Rostov, USSR. I met him dressed in a Russian army uniform with a pistol attached to this belt.

I remained in Lanovits for 5 months then traveled to Gleiwitz, Poland. From there, the "Brichah" (=escape) organized by an Israeli organization helped me to escape to Wels, Austria.

[Page 90]

I left for Israel on 6 June 1949, on the Galilea Steamship (from Trieste, Italy). The rest of the Lanovits Jews that I met while there all immigrated to Israel except Haim Natan Gitelman.

[Page 91]

Lanovits – Majdanek, 1944

Shlomo Pacht (Kendziurs)

(Montreal, Canada)

As with all matters in the USSR, I paid a bribe to arrange military travel papers that requested my presence to appear at the Polish army camp in Zhitormir. Neither the officer that issued the paper, nor I, knew where the Polish division was presently located. We relied on the Soviet trust in military paperwork, hence put down Zhitomir. On the way to Zhitomir, I came to realize that there is no such camp, and never was.

Mendel Brimmer "fixed" my travel papers by changing the destination to Lvov. With the corrected travel papers, my two brothers and I traveled in the direction of Lanovits. We reached Yampol (=Yampil in the Ukraine), 12 km from Lanovits. The rail line beyond Yampol was damaged. The train remained standing at Iskowitz (= Juskowcy). We detrained. It was a clear night. We carried our luggage and walked "home." We got to Grybovo at 6 a.m. The women were already in their fields, working separately from the men folks. My father Berl, who did tailoring for the peasants of the villages, was well known and liked by these villagers. The peasant women recognized us. When they saw us they shouted, "Berl's sons have returned," and cried at the same time.

We knew nothing of the Holocaust that took place; hence we were puzzled why they were crying. They declined to explain. We visited Panasy Yashchuk, a Stundist (- member of a Protestant sect) known in our neighborhood as a deeply religious and moral man. It was with him that we hid some of our goods and goods of others during the Soviet regime. During the last period before the Holocaust, I used to lease land from the goyim (Gentiles). I brought the harvest to Yashchuk's threshing floor. He would thresh the wheat, and keep our harvest separate from his. He did so with almost religious fervor. Now he cried like a baby. His wife came out of the house crying and ran away. "What happened?" I asked. I expected him to tell me that our goods were taken away. "All were killed," he answered.

[Page 92]

"Why?" I asked (a naïve question on my part). I had no idea why all had to be killed. I could not get more details out of him. We left his house.

I entered Lanovits at 9 AM. After all, I knew my town with all its alleys. This time, I did not recognize her. The town vanished. Only a few houses remained standing. Between these houses others lay in ruins. I went over to our house which was still standing. My heart was beating as I approached it. I expected to see my father, my sisters, and my mother, to see the happy past return. Instead, Adamchuk's daughter came out of the house, a young, blond Gentile woman. My father had turned the house to her because it was outside the ghetto, and told her: "We are going to be killed, guard the house in the event my sons will return so that they will have a roof over their head." She told this to us and that was the truth. Then she added, "Do not go out alone. Bandera bands are in the area, murdering all remnants of the previous (Soviet) administration, also former town residents."

She told us that several Jewish residents returned after the Holocaust, among them Itzik Sabaris, Yisrael Brodsky and others. The Soviets inducted them into their army. Six to seven Russians and collaborators are being murdered daily (by Bandera bands).

We entered the house. It was requisitioned by the Raispulbum (District Council). They let the young woman live in the kitchen. Her husband, a soldier, was missing. She and an infant lived in the kitchen. We, too, remained in my parents' kitchen with its inheritors.

We left our parcels in the house and went out. We met the son-in-law of Paweli, the blind. He informed us that Richter, the German Gebiets-kommander was crazy. He killed and hit people for pleasure. He once hit Paweli, when he saw him go out with nine small pigs to a meadow, claiming that he must watch the pigs because the German army needs them. He further told us about 20 pretty local girls that had to be supplied to the German army to clean their houses and do more things..... . He also warned us not to wander about lest we be killed. We went to visit local friends despite his warnings.

We found two trenches, covered with a thin layer of earth. Skeleton bits stuck out of these trenches. Our family and friends rest here. Gentiles stood near us and cried as they saw us. They told us that for two weeks after the liquidation, these trenches moved. Blood would occasionally spurt up from them like a fountain. I fainted. When I awoke, I found myself lying down in our kitchen.

When I recovered, I decided to escape from here as soon as possible. With the help of a Russo-Polish local attorney, whom I had known previously, I willed the house to its present tenant so that it would not fall into the hands of the government. I took the document to the secretary of the Raispulbum, representing the Communist party. The official rose from his seat, pulled his pistol from his holster, and asked:

[Page 93]

"Abominable Jew, the Ukrainians murdered all those dear to you, and you turn your house over to them? There are unusual cases, but your case is dishonorable, and more." All this preaching was meant to frighten me, and to test whether I am indeed the true heir of the house. If not, to persuade me to change my mind and leave the house to the local authorities.

My brothers and I climbed onto the first train leaving Lanovits to escape this place. What the Germans failed to accomplish, the Russians accomplished. I fought in the Red army, was wounded while serving in it (yet I decided to leave the USSR). We reached Zamosc, the border town. We crossed the border at night and reached Lublin, Poland.

Lublin was liberated in September 1944. The local partisans surrounded the city. The Germans and their collaborators were caught in the ring-hold around the city. The small fry escaped, only their leaders were caught.

Before I arrived in Lublin, I saw journalists and important leaders all going to Majdanek, the concentration camp located in a suburb of Lublin. One cannot imagine the sight; that such cruelty can be instituted. An oven was still functioning. Metal racks on which bodies were inserted into the oven stood in front of these ovens.

Before the SS staff escaped from Majdanek, they wanted to obliterate signs of their crimes. They had little time so they shot all the inmates: Jews, Ukrainian collaborators, and Russian POWs. Many of the latter were lying on the ground, wounded, groaning quietly so as not to be noticed by the remaining German staff.

We tried to save those that could be saved. In the rows of the wounded, I pulled out a tall Jewish lad dressed in a Russian-officer uniform. I recognized that he was Jewish and saved him. The gas chamber was a 12 x 12 meter room. Its flooring was still wet from the cleaning it received after the gassing. Nearby, were shacks full of children's shoes, and sorted adult clothing. It was heartbreaking to see the piles of children's shoes. It brought memories of children running, playing catch, and other games. I could imagine these children, pleading to be saved for they are so young. Yet, we could no longer save them. I am not a writer, but to this day, I remember these small children's legs that the Nazis ignored, children who committed no sin.

Ukrainians and Poles rummaged through the men's shoes to search for gold and jewelry that some Jews hid inside their soles and heels. This is how these vultures wanted to enrich themselves. They appeared to have found items inside these shoes. I, myself, found a green paper with Hebrew Letters and a serial number, a Palestine pound sterling money note.

[Page 94]

It must have belonged to a Jew who left Palestine, to avoid hardships, and return to the easy life in Poland. With the pound sterling note he hoped to save himself. I also found 2 damaged greenback dollars bills.

On the second day of my arrival in Lublin, I was informed that its Nazi leaders will be hanged publicly. Politicians and journalists came to be present and photograph this revenge-act. I, who was familiar with the details of their horror acts, volunteered to translate into Polish and Russian all that surviving witnesses testified to. Unwittingly, I converted a friendly testimony to a historic event, with me the main witness. Five hanging posts were erected in a forest clearing. A Polish professional hangman, with white gloves, was at the ready for the best event of his life. A Jewish sergeant of the Polish military police managed the event. His task was a great privilege, to mastermind this act of revenge. Following his order, the five trucks, on which sat the selected "heroes" on a bench with their head covered, entered the hanging area. The Jewish sergeant signaled to the hangman. He climbed onto each truck, had each criminal stand up, and draped the noose around their neck. Next the Polish priest climbed the truck and whispered whatever message he had. This process was followed on each truck. The sergeant asked each criminal if they had something to say to justify their crime. Each one answered, "I have nothing to say." The main criminal, a man of low-stature said nothing. He was shaking, and could not utter a word. The sergeant gave another signal. The trucks moved from the hanging posts and the men were left hanging, crumbling. Whoever had not seen this event has not experienced a tragic gratification. The bodies were left hanging for two weeks, to symbolize the revenge due Nazi criminals. It was a message for future generations.

The mob who wanted to lynch these criminals received some satisfaction seeing them hanging there. The average person was now able to experience freedom after years of daily nightmares.

[Page 95]

How My Daughter Was Saved

Shalom Segal

When I returned from the labor camp [apparently after the war – Ed.] I hurried to Lanovits to search for my wife Idis [nee Rosenberg] and for our young child. The local Gentiles told me everything. I knew I could not find my family in Lanovits. However, from Elenka, who used to live behind the Rosenberg house, I learned that my daughter survived because my wife tried and succeeded to save her before she perished. According to Moshe [Rosenberg, the brother of Idis], my daughter is in the village of Slobidka, near Yampil, with a Shtundist family [a protestant sect].

I arrived in Slobidka on Saturday. When I entered the house of the Shtundist family, the farmer's wife was standing at the oven, baking cakes for the Sunday meal. I asked her where a girl named Clara can be found. The farmer woman was silent for a moment, next asked me who I was. When she heard that I was the girl's father, she explained that the girl will soon return from the field where she is minding a flock of geese, and I will be able to see her, even take her.

After a short time a thin, neglected, five-year old girl appeared, followed by a flock of geese. I recognized her immediately. She looked just like her mother. I ran towards her attempting to hug her, but she, afraid, ran from me. I begged her to come to me. I said: "I am your father, don't be afraid of me!" She cried back "My father is in a prison camp, you are not my father". I offered her candy, and a toy watch. I tried in vain to reach her. The girl kept her distance and looked for her foster-mother to protect her from this stranger. In the meantime it was evening, and I was afraid to stay in the village [Bandera partisans were hunting Soviet bureaucrats and Jews after the war- Ed]. I returned to Lanovits that evening, and returned to the village the next day. I took her to Lanovits by force. Fortunately her "sister", a 17 year-old girl, came along with her. It was due to her sister's help that I was able to take her with me.

The child was dirty, and full of scratches from field weeds.

[Page 96]

Her scalp was also scratched, covered with abscess. When I cut her hair, she cried to high heaven. She did not forgive me for this deed. The next day, while I was gone from the house Clara escaped and returned to Slobidka [How did a five year old find her way? –Ed.] I could not imagine how she could go that far. I looked for her in Lanovits. When I did not find her I traveled to the village [Slobidka] and found her there. She was hiding in the corner of the Shtundist's home, asking them to protect her. I returned with her to Lanovits, and immediately moved to Tarnopol. I anticipated that being far from her foster-parents she will bond with me and calm down.

My daughter was saved thanks to these good people. Today she is a mother and homemaker in Israel. It is good that she has forgotten her difficult past.

* * *

On Saturday, while I was waiting in the Shtundist's house for my daughter to return from the field, the farmer's wife told me the details of our daughter's story.

In the fall of 1942, at the end of December, the Rosenberg's friend Klim forced my wife, Idis, to find an alternate hiding place for our daughter. Otherwise, Klim threatened to throw her out of his house. Klim did make the effort to find an alternate family. He found a Shtundist family in the village of Slobidka, who was willing to receive her. Idis dressed our daughter with several layers of clothing, including a sheepskin coat I purchased for her prior to the establishment of the Lanovits Ghetto. Idis hired a Waggoner and went to the address given to her. They arrived on a cold night. The Earth was frozen, so the noise of a wagon raised attention in the village. Fearful of the attention, Idis placed the girl near a fence she thought was that of the Shtundist house, but turned out to be a different house. She stuffed the remaining dollar bills in the girl's clothing and tacked a note to her dress stating: "My father was murdered, my mother will be murdered. Please take in this girl and the Lord will help you." She did not sign her name.

In the morning, when the farmer woman found the child, she asked her: "What are you doing here?" The child, who spoke a clear Ukrainian, answered "I am waiting for my mother". The child did not want to follow the farmer woman, and did not let her touch her. Only later, when she became hungry, did the girl agree to enter the farmer's house to eat. The farmer woman took all her clothes, dressed her in rags, and went to the Starosta [-village head] to ask him what to do with the child. The Starosta asked her to take her in. He promised to provide her 2 liters of milk per day for the child and her children.

After a few days Idis sent Mitiya to the village to check whether the girl was saved. He found out the mistake in the address when he visited the intended Shtundist family. He went to their neighbor and explained the mistake.

[Page 97]

Klim returned to the village periodically to visit the child and bring her a message from her mother. One day he found out that the foster woman returned the child to the Starosta, telling him that her children have not gotten used to the girl, and have been beating her. She agreed to give-up the milk allocation, and to return the child. Klim took advantage of the opportunity to transfer my daughter Clara-Zhenia to the Shtundist family that offered to take her initially. It was due to their generosity and care that I found her alive when I returned.

* * *

Idis' fate, to my sorrow, was different. A Bandera group discovered her, forcing Klim to ask her to leave his house. These Ukrainian murderers found her in a field, on her way back to Lanovits. They buried her alive together with Shmuel and Aaron Mehlman, Misha Grisham, and the daughter of Sarah Wiesman, the daughter of Shalom Wiesman.

At the edge of the Jewish cemetery in Lanovits there is another small mass grave. It is there that these five persons are buried.

[Page 98]

About Idis' Daughter

Moshe Rosenberg

When Idis [Moshe's sister- Ed] escaped with her daughter from the Ghetto, and hid with Mitiya, the latter did not want to hide them. Instead Mitiya went to locate an alternate hiding place. The man who received her goods told her that he was willing to hide her but could not hide the child. He promised Idis to try and find a hiding place for her and the child. However, no one was willing to accept the child.

In the meantime one evening Mitiya came drunk to his friend and said: "I know that you have Jews in your home. I will publicize your deed unless you share the goods you received with me. The friend became alarmed and asked my sister to leave. She had nowhere to go with the child. In the past she and her keeper had agreed that she will leave the child at the fence of an old [Shtundist] neighbor who was known as a good man. When Idis left the house of Mitiya's friend that night, she remembered the offer of this old man. Idis went to the man's village and left the child in the field next to his house together with a bundle of clothing and a few dollars that she still had. She also added a letter in which she asked the peasant to accept the child inasmuch as she could not raise her. She added in the letter "A day will hopefully arrive when I will return to get her back, at which time I will compensate you for your good deed. The girl was then 2 ½. She spoke Ukrainian as well as any Ukrainian child.

In the morning, when the child was found, she was asked: "What are you doing here my darling?" The child replied: "I am waiting for my mother". The farmer reported the event to the district chief in Didrekala and asked what to do with her. The village head told him it was up to him whether to take or leave the child. The Gentile couple took the child in.

I, who knew what had happened because both I and Idis were hiding with Mitiya's neighbor, tracked the events relating to the child. After three weeks the Gentile's wife went to the village-head and told him that she no longer wished to keep the child. She asked her neighbors if they were willing to take her instead. Her Shtundist neighbor, for whom the child was originally intended on that fateful night, told her: "I am ready to take her. I have three children at home. With her there will be four." The Shtundist farmer woman fell in love with the beautiful child and took her in.

In the meantime a rumor spread in Slobidka and its surrounding villages that a small child in the village was available [for adoption] with the acquiescence of the village head. One of the farmers from Yampil, who was childless, approached the Slobidka village head and told him he wished to adopt the child, having heard that one of the villagers does not want her. The Shtundist farmer-woman agreed to let the Yampil farmer have the child. When her children returned from work [in the fields?] and saw that that their "sister" was missing, they told their mother that they love her and would not accept the separation. The Shtundist children traveled 5 km to the Yampil farmer and took the child by force. They took along a cloth carpet make from sewn-together sacks, and used it to carry the child home on a stretcher. As a result, the child remained with the Stundist family until the end of the war.

When Shalom Segal returned from the labor camp, and heard from me what had happened with his daughter, he went to the Shtundist family in Slobidka and fetched her. As a result the child remained Jewish.

[Page 99]

Horror Details

Byya Goldberg

The house of Rabbi Goldzaker was included inside the Ghetto. Several other families were added to this household and lived there. Yankele, the son of the Rabbi, was a talented child both in his studies and in work matters. During the holocaust period, he realized that a way out of the Ghetto needed to be found. He dug an underground tunnel to a destination beyond the Ghetto fence. It was to save his parents, brothers and him some day.

Mirel Goldberg (nee Kuztseker) noticed his deed, despite the fact that Yankele kept his task a secret, even from his family. He only dug at hours when no one noticed, or when no one was home.

At the last moment, when Yankele revealed his secret to his parents, the family left the Ghetto through the tunnel. Their departure occurred after the Ghetto had already been emptied of its residents. At the last moment, Mirel crawled out after them. Their bad luck was that a Ukrainian policeman happened to pass by and discovered them. He grabbed Mirel, who was already old and frail. He pulled her by her hair and killed her. The Rabbi's entire family was killed as they emerged from the tunnel.

* * *

Rabbi Ahareli went with his flock on their death march to the cemetery, dressed in a white kitel (gown worn on Yom Kippur) and sash. On the way he stopped, stood aside those who were walking and spoke approximately the following words of condolence:

"Dear brethren, we are about to transfer to a heavenly regime. After the great suffering on Earth that we all experienced, I am sure you will reach the Garden of Eden. Therefore, do not worry, go to your fate with the comfort that we all were fortunate to die as Jews, to honor his majesty. Our only sin is that we are Jews. That is why they are killing us. Go therefore quietly, for you will be joining the righteous of this world."

For a moment the Ukrainian guards did not realize what the old Rabbi said, and why his face lit up as he spoke.

When the Rabbi finished his sermon, Ephraim, the son of Krupnitzky tugged at the Rabbi's sash and cried: " Rabbi, don't leave me, let me walk with you, to help me face death."

The Rabbi continued his walk while Ephraim attached himself to him and followed in his footsteps.

In the meantime, one of the Ukrainian (guards) recovered from his astonishment. He went over to the Rabbi and shot him and Ephraim with several bullets as both were praying. Both fell bleeding to death on the road to the cemetery.

As soon as they fell, two farmers came over, and threw the two bodies, like two sacks, on a wagon. The wagon collected all bodies who trailed and were killed on the way.

This is how Rabbi Ahareli was buried with his flock in the mass grave.

[Page 100]

[Poems translated by Mira Eckhaus]
In memory of martyrs

Rivka Perla (the granddaughter of Yitzhak Melamed)

The candle continues to drip
in a long and continuous silence,
so human life dripped and ended
with terrible and brutal cruelty.

We will not forget, we will remember with a tremor,
we will remember the Holocaust and the fire
when we were like a nut shell,
a ship wrecked in a raging sea.

Darkness wrapped the world,
darkness of indifference to the suffering
of the martyrs of our people.
Did no one ask what their crime was, what their sin was?
Did no one investigate why their blood was spilled?

Their memory infuriates me,
the memory of the people, women and children,
and we scream for revenge, revenge
for life that ended and the soul that was taken away.

Memorial candle

Elioz Rabin

A Jewish hand ignited it,
a weak, thin, sly hand.
A hand that has not yet been killed,
two thousand years, years of hope.

And it's burning! It didn't go out by blood.
It did not go out by animals breath.
Because a human ignited it,
a member of a persecuted people, badly bruised.

[Page 101]

Everyone is already dead, there is no one left alive
from the persecuted poor people.
Only the candle is still burning, shining endlessly,
its wick has burned, its wax has leaked,

and it's still burning. As if thousands of years,
years of burning, had not passed through it.
Blood, wounds, terrors did not cloud
its clear light, and his stature is bright.

Memorial candle. Poor memorial candle!
A wounded and humiliated exiled people!
You both live in a world of pain.
You light the path of every unfortunate.

I want to live

Elioz Rabin

Here pass the lines to death,
the children here are always hungry.
Here, everyone is the same - the sons of deep darkness,
with no past, with no present, with no future.

On a moldy slice of bread, they live here,
from today to tomorrow, nothing more.
There is no laughing, smiling, or crying here,
here death eats with no limits!

Here is the executor's gallows, here is the slaughter!
Here is the mass grave of the unknown!
Who walked in lines,
mothers and grandmothers, fathers and sons.

The question is no longer asked here:
"To be one way or the another?"
Only one prayer is carried in the hearts:
"I want to live!"

[Page 102]

Reply to a grandson

You, have asked me how long
will you cry for the communities that have been destroyed?
You said to me - Maybe it is enough
eulogize dead martyrs?

And I will tell you:
you are right grandson in your words
because your living grandfather is more important to you
than your grandfather's father.

But every time I remember my parents
whose blood was shed at the hands
of human animals, my intestinal ache
and tears well up in my eyes.

And I won't tell them:
I've had enough tears!
It was God's order
and we cannot protest against it.

All of you are my witnesses
That I love to live very much
and I don't want sadness to cloud my life
but I can't do anything.

Because I loved all my brothers,
my friends, my girlfriends so much
and it seems to me that it is obligatory and that it is important
to cry for them once in a while.

So that the chain of attachment
of past, present, future
and the bond of the people will thus
be strengthened forever and ever.

[Page 103]

Chapter 3:

In the Soviet Diaspora

[Page 104]

Remembering Lanovits in My Wanderings

By Feirel Melamed (Pnina Perle)

Our town, Lanovits, appeared to me as one in which many interesting activities took place. However, these activities were governed by a stable life pattern that had not changed for generations.

During 1939, our small world was shaken, as was the rest of the world. One morning, we came under Communist rule. Our holy community was in shock. Our Jews started to search for their proletariat ancestry. Retailers, who formerly struggled to make a living,

[Page 105]

began to fear that they will be looked upon as capitalists, and be sent to Siberia. Each one investigated his past so as not to appear as a counter-revolutionary criminal. My father, who was a Torah teacher, feared that the authorities will find out that he taught a religious subject. One resident feared the other, and wondered whether he will betray the other or withstand the pressure of the authorities. The streets became empty. For days, Jews did not venture out of their homes. A tragic calm fell upon the town. The normal discussions about politics ceased. Everyone was afraid.

The Lanovits Jews deserve praise for the fact that no betrayal occurred. Their solidarity held. I, the daughter of a "reactionary" was found fit for the job of head secretary at the Municipality. I was recommended for the job by the local party secretary who liked me. Other Jews were also chosen for key posts in the town administration. These functionaries considered the saving of Jewish residents from arrest and deportation as one of the important administrative tasks. It is worth noting that Lanovits experienced few deportation cases. No more than 2-3 persons were denounced by Ukrainians and deported. There was no way to ransom these persons.

* * *

When the German-Soviet war broke out, the Soviet administrators and we, its staff, retreated. I did not want to be separated from my old parents. I wanted to be available to help them in time of need. However, my mother came to my office and made me swear that I will leave town. She said: "Leave with Batya (my sister) and Shlomo (my brother-in-law). You are likely to be one of the first victims (of the Germans) as a Soviet functionary"

I accepted mother's reasoning and left town. The separation was hard. I cried yet my tears dried-up. I could hardly breathe. I had no time to pack needed items. I left with the clothes on my back.

The travel (by train) was difficult. The weather was alternately hot and rainy. Many passengers developed a fever. There was no medical help. Food was unavailable. We remained hungry. The enemy chased our train and bombarded us.

We arrived in Siberia after a long trip, depressed, broken, and lonely. The Siberian climate was most difficult. I came down with a case of malaria. I went to work despite my illness, to mitigate my loneliness.

For our factory work, I and others, received 400 grams of bread per day. This was the only food we received. When we refugees met, we tried to remember our loved ones that remained far from us. One asked the other: *"Will we ever see them again?"*

[Page 106]

(In the winter) the temperature in town would drop sometimes to minus 30 degrees Celsius. One had to be careful when leaving the house to prevent one's nose and ears from freezing. Local residents warned us of the dangers of this terrible cold. We survived somehow.

At the end of 1944, my manager came to my office, and said: *"Faliah,* (that was my name in Siberia) *Congratulations, the war has ended."* (It actually ended in May 1945 – Ed.) In Siberia, we did not read newspapers, hence did not know what was happening in the world. My manager heard the news on the radio. I did not know what to do. There was no way to get to Lanovits. Yet, I yearned to see or hear from my parents. I thought about them day and night. I wrote letters to various Ukrainian neighbors. Only one person answered my letter. It was Bushka, the male nurse. His letter was unpleasantly sweet. He described the killings that took place. He was full of praise about my father, describing him as an exceptional man. At the end of his letter, he wrote that my father was one of the first to be killed by the Germans.

I came to realize the full dimension of the Holocaust that occurred in Lanovits. There was nothing to return to, nothing worth visiting.

* * *

I remember Lanovits as a small but charming town. I remember, in particular, the daughters of Lieber Bronstein. These women took care of every poor person, fed and washed him. I remember the festive third Shabbat meals of our Rabbis and their followers. I remember the many good deeds of our local men and women. What happened in Lanovits, where so many good people were killed, is doubly reprehensible.

[Page 107] [Yiddish pages 344-351]

From Lanovits to the Soviet Union

By Arye Ginzburg (Atchi)

I was working for Yunek Farber in his egg warehouse when the Soviets marched into Lanovits in 1939. As a worker, I was considered as a "kosher" proletarian. As the Soviets reorganized the municipal administration, I was considered "close" to the regime. The Soviet administration organized a new Police force, consisting of Ukrainians and Jews. Berchik, Hirsch-Ber and I, were selected as Police commanders. My task was to observe all that went on in our town. The task was an unpleasant one because the Soviet administration viewed the Lanovits residents as a "suspect element".

Fortunately, none of the propertied Jews were either arrested or deported to Siberia. This was partly the result of our efforts to prevent this from happening. While we tried to protect local Jews, we could not prevent confiscation of private property altogether. As the Soviet Politruks (managers) became established locally, they proceeded to nationalize significant private property. The first to be affected was Shimon

Glinik. He was rich, and his villa attracted attention. He was ejected from his villa and made to move into his mother's house (Leah Hanah-Atis). Thereafter, his property was nationalized.

The first mayor selected by the Soviet authorities was a Ukrainian by the name of Krawchuk. His wife was Jewish. As a Komsomol leader, she made efforts to help local Jews in various ways. This regime, was half military, half civilian, it lasted for three months. It was replaced by a Soviet civilian administration. The latter administration reorganized the town's local institutions.

[Page 108]

A city council was selected. Andre Kishka, a person who had not completed grade school, became the new mayor. As a proletarian, the mayor had an instinctive understanding of the desires of his superiors. The city administration moved into the Zinberg house, which had a pharmacy downstairs.

After three months, Andre Kishka was dismissed, and Dov Goldberg was named to replace him. The latter lasted in his post only a short while. After two months, he was replaced by Yizhak Shmokh. Pnina Melamed, the daughter of Yizhak Melamed, became his administrative assistant. In the meantime, the city administration expanded. It was again moved (to larger quarters) into the house of Sarah (widow of Shiah) Katz.

The new administration permitted the local retailers to trade as in the past. One day, the authorities decided to raid the offices of the wholesalers and factories in Lvov from whom the Lanovits retailers drew their supplies. The authorities estimated the turnover of each retailer based on the sums indicated by the deferred checks of a given retailer, discovered in their offices. The additional tax levied on each retailer was in proportion to the discovered turnover.

The main victim of this new tax was Uziel Reichman, on whom a 5,000 ruble tax was levied. He refused to pay this tax, was indicted, convicted, and given a five year prison term, to be followed by exile to Siberia. His sentencing brought forth strong communal support. Two local doctors who in the past competed with one another, and who had distanced themselves from Jewish life, Dr. Lutwack and Dr. Lutz Eisenstat, the latter the town's senior physician, examined Reichman and certified that he is too ill to serve his sentence. As a result, he was not arrested nor deported. The fear of the trial so depressed Reichman that he suffered a stroke that paralyzed him. Reichman remained in his house but had to pay the tax.

The youths of Lanovits, Zionist in their orientation, fluent in Hebrew and steeped in its literature, had to stop all their Zionist activities. They joined the Communist Youth organization to assure their political safety. All Zionist political activity was forbidden. Our youths felt like the conversos did in 15th century Spain. At the same time, the registration-of-marriages function was transferred from the Rabbinate to a secular city office. Jonathan Fogel became the registrar of marriages for our town. The Soviet regime did not interfere with communal life in other respects.

Jews continued to pray in their synagogues. In fact, they spent many hours in public prayer, as if to take advantage of something that is about to be forbidden. There was talk about the likelihood that synagogues will be confiscated, however matters did not reach such a point. Our Rabbis continued to serve their religious functions as in the past.

Something, however, shook up our collective spirit. The foundation of our society started to crumble. One felt a change and uncertainty in one's standing in society. All of us suffered from this feeling of uncertainty, including those of us that were now in positions of authority. One felt depressed about life and a certain fog enveloped our thoughts and our hopes for the future. This happened to most of us, though there were a few exceptions. A few of us got married.

[Page 109]

Those about to marry would hire a Rabbi secretly, yet for political safety register their intent to wed with the city registrar. These young couples viewed civil marriage registration as a plague that cannot be avoided. Having a wedding ceremony performed by a Rabbi was still considered by our youths as their primary social obligation. There was a case that annoyed our community. Moshe Kerner married a teacher from Yampil who was a die-hard communist. The couple only registered their marriage with the local civil authorities. When their first son was born, they had him properly circumcised. Our mayor, Yizhak Shmokh, found it necessary on this occasion to dismiss the mother from the party. Her dismissal left an unpleasant mark on her career.

Our youths would meet regularly in the local town hall. This hall, built by the Polish authorities and church, was located next to the old Polish cemetery. On regular evenings, Ukrainian and Jewish youths would meet there for dancing and singing. A band would play to create a joyous atmosphere. This happy setting compensated somewhat for our instinctive reservations as Jews, forced to ally ourselves with a regime and society devoid of tradition.

* * *

One day, we heard rumors that the Germans broke their treaty with the USSR and were attacking Soviet forces on all fronts. The thought that German forces are fast approaching our town caused our authorities to plan a possible evacuation. When German forces were already in Tarnopil, an order was received to pack up and leave. This order was, however, too late to enable us to depart by train. Nearby rail lines were already cut as a result of German bombing. While we sat on our baggage, we had to think of alternate escape means. We confiscated horses and wagons of local Ukrainian peasants and forced them to take us and our baggage eastward to an area still controlled by Soviet forces. Our local Ukrainians hated the Soviet regime. We had no choice but to use force to make them take us eastward.

* * *

About 35 of us left with the Soviet authorities. We knew that we will be the first victims of the expected regime change. We basically ran for our lives. The rest of the Jews refused to leave the town they were born in. To our regret, they even tried to persuade others to remain. I remember Yulik Korolki (Joel Katz), who was considered to be a wise person, dressed in the uniform of a Soviet soldier. He was full of cynicism. He asked me, *"Where are you running to? In the East you will not fare better. It is better to hide here, until the worst has passed. I saw how 'strong' the Soviet forces are."*

[Page 110]

He was not alone. Many thought like he did. One that stood out, thinking similarly was Hirshke Lushik (Hirsh Leizer dem Zaner Shuster). He mocked those that ran away. He was convinced that he was the wiser to stay. Unfortunately, he paid the ultimate price for his "wisdom."

* * *

After four days of travel, we arrived at a village near Kiev. We released the peasants and their wagons and climbed onto a train. The freight train was full of people and animals, with no room to spare. It brought us to Rostov.

On the way to Rostov, we were attacked by German bombers. From time to time, we had to leave the train to take cover in a field or in a drainage ditch. On the way, pardoned Soviet prisoners climbed aboard our train. They were released from prison on condition that they join the Soviet Army. We had to protect ourselves against this criminal, train element. At most train stations, we had the opportunity to buy food. Sometimes we even received food gratis from army commissaries located at these train station. In this respect, our fate was better than the fate of other evacuees.

In Rostov, we separated. A part of the Lanovits group continued to Siberia. I and a few others remained in Rostov and joined a Kolkhoz. With me were "Hirsch Bar-Mazur and his daughter, Byya Goldberg, Hershele Solomon (son of Raisa Shachnes), Berel Plazel the Hunchback, and others. We spent three months in the Rostov Kolkhoz. When rumors circulated the German army is approaching Rostov, we left the Kolkhoz. Each of us went his way. I chose to travel in the direction of Bukhara. Berel, the Hunchback was the only one who joined me going to Bukhara.

We arrived in Bukhara, looked around and slept in the town's main park. We were left with hardly any funds. I sent Berel to a nearby Kolkhoz to purchase matches and sell them at the railroad station. We lived off these proceeds. Byya Goldberg joined us in Bukhara. I developed a trade in vests. I bought them in Bukhara and sold them in Chekalov.

After some months, we met Hershele Solomon, grandson of Shachnes. He was about 20. He lived with us only a short while. He contracted typhus and died shortly thereafter. We buried him in the hospital yard. The local administration forbade us to take him to the cemetery, fearing outbreak of an epidemic.

Our vest trade covered a certain geographical area between Bukhara and Tashkent. During our trading period, we met Shlomo Taitel (Terlo), who brought us news from Batya and Pnina (Melamed).

[Page 111]

Shlomo had, in the meantime, been released from his work camp. In Tashkent, we met the Shmokh family (formerly, Lanovits's Mayor), Jonathan Fogel (Marriage Registrar) and his sisters.

I settled in Chekalov, continuing to sell vests in its market. I was able to support myself from this trade. One day, I discovered Zuni Rabin and his wife at the market. They did not recognize me. I called to them and our meeting was an emotional one. Thereafter, we met again several times. Zuni and his wife joined us. After a while, our trading became more difficult and more dangerous. I decided instead to register for work, to become a worker until the arrival of better days. At that time, I already lived in Yeletsk. I became part of a team that worked in the forest belonging to the Pavelsk district, Chekalov province. In addition to my work assignment, I also did some trading in the local market. One day, I saw Dr. Lutek Eisenstat (the physician that helped Reichman during his trial) trying to sell a wrist watch. I recognized him immediately and asked him the reason why he was selling his watch. He explained that his wife was about to give birth and he needed the proceeds. I lent him 20,000 rubles instead. He returned my loan after a short time, mailing it to Pavelsk. He apparently found a position in the medical field. I never saw him again.

In Pavelsk, I was recruited to join a labor camp located in Magnitogorsk. I bid goodbye to all my Lanovits friends and left for my new assignment alone.

Zuni, Jonathan Fogel, Shmokh, Yizhak Mani, Babzi & Rachel Shmokh, remained in Pavelsk. Jonathan Fogel was already married and had a child. My transfer occurred in 1944. I later heard that these men joined the Polish army so we did not meet again. In Magnitogorsk, I worked a full year in a factory that processed molten iron named "Magniteka". The factory employed close to a million workers. The working conditions were good, but I suffered from the local climate. I contracted typhus and had to leave the place. Instead, I volunteered to join the Red Army. I participated in various battles. I was wounded near Czenstochova, Poland and was transferred to a military hospital in Grudziandz/Poland (near Gdansk) in May, 1945.

* * *

After I was released from the hospital on May 12, 1945, I traveled to Lanovits to see what had happened to our town. In Shepetivka (a railroad junction north of Lanowtiz), I met Shalom Segal and Hayim Nathan Gitelman. Shalom left for Tarnopil and Hayim Nathan and I left for Lanovits. Our town was completely destroyed. Even the remains of houses had been cleared by the Germans.

The only houses that remained standing were the main synagogue, the churches, the house of Shiya Natanes, that of Byrel Pacht - where the tailor's artel was located, that of Moshe Gurewitch Marinkowitz - where the shoemaker's artel was located, the house of Michel the blacksmith – where the court was housed; the house of Hayim Nathan102 opposite Michel Gladner – where the Post Office was located and the house of Benny Hayim Leibes, which housed the government cafeteria.

[Page 112]

Below the cafeteria was the house of Shlomo Plezlis.

None of the Jewish residents remained. We were told that the daughter of Nakhum Kreper and Raisa the hunchback lady had survived. We looked for them but were unable to locate them.

I stayed with Andrian. They bedded me on a mattress that, they said, belonged to Sarah Katz, the daughter of Shiya Natanes. They claimed that they found the mattress on the street. I was unable to elicit from them any information regarding the fate of Lanovits Jews. They even refused to speak about the fate of my mother. Their only comment was that she died and is no longer among us.

I could not remain any longer "in Lanovits." The nightmares I experienced that night drove me to leave the town the next day. Before I left the town forever, I wanted to visit my loved ones at the mass grave. My hosts warmed that Bandera groups are nearby, that it is too dangerous for me to go there. Hayim Nathan did not dare go with me. I left my hometown without visiting the graves of those dear to me.

[Page 113] [Yiddish pages 352-359]

This Is How We Lived In Russia

By Batya (Melamed) Taitel

Chapter I: A Secret Wedding

When the Soviet administration was established (in Lanovits) in late 1939, Shlomo (Taitel) was accepted for a position of bookkeeper in the education department. We knew that under Soviet administration no job is secure, especially in the case of Shlomo. As a former trader, he was subject to be classified under paragraph 11, facing arrest and deportation at any time. Despite this uncertainty, we decided to build a common future, as if the future is assured – we decided to get married.

The wedding was conducted in secret. Our parents insisted that we have a traditional wedding despite the hostility of the (Soviet) regime to such religious practices. For the sake of our parents, our wedding was conducted in conformance with all local customs. My parents' house door was shut and windows barred so no light could be seen from the outside. Only a few persons, those willing to take the (political) risk, were invited to the ceremony. Our joy was mixed with apprehension as to what the future portended.

The wedding ceremony was conducted exactly as prescribed by tradition. We used the same Khupah (a wedding canopy held by four posts) that had been used to wed local couples for generations. The bridegroom recited the traditional blessing and other honorees proceeded with their traditional parts.

[Page 114]

Rabbi Ahareli, the last and most tragic of Lanovits's rabbis, conducted the ceremony.

While the seven blessings were being recited with gusto, the ceremony's proceedings became known outside the house. Next, the door opened and two soldiers in Red Army uniforms entered the house. They sat quietly at the men's table, not uttering a word. Those reciting the blessings stopped in their tracks, terrified of having been caught participating in an anti-regime act. The soldiers rose from their seats to calm the audience, begging them to continue and complete the ceremony. The soldiers told those sitting near them that they were Jews, but had not in the past had the opportunity to witness a traditional Jewish wedding. Their pleas to complete the wedding ceremony failed to relax the tension in the room. The soldiers noticed the fearful atmosphere. Only after the soldiers rose to kiss the men sitting near them, did the audience calm down, enabling the ceremony to be completed. This episode was remembered and recalled for a long, long time.

We returned to work the next day, continuing to wonder whether those two soldiers were planted. The week passed quietly. On Saturday we had a reception for our friends and work colleagues.

Chapter II: Our Exile from Lanovits

Pnina, my sister, worked as a secretary to the town's mayor. One evening she returned home to inform us that she was asked (at her workplace) about Shlomo's background. She admitted to the interrogator that Shlomo was a former trader. We became frightened, certain that we would be deported from Lanovits, exiled to an unknown destination. However, the episode had a happy ending. Shlomo was rejected for army service. His work performance was apparently satisfactory, and he kept his job.

Meanwhile the German-Soviet war broke out. The German army attacked Soviet-occupied Poland. We heard reports that the German army is already 40 kilometers from our town. We could hear the sound of approaching artillery. The Soviet authorities were in disarray and nervous.

[Page 115]

(Local) Jews were uncertain whether and where to escape to. They hoped for a miracle that would save them, as was the case when they faced enemies in the past; they were at a loss as to what to do.

We, as employees of the Soviet administration, knew that we must escape with the rest of the authorities. Our plan was to move to Teofipol for a few days, and later perhaps return to our families in Lanovits. As matters developed, we had to leave hurriedly. I left with only the clothes on my back. I said goodbye to my mother. My father was, at that moment, in the synagogue. I had no time to find him and part from him before my departure.

My mother was in shock, unable to assess quickly the unfolding events. When she recovered, she went to Shlomo's office to have a parting word with him. By the time she reached his office, he had already left. She fainted in his office. Shlomo left before me with the rest of the office personnel. These officials knew better than we did that it was imperative to leave immediately. Shlomo left without notifying me of his departure plans.

Chapter III: Byya Kuzazker

After we left town (by train), it became obvious to all of us that our departure would not last a few days, stopping at Teofipol, but instead a journey to a far-off destination for an indeterminate period. Our journey continued in a confused and depressing atmosphere. More than anything, I felt the pain of separation from Shlomo. I had no idea when and where we would see each other again. Suddenly I was alone, separated from all those dear to me, left to fend for myself.

I found Shlomo accidentally, at one of the railroad stations. He was about to hand out the last paychecks to his Education department employees. He had taken the payroll with him, and was paying each employee his due.

The coachman (who was apparently the one who was forced to bring both Shlomo and Arye Ginzburg to this railroad station. See Arye Ginzburg's story, #15) decided that he was not "married" to this forced exodus. His intuition told him that if he continued to transport these refugees eastward, he would likely be dragged along with the rest of these refugees. To avoid such a fate, he broke some part of his wagon and announced to his passengers that he could not continue further. Instead, he returned to Lanovits.

When Shlomo finished paying his employees, each left for his chosen destination. We were left alone. I broke down and cried. Even Shlomo was bewildered as no one remained with us. At that moment Byya Goldberg (Kuzazker) came over. Sensing my plight he said: "I will not leave you, do not worry, I will travel with you". Moshe Gruber, and Willy, the son of Yossi Kleinman also joined us. On the way, we were joined by Hannah, Moshe's sister Byya who mitigated our feeling of loneliness. I will forever remember Byya's good deed.

[Page 116]

Chapter IV: A Russian Jew Speaks Hebrew

At the Bila Tserkva (south of Kiev) railroad station, we were permitted to board a military train. We did not ask the soldiers for their destination. We were intent to move eastward regardless of the train's destination.

The train took us to Astrakhan (at the mouth of the Volga River and Caspian Sea). The locals greeted us with bread and water. After days of hunger and unimaginable suffering, I will forever remember their great deed. From Astrakhan, we sailed by ship to Makhachkala/Dagestan, a harbor on the Caspian Sea. I mention this town because the locals said that we were the first Jewish refugees to have arrived there. When we were sent from Makhachkala to Khazav'yurt/Dagestan (50 kilometers west of Makhachkala), we had the added distinction of having been the first Europeans that local residents had ever met. [The authoress is perhaps alluding to the fact that locals had never encountered Polish refugees before. Dagestan, a Soviet republic, was relatively isolated from the rest of Russia before WWII. Makhachkala had, according to Encyclopedia Judaica, vol. 12, pp. 478-481, a significant Hebrew-speaking Jewish population. It is likely that Khazav'yurt, a smaller town, had one as well.- Ed]

We arrived in town without any instructions as to who to turn to for help. We approached a municipal official who happened to be of German origin. When he noticed that we were Jews, he was most unhelpful. We were fortunate to meet a Jewish official, a so-called Mountain Jew [Also known as Tats, a Jewish tribe that inhabited this area for centuries, speaks a Judeo-Tat, using cursive Hebrew script. For details see Encyclopedia Judaica, vol. 12, pp. 478-481, and vol. 10, p. 441]. He did not speak Yiddish but, to our surprise, addressed us in Hebrew. He inquired as to problems we encountered dealing with the German speaking official, and warned us against dealing any further with him. When he heard that Shlomo was an experienced accountant, this official found him a job in the agricultural ministry office.

We women were assigned work in an artel (residence) for invalids. We were well treated there. The residence was managed by two local Jews. The invalid residents regularly expressed their appreciation of the good care we provided.

After sometime, Shlomo was ordered transferred to the front as a civilian helper to the Red Army. I felt lonely and confused. The greatest fear one has during wartime is losing contact with one's kin. I knew that the Hebrew-speaking "Mountain" Jew had been assigned to guide the group of civilian conscripts to the front. This Jew had visited Palestine once, to see his father, one of its early immigrants. I decided to accompany Shlomo to his front assignment. I counted on the guide to not stop me from coming along.

The guide was a wonderful fellow. He went so far as to encourage me to come along. The men marched in long columns, and I alongside them. He would walk with me, consoling me, and expressed the hope for better days in the future.

[Page 117]

Chapter V: I Organize An Escape

After we reached the train station, the men were loaded onto a train but I was not permitted to join them. I was forced to return to Khazav'yurt, to my workplace. The next day I became ill, suffering serious pains. The cause of my pain remained a mystery. This condition continued for several days. My friends thought my end was near. In the meantime, the German army continued to advance towards Baku. *(They were stopped at Groznyy/Chechnia – Ed.)* I immediately forgot my pains and regained my energy.

The area defense was augmented by requiring local citizens to dig a wall trench to block the path of a river running through our town, Pnina and I were the only healthy persons at our residence for Invalids to be conscripted.

We worked under extremely harsh conditions. Our bodies were attacked by millions of mosquitoes that inhabited the riverbank. Food was also scarce and the news from the front discouraging. A Romanian Jew, who worked with us, alerted me to the seriousness of our plight. I decided to organize an escape for our residence staff. A stout Caucasian woman showed us an escape route. On the way, we found out that she was a Jewess. We left at midnight on this dangerous mission. The previous day a similar escape plan was leaked to the authorities. The men were caught, and expected to be punished severely.

We ran and hid alternately for 40 kilometers, fearful of being caught by the local authorities. When we reached Makhachkala, we noticed the wide damage to the town that had been caused by aerial bombardments. As we continued (southward) I experienced again a feeling of deep loneliness in the absence of Shlomo. We continued regardless to escape the Germany army. Shlomo knew our escape destination. As his unit broke up, he was able to catch up with us. We signed up to join a convoy headed for Siberia.

Chapter VI: Siberia

We arrived in Siberia in the winter, dressed in summer clothing. We were housed in a barn outfitted with bunk beds. I was assigned to cut down trees in a forest. One day my saw got stuck in a tree. I was unable to dislodge it.

[Page 118]

Exasperated, I sat down and cried, fearful of returning from work without my saw. A burly Siberian saw my plight; with his strong hand, he released my saw, enabling me to return home.

After some time, we were moved into barracks with other Jews, and our living conditions improved.

In 1945 we left Siberia with other (Polish) repatriates and headed for Szczecin/Poland.

From there, we moved to Pfaffendorf/Germany.

For some reason, men and women were housed separately in this Displaced Persons Camp. We felt as if we were again in a ghetto. One woman became hysterical. We all felt desperate that despite having survived the war, we may not be saved.

After 1-2 hours, as we were feeling low, the door to our barrack opened, and a smiling young man, introduced himself as Bolek and said: "Shalom." His magical words and self-confidence lifted our spirits. We again felt at ease, confident that we had reached the end of our said journey. Our destination was the land of Israel.

[Page 119] [Yiddish pages 360-361]

An Addendum to Batya's Report

By Shlomo Taitel

When I was taken to the front as a civilian worker, our camp was attacked by German forces. In the resulting chaos, I chose to escape, to try and return to my wife in Khazav'yurt. The road eastward was being bombarded from the air. Fires chased us as we moved. I ran for hours. When I could no longer continue, I lay down in a field to sleep. When I awoke the next morning, I noticed that my leg became swollen and I could not continue. A military convoy passed me, and a soldier noticed my plight. He arranged for a Red Cross ambulance to take me to a nearby town. From there, I was taken by train to Kharkov (probably Baku, for Kharkov was already in German hands-Ed). The wounded were housed in a nearby military camp. After I recovered, we were told that former Polish citizens may register locally to enlist in the Polish army. I was sent to a medical examination.

[Page 120]

The medical team worked slowly. Twenty volunteers were examined, but only one was accepted. It appeared that they were not interested in Jewish recruits. I was turned down with a person from Visogrudek and one from Warsaw. With our release papers we were allowed to proceed to Tashkent. It was there that I contacted my family by letter and waited for a reply.

We heard rumors that the Caucasus region was being bombarded. The Red Cross helped me again. I received a letter from Batya that her town was under bombardment. She added that they were waiting for me to escape eastward together.

[Page 121] [Yiddish pages 362-367]

My Experience under the Soviet Regime

By Joseph Weiner (Canada)

When I finished my studies in Lanovits, I started working to help my parents. I worked for Asher Brilant in his wholesale business, selling gasoline and lubrication products. In the eyes of the Soviet regime, I was considered a "kosher" proletarian. I was assigned to manage Frieda Shmil's store. Rachel Bobe Uzieles worked there with me. Later I was transferred to manage the nationalized warehouse of Hershel Kagan. In this capacity I had to make frequent buying trips to nearby towns, especially to Tarnopil. A large Soviet supply warehouse was located in that town, serving to supply our entire region.

In 1941 I was inducted into the Red army. At first, I was regarded as a loyal soldier. However, after three weeks I was called back to my former job. My job was declared "essential to the economy."

One evening, as I was attending a dance arranged for the local youths, our mayor, Yizhak Shmokh came over and tapped me on my shoulder. He called me aside, and told me to stop my dancing and prepare to leave for the front. His message was somewhat mysterious. Under the German-Soviet (non-aggression) agreement, no front was contemplated. However, under the Soviet regime we learned not to question orders but to do what we were told. I said goodbye to my mother and brother on that winter morning, (My father had passed away previously, having contracted asthma) leaving with a great feeling of unease.

Avraham, the brother of Motil Pasalsky, the son of the deaf shoemaker, left with me. I have not returned to Lanovits since that departure day. I never saw my mother and brother since that time.

[Page 122]

For a short while, I maintained contact with my family. Having learned from my letters of the poor army food, my mother sent me several food parcels.

I spent two months at a training base, after which I was sent to the front. Next, my army records were reviewed for some reason. I was reclassified as "unreliable" by the army and sent eastward to a town near Moscow.

* * *

When we arrived in Smolensk, the town was already on fire (from aerial bombardments). We were next sent to Vyasma, 90 kilometers from Moscow, traveling on foot, walking at night and sleeping by day. We were promised food, but supplies never arrived. We had to make do with whatever local supplies we could get. Hungry and tired we continued onward for six weeks until we arrived in Vyasma. There we were placed on a train that took us to Gorky.

In Gorky we were given some food and put to work in a machinery factory. The work was hard, and the food we received was inadequate to sustain ourselves. We started to sell our blankets to be able to buy extra food. The black market in Russia was a necessary companion to its fixed-price economy. With the food shortages that existed in Gorky, the black market was particularly active.

Selling our goods was not easy. We were under continuous supervision. We supplemented our food supply as we marched to work. One of us, on the march, would sneak out in pre-assigned order. This person would return to our dormitory, take out a bed, mattress or blanket, and sell these for one or more loaves of bread of pita. At the end of this process we had nothing to sell. Our situation was desperate. We had nothing to sleep on, but that was irrelevant. Our workplace was several kilometers from our dormitory. When we returned, we were so tired that we could sleep under any condition. Our foremost need was for bread, to sustain ourselves.

Our unit Commander was a Moscow Jew, with the rank of army captain. He lent me money to buy food. I am in debt to him to this day. I am certain he has forgiven my debt. He was a Jew with a warm heart, willing to help a brother in need.

After sometime, we started to sell our shirts. We would go to the market and return half naked just to supplement our food rations. One day, when I had nothing more to sell, and was starving, I entered (the Captain's) office. He was not in his office. His shirt hung on the office coat hanger. I put my hand in his shirt pocket. It contained 1,600 rubles. I took them. As I left his office, he re-entered. Having noticed the missing funds, he came to our dormitory, turned directly to me and asked politely if I knew who took his money. I answered him without hesitation: *"You need not investigate further. I am sure that whoever took your money surely needed it, and will repay you at the end of this terrible war, provided he stays alive until then. That is clear."*

[Page 123]

When the matter of selling our bedding was discovered, we were punished. Our work quota was increased. Five hundred of our group were transferred to a forest, 60 kilometers from Gorky, to fell trees. Each group received a production quota. Our food ration depended on meeting our production quota.

I was young and healthy, able to meet and exceed my quota. My food ration was consequently adequate.

I worked in the forest, felling trees, for a full year. It was hard work, under difficult conditions. I tried to find another work assignment, but was unsuccessful.

One day another job opening materialized. A manager, assigned to install telephone lines, came to our work camp looking for workers experienced in such work. I signed up as a person experienced in this field. I worked at this "professional" task for four months. The work assignment was a good one, but the job was about to end. I started to worry (about the future). I dragged out my task on purpose. Instead of completing it in two days, I extended the task to last three additional weeks. In the meantime I had time to spare. I started to socialize with my bosses, and noticed that my bosses liked having more idle time. I came to realize these bosses liked "saboteurs" like me, who do not take their jobs seriously. It was thanks to my delay tactics that they did not have to wander to another job location immediately. From the outside the Soviet system appeared as serious, responsible and effective. The truth was that a productive worker was mocked secretly. Managers preferred a worker that organized his tasks so that both he and his superiors could relax. This was the real Russia. My bosses appreciated the fact that thanks to me, they could remain at their present site for a while instead of having to wander immediately to another location.

I invested in a bottle of hard liquor, and gave it to the top boss. In appreciation I was reassigned to drive a truck that brought supplies to the forest workers. My situation improved, as did my superiors.

I was once tasked to drive to Arzamas, 100 kilometers south of Gorky with our purchasing manager. We stopped to rest a little on that hot day, and purchased a Quass drink (made from sour apples) from a roadside vendor. Two tanks were parked nearby, and next to them were two military officers dressed in camouflage suits. I no longer remember how it came about that these officers started to menace my boss. They called him "Zhid" (he was Jewish), slapped his face and threw his hat onto the truck roof. We were a team of four, so we were able to beat up the two officers. We thought the altercation had been settled. Suddenly we heard a whistle blowing and sixty soldiers appeared from nowhere. We immediately ran away and hid in a nearby forest. From our hiding place we could see that the soldiers left with their tanks. We waited for three hours, uncertain whether to continue in the direction we were going, inasmuch as the tanks left in the same direction. We were fearful, but, at the same time, realized that we cannot return to our base empty handed, so we continued on our way. After driving 8 kilometers, we were stopped by an armed soldier. Our team was taken to the location where the two tanks were parked. Our papers were checked, and the previous altercation investigated. A miracle occurred. Our papers were returned to us, we were allowed to proceed, and an apology was offered to our boss.

[Page 124]

While the matter was being investigated, the two officers removed their camouflage suits. We noticed that both had the rank of colonel. I continued in this assignment until near the end of the war, the beginning of 1945.

Suddenly, I was again inducted into the Red army. The army apparently needed more cannon fodder. In our training camp we slept on boards, using our food bags as pillows. We were so tired from daily training that I did not feel anything when a mouse got into my food bag. The general camp conditions were terrible.

I was fortunate to "befriend" a local captain who for the sum of 2,000 rubles concocted a set of papers for me that showed that I was born in Poland (not in the Ukraine). The papers stated that I wished to serve in the Polish army. His was a farsighted plan, according to which I was to wait for my call-up by the Polish army authorities. The document I was given, stipulated that I was to remain in my present camp until my Polish army papers arrived. My new job was to "make myself useful" to my superiors. With this document, I was able to avoid serving in either army.

* * *

I have a great feeling of nostalgia for Lanovits and all it stood for, as I write my story. I am willing to replace all our modern regimes, to have the opportunity to recapture its lifestyle. Lanovits is still dear to me. While in the depth of the Soviet Union, I longed for its life seven-fold.

[Page 125]

Difficult Separations

By Mendel Brimmer

In the fall of 1939 Lanovits fell into the Soviet orbit as a result of the famous German-Soviet non-aggression treaty. I was 19 at the time. The foundation of our society was shaken. The Soviet authorities nationalized my father's wholesale business. He became the warehouseman of the business.

The Jewish youths had to work to support themselves and their parents. I, who had no profession, created a team of lumberjacks together with Bura Margalit and Leizer Flemchik. The orders for our Artel [cooperative] increased with time. Our salary was more than sufficient to support ourselves, our parents, and provide us some savings.

At the time, Uziel Reichman was indicted as a trader who hid his past and some of his assets. He was tried and convicted. His alternative was to either pay a large fine or be exiled to Siberia. The Jewish community organized a collection on his behalf. Community activists went from door to door to raise the required funds. When they arrived at our home my father was embarrassed. He had no money but felt obligated to participate in such a community effort. He turned to me and asked me to help him with this "Mitzvah". I responded by giving him my entire savings. Reichman was saved, and I lost my savings.

I worked with my team until 1942 (actually, June 1941 – Ed.) The Soviet authorities considered me as a "Kosher" proletarian. I did not have to join the Komsomol in order to deny my Zionist past.

(In 1941) the German/Soviet war broke out. The Soviet administration evacuated Lanovits, taking along its entire staff. Many of the Komsomol members were evacuated with them.

[Page 126]

I, who was not a party member, was not considered eligible for evacuation. Workers like me were left to fend for themselves. I decided to leave Lanovits regardless for two reasons: Firstly, my attitude had changed. The proletariat regime suited me. I saw no problem fitting into it. Secondly, I wanted to escape the German regime. The future under that regime looked bleak to me.

I also wanted to save my friends, especially the girl I had been going out with for two years, as well as her sister and the sister's boyfriend. We foresaw the difficulties our parents are likely to face in our absence. We decided therefore to ask for their consent. The girls were hesitant to ask their parents lest they refuse them. They asked that I make the request on their behalf. I knew I was taking on a difficult task. Both the girl's father and my friend's (the boyfriend of my girlfriend's sister) father were likely difficult persons to convince. The girl's father was Shlomo Zhiliaznik (Pletsele) and the father of my future brother-in-law was Meir Furman, son of Avraham Meshes. I suggested to my friend to join me in approaching his future father-in-law. On the morning of July 1, 1942 (actually 1941-Ed.) we approached Shlomo Zhiliaznik together, asking for his consent to allow his daughters to join us. He was adamant in his refusal. "They are remaining with us," he said, and suggested that we too stay here. His refusal did not surprise us. We expected it.

After we left their father's house, we decided to leave without the girls. Each of us turned to his family to bid goodbye. By the time I reached our house, German aircraft had dropped 3 bombs on the town's outskirts, 2 on the train station and one on Shraga's flour mill.

The atmosphere in our home was tense. I did not dare speak about my decision. Instead, I took my father's military knapsack, the one he came back with after his release as a POW in Austria in 1920. Over the years, this knapsack symbolized for us both wandering and separation. My father understood the hint and said, "You are my last support. What will happen to us will happen to you. Do not leave us." He was sitting at our table, crying like a child. At this tense moment my sister Selva entered the house and said to my father, "Do not take upon yourself such a responsibility. If the lad wants to leave, let him leave, and may God be with him." Father was silent for a moment, and then rose. He blessed me in the traditional priestly manner. I hugged my parents and left. Mother shouted after me to bid goodbye to my grandfather. I went to his house. He opened the book of Psalms, read a few chapters and blessed me again.

[Page 127]

Next, I went to fetch my friend. He lived on the other side of town. As I crossed the town's main street, I noticed it was unusually empty. Only Mordechai Guberman stood at the doorsteps of his house. As I passed him, he asked me, "Mendel, where to?" I replied that I will go eastward to wherever my eyes will take me. He counseled against leaving for an unknown destination.

At Dov Furman's house all eyes were on me as I arrived. They were all crying. Faiga, his mother, demanded to know from me: "Why are you inciting him to leave; he is our only breadwinner." David (Dov ?) listened to his mother, and I left without him.

On the hill overlooking our town, I pondered which direction to take. Which way to safety?

Next, I visited Yashke, a stupid (retarded?) Polish lad, who for years had been renting out his services to the town's residents. I implored him, "Yashke, I am leaving. I beg you to go and help my father. I will remember your good deed upon my return." I bid goodbye to him as if he was a normal person. Somehow I felt a little better about leaving my father.

My instincts told me to change directions near the Jewish cemetery. I took a path through a tall wheat field. I was alone for some time. Suddenly a person dressed in a Russian military uniform appeared. He tried to dissuade me from continuing in my direction, claiming the presence of German troops. I was suspicious of him, so I distanced myself from him, and then ran for hours in the original direction. I crossed the old Polish/Russian order and caught up with a large group of Russian and Jewish refugees.

It was 8:30 pm. While resting, I felt lonely and depressed. I wanted to cry. At that moment one of the coachmen conscripted to evacuate the Soviet staff recognized me. He called me over, and brought me back to reality. Aryon Damchuk used to deliver vats of beer to our store from the train station. He shared some of his water, and let me climb onto his wagon, to recover.

[Page 128]

For a long while Aryon left me alone. Only later did he turn to me and asked timidly, "Why did you run away Mendel? You were not a communist, so no harm will befall you. Tomorrow I will return to Lanovits. You can return with me. I will cover you with hay, and you will return home safely." I did not listen to him even though he meant well and expressed a primitive friendship. My decision to head eastward remained unchanged. We parted, and I boarded a freight train, carrying lumber, to Kiev. Together with other evacuees I continued into the depth of the Ukraine, thereafter Russia. The journey became a long separation from all that was familiar to me.

* * *

In Russia I lived in Voroshlovsk, Ordzhonikidze/Caucasus, and other places. I also worked in a Kolkhoz. At the end of 1942 our group of Jewish refugees was conscripted into a work battalion to serve at the front. I requested to join the Red Army instead, because work at the front entailed the same dangers without the benefits of army provisions such as food and lodging. Four other Jews were in my group. We suffered from hunger and lice. The army authorities however rejected us as unreliable. We continued our work at the front without any means to protect ourselves.

Our task was to dig trenches. When these trenches were inspected by the military staff upon completion they were found to have been dug in the wrong direction to favor the German army. During the interrogation that followed, it came out that our superiors were part of a 5th column bribed by the Germans. A separate army regiment was brought in to disarm the traitors. They were tried and shot. Our group was commended for our work. We were next brought to a public bathhouse where we washed, shaved, and were provided with a change of clothing. From Taganrog, the Red Army withdrew to the Caucasus, and I with them. In the Caucasus I continued as a worker in various tasks.

* * *

During my wandering in Russia, I only met a few Lanovits Jews. These were Moshe Marder, Shaike & Berl, sons of Michael Khirik, and Joseph Weiner. For a short time we were able to spend time together. When we again separated, it was a tragic separation.

[Page 129]

I was in touch with the first three for a long time. Later, Shaike was killed on the Hungarian front, and Moshe Marder was killed in Germany 4 days before the end of the war. I lost Berl's trail, and do not know his fate. I am told he is somewhere in Russia. I corresponded with Joseph Weiner, and was instrumental in persuading him to leave Russia when he was considering settling there. I visited Abraham Weiss in his home in Kiev. I found him indifferent to issues important to me. I therefore decided to sever contact with him.

* * *

In 1948 I visited Joseph Marder at his home in Breclav/Ukraine. He was married to the former wife of his brother-in-law, who fell in the war. I was in regular contact with him after the war. Our dream, to revisit Lanovits finally materialized in 1955. Joseph Marder and I traveled to Lanovits together. We were afraid to experience a shock, so we felt more secure going there together rather than traveling to Lanovits individually. We found the town completely destroyed. The only buildings that remained standing were the main synagogue, the home of Michel the blacksmith, the houses of Shaya Witelstein, Shmuel Bachtel, Shlomo Plazel and a few others.

In Lanovits we met Zvi Mail (He settled there after the war. See his story, original pp 132-136, Ed.) The three of us decided to build a fence around the mass grave of our community. Up to then, our dear ones rested there anonymously. We were unable to purchase bricks for this job. Our solution was to purchase the foundation of Petrus' house, who lacked the means to build on it. I dug out those bricks with my own hands and this way we created our cemetery fence. We met annually in Lanovits to commemorate the slaughter of our families until Zvi and I immigrated to Israel.

[Page 130]

Addendum to my Memoirs

By Mendel Brimmer

Until I actually immigrated to Israel I did not dream that soon I shall have permission to leave the Soviet Union. I corresponded with Zvi Mail on the subject. We both decided to be patient and wait for an opportunity.

In the meantime I married. Our son was born and he started to attend a local school. I had little time to speak with him and learn of his attitudes in this foreign land.

One day our son came home, confused, and asked me: "Dad, are you Jewish?" I replied, "Of course". "And mother?" he asked. I replied "She is also Jewish." Our son then declared, "I do not like Jews, they tortured Jesus the redeemer until he died." It became clear to me that Russia remained Russia: They use Marx to hate Jesus, but they still use Jesus to hate Jews.

* * *

Prior to my marriage, during the confusion that was part of the war period, several of us Jews ended up resting at the home of a peasant woman. It happened on a winter evening. She fed and cared for us in a sincere manner. She let us use her beds. I received the best bed in the house. I shall never forget her gracious hospitality.

In the morning as we parted, we stood there to thank her. We were searching for the proper words. It was tempting to say, "God will pay back your good deeds," but citing God was dangerous. We praised her deeds instead. Her children, who stood next to her, savored the praise we heaped on their mother. She replied, "Better days are ahead for all of us. I expect that you Jews, who are suffering so much now, will also see better days ahead." When her children heard that we were Jews, they asked if we also were the ones who tortured Jesus. While the peasant woman was free from bias, her children were exposed to a different dogma.

[Page 131]

* * *

In the work camp where I was employed, I became acquainted with one of its engineers. He was a wonderful man, but as a party member he was fanatical when it concerned party matters. When secretary general Khrushchev came to visit our camp, he, of all people, was chosen to greet the secretary general. We Jews at the camp were careful to hide from him the fact that we were not party members. We were particularly careful that he not notice when we received letters from Israel.

One time, my normal caution failed me. I received a Rosh Hashanah greeting card from my brother in Israel. It included some of the major panorama and symbols of the new state. As I was staring at the card, thinking: will I ever see these sights with my own eyes, the engineer stood behind me. There was no escape. He saw the greeting card and said: "Comrade, I envy you. I would clearly love to have received such a greeting card." Here too was a Jew, an underground Zionist.

[Page 132]

I was in Lanovits After the Holocaust

By Zvi Meil

On Succoth holiday, September 22, 1940, I was inducted into the Red Army and left Lanovits. I was sent to Vladivostok and the Manchurian border, 12,000 km from home. We traveled for 29 days on a freight train. From Lvov to Irkusk, no food was available for purchase. In Irkusk we were able to purchase a sausage made of horsemeat. It was impossible to eat the sausage. We arrived in Birobidjan [A Jewish autonomous republic on the Manchurian border- Ed] hungry.

In Birobidjan we Jewish soldiers were well received. The local Jews prepared food items familiar to me. They ranged from dumplings with sour cream to a variety of baked goods just like my grandmother and mother used to prepare.

When the war between Germany and the USSR broke out, our unit was sent to Erevan, near the Iranian border. From there we were sent to the Leningrad front. Our unit participated in battles in front of Moscow and Vileki Luki.

In 1943 I was wounded near the town of Nobil, which is near Kalinin. I was brought to hospital No. 53/65 in the town of Yaroslav. I had many wounds. I recovered from my wounds only after the war ended. In my unit in the Far East (from Lanovits) were: Yidele Foiker, son of Moshe the Black, Israel Pacht (the nephew of Kendzur), and Shlomo Shewtz, the son of the deaf shoemaker. When we left for the front, Israel Pacht deserted and disappeared. The three of us from Lanovits stayed together until we arrived at the Leningrad front. Shlomo Shewtz was killed there.

[Page 133]

It happened when our group was crossing through a thick forest. A mortar shell hit a tree that fell on Shlomo and killed him instantly. I and two Gentile soldiers from Lanovits buried him where he died.

Let my testimony about my fallen friends be the equivalent of providing them a Jewish burial.

Two of us were left at the Leningrad front. We were taken prisoner by the Germans when they encircled the village of Vishi-Kotitsa. We were kept in the basement of a private home. After six days, we escaped by killing our German guard. On the way back to our unit, Yidele told me that he decided to desert the army and return to his family in Lanovits. I later found out later from Pavel Hindes that he arrived in Lanovits in late 1941 and perished with his parents in the Ghetto.

* * *

When I was stationed near the border facing Japan, we were ordered to dig defense trenches. Our immediate Commander Medwedew demanded that we work faster, complaining that we (Jews) always want to live from the work of others. When I complained about Medwedew's behavior to our General Commander Simyonow, he did not reply. However, the next day I found out that Medwedew disappeared that night and never returned. Later we found out that Simyonow was Jewish.

* * *

When I was wounded, I was the only Jew in my unit. Shumilow, a Gentile Ukrainian from Lanovits and Bashow, a Russian, rescued me after I was hit. I owe my life to those two comrades.

* * *

It is not my nature to only remember bad incidents. It is, however, a fact that we Jewish soldiers were living under tension that has no parallel in civilian life. The danger to our lives was particularly high if our comrades behind us were Poles or Ukrainians. Serving in a foreign army, far from home, they tended to take revenge on Jewish soldiers.

[Page 134]

* * *

On December 3, 1944, I received a letter from Siberia. The letter was from Hayim Nathan Gitelman. He asked me to visit him in a detention camp where he and other Jews were held. I asked our hospital administrator for a four day leave pass to visit Gitelman. It was granted. I visited Gitelman and his friends at their detention camp. The camp was well organized and its food supply was adequate. A local doctor extended my leave permit from 4 to 18 days. In the camp I also met Shalom Segal. The three of us spent an enjoyable time together. With Segal was his daughter, Klara. They told me that Avraham Weiss is in Kiev. Segal said that he visited Lanovits several weeks ago to rescue his daughter. He was the first person to inform me as to what happened in Lanovits.

In 1945 I received another leave from the hospital administrator to visit my hometown, Lanovits. On the way to Tarnopol, I had to change trains in Kiev. I had to wait in town an entire night. I entered a Jewish home and asked if they could let me sleep there. The next morning I went to the local market to see what goes on there. From afar I saw a person resembling Avraham Weiss. I called him by his last name. He was shocked but did not know who called him. When I approached him and asked, "Don't you recognize me?" he was sure I was a person he knew from Vizshurodok. It hurt me to realize that my appearance apparently changed (due to my injuries). I was, after all, his next-door neighbor.

This episode proved to me that my war wounds may prove to be a bad omen. Weiss was truly happy when he realized who I am. He invited me to his "home". He was widowed after his wife perished in Lanovits. In Kiev he worked in a pharmacy and was happy with his lot. He did not have a room of his own. Instead he slept in the pharmacy and cooked his meals there. I visited him from time to time. He was like a brother to me. When we parted we did not ask "Where to?" Both of us realized that our future destination was uncertain.

On the way to Tarnopol, railway police boarded the train in Podvalochisk and warned us that Bandera bands are still in the destination area, that we passengers must be careful. I felt anguished as I wanted so much to visit Lanovits. In Tarnopol I had to wait for the train to Lanovits until 12:30 in the morning. I went to survey the town. It was completely destroyed. Its streets were blocked by ruined houses (On the train to Lanovits) I traveled with NKVD officials. The train was full of soldiers. I, too, was in uniform. A few minutes after our departure, our train stopped suddenly and all of us flew out of our coaches. It turned out that a Bandera insurgent switched the train to a dead-end rail branch.

* * *

I arrived in Lanovits in the morning (on another train?). We all leaned out of the train's window not to miss anything. While at the Kiskovits rail station we already saw the extent of its destruction.

[Page 135]

The town that once hid the horizon with its panorama; now it hid nothing. Here and there one could identify a few buildings. At the railroad station I met the son of Stefan (the carpenter) Legsiuk. We walked to town together. On the way to town, I recognized a few Gentiles that stared at me, noting a strange visitor. They did not recognize me, and I did not start a conversation with them either. I could not bring myself to speak with anyone. My heart was pounding.

I arrived at the corner of the homes of Brimmer & Sarah Shayes. Suddenly I saw David Schneider coming towards me. It was a tragic meeting for us. We both cried and walked to the cemetery. We spent the whole day there. In the evening I returned to register with the Police. They found lodging for me at the home doctor Zuber (the local felsher= A country doctor).

In the morning, I wandered through the town I loved and found destruction everywhere. I rummaged through the ruins of our house and to my surprise found a photo of my mother. In my wandering, I always carried family photos with me, but did not have a picture of my mother. Here I found it under these tragic circumstances. The photo has remained in my wallet to this day.

That day, Hayim Nathan [Gitelman] and Shalom Segal arrived in town for a visit. Haika Kagan arrived the following day. We spent a week together in Lanovits. We met Ita Karper who returned from Russia and for some reason decided to continue her life in the ruins of the town where she grew up and her parents perished. She lives in Lanovits to this day.

Of all the former houses, the only ones that remained standing were those of Michel the blacksmith, Shmuel Bachtel, Michael Kenfizyur, the bakery of Shmuel Furman, the cellar of Beyla Berg and the houses of: Libergal, Aharon Parnas (Michlis), Golda Berenstein, Moshe Katz, Leibel Shzuleg, Khanah Re'uveni, Shayah Natanes, Manos Zhak, Hazan (including its shingle factory), Eliyah Zabares, Mordechai David Lipes, Moshe Merinkowitz, Berl Pacht, Leah Glinik, Layzi Pletsiles, Yasha the barber, Moshe Kofets, Moshe Fogel, that of Hayim Simcha Reznik (the father-in-law of Kofets).

We parted from our town. Each of us went to his destination. We left downcast, with an empty feeling.

* * *

In 1947, I returned to live in Lanovits. My situation was such that nowhere else was I able to find work and housing. I did not imagine that I would ever be able to live again in my home town, but circumstances forced me to reconsider. I informed all my Lanovits friends that I am back in town and corresponded with them.

From time to time, the remnants that survived visited me. Among them was Yosef Marder who presently lives in Bretslav, Ukraine, and Mendel Brimmer. After some time we discussed the idea, and decided to build a fence around the mass grave of our brethren who perished in the Holocaust. The idea came to me and did not leave me peace of mind for many days.

[Page 136]

However, I did not have the means to carry out this project. We were able to implement it in 1949 when the communist party sent to Lanovits a new secretary-general. He happened to be a Russian that served in my army unit. I told him about my plan. He advised me to implement it as soon as possible, while he is the local authority, and can help me administratively. His successor may not be as cooperative.

In May, 1949, Hayim Nathan Gitelman, Shalom Segal, Mendel Brimmer, Jacob Kagan, David Schneider, Moshe Rosenberg, Yosef Marder and I erected the fence around the mass grave. In 1950, I left Lanovits.

Mendel and Zvi during the installation of the fence

[Page 137]

Yosef Marder
(The Caretaker of Our Mass Graves)

By the Editors

Yosef was not born in Lanovits. He came to the town in 1920, with the rest of the refugees from Kopel and Siniava. He came when the Polish/Russian border was finalized. These Jews chose apparent freedom and escaped to Poland.

Marder was over twenty when he arrived in Lanovits. He worked independently, supporting a widowed father. As a merchant from an early age, he traded in leather and did well commercially. He married, and started a family just like others in Lanovits.

In 1942 (actually 1941 - Ed.), when the Soviet authorities evacuated Lanovits, he left with them. As one previously employed by the Soviets, he feared the Germans. However, he did not want to leave the town permanently so he left his wife Haika and daughter Anzia in town. He and his son, Moshe, escaped eastward. In the Soviet Union, he and his son suffered all the hardships of the war, such as hunger, sickness and injuries.

In 1945, he returned to Lanovits to rejoin half his family that he left in town. On the way to Lanovits, he heard of the tragedy that befell his family. When Bushka, the nurse, advised him to leave town to save his life, he left town broken hearted, resolved never to return again.

In 1948, the Lanovits survivors in Russia decided to come to town and visit the mass grave of their relatives that perished there and Yosef joined them. Together, H. Gitelman, Zvi Mail, David Schneider, Moshe Rosenberg, Shalom Segal, and I (Brimmer) participated in the erection of the fence around the sacred grounds where our dear ones were buried.

In 1964, Yosef returned to the site to erect a monument and a plaque at its entrance. From time to time he returns to the site to make sure it is properly maintained. In the exchange of letters between us (Marder & Brimmer - Ed) one discerns a glimpse of the times, his character, and attitude to our holy place. The following are three of his letters on the subject translated word for word from Yiddish:

[Page 138]

The memorial monument erected by Y. Marder

[Page 139]

3 May 1964

(Date seems to be in error judging by the letter's content; perhaps 3 June 1964-Ed)

"Dear Mendel, Lisa, Children and Grandpa.

I fulfilled my holy obligation by erecting a memorial monument commemorating the Lanovits residents that were killed by the German murderers. I started this work at the end of April and completed it on 23 May 1964. I am enclosing a photo. We do not have a better photographer in Lanovits.

I will describe to you how I accomplished this task. As you know, the gravestones had fallen and the covering earth had sunk. I brought in 150 loads of fill, employing 3 trucks, a bulldozer and a digger. I erected small mounds to prevent the fill from eroding, and seeded the mounds with clover. I also repaired the fence that was damaged in several places, and planted trees inside the fenced area. I poured a foundation on which I erected the monument. The latter is fenced-in from 3 sides. A concrete walkway leads to the monument from a gate that I installed.

The monument has two inscriptions. It was erected midway between the two large mass graves.

Editor's Comment: The inscriptions are in Russian and Hebrew:

'Here lie Lanovtse residents that were killed by Fascists on 29 Av and 1 Elul Tashav 13 & 14 August 1942'

6 January 1967

Dear Mendel, Lisa, Children & Grandpa:

Mendel, why are you not answering my letter? I wrote you that there is a need to write a book about Lanovits so that it will serve as a memorial for future generations. The book will inform them what Lanovits was like, also how its Jews were killed by the fascists.

If it is difficult for you to publish such a Yizkor book, seek help from those from Lanovits living in the Diaspora. After all, they, too, had relatives that perished in the Holocaust, yet did not help to erect the memorial. Let them at least help with the publication of such a book.

12 September 1967

Dear Mendel, Lisa, Children & Grandpa:

On September 4, 1967, the first of Elul, I traveled to Lanovits with Hayim-Nathan Gitelman on the anniversary of the Ghetto's liquidation. We went to the mass graves and arranged a memorial in town. The monument and the graves are in good condition. I arranged a 'Yarzeit' and said 'Kaddish.'

27 May 1968

I congratulate you on your decision to publish a Yizkor book commemorating our dear ones that were killed by the Fascists; may their sins be remembered forever. Remember to mention my wife, daughter and son that perished (in the Yizkor book)"

Editor's comment: These letters testify to Marder's great dedication to our project. We are fulfilling his wish

[Page 140]

Moshe Marder

By Mendel Brimmer

Moshe, Shaike

Moshe was the son of Yosef and Haika, born in 1923. He received an education typical of that given to Lanovits children. He was a quiet and serious child who felt close to his parents.

When World War II broke out, Moshe was 16. At age 18 he left his mother to join his father and help him in his wanderings after his flight eastward. At age of 19 he was inducted into the Red Army. He was wounded at the Ukrainian front. After his recovery from the wounds he was sent to the rear. However, after several months of recuperation he was again sent to the front.

In 1944, I met him by chance at the Armavir/Kuban railroad station. We spoke together at length. He gave me his father's address, which was previously unknown to me. We parted, not knowing that I shall never see him again.

In March, 1945, he fell during an attack on German forces in Czechoslovakia. He was 21 when he died.

In the accompanying photograph, he is on the right (on page 140) with Shaike Schneider on the left. Shaike was the son of Michael Kenziyur, a friend and of the same age as Moshe. Shaike helped his father in his tailor shop. He was drafted into the Red Army in 1944. He, too, fell on the Czech front in 1945 and the location of his grave is unknown.

[Page 141]

Chapter 4:

In the Thicket of Redemption

[Page 142] [Blank] [Page 143]

Each Generation and Its Zionists

By Moni

The Lanovits community was concerned with "Parnoseh" [= The ability to support a family] to an extent that it eclipsed to spiritual life. "Parnoseh" was the criterion by which the seriousness of a young man proposing marriage was measured. It was also the criterion applied to our generation. When leaders of the community spoke about important matters they would remark, "Where do you find young men in this generation that are willing to submerge their honor, and seek to make a living in agriculture? Today, there are none. Instead they want to reform the world or express other fantasies."

With this prevalent attitude, Zionism was characterized as a quasi-serious idea. Zionists were considered to be persons who are not serious, or those collecting for Zionist causes.

The community found spiritual uplifting in Hasidism, something above "Parnoseh". In each past generation, a Hasidic Rabbi found a way to fortify Judaism (against assimilation) on the premise that "We have to wait a little longer for the Redeemer to arrive."

The community saw in Zionism a road to a different future that had no spiritual content as compared to that offered by their Hasidic Rabbi.

To be a Zionist in Lanovits meant to take risk in two respects; being considered an unrealistic person and one unwilling to wait for the Redeemer.

One could not be a Zionist in our town unless one had a strong personality, income, and spiritual vitality. His personality had to be strong enough that no one would dare accuse him of being wedded to a silly idea. As a result, the town's Zionist activists were also community leaders.

Among the first were Joseph Warach and Leibish Orbuch. Both emigrated to the U.S., but Joseph Warach continued his activity on behalf of Israel from the first day of his arrival in America. His 48 years there have been dedicated to raise money for the Zionist organization which he continues to do today. He also helped us in creating a Hebrew Free loan society and in the raising of funds for this Yizkor Book.

The next generation included Yudil Buchstein and Eliezer Katz. Yudil Buchstein would leave his store, dress up in his holiday clothes, and, as chairman of the Jewish National Fund (JNF), solicit donations for the organization. He did so without demanding any recognition for his effort. His belief in the importance of this task was unshakable.

[Page 144]

For us young men he was an example of a respected father that understands the spirit of our generation. He found his satisfaction in his support of the younger generation.

Eliezer Katz and wife   Yudil Buchstein and his wife

Eliezer Katz loved people. He was fastidious about his outer and inner cleanliness. He added his Zionist activity to his other tasks. His activism demonstrated that Zionism was not restricted to a particular age group. He was elderly, yet as a wholesale trader he saw in Zionism a mission whose time has come, hence should not be ignored.

Zionism reached its peak influence in Lanovits when Peisy Buchstein and his brother-in-law, Shlomo Berman became active in the community.

[Page 145]

Peisy was a quiet person, solid in his convictions regardless of public opinion. As the only child of a well-to-do father, who also had important social standing, Peisy devoted his talents to community work and the promotion of Zionism . Peisy spoke a perfect Polish, providing him a respected standing within the Polish community. He was also knowledgeable at public accounting. Having these two attributes, Peisy was the logical candidate to represent the Jewish community in its dealings with the Gemina, the local administration whose officials were exclusively Polish. On the strength of his personality he became the conscience of the local administration. Local officials responded to his requests, in appreciation for the accounting and organizational advice he gave them. Town councilors listened to his advice when addressing local problems. When Peisy became identified as a Zionist, those who opposed it questioned their own judgment in view of his strong convictions. His conception of Zionism was less pro-active than the conception of those who wanted to become pioneers in Palestine, nor did he deny the importance of the Diaspora. However, his support of Zionism sustained the idea locally, providing it continuity. Peisy also established the first local cooperative saving and loan society, one that was certified and audited by a government agency. This cooperative institution was viewed over the older community charity organizations.

Shlomo Berman was a talented public speaker. In his speeches he would raise the imagination of his listeners offering them faith in matters above their concerns for daily bread.

The community loved him despite some of his financial failures, which also caused losses to others. He was always forgiven. Tall, with thick black hair, he was regarded like a prince despite his crazy ideas.

Shlomo was not an official of any Zionist organization, but nonetheless often their mover and shaker.

He had new ideas of how to dramatize the Zionist cause, and a feel for what the public will respond to. He pulled the Zionist issue out of its corner, and made it a central, subject for speeches from the synagogue pulpit. In his speeches, he sketched a vision of the future that lifted the spirits of his listeners. He was also the one to arrange JNF dinners at the Polish community center, providing the center with extra income.

Shlomo used his talent as a dramatist to improve local theatrical productions to give them a professional quality.

We could not ascribe to Shlomo any concrete achievements on behalf of the Zionist cause, yet, indirectly, he opened the hearts of the local public to accept wider horizons, and wider life choices.

It is fair to say that with Shlomo, Lanovits became open to new ideas. However, he did provide leadership for new ideas. The expectation people had that he would change attitudes remained unfulfilled.

The tremor in the community he initiated, due to his talents as a public speaker, were exploited by those who followed him. With their personal example these followers inspired others to become pioneers. Shlomo's contribution was remembered long after his star faded.

The next set of activist were Yizhak Zingel and Yizhak Buchstein. The first was a person that showed the way to attract others to the idea of "building the land (Palestine)". The second person provided the wherewithal that facilitated Zingel's social activity. The two had opposite talents, thus complementing each other's strengths.

Yizhak Zingel was all movement, action and initiative. He reorganized the Zionist funds so that fund raising occurred on a regular basis. Due to his efforts the small Hebrew library was enlarged significantly, as was the number of readers.

[Page 146]

He dared to rent halls for Zionist functions without knowing where the rent payment will come from. Lanovits became a beehive of social and cultural activities. At Zingel's initiative, emissaries from Israel were invited to speak to local congregants, explaining both the difficulties and rewards awaiting them in the land of their dreams. His great achievement was the founding of the "Hehaluts" branch [=pioneers], so that Zionism now meant preparing for immigration to Palestine.

Yizhak Buchstein accompanied Zingel in all his Zionist activities. He was the type of person that carried out his tasks quietly and thoroughly, knowing his own limitations. While supporting two families, his and his mother, he was limited in the initiatives he could undertake. His advice did, however, prevent many activities from failing; that was his contribution.

When the idea of pioneering took root, the two parted ways. Zingel had to develop the Hehaluts branch with the help of others. These pioneers eschewed the old Zionism of words. Instead they wanted to prepare themselves to immigrate personally.

This period, when the Hehaluts movement got started was also a period when the old activists moved over to stand in their shadow. Instead, a new generation of activist arose lead by Israel Glazer and Yizhak Kirshon (who were the first to immigrate to Palestine).

[Page 147]

Their rise meant that former fund raisers became secondary players to the pioneers. They prayed for the pioneer's success and marveled at their conversion to productive and agricultural workers.

* * *

This article will be truncated so as not to duplicate other articles on the activities of Hehaluts Hatsair [=young pioneers]. However, we need to make an observation.

The founding of the young pioneers movement caused a real revolution in our town. The youths started to direct their thinking and planning towards immigration to Palestine, rejecting the idea of staying in the Diaspora. Old Zionism became the activity of the town's elderly, and an empty shell. The youths now focused on the idea of immigration and how to prepare for it. The leaders of the young pioneers defined a clear goal and ways to reach it. The Town's youths were redeemed from old thinking, preferring to reject the Diaspora in favor of immigration. They hoped to be able to bring along the rest of the family at a later time to a secure place where sudden turmoil is avoided.

Unfortunately, the British mandatory immigration restrictions precluded most of them from reaching Palestine, thus most of them perished in the Holocaust.

[Page 148]

First He'Halutz Branch In Lanovits

By Israel Glazer

I was 16 at the time, a year or two after completion of the customary schooling in Lanovits. Adulthood depressed me. My energies called for something to do. My uncle, Asher Brilant, offered me a job in his wholesale store selling food and fuel. I was happy to accept his offer. I felt relieved being busy and useful during the day hours. In the evenings and on Saturday, when a person thinks about his future, I felt certain emptiness; the future did not look bright. I realized that this image of the future is not good for me or for my friends who were even less occupied with work than I was. We could not free ourselves from thinking about our local future. We realized that it was not the future we desired, yet we also realized that local conditions and the structure of our community were unlikely to change.

It was then that the idea of immigration to Palestine became an alternative.

He'Halutz branch in Lanovits

The traditional education of our youths focused exclusively on relations between people and ones relation to his community.

[Page 149]

It created a youth that was well equipped to deal with internal community problems, but ill-equipped to fight for broader job opportunities. This type of upbringing influenced our thinking. We discussed and argued among ourselves the place Judaism plays in our lives in the diaspora. We also discussed the future of diaspora Jewry. The problems we saw within our bleak future lead us to the larger question: "How long will generations of Jews continue the sad pattern of trusting their luck to make a living under the same uncertain conditions they live under presently?"

Immigrating to Palestine was not considered an immediate solution to our perceived future problem. Instead, it was viewed as an alternative for the distant future. It was regarded as a solution that bypasses present problems, aiming to pay off in the future. Immigration to Palestine was not only seen as a solution for us; it was a solution for all diaspora Jews.

The annual memorial lecture commemorating Dr. Herzl, which commenced in 1921, added to the recognition of Israel as a viable alternative for the future. As such, the annual lectures in our synagogue were unimpressive. The speakers repeated the same visionary stories and the legacy he left to us, without any intention to carry out his vision. Nonetheless these lectures exerted a powerful pull on our thinking. We came out of this lecture resolved to carry out his dream. We asked ourselves: "How do we start?" We started by founding an undefined organization that we named "Hashomer Hatsa'ir." The germ for this idea came from Yoskeh Shapira, and from me, the younger of us two. Zeidel Goldman (now in Argentina), Meir Rosental, Hannah Mahler, Devora & Friel Shpieler, Gitel Glinik, the Brimmer sisters, Mordechai Kofets, David Gurewitch, Hershka Weiss, Avram Weitzman-Folker, and Cherna Wohl (now in Argentina) joined us.

The tie that bound us together was our teacher, Raphael Sfarim, one who taught us to reject life in the diaspora. He, himself, made his own secret plans to immigrate to Palestine. He implored us not to sink roots locally.

Within the Hashomer Hatsa'ir organization, we created a soccer team with the intention of developing our bodies, and preparing ourselves for the physical work we anticipated in Palestine.

* * *

In 1923, we contacted the Hehaluts central committee. The latter sent us guidelines, bulletins, and instructions on how to transfer money collected for the "Israel Workers National Fund" (IWNF). The objective of this fund was to solve the unemployment problems in Palestine by creating new job opportunities for Jewish workers.

In discussions with Jewish National Fund" (JNF) activists, we made the point that development of Jewish settlements in Palestine is probably more dependent on IWNF funds than on JNF funds.

Through our various activities, we learned to work together as a group, one that has an important future objective. Our town's affairs became of secondary importance to us. At this juncture (the start of Hehaluts activities) our Hashomer Hatsa'ir function, as well as soccer lost their significance.

[Page 150]

Our main aim turned instead to preparation for implementation of our Zionist idea: Immigration to Palestine. On our own initiative, we created a work group that sought jobs in town. We accepted all manner of jobs, from felling trees to cleaning yards. We refused no task that would get us accustomed to physical labor. Above all, we wanted to demonstrate our willingness to change our personal lifestyle to prepare ourselves for a great future – immigration to Palestine.

We were regarded as dreamers in the eyes of the town's burghers. They wondered how their sons and daughters could forsake a mercantile future for a life of physical labor. Was this a sensible way to earn a living? Our parents regarded us as having lost our way.

In 1924, we decided to improve our physical training by seeking agricultural work. Instead of accepting any job, we sought work in the fields and villages. In the first 2 years, the community and its youths wondered whether we were realistic. However, when we went to work in agriculture, our community members became interested in us and helped us, especially the town's youths. We became a center of their attention. They were eager to be seen as supporting us publicly. It appeared that Zionism meant little to our youths unless it was associated with working the land.

* * *

After some time, we decided to become independent farmers. We leased land from Mr. Ladiniuk, plowed it, and seeded it with sugar beets. We purchased three horses that we used for plowing. When this task was completed, we used the horses to transport goods as wagoneers. The latter was our original idea. Dealing with horses, fodder and harnesses seemed in our imagination to be part of the redemption process. We decided to serve the Kremenec-Lanovits route as wagoneers. We contacted local retailers who needed to have goods delivered from the regional distribution centers in Kremenec. We also transported people. This competition angered the local coachmen and wagoneers, whose business suffered. Their income was meager enough. A fight developed between them and us. Michael Itzik Shmueles cut our horse harnesses at night and threatened us in other ways. We knew his violent nature and took his threat seriously. We discussed the above problem in an internal stormy meeting without any outside pressure. We concluded that we must stop our transport business. The local coachmen and wagoneers were unaware of our decision. They were still angry at us. For some reason, they declined to contact us to seek a solution. We, however, decided to terminate our wagoneer work so as not to compete with our fellow Jewish workers.

[Page 151]

We viewed our fellow wagoneers as the only group in our community belonging to the working class; they were, in our eyes, like the salt of the earth. They, unlike most members of our community, earned their living doing physical work. We did not want to hurt the proletariat element of our community. This bit of Marxism, in our attitude, precluded us from becoming a factor that depresses wage levels, or breaks strikes. We informed our fellow coachmen and wagoneers that we were their allies, and will no longer compete with them. We abandoned wagoneering and settled on working solely in agriculture.

Our work became the talk of the town. We transported our sugar beets to Preminger's weighing station for delivery. Preminger was the representative of the sugar company located in Khodorov. We lined up together with the Gentile wagoneers who transported the sugar beets raised on land leased by Jews, but not worked by them. Their traditional blessing over vegetables as "The Fruit of the Earth" referred not to the results of their labor, but, instead, to the profit made in raising this crop. We, on the other hand, transported the produce of our own labor and sweat, thereby risking our standing in our community.

Our evenings were spent discussing the day's events, the waiting in line to unload and the women we met. Our members were proud of their accomplishments – raising agricultural products that we harvested and sold on the market. The proceeds more than covered our expenses. Our accomplishment was an example for the town's youths, an example worth copying. More of them joined our group, especially those older than us. These new members were the town's leaders of yesterday, who, in the past set the tone for the youths of the community. Now, having been eclipsed by our achievements, they endeavored to join our efforts.

The leaders of those who joined us at this juncture were Y. Buchstein, Sh. Glinik, Sh. Reichman and Yizhak Kirshon. The person that stood out among them in his enthusiasm was Y. Zingel.

We knew him as a progressive and active leader who helped our youths previously to search for new solutions to their perceived problems. He introduced them to secular literature and education. He established a large library in town, enabling its youths to become familiar with new ideas and exposing them to the thinking of Gentiles and Jews alike.

This group of late joiners experienced a two-fold social problem. They became a second fiddle in the community's life. The also had to accept the fact that the beautiful girls their age no longer sought them out. Dressed in overalls, with blistered hands, they no longer belonged to the town's intelligentsia. They were, however, able to cope with those problems and mixed well with the early members of our group. With their public support of our activities, our group became the center of interest of the community's youths. Immigration of their young adults to Palestine became an acceptable alternative in the eyes of the town's families, even among the more sophisticated ones.

The enlarged Hehaluts group held a meeting at which a new executive committee was elected and its functions defined. Y. Zingel was elected Chairman, and I was elected secretary of the organization. Members of our organization were also elected to the library committee in a democratic election.

[Page 152]

I viewed these two elections as one of our more important accomplishments.

* * *

At the end of 1924, Pinhas Rashish, an emissary from Palestine and member of the Central Committee of the General Hehaluts organization visited our town. We spent an entire evening with him, eager to hear his message.

Rashish was favorably impressed with our organization's accomplishments. I do not know exactly why. It may have been the fact that we had our own meeting hall and that the hall was suitably decorated with pictures of the new Palestine. He may also have been impressed with the detailed accounting of our fund-raising on behalf of the Israeli Workers National Fund and with our agricultural training. Based on his observation, Rashish apparently concluded that our organization was alert to current events and serious in its desire to immigrate. When we parted in the early morning hours, Rashish promised to provide us with 3 immigration certificates for our youths.

This was a large initial allocation for our small branch, but it was also small in comparison with our needs. Many of us wanted to immigrate, and a large portion of our group had completed suitable agricultural training.

Rashish left, and we were delighted with his promise. As news of his commitment spread, our troubles started.

Our executive committee dealt with the selection of candidates during several difficult meetings. We were faced with many needs and so few means to satisfy them. Some members complained bitterly about our selection process. A particular complaint was voiced by Zina and Feige, the Kuziles sisters. They joined our group as individuals, separating themselves from their former friends. The conditions in their home would have justified assigning them priority, though their economic condition was not an issue. Their selection would have turned the tables on who is important in our town.

What to do? We spent many hours at meetings to arrive at a fair selection. In the end, 3 candidates were selected: Y. Kirshon, M. Rosental and the author of this article. We immigrated the same year (1925), being the first to arrive from Lanovits as a group. Feirel Yishpa actually preceded us; however, she left our town by chance, without announcing her intention to immigrate. We were the first pioneers sent by our town to settle in Palestine. The parting celebration turned into a significant event, comparable to a wedding between a lost nation and its motherland, a party that is difficult to describe.

* * *

The going-away party took place in the home of the young Rabbi from Horokhov. Our community leaders and its Zionist activists (those who formerly mocked us and handicapped us) came to the Rabbi's house in the early evening hours. Many cried. Parents were overwhelmed by the thought of their son leaving for a country that does not exist. We listened to fiery speeches and our hearts pounded in the excitement. Local women prepared cakes and others brought drinks to celebrate this momentous occasion.

[Page 153]

The event resembled a wedding party whose principals were the " Hehaluts " members. The latter were at a loss as to how to respond to the honors bestowed on them. The community members in attendance, accustomed to celebrating the visit of a Hasidic Rabbi, saw to it that this event would be remembered for years to come.

In the end, we parted with hugs and kisses. Women cried and the men said, "They want to leave? Let them leave." The rest of the community members, resolved to make the best of local conditions, returned to their homes.

* * *

On May 3, 1925, Polish Independence day, we left Lanovits. We three walked in the middle of the street that passed below the houses facing it. Our parents and relatives walked behind us. As we passed their houses, its residents waved to us. Some were so moved that they too came down to join the procession to the railroad station.

We parted from those who came along. We did not realize that this would also turn into our final parting.

[Page 154]

He'Halutz Hatza'ir in Lanovits

by Zvi Brimmer

Lanovits was a dynamic town. While it was faithful to its traditional customs, its residents yearned for changes. I remember our townsmen as persons who conducted their business calmly and worked quietly, yet would erupt during occasional arguments in their spare time. There were no altercations in our synagogue as repeatedly happened in other towns. Yet, the synagogue was the site of frequent heated arguments between one faction and its opposite side, dealing with their attitude towards Zionism and immigration to Palestine.

In our days, the disputes concerning the choice of a new Rabbi and the proper level of orthodoxy had subsided. Opinions in town differed primarily concerning nuances in interpreting Dr. Herzl's legacy of how to implement his ideas.

The town's youths, exposed to the atmosphere of frequent disputes, typically adopted their parent's position on the above subject. They added to their views the element of implementation, as if to say: "You can think one way or another about Zionism, but you are not free from implementing its consequences. You must plan to immigrate to Palestine."

The local "Tarbut" school provided its students' knowledge of the Hebrew language and culture. It also functioned as an educational institution that directed our thoughts towards the implementation of Zionism. Our youths came to view pioneering as the solution to the problems of our generation, a view that differed markedly from the view of the adult members of our community. Enrollment in the "Tarbut" school lead naturally to consider pioneering.

The youths, who organized the various Zionist groups, reached their peak success with the founding of "Hehaluts Hatsa'ir". Within this organization we crystallized our thinking in discussions about the problems of Palestine and our role in promoting Zionism. As time passed, Hehaluts Hatsa'ir became the address to which adult Zionist activists turned to with requests for help.

We were the ones that went from house to house to empty "Jewish National Fund" boxes. When we found an empty box, we dared to explain to the donor their elementary duty to donate, and why. We also collected for "Keren Hayesod" (=Infrastructure Fund) and carried out other tasks requested of us by Zionist activists. Our branch became the body that carried out the detailed Zionist activities.

We participated in the preparation of local shows, recognizing the income they provided to support local Zionist activities. Who cannot remember the dirty work of cleaning the Kuziel horse barn, installing a stage in it and arranging seating places for the local show?

[Page 155]

This volunteer work created a spirit of teamwork among us that made our lives more pleasant; however, the tasks themselves were often difficult causing occasional bitterness. We basically served as attendants to the adult actors, freeing them from accessory tasks. On the day of the performance, we stood at the hall entrance collecting tickets and preventing freeloaders from sneaking into the hall; a task that required steel nerves and risked a beating. The day following the performance, we dismantled the stage and returned all the items that we borrowed from various homes. We viewed these portage tasks as a means of promoting active Zionism.

During the late 20's and the 30's, the town's economy suffered an artificially created decline resulting from new anti-Semitic laws (passed by the Seym=Polish parliament). As a result, some of the town's leading activists departed or reduced their level of involvement. Members of our group took their place, raising the local Zionist profile that was temporarily neglected.

It was at this time that we inherited the custody of the large local library which was unused for several months. We dusted off its books, rented a hall and created an attractive reading room. It doubled as a lecture and social hall. Members of the community responded to our restoration effort by using the library and attending scheduled lectures. We won recognition as Zionist activists.

Our enthusiasm inspired senior community members who were discouraged as a result of deteriorating economic conditions. They likened our enthusiasm to charcoals that warm up a house. We actually used charcoals to heat the hall's furnace on cold winter evenings to take away the hall's chill. These cold winter nights deepened our feeling of despair, a feeling that changed to hope as we gathered in our warm clubhouse hall.

The clubhouse hall allowed us to renew the scheduling of outside speakers and preachers who came to town bringing news from our potential homeland (Palestine) to a bewildered community. We invited members of the Hehaluts central committee to town, and arranged for them to speak in an attractive hall to keep the subject of Zionism focused in the minds of community members.

The Zionist youths who followed us (after we immigrated) continued this promotional effort, a fact that left a deep impression on me. We youngsters understood what had to be done culturally to minimize the social boredom that affected our parent's lives.

We matured as a result of these efforts. Our organization was transformed into a Hehaluts branch. Children of yesterday became adults who strove to immigrate to Palestine. A war started between parents and children who demanded permission to immigrate. Our dear parents, who saw us mature, expected us to support them both as household contributors and, later, in their old age. They were thus loath to yield to our demand in spite of their realization that pioneering was the wave of the future for them and for their adult children.

[Page 156]

They were too weak and too discouraged to accept this reality. The resulting domestic friction was a difficult test for both parents and their children.

It was in this period that our group decided to make the "plan to immigrate" a precondition for remaining a group member. Whoever declined had to leave the group. It was heartbreaking to see dear friends part ways. Years of friendship were torn asunder. We were all drawn into emotional difficulties that cannot be described. However, a significant change occurred in our community; immigration to Palestine became a singular topic that affected everyone. It was a topic discussed in homes at mealtime, and among congregants in the synagogue. The community was faced with a fateful decision. There were days when the opinion of those who opposed permitting youngsters to immigrate prevailed and we were almost excommunicated. However, we refused to give up. On the contrary, as more of the parents opposed us, we took steps that were novel to our town. In meetings among us, we discussed ways and means of dealing with our parents; how to explain to parents our dilemma. We promised financial and moral support to whoever was forced to leave one's parents without their permission to join a Hakhshara (=agricultural training). The slogan "Immigration" became our daily byword.

The author of this article remembers his and Bluma Miller's difficulties with their respective parents who followed them out of town in an effort to return their children from these training centers. I can recall instances of escape through a window at night and of transfer of clothing to friends all in an effort to escape from home and reach a training center.

In the end, we organized a Hakhshara center in our town. Our purpose was twofold: it was to demonstrate to our parents that parents of youngsters from other towns do allow their children to train in Lanovits, away from the parental table; also to demonstrate that a Hakhshara center is not a licentious place, nor does it entail bone-breaking work. By having our training center located in Lanovits, we wanted to compel our parents to allow their sons and daughters to train locally if they are loath to let them leave town. Lanovits was not an industrial town; establishment of a local training center was primarily based on the above-mentioned considerations.

The establishment of the local training center to prepare us for immigration to Palestine defined our conception of the meaning of Zionism. It is possible to summarize: our above-mentioned conception of Zionism and our persistence in adopting this point of view was a new phenomenon in the lives of generations of our town. It was also a new concept for the old Zionist activists. Had many in our community adopted this viewpoint, our community would have been more content.

Unfortunately, few from our town immigrated to Palestine. Those who survived perhaps survived due to the idea we planted in their minds. While we feel satisfied with our past accomplishments, we know in our hearts that our success was indeed minor when compared to the destructive violence of the period that followed our departure.

[Page 157]

My Pioneering Days in Lanovits

By Sonia Shar (Shifman)

In the winter of 1933 I left for Hakhsharah (= Pioneering). The (Hehaluts) secretariat directed me to the Klosova group located in Lanovits. I was familiar with Lanovits, hence I was surprised that this town was chosen for pioneering work. I asked myself: "Where are its work places?" It turned out that the local Hehaluts branch members succeeded in persuading the central secretariat that the loading of grain at the local railroad station will provide sufficient work slots for the group's members. The group had yet to form. It was our task to get it organized. We had no funds. Our first problem was to find housing. Later we would look for job opportunities.

We arranged a meeting with other group members. I, Korakh Yosef, Zinamon Yosef, the three founders of Kibbutz Lanovits posed the immediate question: "Where to sleep?" The local members solved this problem nicely. We came to realize that such problems have local solutions; that the Hakhsharah will succeed.

We were housed at the home of Shmuel & Leah Bachtel. They gave us one of their rooms gratis. We were surprised at their generosity for Shmuel was known as a BUNDIST. We lodged with them for one week free of charge.

Later, we were moved to the home of Michel Kowel, (the blacksmith). The two young men of our group occupied the rented room, whereas I slept gratis with Sisel and Edith (Edel), the blacksmith's lovely daughters. These were terrible days for me.

[Page 158]

The toilet was located in the barn behind the house. At night, when I had to use the toilet, I would meet Michel's crazy sister who sat regularly next to one of his cows.

* * *

Our first work assignments were the felling of trees and clothes washing. We realized that our group would fail unless it grew in numbers. We strove to increase our group so as to create a normal social environment. But, who will provide us work assignments?

It was Ladiniuk, an eccentric person who no one knew if he was Polish or Ukrainian, who became interested in our group as potential employees. He employed us in the planting of cabbage on his large farm, which he cultivated intensely. It appears that we did not disappoint him. He would move from one planter to the next advising each of us on the proper planting procedure to use. After the planting project was completed, he employed us at various tasks for several months.

The work was not easy. He had no water distribution network with which to water the plants, yet he believed in intensive cultivation employing water and manure. We were the ones to carry the water from the local well regularly. I was tasked to bring manure to the vegetable beds with a wheelbarrow. While he was a learned farmer, he declined to invest in the construction of a water network, employing our labor instead. We were the substitute for a sprinkler system and a manure spreader.

Zvi Brimmer joined us later. His joining our group left a deep impression on the local community. Here was a young man who moved out of his parent's home to join a group of adventurers and declare his intentions to change his lifestyle. His joining brought additional members to our group; Johnathan Rosenberg and Golda Todt from Kremenec, and Sandor Korin from Brestichitsky. With our enlarged group, we could now call meetings, hold dances and songfests. We developed into a functioning group.

We were only 7-8 members, yet the local Hehaluts members always came to our aid whenever we needed help. With their assistance, we fulfilled all jobs offered to us.

Aside from material assistance, the Lanovits Hehaluts members lent us emotional support. Malka Brimmer taught me how to bake bread, so that we could supply our own needs and save money. One day a week I did not go out to work. Instead, I baked bread for our group. We enjoyed the taste of our own bread and the independence it symbolized. The parents of Zvi Brimmer viewed themselves as "wedded" to our group. They came over every evening to visit, be of help with various arrangements, and line up work assignments.

As the group grew in numbers, we moved to the Grawitz house in the new section of town.

[Page 159]

It was the time that the pioneer group that was living and working in Melinsky was liquidated. A portion of their members joined our group. Our group grew to 20 persons.

As I recall those days, it seems to me as if we were the local attraction for the Lanovits Hehaluts members during their leisure time. Bluma Miller, Yitzhak Gluzman (Potsi), Yosef Buchstein and others spent most of their evenings with us.

I laundered clothes for locals. At first, I was hired as an assistant to the Gentile washerwoman. Later I was hired directly. I felt like a certified washerwoman. In reality, my employers wanted to save the added expense of the Gentile washerwoman. I remember an episode that occurred with my relative Yente, the wife of Eli Schneider. She gave me a big load of laundry to wash in the local river. It was the time of year when the snow had already melted and turned to mud. After I finished washing and rinsing the laundry, it gleamed in its whiteness. I placed the load on my back to return to her house. On my way back, I slipped on the mud, soiling the entire load. After that event, she no longer hired me. The same happened to me with Rivka, the wife of Moshe Kuziel.

Our men worked at felling trees, as assistants to teamsters, and as clerks and stockmen in local stores, especially in the metal stores. Their main occupation was the loading of grains onto freight cars. It was the work life they sought. Many of work assignments came from Moshe Gurewitch and his sons, Benik and Azriel. We also worked at the lumber yard of Golda Berenstein. I don't remember days without work, thanks to the constant referral-help we got from the local Hehaluts members. They treated us with respect, as persons who regarded the implementation of the Zionist idea seriously. The local youths saw us as persons who succeeded in changing the status and values of others in the community. Their parents exhibited a more ambivalent attitude towards us: on one hand, they wished that their children would respect work as much as we did; on the other hand, they feared that their children will wander to a faraway place, where their experiment may not succeed, the British may not let them into Palestine and all their years of labor will have been for naught.

We were fortunate that our group did not include atheists, so that we all kept the Sabbath and Kashruth. This gained us the respect of the orthodox members of the local community.

[Page 160]

Eight months after our arrival, a group of "Beitar" pioneers was founded locally (=revisionists, followers of Jabotinsky). The Revisionists noticed that due to our presence, the Zionist focus was on Hehaluts. They decided to employ the same strategy to gain a political advantage. The days of that pioneer group were numbered. However, while they were active, we experienced tension and competition in obtaining job assignments. After a short period, their group broke up and we continued in our work efforts, regaining the full sympathy of the community that we had in the past.

When I think back of my days in Lanovits, I see a town and a community that had a strong Zionist orientation; one that was pragmatic in solving political problems. I do not understand why despite this positive local atmosphere so few of its youths left for Palestine. My heart bleeds for the dear friends that I left there, who perished.

[Page 161]

Beitar Hakhshara in Lanovits

By Sarah Kitikisher
(Vishnivits – Jerusalem)

Lanovits did not have a Beitar (= youth organization of the Revisionist party) branch. I do not know why our movement chose this town (Lanovits) as a place to train pioneers. We were ordered to move to Lanovits so we did. We arrived there on Hanukah holiday 1934. When I arrived I found 20 pioneers that preceded me. An apartment had been rented for us in the meantime. Those who preceded me had no lodging for awhile.

We lived in the house of David and Feige Michlis in the center of town, where we were for awhile a subject of curiosity to the town's folks. The community looked upon us as nice Jewish youngsters that needed "Nebekh" (=unfortunately) to do manual labor. After awhile, the community realized that we worked not only to support ourselves; that work was part of a pioneer's vision. With this attitude change, we gained respect, even envy.

We (women) worked as housemaids in the homes of Bina Buchstein, Berchik, Yosef Baratz, Hayim-Nathan Gitelman, Shlomo Berman, and others. I worked as a saleslady in Kurchak's store. The men worked at felling trees.

We were fortunate to encounter a warm-hearted Jew, Moshe Kopitz father to 11 children, who provided us work in his fields. Sometimes, he created jobs for us, to assure steady work for us and food on the table.

The Lanovits youths divided their sympathy between the two Hakhshara groups, ours and Hehaluts. On certain evenings, they arranged common discussion and singing sessions. As a result, the political animosity between the two groups fell markedly.

I recall Zoniah Rabin, a good looking and kind young man, whose personality rose above party differences. While a Hehaluts activist, he felt obligated to visit us regularly and listen to our needs. He tried to minimize our public loneliness that might result from those who shunned us because they were politically against us. His regular visits left me with pleasant memories and the hope of real friendship among Zionist groups.

During Hanukah 1935, we arranged a banquet in "Dom Lodovi" (=the Polish town hall). I think it was Byya who tried on that occasion to redeem our honor which, he thought, was sullied. An altercation with some youths resulted, but it all ended peacefully. This was the only altercation with us that I recall to have occurred in Lanovits. The remaining days in Lanovits were pleasant ones. We lived among warm-hearted Jews who made us feel welcome, considering our (= the Revisionist's) forced isolation within the Zionist movement. I will always remember them fondly.

[Page 162]

Redemption That Ended Poorly

By Etil Adler (Shpieler)

Not everyone has the same memories of one's hometown. There are those whose childhood involved hardship, suffering and poverty. In my case, I also lost members of my family while a youngster. Despite all this, when I think of Lanovits, I yearn for her.

Israel attracted me like a lover who will redeem me. Once here [in Israel], I always dreamt of returning to Lanovits for a visit to experience once more the great love I had for my community.

It seems to me that each of us, who left, imagined the experience of homecoming, when neighbors and friends would stop their daily chores, to sit with the guest and hear what it is like "over there," and savor his success of settling elsewhere.

The thought of a future visit to one's hometown encouraged a person and tied him to his roots, to his family that wants the best for him.

When a person emigrated and succeeded to put roots in a new place and freed himself of its handicaps, he started to think of how it was back home. He thought of his family and friends; it was the one place that wanted him, whose community wanted to see him again and wish him well.

I never got to see my community again. At the time of the Holocaust, I received a postcard from a Lanovits policeman, informing me that all the town's Jews were killed by the Nazis (in August, 1942). I knew then that the privilege of a happy return was taken away from me. I thought, in my heart, of these good people. Had they also immigrated to Israel, they would have made a positive contribution to our state. When they died, our redemption suffered a great loss that will take several generations to replace.

[Page 163]

Dramatics in Lanovits

By Moni
(In honor of Shlomo Berman)

The Jewish Community of Lanovits, surrounded by Ukrainian villages, provided ready material for dramatic tragedies. The older audience, however, was not enamored with plays. Our youth wanted to introduce a bit of dramatic freshness and self-expression into the dry cultural life of our community. In the past nothing helped. There were no objective conditions to put on plays, not even Purim plays. These sad conditions prevailed until Zionist activity opened the door to dramatics.

The self-criticism expressed in Shalom Aleichem plays gave legitimacy to the rejection of shtetl lifestyle and the corresponding yearning for the Zionist alternative. These plays made a caricature of our lifestyle during the last 2000 years, emphasized its lack of purpose, and suggested the need for reform. All these factors created an excuse to produce plays in which each person in the audience could see himself in the context of world events, as an object susceptible to inevitable changes if he wants a normal life. The stage became a medium on which to depict the terrible vicissitudes of recent times.

Zionism could not be explained to the simple folks except in the form of a drama play, where the attendee could focus on the issue in a limited time and space. The stage became an audio-visual vehicle with which to explain Zionism and the need to change local values soon lest Zionism will come too late.

The drama group was thus created as a means of explaining Zionism; a way of convincing the community of the merits of the redemption idea prior to the Holocaust.

The stage directors were the best talent in town, who worked tirelessly to transform local values via stage productions.

* * *

Our directors were serious men who were best at staging tragedies that depicted doubt, delusion, pain and suffering.

[Page 164]

The available repertoire was not composed by Zionists; however, it was written by talented Jews and met Zionist (propaganda) needs.

Plays by Shalom Aleichem, such as "Tuvia The Milkman", and "A Bloody Joke," "God, Mom & the Devil," "Miraleh Efros," and "Moti the King of Woodworkers," were staged by Jacob Gordin. These plays by Shalom Aleichem and Gordin depicted the gloom of present life and shook the audience out of its tranquility. The play "Tuvia the Milkman" exposed the shallowness of Tuvia's "Betukhen" (=trust) in his lot. It implied that his confidence will not hold when pogroms occur and his daughters are raped; it will be shattered instead. The play, "Mirale Efros" taught the audience that those who put their faith in the present regime and in the security of their wealth will raise children that leave their faith. The play "Bloody Joke" and "Moti the Woodworker" dealt with the futility of integration and increased reproduction in the diaspora. None of Goldfagen's plays were produced, nor others of Mendele. The emphasis was on plays that had a Zionist orientation.

* * *

When attempting to depict the social character of our town for this book, several talented persons come to mind who were involved in producing drama plays in our town. The most memorable of the set was Shlomo Berman.

He was a shining public figure, yet he was even better at stage directing. It was he who gave the local plays an almost professional polish. The actors were successful in identifying with their character in a convincing manner. Each play that he directed stood out in its smooth execution. The accompanying ballads were also composed by Berman. He contributed significantly to an atmosphere of empathy for the Zionist dream in our community.

For a short period we became acquainted with Bernzil, a man from Warsaw and a promoter of Y.L. Peretz's (1852-1915) literature. He came to our town as a bookkeeper for the Greenberg-Kagan firm. The plays he directed were noted for their creative staging and costumes. These tools helped to explain the period the play dealt with. They also facilitated getting the play's moral message to the audience. Bernzil arrived in Lanovits, with no clear literary conception. Raised in a Yiddishist seminary, he was searching for reformist ideas. It was his interaction with our youths that turned his thoughts away from those expressed in the literature of Y.L. Peretz, and towards Zionism.

Younger local talent followed Berman and Bernzil. Their stage productions made it possible to collect funds for Zionist functions and help financially those young emigrants that needed financial assistance for their travel to Palestine.

The town became accustomed to the process of performance preparations followed by a play.

[Page 165]

When a period passed without overt preparations for another performance, locals asked for an explanation. In this manner we attained an important objective. The community became interested in such plays and in the Zionist ideas expressed in them.

* * *

For the local actors the rehearsals were a significant experience that reinforced their realization that their efforts to properly depict a character were not in vain. The plays gave these actors an opportunity to stand out and show their creative talents.

Lanovits loved its actors and kept a proper distance towards them. No one mocked the actors the day after a play; on the contrary, they showed them respect.

Several local actors won the hearts of the audience: Sonia Burstein for her lovely singing, Nasia Trelo and Mania Rabin (Zingel) for their acting, and Motke Roichman for the humor he inserted into his acting roles. When Byya Kazatseker or Yokel Schuster acted in a play, the town celebrated their successful performance. Likewise, great sorrow was felt when the town lost its great comedian, Shmulik Futerman, the son of Motel Dayan, formerly from Zhuhan.

The dramatic talents in our community helped create an atmosphere in our town which made the Zionist solution credible. We need to credit these stage actors with this important achievement.

After a show in town
S. Berman sits fourth from the left

[Page 166]

Changes In Class Standing In Lanovits

By Josef Buchstein

The social values of the Lanovits community changed greatly in the years I lived in this town. This change was (largely) due to the influence of the Zionist organizations: Hehaluts Hatsa'ir, No'ar Ziony, and Hehaluts.

I arrived in Lanovits at the age of 11. While relatively young, I was nonetheless old enough to discern social patterns and note local values.

The community was divided into a number of social classes. The most respected were both learned and wealthy for generations (Of course this assessment is relative. A person that was considered wealthy in Lanovits would only fit into the middle-class of a larger city). In my time, these respected residents were no longer rich, but their self-esteem as upper-class member remained. Their sons all had acquired either Torah education or general learning.

The next social layer consisted of tradesmen and retailers. These families were able to provide their children a comprehensive education. After their children learned the basics in a heder [= a one-room school with one teacher], their sons were sent to another school or tutored Gemarah and, sometimes, were also taught Polish. [An amazing set of priorities for Polish Jews – Ed.]

After the tradesmen and retailers came the local artisans whose economic status was often precarious. The average artisan or craftsman could not afford to finance his children's education for more than a few school years. When his boys learned to read the Hebrew prayers, even without understanding their meaning, their heder education ended, and their craft training started. In the eyes of one's parents, and in the eyes of the community, a person that could read the prayers in the prayer book was no longer an Am Ha'aretz (= An ignorant person). In most cases, after completing his heder studies, a son would learn his father's craft.

Among the tradesmen and craftsmen some were more, and some less, well-off. Those who were good craftsmen had many clients. Such a craftsman could afford a tutor for his sons and perhaps an apprentice in his shop. His living standard was typically better than that of a retailer. Other craftsmen hardly made ends meet.

The town's living standard was low, including the standard of those who made a good living. Everyone was intent on saving money for either a dowry or to finance future illness. [No safety net here – Ed].

There was also a segment within the community that had no trade, nor enough money to establish a small store or a small grain-storage room. These men lived off the small income earned during the weekly market day. They would buy a quantity of raw linen, a bit of Hog's hair, process it and resell the product. They lived from this income for a week until the next market day. Their plight was a difficult one, yet I do not remember a single case of fraud or theft. These poor people were simple and proud, unwilling to accept financial support from others in the community. At most, they accepted interest-free loans from the local organization, or would charge their purchases at the store they patronized. I do not remember a case where a debt remained unpaid or that a person declared bankruptcy.

[Page 167]

There were no (Jewish) beggars in Lanovits, though there were families without food. Others in the community collected funds for these families and provided them with confidential assistance.

* * *

Each of these social classes had its own social and religious institution. Even our synagogues tended to serve a given class. The most respected and affluent community members attended their Kloizl [=a small synagogue frequently restricted to an occupational or social group]; the less affluent prayed at the Beith Hamidrash. The more successful artisan families prayed at the main synagogue. The less successful artisans prayed at the synagogue's annex called "Das Kleine Schulchel". Both the Kloizl and Beith Hamidrash attracted a number of poor congregants. These were primarily neighbors of affluent families. They were tolerated in these prayer halls because they could be called up to the Torah readings as the "fourth", a position that others shunned traditionally.

The community's social classes were served by two pulpit Rabbis, one serving the well-to-do, another serving the less prosperous community members. The community's religious orientation was entirely Hasidic, yet within it there was a further segmentation; some followed the teachings of the Trisker Rabbi. Another group followed the Rabbi from Ostarah, and the artisans had a third Rabbi.

A person who supported himself doing manual labor was looked down on. I know this from personal experience. When I became a member of Hehaluts Hatsa'ir, immigration to Palestine was a serious option. I reasoned that I would need to learn a trade that would be useful in Palestine. I liked woodworking, hence decided to train in this craft. I discussed the matter with my late father. He agreed with my plan, and I apprenticed myself to Mr. Glick. The apprenticeship was cut-short when Mr. Glick himself immigrated to Palestine after a few months. I, unfortunately, did not find another suitable journeyman to work for. I also needed to help my parents in their store. However the short apprenticeship was sufficient to keep me in this professional to this day. The gossip in our town centered on the idea that we youngsters saw in manual labor a sort of heroism or patriotism whereas the community's adults saw it differently. This clash of values is illustrated by the following example: My father had a sister in Lanovits, named Sarah, the wife of Pini Wiger. For some unknown reason, she was cross with us all the years that I remember. When she heard that I switched from retailing to manual labor, she went to her Rabbi asking him to lobby my father to disallow me to learn woodworking. She reasoned that my act was staining the reputation of our family.

A manual worker was considered a lower-grade person. This value assessment changed in the 1930's. As I leaf through a photo-album depicting my friends of that period, I find a composite of youths from several social classes assembled together on the hill above the seven springs (outside our town). I find other photos of groups consisting of youth from all social classes lounging on the front porch of Shmuel Forman's house on a Sabbath afternoon.

What brought about this change (reform)? Why did it start in my generation? I am of the opinion that the reform came about primarily due to the education we received at the Tarbut School. We were the first graduates of this school, hence the reform in local values started with us.

[Page 168]

What was the situation prior to the opening of the Tarbut School? All the local boys were taught by "teachers-for-beginners". Their salary was low. As these boys grew up, more experienced and expensive teachers were hired for them. Not all the parents could afford the extra tuition-expense. Thus only sons of affluent families were taught at these higher levels. The lot of the girls in a family was even worse. They could not attend a Heder, hence needed private tutors. These added tuition expenses were significant; hence this education luxury was available only to children whose families could afford it. In contrast, once boys and girls could get their education at the Tarbut school, the economics changed. The school's classes were larger, and the tuition fee was fixed at an affordable level. The school was supported financially by a local committee. Now almost all the community's children received the same level of education plus recourse to a library. Its monthly lending fees were minimal, so that virtually anyone was able to borrow books to read. Having the benefit of a better education than available in the past, these youngsters benefited further from the availability of Zionist club houses. Each of the aforementioned Zionist youth movements had a clubhouse opened to all comers. The youths would meet on evenings for a chat or a dance. A new environment was created where an individual was no longer a "finished product" defined by his family's social standing. In the clubhouse, a youth had to prove his social skills to fit into this new youth-society. It was, therefore, natural that a new social group emerged that transcended the former stratified classes.

The attitude towards manual labor also changed, influenced by the presence of the Hehaluts organization. Sons of wealthy parents sought physical labor jobs to accustom their bodies to the tasks they expected to find in Palestine. Their wages went to support their clubhouse. Likewise members of the Hakhshara group tried to earn enough to cover their food and lodging expenses. These youths were no longer ashamed to be laborers.

I do not recall cases of youngsters changing from trade to manual labor who were not involved with immigration plans. This was so because day labor rates were so low that one could hardly live on such wages. Even the Hakhshara member's wages were barely sufficient to pay for food and lodging of one room, sleeping several men. Nonetheless, a person who carried water or felled trees was no longer ashamed of his job amongst his family members. It follows that the Zionist youth movement not only prepared its members for working life in Palestine, it also transformed the value-system within our community.

Had our Shtetl not been destroyed, we would have likely been a witness to a radical change in social values within the Diaspora communities, influenced by the presence of Zionist youth movements. Unfortunately we were not privileged to witness this reform.

[Page 169]

Youth And Its Yearnings

By Shalom Avital (Kwaitel)

As I attempt to put on paper my memories, I recall a wonderful period during my childhood and youth. I remember dreams that came to fruition and others that remained unfulfilled. As I think back, I can visualize my town's features: its straw-covered houses, and others that had tiled roofs; its wooden sidewalks and unpaved streets. The town's Jews faced occasional dangers and a constant struggle to earn their daily bread. All (who remained) disappeared from the face of the earth. Only a few of us remained, like firebrands snatched from a burning fire, to bear witness to the fate of a community whose members were tortured and slaughtered, and are no more.

The town had neither a kindergarten nor a nursery for its children. When a boy reached the age of 4-5 he was brought to the local heder by a belfer [= assistant teacher in a heder]. The child first learned to read, write, Humash [5 books of Moses], Rashi [=commentary], Gemarah, etc. Learning these subjects we spent our days in a narrow and dark classroom. During the summer we studied in two shifts. In the winter a third evening shift was added.

In the 1920's, the first sign of Haskalah [=secular reform] penetrated our Shtetl. A Hebrew language teacher appeared in town who taught Hebrew to both boys and girls, as well as grammar and some arithmetic. This new teaching [In the Tarbut school] was offered in small measures so as not to disturb the town's life-pattern that moved inexorably like the steady stream of our river Ritsheke past the main entrance to our town. Children advanced from class to class, changing teachers. Those teenagers who continued their studies tackled the study of Talmud. Those who persisted in their studies ended up in the Kloizl where Reb Motel Melamed taught them Torah, Ethics and love of the Jewish people.

The Hebrew language Tarbut School strengthened its standing within the community with the help of local Zionists. Its teachers, who changed frequently, drilled us in both Torah and secular studies. The most talented and respected of our teachers was Rafa'el Sfarim who is still with us in Israel.

This institution shaped our education and outlook. Unfortunately, only a few of us students were able to implement the Zionist ideal and immigrate to Palestine or immigrate elsewhere. Most of my fellow students perished with their parents in the Holocaust.

An important factor that shaped the intellectual image of our town's youth was access to our Library, consisting of circa 10,000 books. Its scope developed significantly under the direction of Yitzhak Kirshon when the latter was back at his parent's house in Lanovits from Palestine recovering from his illness.

We acquired and read books in Hebrew and Yiddish ranging from fiction (both original and translations) to philosophy. We also obtained publicity journals. After new books became available, discussions were held regarding the values, trends and images developed in them. The Library was a constant source of material for special projects such as fundraising, publicity and stage productions.

The rehearsals, usually under the direction of the talented Shlomo Berman continued sometimes for months. Those of us who had acting skills got key stage assignments.

[Page 170]

Others assisted in various tasks ranging from one that whispered forgotten lines to one that designed publicity signs. One needs to credit the efforts of hundreds of youngsters who became involved in the preparations for a given stage production. The performance took place at the horse-barn owned by a local lord who also owned the only flourmill in town.

The town's youths were also active in fund raising for the Jewish National Fund (KKL). These activities symbolized for our youths the shaking-off of older Shtetl lifestyles, and a fundamental change in Jewish life-pattern and individual values while still in the Diaspora. We accepted the notion that KKL money will purchase dunam (=4 acres) after dunam (of Palestine soil) bringing us nearer to the redemption we had sought for so many centuries. Once a month, two of us would go to each house to empty the "blue" (KKL) collection box, asking the head of the household to "round up" the content's amount. We regarded these collections as akin to holy work. In the evening we brought the few Zlotys we collected from the town's poor and rich to the KKL treasurer. We "compared notes" about the results, satisfied that Lanovits was doing its share in building a homeland (in Palestine).

For us, this was a period of yearning. We were seeking new channels for our youthful energy. We were no longer satisfied with romantic ideas or just symbols. A new wind began to blow in the Jewish world. The Zionist youth movements struck roots in the Shtetls of Eastern Poland. Competition between Zionist groups was intense. Each group opened a clubhouse trying to pull the town's youth to its movement. In the process our youths matured and started to think in terms of implementing the Zionist dream. They joined a Hakhshara (=pioneer training), and prepared their parents for a future separation when they immigrate to Palestine. Regrettably only few of us managed "implementation" and immigrated to Palestine. Many of us who matured and joined a Hakhshara, and others who remained at their parent's table, all perished in the Holocaust.

Let these words and the collection of stories that accompanies this article be a memorial to the dear youths of my Shtetl Lanovits who dedicated their lives to build another home in Israel but did not reach the Promised Land.

[Page 171]

In Memory of Those Friends Who Perished

By Cherna Rabin

In memory of Meitzy Shpiler

I chose the Hehaluts movement from among the Zionist movements active in our town because it was the pioneer movement among them. Its members who passed Hakhshara training became true pioneers, implementing the Zionist dream by immigrating to Palestine. Hehaluts did not spoil its members with promises. I was drawn to its ranks largely because the Movement was also egalitarian, whereas our community was divided between rich and poor. I disliked the community's social outlook. I regarded each youth as an individual, regardless of his parent's social standing. Our movement also prepared us for a practical life. At home none of us had an idea of what physical labor entailed. This idle lifestyle was easy for our youths, but hard on their parents. The aforementioned pioneer training prepared our members for a life of labor in Palestine. Having passed through Hakhshara, they were able to adjust, and withstand workplace difficulties avoiding a personal crisis.

The movement had other aims as well. It taught lessons in Zionist ideology to youths who otherwise tended to idle, or drift away from Judaism copying Gentile lifestyles. We members had periodic discussions on the subject of Zionist and Hehaluts history. In this way, our youngsters received both physical and spiritual training. A youngster who passed through pioneer training knew its purpose and its advantages as concerns his future in Palestine. Of our graduation class, not all were members of the Hehaluts movement, nor did they regard its aims seriously.

[Page 172]

Some of us did not join a Hakhshara. They had various reasons: one was afraid of hard labor, another did not want to rebel against his parents, and a third did not wish to leave his comfortable home. After all, who could have imagined such a bitter end? It would not have occurred in one's worst dreams. My heart breaks when I remember all my friends that remained in our town. At the time I am describing, only Meitzy Shpiler and I passed pioneer training. We both filled out questionnaires and were accepted as Kibbutz candidates.

I shall never forget the day of our departure. I remember the goodbye from my father whom I loved and so respected for his wisdom and intelligence. Additionally, there was the difficulty of taking leave from all my friends and neighbors. It was not an easy goodbye.

As my father's only daughter, many wondered how was it that he agreed to my departure from home. The Hakhshara was no surprise to my father as he was a dedicated Zionist, supportive of the idea of immigration to Palestine. He realized that our youths had no future in the Polish Republic; hence it was not difficult to convince him to let me immigrate. I did start to talk about joining a Hakhshara at a rather young age, a fact that bothered my father. Once I was accepted as a kibbutz candidate by the Hehaluts central committee, there were no more objections to my immigration in our home. As I stated earlier, the separation was difficult. We all knew in our hearts that this is the beginning of the end… [Did they know that at the time? – Ed.].

I shall never forget the actual departure day. The train pulled away, while all present at the platform remained standing. We were all frozen in our place as our dear ones disappeared. Each of us sat in the train coach deep in thoughts. We left behind a youthful period full of joy and sadness. We were entering an unchartered but interesting period that promised a better future.

We arrived at our destination [apparently Warsaw – Ed.] hopeful about our immediate future. We were immediately taken to the Kibbutz doctor. I was the first to enter the examination room. After a short examination, the doctor declared me fit for any physical work. Meitzy Shpiler was the next one to be examined. He came out after several minutes very sad. He was not accepted because he was found not healthy. The doctor did not give details as to Meitzy his ailments, but told him that he was rejected. It is hard to describe Meitzy's shock when he heard the doctor's decision. After a few hours, Meitzy recovered. He decided not to give up on his candidacy. Instead he drafted a plan to visit a specialist in Lvov who would likely be able to help him. His plan was to recover from his illness with the help of this specialist and reapply, in order to implement his immigration dream.

We parted with a heavy heart. I somehow had the feeling that Meitzy would never return to the Kibbutz. His fate remained in my thoughts for a long time. Not many of us realized that this tall, strong-looking man was like an over-ripe apple, already spoiled.

His family, who arrived in our Shtetl as refugees, settled-in after some time. Their first years were difficult ones until they integrated into our town's economy. Their children were divided into two camps. One set stayed in town, the other rebelled against the local grey life that was without content and decided to leave the Shtetl. Meitzy was among the rebel children until that sad trip to the Kibbutz doctor. Unlike his father and brothers, he refused to join them as a trader.

[Page 173]

He earned his living instead teaching how to play the mandolin. Where he got this musical talent, G-d only knows. He was talented, had good hands and was good at music.

Dreaming youth
Meitzy is leaning on a tree trunk

[Page 174]

Meitzy did not return to the Kibbutz. It appears that his doctors did not give him much hope. He accepted his fate and remained in his Shtetl. Here and there, we heard rumors about Meitzy's doings. He himself did not write to us. I heard that he became an idler and stopped changing girlfriends. Some of my girlfriends married, others left our town. Meitzy continued to dream of immigration to Palestine, waiting for a miracle…

In the meantime, winds of war arose, and then WWII broke out. The Russians entered our town, and (after 2 years) left suddenly taking with them whoever wanted to save themselves. Why was he not among those who left with the Russians? The Germans meanwhile occupied the town, sealing its fate. After the War, Meir Bakar visited with us. He told us that he escaped from the cemetery where the Ghetto Jews were murdered. For a full week, he gave us details on what happened to our friends and relatives. We were broken hearted at what we heard. It was hard to accept the tragedy and humiliation that our families suffered daily. He told us that some in town advocated rebellion, others just accepted their fate. I was particularly interested in Meitzy's fate since he was the only one of our group that remained in the Shtetl. Regarding Meitzy, Meir Bakar told us a different story. He was killed earlier by local Gentiles. They settled accounts with him bringing him to a bitter end. We knew these Anti-Semites who behaved like animals. They beat Meitzy with sticks, leaving him in a field to die. May his memory be blessed.

I want to take this opportunity to remember those of our friends who did not live to experience the founding of the State of Israel: Hannah Margalit, Manya Katz, Sunia & Fania Shpiler, Gitel Malka, Slova

Brimmer, Edel & Zisel Chisda, Risel Wiesman, Fierali & Yosky Weiner, Lieber Blank, Shalom Maharshak, Brandeli & Motil Buchstein, and my brothers-in-law, Shaike & Zuni. I also wish to remember my beloved parents, relatives, friends and neighbors. Let their memory be blessed.

[Page 175]

Chapter 5:

Significant Persons and Dr. Zinberg

[Page 176] [Blank] [Page 177]

The Legacy of Lanovits in the Writings of Dr. Y. Zinberg

By Hayim Rabin

Dr. Yisroel Zinberg

Dr. Yisroel Zinberg was born in 1873 in Lanovits, Volyn, when this town was still small.

At the time, 950 Jews lived in our town, surrounded by a sea of Gentiles. Two of their villages bordered on the town. Lanovits was a relatively new community planted in the midst of Gentiles whose way of life remained unchanged for generations. Nor was there a desire on their part to change it. The Jewish community of Lanovits was in contrast a dynamic community that re-examined its purpose regularly.

At first look, the two societies appear to be similar, both frozen in time. Actually, the difference between them was large. The village Gentiles lived in the present, where the struggle for their daily bread shaped their social outlook. They did not strive for a different life nor did they have a vision of what it could be like. At the same time, the Jews of Lanovits, whose memory of the past shaped their lives and marked their preferred values, looked at their past differently.

[Page 178]

The present was for them a laboratory in which to use the best of the past to chart a better future.

This was a new concept in our town, to conceive of the future as a continuum of the present, measured not by individual achievements, but instead by society's achievements.

When we consider the Lanovits community as a geographical or demographic entity it is miniscule. However, when we recognize its ability to inspire its residents to think and innovate, we discover its greatness.

The striving for a moral community was expressed in various traditions. Within the family it was expressed during the Sabbath and Holiday meal. On the community level memorial dinners were held to commemorate an important person that passed away. The dinner was a means to an end of shaping a moral community. This striving was also expressed by strict observance of Jewish laws in the home, by honoring one's parents, and by regular prayer.

* * *

When we compare the community's social life to the social life and worldliness of the Gentiles in the surrounding villages, we can readily appreciate the high standards of our community. The establishment of the Lanovits community represented a preference for the deeper Jewish Life in a Shtetl as compared to the convenience of life in larger towns [The author seems to ignore the historical restrictions that precluded Jews from being allowed to reside in larger towns – Ed.] The Shtetl Jew was able to eschew the Gentile's life style of excessive eating and drinking because of his attachment to his past as reflected in our Jewish literature. This literature contained the people's spirit and values. Acquaintance with this literature not only made our resident a good Jew. It also created a good person, loyal to his society. This goodness was the result of the person's devotion to the values of his ancestors as reflected in our past literature.

* * *

[Page 179]

Dr. Zinberg did not study in a Yeshiva. His biographer points out that his knowledge of Hebrew did not stem from Torah learning. It is surprising that a person who studied secular subjects and science in a foreign (Russian) language was later drawn back to the study of Hebrew and Yiddish and its literature.

For many years Dr. Zinberg lived far away from Lanovits, dealing with subjects that had nothing to do with our town. Nonetheless, he seemed connected to Lanovits as if by an umbilical cord through which he drew secret nourishment. In time, this nourishment enabled him to compose and publish his literary history and research the values reflected in its works.

His attachment to Lanovits stands out in his eclectic approach to his collection of Hebrew literature. He chose to emphasize those literary works that dealt with values. In his approach, he illustrated the legacy our town left in his writings.

The legacy our community was expressed in 5 aspects of his writings:

1. The language he chose.
2. His methodology.
3. His work style.
4. The emphasis he placed on certain topics.
5. His analysis of the purpose of our literature.

A. **Writing in Yiddish**

Zinberg wrote his monumental multi-volume book, containing a set of Hebrew references in the Yiddish language. He saw the need to excerpt part of this literature into Yiddish in order to provide his brethren an understanding of these works, yet screen this material from the secular world.

Just as the Lanovits community prayed and wept in Hebrew, but used Yiddish as its vernacular, so did Zinberg bring the Hebrew literature to his people in their day-to-day language – Yiddish.

B. Methodology

Zinberg documented in his encyclopedia the history of Jewish literature starting with the publication of the Talmud and culminating with current Hebrew works.

[Page 180]

He regarded as literature all works from poetry to prose and philosophy. He viewed these literary works as an expression of Jewish continuity through the generations. He included references to all these literary works in these encyclopedic volumes. His comprehensive approach mirrored the attitude of Lanovits Jews who would open their Siddur, or Makhzor, or Midrash or Ein-Ya'acov book to study and absorb its poetry or prose, thus satisfying their religious thirst.

Zinberg did not skip over any published works, citing all of them. He even regarded the "Shulkhan Arukh" [Code of Jewish Law] as a literary work that creates in Jews a yearning for their homeland and an abiding faith in the merits of following the law. This book, which demands service to our creator, Zinberg saw as inspiring a desire to preserve one's good image by keeping each of the cited laws. He included in his citations poetry dealing with daily life, wine, love, meditation, polemics such as "Moreh Nevukhim" [Guide to the Perplexed], The Kuzari, books on travel and medicine, works by Alharizi, Moses Mendelson, Spinoza, Shabtai Zvi, Jacob Emden and Jonathan Eybeschutz.

The Jews of Lanovits, like Zinberg, tended to study from all available sources in order to understand their heritage better.

It is difficult to characterize Zinberg's writing methodology. He wanders between different fields. He is both a lexicographer and a historian in one chapter, and a critic and researcher in another. He examines and critiques some works, and with others his esthetic dictates that he merely categorize the subject of a monograph or book. He merely describes the content of some works, and analyses in depth other books. It is not my intent to provide detailed evidence of these observations. Instead, these comments are intended as a review for posterity, in an attempt to link Zinberg's and the Lanovits community's attitude towards Jewish literature. What is of interest to us is not his formal method, but rather, his writing approach as a Jew, intent on preserving his unique (Jewish) identity.

His focus on the 1000-year European part of our history was not due to particular research, but rather due to his deep concern for the preservation of our national identity. Zinberg was concerned that the specter of a liberal Europe was liable to be a strong attraction to young Jews, as a means of freeing them from the chains of the past, hence could serve as a model for desired changes. The parents of Lanovits youngsters shared this concern. Some parents were fanatical in their struggle against the liberal inclinations of their children.

C. Writing Approach

Zinberg's writing took place under interesting circumstances, testimony to an almost religious approach to writing. He worked at his job during the day to support his family. He spent his nights organizing his references, reading available books and writing chapter after chapter. It reminds me of the custom of some Lanovits Jews who would get up before dawn, or stay up after midnight, when family members were asleep, to focus on the study of a particular subject.

In 1914 the world was shaken by the events of WWI. It was a time of mass population transfers, hunger, and the promise of a better (socialist) future. Zinberg was a dedicated socialist, yet one with a European secular education. He was at that time far from his hometown and starving. Nonetheless he continued to write. It is hard to understand his attachment to an old literature in the face of a new (revolutionary) world. One can only speculate that Zinberg sensed that the new (Communist) Society was likely to discard the old without creating anything new that is worthy. He apparently sensed the likelihood that the new regime will swallow small nations, their culture and literature. He must have sensed that this danger existed for his people as well. In view of this perceived danger, Zinberg spent his energies completing his monumental work, in an effort to save our literary and religious culture. He, like others in Lanovits, believed in the saying, "This is our Torah, while a person may die…" He believed in the future of his people just as he believed that Lanovits was a long-term experiment that will continue and survive.

D. Emphasized Topics

In his review of middle-age Jewish literature Zinberg devotes long chapters to the writings of Yehuda Halevi, Ibn Gvirol, Alharizi and Ibn-Ezra. Instead of his normal practice of listing facts and topics, we find Zinberg suddenly writing essays and involved critiques of their writings. These occupy a disproportionate space in his multi-volume book. Dr. Zinberg takes advantage of the nature of these compositions to explain his analytical approach. These compositions, by the aforementioned authors, reveal a tendency to preserve a humanistic social image. When he notes this, Zinberg, in effect, checks his own emotional make-up against the objective logic of their vision.

These composers and thinkers of the middle-ages, who composed drinking songs and poems of desire, sought help from time-to-time with Torah interpretation to check the merit of their own literary works. Zinberg saw this phenomenon as an excellent example of how one validates poetry as appealing to the emotional needs of one's people.

Zinberg realized, when reviewing past literary works, that one needs to verify that these works have an eternal appeal to a Jew at all times and in all circumstances.

He saw the existence of his hometown as a truly Jewish Shtetl whose community defended its unique society against waves of outside changes. He regarded its success as a reason to devote his life's work to the study of Jewish literature.

[Page 181]

E. Literature as a Bridgehead to Statehood

Zinberg relates (in his writing) that Shlomo Molkho [= a 16th century convert and Jewish Kabalist leader] came to him in a dream and asked him to write his work. The Molkho episode is an interesting chapter that does not concern Jewish literature. Molkho's story is perhaps an ideal subject for a drama that illustrates the large conflicts in his life and his tragic end [=he was burned at the stake in 1532]. Molkho was not a writer, but Zinberg saw in him the product of Jewish literature. He was a convert who stumbled into the winding paths of Jewish thought. In his walks through the spiritual expressions of the Jewish people, Molkho saw himself as a leader marching with them towards their goal -- having a land of their own. This man (Molkho) accompanied Zinberg as a (tragic) example during his long creative period. Molkho's example provided Zinberg with the stamina to labor at the preservation and recording of Jewish literature. He saw in literature not just a means to entertain one's mind and heart, but more as an asset with which the Jewish people will march forward to their objective - a homeland of their own. In its literature, Zinberg saw a guarantee for the people's continued existence and hope.

In summary we can state: Yisroel Zinberg, the chemical engineer, the young socialist, the steadfast genius, did not succumb to the attractions of his era and its benefits. Instead he devoted his full talent and energy to the documentation of his people's literature. He was fascinated by the experiment that demonstrated the ability of literature to maintain a people's vision of the future, shunning short-term diversions, and maintaining behavior limits. We Jews would not have been worthy of such a great editor without the existence of a shtetl community as we knew it. In this instance we are proud that it was our shtetl, Lanovits.

[Page 183]

The Author and His Project

By David K'na'any

It seems almost paradoxical that a book that covers the history of our literature over the last 1000 years, entitled "The History of Jewish Literature" by Yisroel Zinberg, should have been written by a person under such unfavorable circumstances. It is doubly surprising that the book was written by a Chemical engineer employed at a large factory in Leningrad for several decades. The book, which emphasizes the continuity and uniqueness of Jewish history, was written in a country that banned use of the Hebrew, and later the Yiddish languages. Its authorities created a spiritual climate designed to cause Jews to forget their past and their heritage.

There have been many cases in our history and the history of other nations of writings to mark the end of a specific era or social process. These writings served to commemorate and show respect for their significance. This was not the motive that guided Zinberg in his literary effort. He did not see himself as the last person to survey Jewish literature, nor did he view it as the end of an era. On the contrary, he saw his work as a chronicle at a way-station of the history of Jewish literature. As a historian who viewed his people's history from a long distance, he did not attribute special weight to the present period vs. previous periods. He was aware of the ups and downs of a culture, hence based his writings on the premise of its periodic renewal and eternal qualities.

Only this love of the past and his historical consciousness gave him the strength to complete his literary work which he conceived already prior to World War I. All his friends agree that they had never come across a person who was as steadfast in his work as he was. During the day he worked in his chemical lab, and at night he continued his writing and his historical research at the Asiatic Museum in Leningrad. He continued his literary effort in this pattern during the war, during the Bolshevik revolution and the civil war that followed, and under the new regime, aware of his spiritual isolation from other Jewish research centers (e.g. Warsaw and Vilna). He was quoted as having written to a friend: "I am one of the last Mohicans…dealing only with the past. Today I am writing only about our past and the heritage of our forefathers…While I do this, I have a desire to speak to live people."

He was aware of the anachronism of his situation. (While the regime wanted its Jewish citizen to believe in a better future he was researching their past); that his work was regarded as "superfluous", that the regime knew he needed to contact persons in other countries. He also realized the irony in the situation when literary characters appeared in his dreams while he was about to publish a paper on the subject of "The issue of love in Jewish literature of the Middle Ages", or when he studied in depth the quarrel between Rabbi J. Eybeschutz and Rabbi Y. Emden.

[Page 184]

One must admire the range of his intellect.

While we admire the person, we have not shied away from the shortcomings of his literary work. His writing lacks consistency. Some chapters include detailed analyses, and others mere studies and descriptions. In some parts, the author acts as a bibliographer, and in other parts as an esthetic and social-critic. These shortcomings are connected to the range of subjects handled by a single author. It is doubtful that he could have dealt with these subjects differently.

The book, in reality, covers the history of Jewish literature during its European period. As is customary, a book entitled "History of Literature" covers fiction, prose, poetry and plays. Zinberg, however, saw Jewish literature as covering a wider range. He chose to include other literary works that expressed the spirit of our people, that had value for future generations, though written in other languages. He included works in Hebrew, Aramaic, Yiddish, Arabic and German. Had he restricted the book's scope (to Hebrew and Aramaic) the result would have been one-sided. It would not have shown the literature's unique characteristics.

For a long period in our history, fiction was "out-of-bounds". It was regarded as an unnatural phenomenon. The struggle to make fiction legitimate is an important chapter in our literary history. The range of subjects Zinberg selected for his book did not just widen the traditional scope for an encyclopedia; it was all inclusive. The selections included prose, poetry, plays, liturgical and secular songs, rabbinic writings and debates, philosophy, theology, ethics, sermons, historiography, linguistics, travel literature, historical documents and papers dealing with subjects in the natural sciences. He introduces his readers to a range of subjects as for example: The collected writings of Emmanuel and the "Zohar", the travel accounts of Benjamin of Tudela, to the writings of Rabbi Moshe Isserles, to Moreh Nevukhim [Guide to the Perplexed" by Maimonides], to "Miracle Tales" by Yosefa Shamash, to a glossary of Yiddish words from the Middle Ages, to "Shulkhan Arukh", to "Paris un Wien" [in Yiddish], to the Sabatean literature, to Maquamat of Al-Harizi [= a system of musical classification of liturgical melodies], to Moses Mendelson, to grammar books, to excommunication edicts, the writings of Zbarah, Krashkash and Joseph Spiel.

There is no doubt that this rich gallery of creative writings that included both ancient and contemporary works had its shortcomings (Zinberg read most of these sources. He never shied away from stating: "I did not read this book"). Some subjects lacked an adequate coverage or a clean explanation of their unique quality [that justified its inclusion – Ed.]. Topics were covered in unequal proportions. Some literary periods were merely skimmed over.

[Page 185]

However, he portrayed many writers in a skillful manner, especially the early ones that were dear to his heart. These personalities are richly described from several viewpoints. His analysis is sharp and exhaustive, as for example his essays on Abraham Abulofiah, Ibn Gvirol, Vilna Gaon, Moses Mendelson, Abraham ben Ezra, Aryeh Dimodina, Gluekel of Hameln. Eliyahu Bakhur and others.

The book was targeted to appeal to the Jewish masses. It has an intimate writing style that expressed the author's love for Jewish culture. Zinberg did not apply a formal esthetic measure [to his selections], instead he believed in a scale of moral values which he regarded as the main attributes of Jewish culture. It consists of a striving for redemption, for Tikun Olam [= reforming the universe] and for the uplifting of man. He chose writers and writings based on their ability to create and depict values that satisfy the heart of the reader, and influence the masses. He chose the writers based on their ability to project a vision, on the range of their intellectual horizon, and the depth of the emotions they projected. He also looked for those writings that showed a strong striving for social justice and the depiction of a full personality. The essence of his humanistic outlook was, in his own words: "The building of a socially just political system is the most noble of projects; hence a moral story is the crowning achievement of a literary person." By using this criterion, Zinberg - who loved his people - was saved from the dangers (attractions) of love, of eclecticism and of apologia. He criticized and/or praised writings based on his conception of the forces that shaped Jewish history.

Zinberg stated that in his youth, he prayed using a Marxist Siddur. After a while, he dropped out of the Yeshiva that he attended. However, the Talmud lessons were valuable. They increased his awareness of the connection between life and literature. He does not maintain that the spiritual development of his people was solely based on immanent (remaining in place) laws. He emphasizes the social and economic factors that influenced these laws. Thus he explains the spread (though not the start) of the rationalism of Maimonides and that of his disciples as fitting the interest of the upper classes of the Jews of Spain and Provence [Southern France], and the opposition to rationalism as reflected in the Kabalah. He emphasized the social roots of the Hasidic, Misnagdic and Haskalah movements, and the decay in the stature of Rabbis. He saw a strong connection between the political reaction in Europe [after Napoleon's defeat] and the spiritual decline in the Jewish world. He pointed to the dialectic with serious repercussions that occurred when centers of Jewish life moved from Western Europe to less developed areas (Eastern Europe and Turkey) at a time when the West gained political freedom and made great economic strides. He employed Marxist determinism in his thinking but shunned its rosy predictions for the future.

Zinberg's focus was on the historical process, on the past that seems to shape the present, on the influence of a people's heritage. He emphasizes the historical distinctiveness of each nation, how it absorbs and reacts to changes. He saw Jewish history as a continuous process. Thus, early periods influence later ones, explaining the resulting changes. Sometimes, he sees eternal repetitions in this pattern. Surveying our history, Zinberg saw an unending struggle between "Emotional Judaism" and "Intellectual Judaism." He stated that these were two approaches that fought for Hegemony. One side was a democratic "emotional religion" and the other side, an "intellectual aristocracy" in the shadow of rationalism. These were two movements that fought each other at times and at other times compromised.

[Page 186]

Zinberg developed his monumental book to reflect what he saw as a long-term struggle within Judaism between Aristotelian rationalism and the anti-rationalism of the 13th and 14th century, between the Judaism of "Shulkhan Aruch" and that of the Kabalah, between the Haskalah and the Misnagdim movement and Hasidism. Typical are his treatises on the intellectual confrontation between Rambam and Judah Halevi, Spinoza, and Shabtai Zvi, the Vilna Gaon and the Ba'al Shem Tov.

Zinberg was clearly on the side of those who favored the Musar movement, the Yiddish language and Hasidism. He justified his position not as a mystic or anti-rationalist. Instead, he saw "emotional Judaism" as the central force that built Jewish history and that satisfied the spiritual needs of the Jewish masses. Hasidism provided them a sense of purpose and consoled them at time of need. In contrast, the "dry rationalism", as interpreted by its intellectual rabbinic followers, gave the Jewish masses nothing. It actually put the future of Judaism at risk. It is not difficult to recognize in this set of arguments, in this simplified humanism, an echo of the conflict in the hearts of the Jewish elite during the first half of the 20th century as they witnessed a traditional way of life in a struggle with assimilation. The Jewish elite (intelligentsia) were afraid of secularism and its attractions.

* * *

Yisroel Zinberg wanted to cover in his "History of Jewish Literature" the recent writings ending in World War I. He did not finish his life's project. [It was published posthumously in 1965 – Ed.]. In 1938, he was arrested by the Soviet authorities. According to rumors, he was exiled to Siberia and died there in

1943. [His nephew, in an article on p.187, visited Zinberg's widow and daughter in 1966. He writes that Zinberg died in Vladivostok in 1939 - Ed.] Jewish creativity in Eastern Europe ended in 1939, and the "European Hegemony" in our history ended in 1943. It is almost symbolic that the end of this era and the death of its recorder occurred at the same time.

The hegemony of Jewish life has shifted to Israel and to the Hebrew language. The educational importance of Zinberg's book has not diminished even today. This encyclopedic compilation is unique and the first in our language [translated to Hebrew, 6 volumes, 1955-60 - Ed]. Even a "good" Hebrew reader [i.e. well educated – Ed.] is not usually familiar with Jewish literature published between the 13th and 19th century. His knowledge is usually restricted to the bible, Sephardic poetry, and the Haskalah- period literature. This unfamiliarity on the part of the Israeli reader is a factor in the tendency of Israelis to disparage the value of Jewish Diaspora literature. Zinberg's book provides the Israeli reader for the first time a comprehensive view of Jewish literature. The reader is exposed to poetry, meditation and research, to the intellectual struggles that took place within Judaism during the last 1000 years in such areas as Europe and the Middle East. All these literary works are described against the background of their local secular culture and their national social struggles. The Editor points out the literary background that inspired these works and the connection between them.

The publication (of the Hebrew translation) of this book is a great blessing. A book that was born in great isolation (written in the USSR) has been returned to its Jewish homeland where it will perform the mission meant for it at its inception

[Page 187]

In Memory of Dr. Yisroel Zinberg

By Eliezer Zinberg (Kibbutz Nir David)

In January, 1969 we will commemorate 30 years following the passing of the historiographers and writer Dr. Yisroel Zinberg. He was born in Lanovits. It is there that he developed his deep affection for his people and their culture. New intellectual ideas (e.g. communism) failed to dissuade him from his tie to his people.

His daily work was in the Chemical Engineering field, a profession he loved. However, his free time and evenings were dedicated to research of the history of Jewish culture in its various Diasporas. He learned the science of Chemical Engineering at the University [of Karlsruhe/DE and Basel/CH*]. His affinity to the culture of his people and the desire to research this field he inherited from: his learned father, the atmosphere in Heder he attended, and the general culture of his town. As a result, he regarded his scientific work as a duty, and his social research as a work of love.

Dr. Yisroel Zinberg became one of the more famous researchers of Jewish literature. He contributed his deep knowledge of this subject to his people. His published works are nowadays a primary source for those who wish to research the history of our culture. His multi-volume study is the product of a long and continuous effort that only few of us can persist in. He gave up his private life, his leisure and rest in order to complete this literary work. For his dedication to its completion he paid with his life.

Zinberg belongs to Lanovits. His legacy is a link in the legacy of our town; hence his story belongs in our memorial book. Additionally, it is symbolic that the anniversary of his passing parallels the 30th anniversary of the tragic demise of our town. I, Eliezer, his nephew, the son of Dr. Joseph Zinberg, wish to dedicate the following chapters in my uncle's memory.

* * *

Three years ago, I was able to carry out one of my dreams. I visited Leningrad: "I arrived in the city. In less than one hour I shall be in the apartment of my late uncle, Dr. Yisroel Zinberg. I will meet the remnants of his family and hear about him from them.

Excitedly I walked along the alley that my uncle probably walked daily for 40 years. I arrived at his house, climbed the stairs and stood in front of a darkened sign that read: S. L. (Sergei Lazarovich) Zinberg. In a moment I shall be inside his apartment… I wondered as to who I will meet?

[Page 188]

I was received by his daughter, Tamara, a famous local painter. Zinberg's widow, aged 91, does not react to my 'Shalom' greeting. She has left this world while still alive. Now she lives in her own world, the world of the past. It is unfortunate that I do not have an opportunity to speak with her. She was, after all, Zinberg's loyal assistant, hence could have added interesting details concerning his life's work. My family was able to exchange letters with her during the terrible siege of the city (during World War II). I read those letters eagerly. She wrote interesting letters in a beautiful handwriting… now it has all ended.

The writer sits third from the right

His daughter wisely received me in her father's study. This was my uncle's work place. The apartment appears to have been renovated as most Leningrad apartments have been after World War II. On his writing desk stood a rare photo of the writer (he did not like to be photographed).

It was at this table that he sat for long night hours pondering over the history of Jewish literature. He dedicated half his life to this effort. The other half he dedicated to the science of chemistry.

[Page 189]

Zinberg published a large number of articles and books, some of which are still used to teach chemistry in the USSR. In this room he created "The History of Jewish Literature", his life's work. His effort was suddenly terminated at the end of 1938. I also found out that the poet Rav Rabi, who started to translate Zinberg's book into Hebrew, died in Siberia at about the same time Zinberg died. The authorities were successful in eliminating both the author and his translator.

My uncle left a huge archive and library. Both were left untouched by the authorities.

His friend, Hillel Alexandow, was exiled with Zinberg. Alexandow was both a writer and lecturer at Leningrad University. When Zinberg was hospitalized (after a difficult journey of many days on the infamous "prisoner's train" he arrived in Vladivostok fatally ill- Ed*) he asked his friend, Alexandow, to take care of his archives should he, Alexandow, return safely to Leningrad. Alexandow honored this request upon his return. Zinberg's archives were given by his daughter to the Institute of Asiatic People. His book collection was donated to the local public library at the request of his many friends who wanted access to his collection.

Hillel Alexandow kept his promise to Dr. Zinberg upon his return to Leningrad from his Siberian exile. [Most of those who were exiled in the 1930's were rehabilitated after Stalin's death in 1956 and allowed to return to their home towns - Ed.] With the support of the "Institute of Asiatic People," Alexandow was provided with the means to catalog Zinberg's archives, a task he has carried out voluntarily with great devotion.

Among the unpublished manuscripts in these archives was the draft of the last volume of his multi-volume encyclopedia. This volume is due to be published by Brandeis University in the United States, edited by Professor Michael Astour. Professor Alexandow has edited several other manuscripts from these archives, publishing them in the Soviet Journal "Sovietishe Heimat" (in Yiddish). He is also compiling a bibliography of these archives, hoping to publish these in the near future. In my discussions with Professor Alexandow, I got the impression that these archives are in trustworthy hands.

Dr. Yisroel Zinberg asked his friends on his deathbed [in the prison hospital] to remember him and his contribution. This was his unwritten will. Let this article be a part in fulfilling his wish that I took upon myself to do. We shall try not to forget him nor his literary contribution. The latter will be remembered for a long time.

*Ref. "A History of Jewish Literature" by Y. Zinberg, translated into English by Bernard Martin, 1972, vol 1, p. ix: translator's introduction.

**

In January, 30 years ago, my uncle passed away. I feel obligated to publish in his memory a lesser known article that was previously published in the Journal "Die Yiddishe Welt" (The Jewish World) in 1912 in St. Petersburg, Russia. This article exemplifies the author's love for his people and the land of his ancestors [Israel].

[Page 190]

The article is entitled "The Land Book" by Y. Zinberg.

The book was sent to us by one of the (Jewish) workers in Haifa. He previously worked at the Putilov factory* in St. Petersburg [*see above reference] where he shaped metal structures. This person spent all his working hours among Russian Workers. He knew neither Hebrew nor Yiddish. Nonetheless, he dreamt about the land of the Prophets, and immigrated to its shores. He now works in Haifa, Palestine.

The book, entitled "Yizkor" is a memorial book commemorating the lives of eight Jewish guards who were murdered, one after another, by their Arab neighbors. The book, dealing with these eight deceased workers, is full of life, the life experiences in our Holy Land.

Hundreds of articles have been written about the merits of settling the Holy Land and about "Workers in Palestine." Yet reliable information about actual work conditions in the land of our forefathers is scarce.

We only know that hundreds of our youth, who dreamt of a free life, devoid of the limitations pertaining to life within the pale of Settlements, have immigrated to Palestine, full of hope for their future. We also know that many of these immigrants lost their golden dreams. The day to day reality suppressed their noble hopes. They left the land disappointed and bitter, their hopes shattered.

However, not all leave the land. It is not a grave for hopes for all. There are those who are content, those who have succeeded. For these, the aforementioned dream remains a life of hope and challenge. The book sent to us from Haifa introduces us to a few who have succeeded, and were happy.

[Page 191]

We are introduced to Berl Schweiger who immigrated from Odessa full of enthusiasm. His heart went out to the natural life of local Arabs. He saw them as complete persons, free men, exhibiting healthy instincts and attached to their land. Berl accepts a job guarding Jewish vineyards to protect them against hostile neighbors in the south of Palestine. We are next introduced to Avraham Joseph Berl, a brilliant scholar and ordained Rabbi who discards a promising career, immigrates to Palestine and becomes a guard in the Galilee. Next is Yeheskel Nisanow, born in the Caucasus Mountains to a family that always felt free. Yeheskel could not understand how one can meet an enemy who hits one stealthily, while pretending to be your friend. Next is Ya'acov Plotkin, a middle-aged man who after (The Russian 1905) pogroms found the strength to eschew his old lifestyle and start a new life in Palestine, becoming a farmer. Life was a struggle, but he felt the struggle was worthwhile.

However, in life, its beautiful aspects sometimes are connected to tragedies. Like the aforementioned local Arabs, these young men wanted to shape their lives on their land without compromise. This concept the local Arabs do not want to accept. They view (the Jewish settlers) as illegal immigrants who have come to their land with a doubtful ancient claim, whereas they (the locals) have lived on this land for countless generations, and regard themselves as its exclusive owners.

The fallen men worked and soaked their forefather's land with their sweat. Now they have soaked it with their blood. In the words of the prophet Yeheskel (Chapter 16 verse 6), "Yea, I said to you: live in spite of your blood." With their sacrifice, there is hope for a better future. One feels this sense of hope as one leafs through the aforementioned Yizkor Book (for the 8 murdered guards). I do not judge the literary merits of this book. Its value is not as literature but, instead, as reflection of the inner strength shown by its protagonists as they carry on the difficult settlement task.

Do not ask whether these men will succeed. Reaching their objective is not the main issue. It is the desire and resolve in this struggle for a better future that matters.

[Page 192]

Their resolve illuminates their lives. When some of their friends fall in this battle, the rest place flowers on their graves and continue to march (to their objective).

Blessed be the living; let those who fell be remembered for a long time.

Translated from Yiddish by Shechna Nashkas; Published in the monthly, "Die Yiddishe Welt", No. 1, St. Petersburg, 1912.

[Page 193]

Zinberg's Heritage and Posterity

By D.A.

Ninety years have passed since the birth of one of the greatest Jewish historians in this century. Shortly afterwards, we were informed of two related events:

1. On 26 April, 1964 an article appeared in the NYC newspaper "Neue Freiheit" (in Yiddish), by Abraham Belew (or Beluw), its Novosty correspondent, regarding Dr. Zinberg and his archives. Among other news, he mentioned briefly that Zinberg was the victim of Stalin's persecution and died in 1939, and was rehabilitated posthumously in 1956, after the 20th Communist Party Congress took place.
2. On 30 April 1964, Professor Astour of the Yiddish Language Department of Brandeis University wrote to researcher Eliyahu Shulman [whom he asked for political help in releasing the Zinberg's archives] that he, Astour, found a handwritten manuscript of the last volume of Zinberg's "History" series that Zinberg was unable to send to his publisher in Vilna, Lithuania [Zinberg's archives are presently held in the Institute for the Study of Asian Nations of Leningrad University] because of his arrest in 1938.

A Chemist who was a Great Literary Historian

Yisroel Zinberg was born in 1873 in the town of Lanovits, province Wolyn, Poland. He was trained as a Chemical Engineer. For over 30 years he directed the Chemical Laboratories of the Pulitov Company, later renamed "Kirov plant" in Leningrad. In his capacity as director, he published numerous articles and text books including one entitled "How to conduct a Chemical Analysis". The latter was re-published in 1929 and again in 1931. Outside his profession that provided him with a livelihood, he was drawn to the study of Jewish Literature and its historical development. It was in this field of study that he developed his monumental project. His first publication in 1900 was a monogram dealing with the writer Yitzhak Ber Lewinson. In 1901 followed his book entitled "Shylock's Successive Relationships." This book was followed by: "Two Avenues in Jewish Life," "The Founders of Jewish Journalism," plus other books and articles. In 1908-13, he was one of the editors of the 16-volume "Jewish Encyclopedia." In the 1911-1913, Zinberg gave a series of lectures on the history of Jewish literature at the Institute for the study of Asian Nations. He started his lecture with "Jewish poets residing in Palestine." These lectures were later rewritten to fit into his 12 books and 9-volume monumental encyclopedia.

[Page 194]

Recently, a draft of part one of volume 7 has been found in Zinberg's archives.

The first volume of his encyclopedia was still written in Russian. When Zinberg realized that much of the later Jewish literature was indeed written in Yiddish, he concluded that the encyclopedia should likewise be written in Yiddish. He also rewrote he first volume into Yiddish.

Zinberg wrote a number of critiques of current books. These included: "The History of Jewish Literature" by Max Weinreich & Marek Erich; Shiefer's "History of the Jewish Theatre"; the writings of Y. L. Peretz & Shalom Aleichem. He contributed to the periodical "Sammel Heften" published in Petrograd. He also published several semi-fictional articles.

In his writings, Zinberg described the history of Jewish literature as a continuum starting in ancient times always reflecting the nation's fate. He singled out the European environment's influence on Jewish literature as an example: The development of Moslem poetry and philosophy during the Spanish Golden Era; The Italian Renaissance, and later, the Haskalah and Humanism of the 18th and 19th Century. He illustrated these influences by citing the following examples: The effect of the environment on "Emanuel the Roman's writing; The influence of German philosophy on the writings of the 18th Century. A special place in his encyclopedia was reserved for Yiddish literature which, for the first time in Jewish history, included fiction and translation from secular works in the field of Ethics and Philosophy.

Ant's Labor After Regular Work Hours

Zinberg wrote his reviews and critiques after conducting extensive research and reading of original works, as evidenced by his numerous references. Only seldomly was he content with a secondary source. He conducted his research under difficult working conditions while living in the Soviet Union, disconnected thereby from a larger segment of East European Jewry (residing in Lithuania, Poland, Hungary and Romania). He was likewise separated from literary sources unless they happen to be available in Soviet libraries. He sent his output to his [foreign] Vilna publisher. It appears that this isolation did not affect the quality of his literary work. The supplementary material that appeared in the (recent) Hebrew translation of his encyclopedia dealt with material that Zinberg had no knowledge of. These supplements merely add to the information contained in the original (Yiddish) volumes. They do not contradict its original content.

Zinberg planned to complete his history volumes to cover all the literature up to First World War, but alas, he did not accomplish this. The Soviet authorities were aware of his literary work. For a time, they tolerated its publication. The same tolerance applied to his extensive correspondence with persons outside the USSR, connected with his literary effort. However, in 1938, during the period of show-trials against Soviet Jewish leaders and their elimination, Yisroel Zinberg disappeared. In early 1938, he was able to report to his publisher the completion of the first part of a book entitled, "The Blooming of Haskalah Literature". The manuscript, however, did not reach his publisher because Zinberg was arrested and later "eliminated".

[Page 195]

Attempts to Save Zinberg

When news of his disappearance reached New York, a committee was formed to try and save him. The committee included the following Yiddish writers: Hayim Greenberg, Joseph Haikin, David Pinsky, Jacob Fishman, Eliyahu Shulman, the Jewish-American writer, Leon Danan and Judge Isidore Glowerman. The effort was judged to be politically risky in those days. Some writers thought that these appeals would actually hurt Zinberg's chances for parole, and therefore refused to join the committee. In the end, Hayim Greenberg, the committee chair met with a New York Times editor. The latter promised to investigate Zinberg's fate locally (in Leningrad). These efforts proved futile. Zinberg's neighbors denied knowing a neighbor by that name. The local police also denied knowing anything about him. In the end, the committee decided to contact the Soviet Ambassador in Washington, DC. The investigation that ensued dragged on for months. In the meantime, World War II broke out. The committee members continued their efforts but succeeded only to save his archives.

Years later, when Stalin died, a new liberal policy was instituted in the Soviet Union. In this more favorable atmosphere, a Jewish-American scholar by the name of Abraham Katz was given permission to microfilm many Hebrew & Yiddish archives in Soviet Libraries. Upon his return, he reported that in the Leningrad public library he found a collection of works by Friedlander, Mirkovich, Antony Harwan, David Ginzburg and the archives of Zinberg, David Magid and others.

When committee member, Eliyah Shulman read Katz's report, he opined that Zinberg's Archives are likely to include a draft of his last encyclopedia volume; also, that he does not expect a favorable response to any private request for this material from a Soviet institution. Instead, he asked Prof. Michael Astour, of the Yiddish Languages Department of Brandeis University to initiate such a request via the University. In addition, Shulman wrote an article in (the Yiddish periodical) "Zukunft" asking for help from anyone re. this subject.

The Volume and its Content

Brandeis University contacted the Saltikov-Chzhderin library in Leningrad asking for microfilm copies of Zinberg's archives. It turned out the above address was in error. The above mentioned library forwarded the Brandeis request to the "Institute for the Study of Asian Nations of the Leningrad Academy of Sciences." Once the microfilm material was received in the U.S., the draft of Zinberg's last volume was among the copied material that was sent to Prof. Astour. As reported to Shulman by the latter on 30 April 1967, significant editing is required before Zinberg's last volume can be submitted for publication. Prof. Astour reported furthermore that he had already secured a publisher, Chico, who agreed to publish this last volume.

Per Eliyahu Shulman in an article published in the May-June issue of "Zukunft", the photographed handwritten manuscript is part 1 of "The Blooming of Haskalah Literature" mentioned above.

[Page 196]

Besides a critique of Jewish Journalism that Zinberg published previously, the subject volume contains a review of the works of Issac Meir Diek, Linsky, Avraham Uri Kowner, Moses Lilienblum and Mendele Mokher Sfarim.

Discovery of Significant Archives

This is a suitable opportunity to describe the other findings among Zinberg's Archives. These include letters from the following poets and writers: Shalom Aleichem, Y.L. Peretz, Shalom Ash, Ch. N. Bialik, David Frishman, Zalman Shne'our, Ya'acov Dinezon, Joseph Opatoshu, Morris Winshewsky, Uri N. Gnesin, Historian Yosef Klausner, Publicists Shmuel Niger, Reuven Brenin, Hillel Zeitun, and Playwrights Peretz Hirschbein, Sh. Ansky, Lexicographer Zalman Reizen, Author Shmuel Horodetzky and Publicist Ya'acov Horowitz.

Y. L. Peretz mentions in his letter to Zinberg that his Hasidim stories were written without any personal ties to the Hasidic movement nor to any of its leaders. He furthermore states in his letter that he initially wrote his stories in the Polish language, but decided to switch to Yiddish and burn the Polish manuscripts. His writings in Hebrew also displeased him, hence he switched to Yiddish at an early age.

The correspondence with Ch. N. Bialik deals with weighty literary questions. In his letters dated 1921-1927, Bialik deals primarily with his preparation to publish the Hebrew translation of Ibn Gvirol's poetry on which he worked for several years. The State Library in Leningrad had a copy of the Ibn Gvirol handwritten poetry. Bialik asked Zinberg's advice as to how to get a hold of this manuscript.

The five letters from Opatoshu deal with relations between Yiddish and Hebrew language writers. Ber Borochow asks if he could participate in the editing of the Jewish Encyclopedia. Winshewsky sent Zinberg material relating to the history of the newspaper "Wahrheit."

[Page 197]

Finally, two letters from Shalom Aleichem, one dated October, 1909, sent from Switzerland, written in a beautiful handwriting, deals with the composer Marek Warshawsky (1848-1907). Shalom Aleichem writes glowingly about Warshavsky's talent and musical works. The second letter, written in Russian, dated 3 November 1909, he refers back to the October letter asking to make a correction re. the Warshavsky Story, to whit: "In his performances in the provincial towns, he was (not we were) quite successful." The letter demonstrates Shalom Aleichem's modesty, not wanting to take credit for someone else's success.

This summarizes the article written by the correspondent of Novosty news agency. It is known that Zinberg also wrote a manuscript on the history of the Jewish Theatre. We hope his manuscript will be found and the book published either in Leningrad or New York City, completing the content of his archives.

[Page 198]

Our Late Rabbi Motel Speizman

By Ozer Lerner

He was one of the leaders of our community, a shining representative of our town. He was our leading source of Torah learning. Thanks to him, class after class of students received a thorough Torah education. He helped create our legacy bearers. His monetary compensation was meager. He lived in a rented room. His food consisted of bread, potatoes and a glass of milk, sufficient to sustain his health, and continue teaching.

When he suffered from a headache or a toothache or a sore throat, he would wrap his head with a kerchief and continue teaching. He regarded himself as a public servant, hence tried to repay the community in various ways. He served as a Dayan (Religious Judge), as a prayer leader or scripture reader without added compensation. Rabbi Speizman was poor, but in his heart he felt satisfied serving his community.

He once observed Jews working in a warehouse on a Sabbath, weighing grain and recording the weight of each grain sack in order to prepare these sacks for rail shipment on Sunday. The Rabbi shouted "Fire". When asked where the fire is, he replied "It's the Sabbath building that is burning". You are asking where the fire is: You are violating the Sabbath." The assembled crowd understood the issue. They entered the warehouse and persuaded those inside to cease their work. For a while, the Rabbi remained on the spot, leaning on his cane, lest the workers return to their workplace after he left. Only after he was promised that they will not return today, did he agree to go home.

Once a poor man, who was physically handicapped, came to our town. The Rabbi did not let him collect. Instead he told the man to "sit and study Gemarah". "Your legs will probably not carry you. I have young students who can run after a ball; they can do this Mitzva." The man stayed at the Rabbi's home for several days. When we turned in our collection on his behalf, the man saw that our Rabbi added his own contribution.

[Page 199]

The man refused to accept the Rabbi's contribution saying, "It is enough what you did for me already." The Rabbi became angry and told the man that his attitude will be forgiven only because he is ignorant about the deed that was done. "You prevented one Jew from doing a Mitzva to another Jew."

The man apologized, explaining that he only wanted to suggest that after what the Rabbi did, adding a contribution of one kopek would have sufficed. The Rabbi retorted saying "You are telling a Jew to do a small rather than a large Mitzva?" The man apologized again. "I can see that I cannot win an argument with you, do as you wish." The Rabbi took out all the money he had in his pocket and gave it to the man following the dictum that a man should give "according to his ability." The Rabbi interpreted this dictum to mean "what one has at the moment."

When a refugee came across the border [Lanovits was a few km from the Poland/USSR border], the Rabbi went out of his way to help such a man. He considered such help akin to saving a Jewish life from extinction. [The Rabbi apparently realized the pressure on orthodox Jews in the USSR.]

I remember the case of one refugee for whom the Rabbi "organized" several pairs of students to collect money and food on his behalf and bring these to his new lodging. This refugee stayed with us for over a week. When he decided to leave us in order to distance himself from the border area, he asked the Rabbi for advice. The Rabbi told him to follow his instincts. As soon as the refugee left the Kloiz, he was arrested and sent back to the other side of the border. Following his arrest, he was shot without a trial at the border point, so as to be a warning to others who may contemplate crossing the border illegally. When we told the Rabbi what happened to the refugee, the latter went behind the stove and cried. He hid his face lest we see him in his despair. We waited for him to calm himself. He continued to torment himself saying: "I did not tell him to leave, but I also did not tell him not to leave, therefore, I am not free of contributing to his death." He faulted himself for not advising the refugee to leave at night; for not sending his students to show him the way. "Had I done this small thing, then he would not have gotten lost at the border and would have been saved."

His teaching methods were modern, even though he arrived at them through intuition. He was able to bring a student to think for himself and to sharpen his thoughts so as to arrive at an answer readily. When we studied Gemarah, he would say to us: "Do not look sideways, look straight and absorb the Talmud commentaries. Explain the material to yourselves, next re-read the commentaries for a better understanding for the authors spent many hours developing their commentaries."

When the Rabbi noticed that we stopped learning and diverted to speak about another matter, he would ask each one of the students how he got from the commentary he was learning to the issue being discussed. Each of us had to find an excuse as to the reason for his diversion from the study topic. It was done without threats. Instead it was meant to discipline us to focus on our studies. When we tired of learning, the Rabbi would introduce a riddle or a story in order to encourage the student to express himself. The Rabbi preached that behavior is important outside of learning. While learning, if one comes across a person older than him who makes a study mistake, disregard his credentials even if he is an adult and stick to your opinion. Only in non-learning situations let politeness influence your behavior.

[Page 200]

Some of the Rabbi's secular remarks were a topic of conversation amongst us, a sort of oral law. One time the Rabbi agreed to join a nominating committee for a set of Gabays (Sextons) provided the committee meets in his Kloiz so as to minimize time taken away from learning supervision. He opposed one nominee whom he did not consider as suitable for a public position. He told the committee members, "Do not choose him for one should not practice idolatry or bow to an image. I was too young to understand the connection so I asked the Rabbi the relevance of idolatry to the Sexton's job. He explained: "When a person is selected for a public position, the public bows to him, does his will and flatters him. If the person is not worthy of such attention, such behavior is akin to idolatry. It is said that a goy that became rich and rose in stature is like "he became a Jew."

I forgot the refugee story for a long time until Zvi Beker, our sole survivor of the Lanovits massacre reminded me of it. I asked Beker what happened to our dear Rabbi. "Was he massacred with the rest?" He replied that Rabbi Speizman was the first war fatality in our town. When the Soviets entered our town (1939) they declared a curfew until the late morning hours. That morning our Rabbi rose as usual and forgetting about the curfew, he put on his tallith and proceeded to walk to the synagogue. The guards who saw him disregarded the curfew shot him. He died on the spot. The guards left him lying on the street. Some of us did not see him; others saw him but were afraid to leave their homes. As I heard of my dear Rabbi's tragic death I was reminded of all those aforementioned episodes including the story of the refugee.

The Rabbi's attitude to Zionism was an enigma to us (while we were his students). He avoided this subject as if it was not a proper subject for discussion. However, before I emigrated, my mother ordered me to say goodbye to Rabbi Motel, my esteemed teacher, though I had not attended his Yeshiva for the last several years. When I arrived at his home I could see he was happy to see me at first, but soon his face saddened either due to tears or due to an effort to control his emotions. He confided in me, saying: "I always thought that my place was among my students, that I ought to go where they go. Moreover, I should do this sooner rather than later. Nonetheless I tarried. I said to myself that I might need them (economically) so it is better that many of you be there so their burden will not be a high one, should I no longer have pupils to teach." When I asked him why he never confided this wish to us students, he replied that he always wanted to be with his students, which was his obvious if unstated wish. He claimed that he was just waiting for a proper time to implement such a plan and join us.

He never reached this goal. We never had the pleasure of his company in Israel. May his memory remain with us eternally.

[Page 201]

The Late Aharon Rabin
(The Last Lanovits Rabbi)

By Rabbi Dr. A'haron Wertheim

With fear, trepidation and deep respect, I will write a few words about the life of my father-in-law, the late A'haron Rabin.

We have become accustomed in the last few years to encounter publications of Yizkor books that describe, in detail, the horrors of the holocaust. These books detail the destruction of whole communities together with their leaders, the killing of young and old. They tell us that "Jews went to their death like sheep together with their leaders." To those who perished we declare: "You are all loved, and are holy to us, survivors." In their steadfast dedication to Judaism, while clearly expecting the worst, we need to regard these leaders as holy persons. Among those we can still discern persons who were examples to us while they lived, and when they died. One of these shining examples was Rabbi Aharheli (his nickname - Ed.)

Those who got to know him well came to realize that he was a special person, holy in his manners in life even before he was murdered.

I regret that I got to know him for only a short time, so I am incapable of elaborating about his spiritual level. Let me relate what little I learned about this special person.

* * *

He was born in 1870, son of Rabbi Moshe Rabin, a scion of one of the most important families of Eastern Jewry. His ancestor was Rabbi Israel Ben Eliezer Ba'al Shem Tov, the founder of the Hasidic movement, from Mezirech. He was a sixth generation Hasid, named after his late grandfather, Rabbi A'haron from the town of Titiyov, whose writings are well known in Hasidic circles.

[Page 202]

Already, as a young man, Rabin concentrated on daily Torah learning. Even after he married the daughter of Rabbi Mordechai of Shumsk, a scion of the Magid of Zlochev and Radzivil, he continued his learning schedule to become proficient as a pulpit Rabbi.

At the age of 30 (1900), he was named the Rabbi of Lanovits, a post previously filled by his wife's grandfather, the famous Rabbi Yosef of Radzivil. In Lanovits, he got acquainted with many people who remembered his forefathers. These people became respectful of his way of handling religious issues.

Mrs. Yochevet, a wealthy woman of the Geldener and Zinberg families bought him a beautiful brick house that became a local center of learning. To that end, Rabin built a Beith Midrash, (house of learning) in his courtyard, available to any young man wishing to study Torah. Rabbi Ahareli also hired a learned tutor to teach his sons and other youngsters. In those years, his house became a center of religious learning.

His days of joy ended in 1913 when his wife, Eta, died suddenly, leaving him with six orphans to take care of. His wife was both beautiful and modest. I am at a loss to describe the seriousness of this turn of events. The Rabbi succeeded despite many difficulties to raise his children in an orthodox manner.

His exemplary behavior and stress on Midoth (man-to-man behavior) enabled him to exercise strong local leadership, like that between a Tzadik and his followers. However, his double role as both an interpreter of Jewish law, and that of a Hasidic leader caused him numerous problems. The Lanovits community became divided as a result. They wanted an additional Rabbi that dealt with problems of secular life, one that does not demand behavior that is beyond their capability.

* * *

I have mentioned previously that he was a modest person. He seldom raised his voice, honoring the saying, "The ways of the wise sound pleasant." He was not only respected by his townsmen who sought his advice, as is the custom of Hasidim, but also by Jews of nearby villages, as well as by Gentiles.

[Page 203]

It was the custom of these Gentiles to ask for his blessing, regarding him as a holy person.

His home was open to guests not only for food and rest. He also helped his guests with money that he collected from his townsmen in accordance with their financial ability. As the town's Rabbi, he did his duty to help the community's poor as much as possible.

When my wife and I came to visit him on a visit from the U.S. to Lanovits in 1935, he asked us to use our influence with the committee of Lanovits expatriates in New York to help Lanovits's poor. Following our request, a help committee was formed, chaired by Mrs. Rose Shtepshagel that arranged for weekly flour purchases in Lanovits meant to be distributed to its poor members. The weekly purchase and distribution was implemented by a committee under the supervision of Rabbi Rabin.

I remember that following my first year after my arrival in America, I mailed my father-in-law a $50 money order. After some time, the money order was mailed back to me together with a letter. In his letter, he expressed his appreciation for my good intentions, but, he added, stated his opinion that financial help ought to come "from top to bottom", i.e., from fathers to sons, not from sons to fathers. In spite of his limited income, he declined to receive financial support that did not come "from top to bottom".

We learned via a rumor that several months before the terrible massacre, the local authorities decreed that all prayer halls be shuttered. Rabbi Rabin arranged a secret minyan. The minyan meeting was discovered. Consequently, he and other Jewish notables were arrested and threatened with a death sentence. After energetic negotiations and payment of a bribe, the Rabbi and the notables were released. The total annihilation of the district's Jews occurred shortly thereafter. According to a reliable witness, one of the few that survived this massacre, the old Rabbi encouraged his flock to recite the Vidui (Shma Yisrael), to prepare themselves for execution. Machine-gun fire cut them short as they were praying. He died with his flock. Israel is redeemed thanks to their sacrifice.

[Page 204]

The Late Reb Yisroel (Srulikol) Rabin

(Author not stated)

He was the third son of Rabbi Aharon Rabin. He had a sharp mind and was well versed in both secular and Torah subjects. In 1922, he was conscripted into the Polish Army, where he suffered greatly in his attempt to keep the Sabbath and Jewish laws. Despite these difficulties, he finished his military service without violating either Sabbath or kashrut laws.

One such episode occurred on a first Seder night, when his cruel commander prevented him from attending a Seder by assigning him to guard duty. The order pained him so that he left his post to enter a Jewish home to carry out the blessing over Matzo and Morror. His superiors discovered that he left his post and threatened him with a court martial. It was only through the strenuous efforts of local Jewish leaders that he was saved from such a fate. This happened in Lutsk, the capital of the province of Volynia. The episode was spoken about for a long time.

He married the daughter of Rabbi Levi of Brody. Reb Yisroel had two beautiful children. He remained in Lanovits living with his elderly father, helping him with his religious duties. When the angel of death arrived, he perished with all the other innocent young and old in evil Poland.

[Page 205]

The Late Zeyda Katilansky

By Lola Friedman Katilansky

Zeyda came to Lanovits from Odessa, where his father served as the city's chief Rabbi. It was his father's idea that his son should marry his cousin Rachel, the daughter of his brother Yeshaya Katilansky. His father hoped that his son would in the future replace his father-in-law and uncle to become the chief Rabbi of Lanovits. Zeyda, who was an ordained Rabbi, did not strive to become a pulpit Rabbi. Instead, after marrying his cousin Rachel, he joined Shmuel Buchstein as a partner in his metal retail store. He became a successful partner. Later, he became an independent retailer.

He integrated easily into the Lanovits community and became one of its leading citizens. His home became a meeting place for the town's couples. He was well liked by both his married and bachelor friends.

Slowly he also became proficient as a local lobbyist. His good appearance, his knowledge of the Polish language and its nuances all guaranteed his successful interventions with local officials on behalf of community members. Yet his local success bothered him until he decided to move to another town. His ambivalent feelings vis-a-vis the Lanovits community almost led him to have a medical crisis. On one hand, he wanted to live in a larger town, but, he repeatedly delayed a move because of his love for the Lanovits community. Eventually, he moved to Lvov.

In Lvov, his anguish deepened. His small Lvov apartment compared unfavorably with the beautiful house he had in Lanovits. He found the Jews of Lvov, he got to know, to be primarily interested in making money, unlike his warm-hearted Lanovits friends. Feelings of regret engulfed him. His friends expected him to move back to Lanovits soon.

However, this did not happen. Zeyda became engrossed in the trading activities of Lvov. The Lanovits traders, and those from neighboring villages came to increasingly rely on Zeyda's business connections.

This activity supported him financially. He worked mainly with Reb Moshe Weinshel who later became his partner in clover marketing. While his business developed, Zeyda continued to maintain his Lanovits contacts.

[Page 206]

Lanovits visitors would regularly lodge in his small Lvov apartment. The Katilansky couple's greatest joy was to host guests from "there", from their former shtetl.

At times Zeyda was awakened from his night's sleep to receive "Landsmen" who arrived in Lvov aboard the night train [from Kremenec- Ed.]. Despite the early hour, he received them warmly and dealt with the tzores they related to him. He took them to hospitals, to Lvov's medical professors, to high officials and/or lawyers, all according to their respective needs.

When Zeyda became well-off, he devoted a significant amount of his charity giving to the poor of his shtetl, Lanovits.

These details I know well. Rachel and Zeyda were childless. As Rachel's niece, I was hosted by them in Lvov. They also paid for my high school education. Living with them, I got to know them intimately. Zeyda was like a father to me, and Rachel like a friend. Both loved their Lanovits' friends and were always at the ready to help them when a need arose.

The Jews of Lanovits regarded Zeyda as an educated person who was both orthodox and modern. He was conservative in his behavior, yet always friendly to those who needed him. The Lanovits community forgave Zeyda for his European attire, for his lack of head cover while at home, or even going at times hatless outside his home. They valued his intelligence and culture and the fact that he offered them both traits at their level.

To Lanovits women, Zeyda symbolized the kind of husband who knows how to respect his wife and share his social standing with her. Rachel Katilansky deserved this respect. She was smart, and devoted to her husband. The sense of nobility in their family life was, however, largely attributed to Zeyda

Reb Zeyda Katilansky and his wife, Rachel spent their remaining years in Lvov, but their hearts were with the Lanovits community. Both deserve to be remembered with all the others from our shtetl.

[Page 207]

About Shaiky & Zuni (Rabin)

By The Editor

I waited until the end of the period for call-for-papers for our book. I expected that someone will surely write about (my brothers), Shaiky and Zuni Rabin. After all someone whom they helped must owe them a personal debt. I expected several articles based on their respective experience with my brothers. Even if a person was not in debt to them personally, I expected him to write an article as a character reference. These two brothers of mine did much for our community; teaching, organizing and helping the community's needy. I expected someone to sketch their personality and contributions.

[Page 208]

To my regret, no one submitted such an article, perhaps because he was unable to tackle the subject. I was thus forced to do this task myself even though these are my brothers. As an editor, I wanted to avoid any appearance of favoritism. I write this because many of my colleagues asked that I fill this void. I pray that I shall avoid small family differences; that I shall not exaggerate their contributions due to my great love for my late brothers. It is my hope that my article will reflect their contribution as others in our community remember this to be.

Shaiky Rabin

Already at an early age, Shaiky became opinionated and willing to fight for his point-of-view. As a 13 year old he questioned the divine. His arguments with our father continued for a fortnight, marring the solemnity of our Sabbath meal.

He absorbed various theoretical viewpoints. Using his analytical mind, he combined these into the Zionist redemption idea. To Zionism, he came as a leader, able to help doubters clarify their thoughts and give their beliefs a clear direction. He helped clarify many skeptical minds.

He was a complex person. When with friends, looming problems were clarified, and the chance of successful resolution suddenly improved. Skepticism gave way to optimism

Whenever he dealt with a Jewish problem, such as the chance of future redemption, he raised the issue to its highest level, applying all the research tools at his disposal.

During a typical discussion, he tended to keep his distance. The initial impression one got was of an egotist, a narcissist. Yet when you warmed up to him, and entered his social circle, you found yourself with a warm friend who wishes the best for others.

He was a regular joker. When he lacked a familiar joke for the occasion, he would create ridiculous situations and exploit these to the fullest. Yet at other times I found him serious and sad, concerned with the world's problems. I came to realize that his joking was an escape from reality.

[Page 209]

Already as a child he excelled in reading and general studies. If you wanted assistance with a homework problem, he was always willing to help.

* * *

For years Shaiky appeared to us as a friendly and complex child. One day I found him graduating from childhood and mixing with adults. At first he followed certain community leaders as a blind follower, which was viewed by us with apprehension. Yet, after a short while he developed into a leader. Shlomo Berman and Hayim Nathan were eager to hear his opinion and sought his advice. He became a splendid public speaker, who was able to enliven an audience. The community loved to hear his lectures from the synagogue dais. While short and thin, the synagogue audience was captivated by his clear voice and lofty thoughts. His speeches gave their lives a purpose and hope. His lectures drew crowds, while the town had no prophet, it had Shaiky, who lifted their spirits.

* * *

He saw his future in mass education, as he stumbled into this field. He was mistaken in thinking that a professional education will enable him to lead a full life and develop his effervescent personality. Nonetheless, he delved into this field and never left it. He taught at Vlodimiretz, then in Rosyshch. In the latter town he became a school principal. In these places, he educated a generation of Hebrew speakers and Zionist sympathizers. His enthusiasm left its mark on each of these communities.

His deep commitment to his family and parents led him to self-sacrifice. When he had the opportunity during the war to leave Eastward with the Soviet authorities and survive, he instead turned back midway to be with his wife, daughter and parents. As a result, he perished with them. Let his personality and worthy image remain in our hearts and memories.

[Page 210]

Zuni Rabin

Zuni grew in the shadow of his older brothers, hence was inconspicuous. However, in a few years his winning personality became better known. His good looks and height impressed town folks. At times he acted like a guest in our town who sees others from the sidelines but keeps to himself. Yet, when their questions touched his heart, he helped them to the best of his ability.

Unlike his brothers, Zuni felt unshackled by the political constraints of local Zionist organizations. He believed instead in the unity of Zionist aims. He started his educational activity in the Zionist Youth organization together with Shalom Maharshak and was successful at this effort. The two led a generation of youth having a Jewish national commitment. Two years later when he came to realize that the "Zionist Youth Movement" was a front for a petty-bourgeois ideology, he left the movement to work instead for the "Hehalutz" organization. His friends remember him as a capable organizer and lecturer who captured many hearts.

When the Soviets entered Lanovits in 1939 he was already a certified teacher, having graduated from the Lvov teacher's seminary. He was immediately hired by the Soviet authorities to direct the newly established local Russian elementary school. His fluency in Polish and smattering of Russian won him a free hand in his new position. He developed good relations with Ukrainians, Poles and Jews and was adored by his students as a professional educator.

Zuni and his wife left with the Soviet authorities when they withdrew eastwards in 1941. He later volunteered to join the Polish army and returned to Poland in 1944. Near the end of the war, he stepped on a mine and was killed. There are those who claim he was killed by fellow Polish soldiers who wanted the glory of factory to themselves. Zuni was born in Lanovits; he was one of us. Let us remember his radiating personality when we commemorate our losses.

[Page 211]

Yosef Ozer Shpirt
[Our Last Hebrew Teacher]

By Lola Katilansky

Yosef Ozer Shpirt was born in Yermilintz to very rich parents. His father, Yisakhar Shpirt was a large trader who was well connected commercially with other traders throughout the world. These contacts enabled him to provide his children with a European education with emphasis on the knowledge of key languages. His five children learned and knew English, French, German and Russian. Yosef Ozer, his youngest child, was the most learned. While he lived in Podvolochisk, the locals learned to appreciate his language skills and relied on his translation help.

A road full of obstacles led him eventually to Lanovits. In 1917 his parents left Yermilintz in the middle of the night and escaped to Podvolochisk. Their past as wealthy merchants put them at risk under the new Bolshevik regime.

[Page 212]

They left their entire belongings in place to save their lives. Their next travails were both economic and political. As former Russian citizens, the Polish government refused to grant them Polish citizenship. Instead it exiled the family to Novi Sundig near Poznan. The locals of the area persecuted them, preventing the family from supporting themselves locally.

Without an alternative, they had to leave Poland. Their eldest daughter, who lived in France and was a University professor, was able to secure entrance permits for her unmarried brothers and sisters. She could not, however, obtain an entry permit to France for Yosef Ozer, her married brother.

Yosef escaped instead back to Podvolochisk, then illegally to us in Lanovits. We transferred him immediately to Zbarazh [near Tarnopol] where we were able to bribe a local official to grant him Polish citizenship. With these papers in hand, my uncle Zeyda Katilansky rented him an apartment in Lanovits.

The book's editors provided the following addendum:

"Shpirt's life in Lanovits was a difficult one. The local "Tarbut" communal workers were loath to create a (Hebrew) school for him to teach in. The student's parents could not afford the extra payments to finance such a school. Yosef Ozer accepted the task of organizing the school, soliciting funds, purchasing text books and teaching Hebrew to his students. He paid his rent and supported his family. He was the key person who maintained Hebrew culture in our town.

His limited income did not affect his spirits, nor did he show signs of bitterness. Those whom he met, he always received with a smile, and a friendly chat. He was unassuming with local folks. Little did they realize how knowledgeable he was in both secular and religious subjects and in languages.

His students recognized him as the only teacher who did not raise his voice to them, nor shout orders. Even his occasional reprimands were accompanied by calming words. When a student failed to do his homework, Shpirt would remark about it but not show anger. There were times when the students wished to have a stricter teacher; however, they understood the reasons for his reticence to be strict.

His wife, Rachel nee Katilansky was always well mannered, almost aristocratic. Nothing was too difficult for her in caring for her husband and son Pinchas. No one in the community ever heard her complain about her fate. Her wisdom and self-respect assured her standing in the community as a daughter of well-to-do parents who is content with her lot. She watched over her husband's pupils making sure that when they went out in the winter, their coats were buttoned, and in the summer, that they were not sweaty.

The Shpirt family while familiar to suffering was well respected. Their son had a character similar to that of his father.

[Page 213]

Yosef Ozer was the last torch bearer that promoted Hebrew culture in our community. He prepared his students for "Aliyah" to Palestine by teaching them Modern Hebrew. Some of his students left for Palestine. While parting with them was painful, he was proud that he prepared them well for their new life. He perished with the rest of his students in his final class in the Holocaust. May his memory remain our hearts."

[Page 214]

Lanovits and its Notables

By Rabbi Y. Opatowsky (Manchester, UK)

Shaiky and his outstanding mother

In May 1931 I was sent by Keren Hayesod [=Palestine Foundation Fund - to finance immigration and colonization] to Volynia to promote this institution in the province. The original plan for my visits did not include Lanovits. However, I requested from the Central Committee that Lanovits be included on my "circuit"

Why did I make this request? There were two reasons: The first was that in Warsaw we heard that the Lanovits community was divided between two camps. One camp believed that now is the time to build settlements in Palestine, i.e. support Keren Hayesod, while the other camp supported the purchase of additional land via Keren Kayemet [= Jewish National Fund]. It was feared that the controversy will lead to a decrease in contributions to both funds. The second reason was a letter I received from Yeshayahu Rabin, urging me to come and speak to his community. As a member of Mizrachi [=Religious Zionist organization] I was not involved in this controversy. However, the fate of Keren Hayesod contributions was dear to my heart. Secondly, I was intrigued by Rabin's letter.

I arrived in Lanovits sometime in the afternoon. I no longer remember when the train arrived from Tarnopol. Six community notables and a shy, bespectacled 20 year-old met me at the train station. I presumed the young man was the one who wrote the aforementioned letter. I shook hands with the delegation members. Next I approached the young man and said with a smile "My name is the same as your name". He smiled as if he understood the hint, that I knew him to be the letter's author.

The delegation included two Buchstein brothers. One was short and corpulent, the other had thick lips. The latter's name was Pesach. He was at my side throughout my visit. The name of the other Buchstein I no longer remember [probably Yitzhak - Ed.].

[Page 215]

When we climbed onto the wagon, Pesach Buchstein seated me next to him on the back seat, reserved for important guests. I arrived in town shaken by the rough ride. Alter Feiga Zinz was my host. The reason I remember his name is that my stay at his home was a great pleasure. He was the first person I met who was well versed in Torah learning, yet understood the mood of the younger generation. I was impressed by his wisdom, the cleanliness of his home, and the sensitivity of his daughter. They all added to the pleasure of my stay.

I prayed Mincha at the home of Reb Alter, without a Minyan. In the evening I was taken to the home of Pinny Buchstein for a festive dinner. After dinner, the committee, headed by Pesach Buchstein, met. They discussed the meeting's agenda at which I was to speak, when to schedule the fund-raising, and how to make it most effective. I was to speak on Saturday night after the Sabbath.

That evening I got to know the community. Those attending were serious and thoughtful people. One after another in the audience asked to speak. Their words were sweet. For a moment I thought I was back in Warsaw at the central committee meeting listening to comments of our elder statesmen. Their comments were of a similar caliber.

I visited many towns in my day, and each left an impression. However, this evening left a particularly deep impression. The discussion created tension but civility was maintained. The arguments were well reasoned and clearly presented. There was nothing provincial about them. Yeshayahu Rabin's arguments could be said to "best" the others.

The discussion dealt with the preference given to Keren Kayesod over Keren Kayemet (to buy land). Most of those present spoke of the importance of Keren Kayemet. Yeshayahu, who was known to all as Shaike Rabin, spoke on behalf of the importance of Keren Hayesod. His arguments were polished and to the point. I was several years older than Shaike and a regular circuit speaker, yet I felt I could learn from him. To me, he was a rising star. Unfortunately he too perished.

While all the community leaders were kind and helpful, his support was outstanding. The meeting took place in the Beit Hamidrash [= learning center, attached to the synagogue]. The sexton did not want to open the synagogue for the occasion. The meeting place was crowded.

[Page 216]

In the audience were Jews eager to hear new ideas. No one wore a Shtraimel [=fur hat]. It was said that the local Rabbi is the only one that has a Shtraimel. The rabbi did not come to greet me because of his hate of Zionism. He neither received me as a guest even though he knew that I also was a Rabbi. Those who came to listen to me put on their best clothes, whereas he came plainly dressed. I knew that among the audience were many anti-Zionists. I did not argue this issue. Instead, I told them of the happenings in Palestine. That is what the audience came to hear. At the end of my lecture, the audience surrounded me, wishing me a "Yesher Koach" [expressed their appreciation for a good speech]. This was not the custom in other towns. The love of Israel could be seen on the faces of this audience.

I stayed in your town four days and each day I felt uplifted. I was not troubled by local quarrels or by petty differences. The cause I came for won their respect.

Even in the manner of fund-raising, Lanovits was different from other towns. I was not obliged to meet individually with important contributors. All in the audience contributed including anti-Zionists. They did not want to express their opposition by withholding a contribution.

This is how I remember your town, small in number, but great in its quality, full of wise and considerate people.

[Page 217]

Feiga, the Bath Attendant

By Ch. Liwerant

"Feiga Die Baderin" [= Bath House Attendant] or "Mome Feiga" was how she was known in Shumsk. She moved from there to your town Lanovits when she remarried.

She was known as Feiga Die Baderin because she owned the Shumsk bath house. She was also known as "Feiga the Aunt". Locals regarded her as their aunt because of her love and devotion to them.

I knew her from my childhood days inasmuch as she was related to my late stepmother Beila Yokelson. My stepmother's first married name was Galperin, the same name as Feiga's first husband. My stepmother's maiden name was Hazan. The latter was a large and respected Shumsk family.

Feiga was a regular visitor to our home and I was a regular visitor to her home. Even after she moved from Shumsk to Lanovits, her visits to our home were a stormy and noisy occasion. She came laden with gifts. For us children it felt like a holiday. During her visit there was a constant commotion. Visitors came to see her. There was the accompanying smell of cooking and baking, a wonderful mixture of smells that lingered for days after her departure. My child instincts told me that this woman was different from other women. I remember her as beautiful, and dressed in the latest fashion. Loud, but friendly, she spoke freely with men and women, a custom not common in those days. She addressed us children in the same friendly and direct manner.

Her apartment was above the bath house. The bath house, an important local health institution, was known for its cleanliness. Its procedures were followed faithfully so it was considered a high-quality bath house by both Jews and Gentiles. The local rich paid well for its service. Those who could not afford the fee were let in gratis by "Mome". Even though the latter were many, she made a good living from the bath house. So much so that she was able to help the local needy as well.

Her apartment above the bath house was spotless. Its living room was always full of men who came to discuss various topics with her. On the dining table were delicious juices that her guests appreciated the taste of for several days.

[Page 218]

Her poise and her full knowledge of Polish, the state language, helped many locals who needed her mediation with authorities, or when dealing with the local estate owners.

I remember a visit to her home accompanying my father, Alter Yokelson. The image I remember is a person resembling a queen whose subjects adored her.

Many years later I saw a performance of "Miraleh Efrat" [a famous Yiddish play]. The way the main actress carried her house keys, and the jewelry she wore, reminded me of Feiga. In Shumsk Feiga had a special standing. She took personal charge of helping the poor in special situations. Other needs were served by local people she organized for these tasks.

* * *

I cannot gloss over how well Feiga organized the wedding of my stepmother's sister Roza. Its memory will remain with me forever. For several days prior to the wedding our home was a beehive of activity organized by Feiga. The Lekakh, the strudel, the cakes, the "golden soup" and sweets were all either prepared by her or under her direction. She was known for her prowess in these affairs. After the wedding service the partitions between men and woman were removed. The service was followed by Quadrilles, waltzes and Mitzwa dances under Feiga's direction. The high spirit of the wedding brought true joy to the wedding couple and guests. This wedding was talked about in our town for a long time.

Feiga did not have children of her own. Instead she was an "aunt" to many locals. She was a noble woman, the likes of whom are few.

[Page 219]

Leizer "The Greener"

By B. Harin

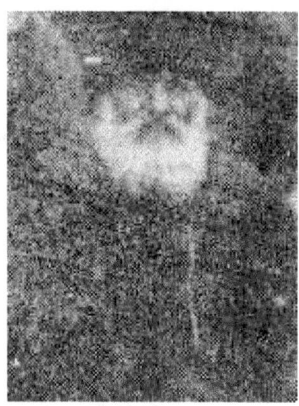

The nickname stuck to him because of his green complexion. He looked like a man near death. Despite such appearance he was in reality a lively and responsive person. I once saw him walking as if in a fog, about to fall asleep. Yet, when he met with another person the image changed radically. One could not fail to enjoy his eternal humor.

He won contests with stronger men through his humor, strong intellect, and imagination. My memory of him recalls the character Schweyk in the famous play by Jaroslaw Hasek, who withstood all life's vicissitudes with his wisdom and positive attitude.

* * *

One time Leizer decided to enlarge his narrow and dark house. He had no alternative than to encroach on the area of the old Polish cemetery that bordered on his yard. During the digging, he unearthed several old graves. The Ksiandz (local Catholic priest) reported the incident to the local police in an attempt to turn the affair into a religious scandal.

Leizer lived across the street from us. We youngsters, having read about pogroms, were at first afraid of the procession of people coming towards us. At the head of the group was the priest, followed by the police chief, several policemen and assorted followers. Curious, we children became oblivious to the danger while present at this gathering. We expected Leizer to beg for a way out. The police chief asked the policemen to stay behind him.

[Page 220]

While the priest stood pat, hands folded, Leizer appeared. He bypassed the priest, in his hand a cigarette lighter of older vintage. Approaching the police chief (who loved him dearly) he held the lighter like a pistol and shouted jokingly: "Move away, I am shooting". The police chief burst out laughing with the policemen joining in. The priest stood alone, not knowing what to do. The crowd enjoyed the resulting comedy. The episode caused a long period of friction between the police chief and the priest. Leizer's house remained untouched. No altercation ensued.

* * *

His ability to get out of complicated situations was the most famous and surprising of his exploits. He seemed fearless, not only when dealing with Gentiles.

Leizer once had a dispute with Reb. Leizer Starick, the respected husband of Feiga Michlis. Starick, a simple man, found himself one day on the street facing Leizer.

[Page 221]

He had no choice other than to defend his honor. A string of accusations against Leizer followed. We admired Leizer, and eagerly waited for his response. Leizer, unflustered, waited for his rival to pause and said:

"What you said, Starick, is all true, but whoever asks for forgiveness is multer [= a trough for kneading dough]. Is it true? Answer me!" Starick, confused, replied:" What is multer? Am I multer? Since when?"

The assembled crowd needed no more. The secret is out, that Leizer Starick, the respected person is multer. One asked the other: "What is multer?" What has a kneading trough to do with this dispute? No one knew the answer, but if Starick was shaken by this disclosure, there must be something to it. Starick meanwhile turned to the crowd around him and said:

[Page 222]

"Fellow Jews, let him say what he has to say, but not call me multer!". The crowd, however, was merciless, saying: "You are multer, you decide the merits of this case." Starick lost the argument.

Leizer meanwhile turned to go home, proud of having won. We left the defeated Starick, despising him for keeping a secret from us. We, too, did not know what multer meant. When we reached Leizer's home we asked him: "Tell us about this 'multer' business, and how did you discover it." He replied: "I don't know its meaning. There was nothing I could do or say about him., so I chose 'multer' to defeat him." It was a simple, crazy, invention on his part.

* * *

Leizer was ignorant of languages. Even Yiddish he spoke poorly. Though he was a son of a teacher from Rachmanov, near Shumsk, he had difficulty with words and letters. Despite such handicaps, he was sometimes sent by our town leaders to the province governor to appeal an anti-Semitic act or an increase in taxes that Poland was known to impose on its Jews.

He succeeded most of the time, even when others, with a more polished approach, failed. In one case, two of our learned men, Pesach Buchstein and Shlomo Berman returned empty handed from Lutsk whereas Leizer accomplished the task. It happened as follows:

He left with a horse and wagon, reaching the governor's building after a two day journey. At the entrance, he had to argue with a pompous guard, but in the end succeeded in entering the building. He went straight to the governor's office. The governor sat at a large desk at the end of a long room symbolizing the separation between authority and its subjects. Leizer stood for a while at the other end of the room, next to the heavy, ornate, entrance door.

[Page 223]

He waited next to the heavy purple curtains. When the governor lifted his head and saw him, he wanted to cry out: "Who let you in without my permission?" Leizer went towards the governor's desk, part in supplication, part boastfully. Lifting his hand as he reached the governor's desk, he said: "Let them be. Listen to me as you would to a friend to whom you wish to offer good advice. I am from your province, from Lanovits. It is worth your while to visit our town. We are dying to see you. When do we ever see a governor? I want to invite you. Now I can return to my town and say proudly that I stood next to you."

The Pole's serious countenance softened in spite of himself. Subject to flattery, he opened up, discussing Lanovits's problems with Leizer. The road to his heart opened. Leizer described the difficulties he had on the way to Lutsk, and the problems he had entering the building, and the subject of his visit. The governor reconsidered, and the new law was rescinded.

* * *

Leizer died a natural death before the Holocaust. For me, he is a prototype of the tragedy of Jewish Lanovits. We need to promise ourselves and generations that follow us not to return to situations which require talents such as submission, cunning and arrogance as Leizer needed. This is the legacy his story conveys.

[Page 224]

Arenda Holders

By Yeheskel Shmukler

Village Jews, also known as Arenda Holders, did not merit special mention in the memorial books about communities that were wiped out.

These Jews were unique. All the town Jews were like prisoners of war in the midst of Gentiles. Town Jews, however, were a united group that could defend itself against a sudden catastrophe or a personal vengeance, whereas village Jews were isolated, subject to sudden dangers that could not be foreseen. They were on their own. Despite these risks, village Jews accepted their fate as a "Diaspora within a Diaspora" and maintained their full Jewish identity. One can mock their depth of knowledge, but not their dedication which they maintained despite emotional and physical discomfort.

I, myself, was the son of an Arenda Holder, Moshe Kiskiwitzer and his wife Judith. I was one of eight children that were raised in a warm Jewish home in the midst of an unfriendly Christian society.

Ours was a large village full of Orthodox Gentiles whose concept of society and personal behavior was based on homilies that they heard in the village church.

Two more Jewish families, Moshe Tepper and Meir Fishman lived in our village. These three families earned their living leasing and operating the local flour mill from Count Poplowsky, who later became the district chief of Lanovits County. He was happy to turn over the mill's management to these local Jews. They, in turn, provided him a guaranteed monthly income.

* * *

From an economic standpoint, we had good and bad years. These economic changes depressed the family's spirits but never led to despair. Our parents dismissed these changes as due to "luck" or "fate". What pained our parents more was their struggle to raise their children properly, how to install "Yiddishkeit" in them. They were not referring to Torah learning or to good deeds, but instead, to proper "Jewish behavior," while living among a sea of Gentiles. Our parents' influence was limited and their economic concerns limited their ability even further.

[Page 225]

In family discussions we shared their concern as to how to maintain our unique behavior. When our family deliberated on ways to maintain our Jewish identity, we children felt "big" as if we were sharing a serious secret with adults. Going outside we became serious, proud to keep a secret from Gentile children. At first, we kept apart, proud of our differences, but seeing them playing happily, paying no attention to us, our hearts were drawn to them. The initial pride gave way and the "Yiddishkeit" separation folded. We were like them after all.

Our childhood was difficult. Life was equally hard for our parents. We loved our surroundings and could not easily isolate ourselves from its charm.

Our parents' ability to provide a Jewish education was limited. Teachers willing to live in our village were not always available. To travel to a nearby town involved great difficulties. We were caught between an attractive secular childhood and parental restrictions. We loved our parents, hence could not fathom their contradictions.

Meanwhile new ideas reached Ukrainian society. To their religious fanaticism, Ukrainians added a separatist propaganda that included active terror against the Polish authorities and Jews. Our security situation turned serious. To this day, I don't know how these isolated Jews found the courage to remain in their villages. Yet they stayed. Every week or fortnight they traveled to Lanovits, absorbed the friendship they experienced there, but they also heard of troubles and elected to stay in their village.

* * *

Our visit to town on the high holidays was our great experience. It involved elaborate preparations. The three families met several weeks prior to our departure to detail travel plans, such as who will travel in whose wagon, who will guard our house and other matters. It was a team effort. We could feel the holiday spirit as the preparations proceeded. Daily economic issues took second place to the travel preparations.

The big moment in this event came when all our goods were assembled, including blankets, pillows, pots and pans, dresses and coats. We all pitched in carrying them to the wagon while the men loaded these items each in its proper place, leaving space for passengers. This was an act of self-sacrifice and physical effort on the part of our parents, for an idea, the details of which may not have been clear to them. Our Gentile neighbors watched us, wondering what the commotion was all about.

[Page 226]

This was the Jewish soul of village Jews, their way of maintaining their identity.

We arrived in town as strangers coming to visit strangers. Something separated us from our Lanovits hosts. Our ideals and customs differed from theirs. Ridiculed by the local children and feeling alienated from them, we children suffered greatly during these visits to the town.

Our uncle Idel Kiskiwitzer, who moved from our village to the town, provided us with a warm family-like atmosphere for he still understood the village culture. His home had a special attraction for he also hosted the Rabbi from Chortkov. The Rabbi's teaching and the festive atmosphere he created added to our enjoyment. It lifted our spirits for many days after our return to our village.

The synagogue prayers, the Jewish holiday experience and associated pride all added to our resolve to withstand the secular pressure we experienced in the village.

The trip to town was a sort of exodus from Egypt. It gave us pause to think of the purpose of our lives in the village. The trip back felt like a return to an uncertain, perhaps hostile, environment after we tasted the freedom of being with our own people in Lanovits. Despite all the doubts, our family remained in the village.

Our visits to Lanovits introduced us to the Zionist alternative. We left our poor parents to their fate. Instead of holding on, we youngsters opted to receive agricultural training and immigrated to Palestine.

We dreamt of having our parents join us, but failed in this effort. It seems to me that the story of the Arenda Holders of the area belongs together with the Lanovits story. They, more than others, suffered from the problems of the Diaspora.

Together with the Lanovits Jews, they experienced moments of elation in their erroneous conception of Diaspora Judaism, the idea that one can live a Jewish life among Gentiles.

[Page 227]

Chapter 6:

Lanovits in Legends

[Page 228] [Blank] [Page 229]

Lanovits Legends

By Ch. Rabin

Translated by Joseph M. Voss z"l

1. Hayim Mordechai Became a Trader

Hayim Mordechai was meant to be a Rabbi. He studied regularly and attended the synagogue between lessons. His wife supported the family in the intervals between childbirths. When she could stand it no longer, she told her husband that her talent is household work and cooking, that he is the one who needs to support the family.

She sewed a money pocket into a book he was reading and the book into his vest pocket. Next, she dispatched him to the Yermolinitz fair and told him: "The money I gave you is our main asset, the result of our labor. Guard it on your journey. In order not to divulge its hiding location, do not touch it until you arrive at the fair. Look for suitable merchandise at the fair,. Purchase only an item that you like."

When Hayim Mordechai arrived at the fair, he sought a spot far from its noise. He sat down in the shade of a fence, spread out his jacket, took out his book and read it until sundown. As the fair visitors left and the place fell silent, Hayim Mordechai arose for his evening prayer. He stood up to pray "Shmoneh Esreh" [= 18 prayers], his eyes closed, with his book and money pocket under his armpit. At that moment, a thick-bearded Jew, carrying a parcel covered with an old sheet and a belt, passed by. He noticed the book and the money pocket protruding from the book under Hayim's armpit. He began to plan how to remove the book and money pocket, and then return the book to its owner. He tried to pull the book from Hayim's armpit but failed in the attempt. Hayim Mordechai's arms held it tight. The man waited for Hayim to complete his prayer and said: "A Jew does not come to the fair only to sell. If you bought nothing with your proceeds it is like going twice in one direction."

[Page 230]

Hayim, remembering why he came to the fair, replied in kind: "You, who came to sell your merchandise and did not, nor buy anything, did you not waste your time?" The man, agreeing with Hayim's logic, offered his wares to Hayim, suggesting he would benefit from a trade. The man opened his parcel, pulling out a beautiful red kerchief.

Hayim's eyes lit up as he admired the green and blue flowers of the kerchief. He remembered his wife's instruction to only purchase items that he liked. Hayim was eager to purchase the item. The man sold him hundreds of identical colorful kerchiefs. Hayim paid him with paper money of identical color, each having the king's image on it. Together they left for a restaurant feeling like old friends. In the morning, they parted warmly, Hayim to Lanovits and the other Jew to Yampol. On the way home, Hayim was saddened that this friendship ended so quickly. He was consoled by the thought that his wife will be glad that he is now a trader.

* * *

When his wife saw the merchandise, she shuddered. She wondered as to whom will they sell so many kerchiefs of the same design, or where will they find so many women customers. She was consoled by the fact that the cost of kerchief was one quarter of the normal price. But, her heart sunk: "Where will I find willing buyers?"

When the first Shiksah [=Gentile young woman] bought a kerchief, her friend, who pined for the same boyfriend as the first, became envious. She, too, bought one. Her neighbor saw her, became envious and bought one as well. After a few days, all the kerchiefs were sold due to their popularity and the envy of other Shiksas.

The village lads loved the new looks and were content. Hayim Mordechai made a good trade and his wife was proud of him.

[Page 231]

The story serves to demonstrate that help from G-d can come quickly when consumer desire runs wild.

2. Baruch Peretz and the Bear

Baruch Peretz was one of the strongest men of the town, built like a cedar trunk. Muscle bound, he was also one of the most courageous men of the area. Just as there is merit to courage, excess courage can also be a liability. His story is as follows:

When Baruch married Rivka, he promised to build her a house in Lanovits. He could not afford a plot of land in the center of town. Instead, he opted for a plot next to the Catholic Church. The plot was available because no one wanted it. A large bear was reputed to appear at this plot at night. Baruch ignored the advice of his friends not to challenge the night animal. They considered the animal to be a kind of messenger, to dissuade Jews from living adjacent to the Catholic Church.

Baruch said to himself: "If my wife is afraid of the bear, let her stay at home in the evening hours; that suits me. I am among those who finish their evening prayers at the synagogue early and returns home early. Should I be late some day and meet the bear, I will trust the Lord to help me in such a situation."

One day he left his home in the early night hours to go into town, completely forgetting why he avoided departing at night heretofore. He returned from town that night, forgetting the danger, as the bear came towards him. Days later he admitted his racing heartbeat when he saw the bear. However, his version the day following the incident was different: "As I approached him, he came towards me. When I arrived at my house, he disappeared, having realized that I was not afraid of him."

On another occasion, Baruch left his house on Saturday evening to participate in a Sabbath celebration at the house of Michel Geldener. It was the birthday of Melvina, his wife, nee Lida. The house guests enjoyed their meal and the company as the hours passed. The guests departed in the wee hours of the morning. Baruch Peretz left, forgetting about the bear danger. Baruch's house was close to the Geldener house. Soon a horrendous cry was heard from the direction of Baruch's house. All the guests were frightened. The men in the group turned around to try and save Baruch.

[Page 232]

When they arrived at his house, the men noticed that Baruch was holding the bear's ears. The bear, the size of a wild pig, was attempting to pull Baruch to him, but Baruch held his ground. Baruch, in turn, tried to let go of the bear's ears but his hands failed to respond. They stuck to the monster's ears. Finally, the men cut off the bear's ears. The animal disappeared. Baruch was carried home having fainted, with the monster's ears stuck to his hands.

3. If One Tells You About Naked Ducks, Believe Him

Eti Hayas was always able to support herself. What occurred took place when she was selling liquor directly from vats. The customs office gave her a liquor sales permit. Inasmuch as the production of glass in Russia at that time was in its infancy, and bottles were in short supply, she was permitted to sell directly from her vats to fill customer's glasses. The vat's faucets, made of wood, always leaked a little. The resulting vapor caused nausea so the vats had to be kept in her barn. Eti, who for tax reasons had to account for the vat's content, decided to collect the dripping liquor with a saucer and return it periodically to the vat.

Eti earned a good living from this concession; hence she decided to add another item to her household, geese. She planned to fatten them in the winter, to slaughter them on Purim and preserve the meat, and then use the goose fat on Passover. Twenty geese were purchased on Hanukah and placed in coups to lessen their mobility. This was meant to help them gain weight rapidly. It was hoped that they will have grown and be fat, ready for slaughter on Purim. The plan was to hang their bodies in her attic so that the meat freezes rapidly. Each week, one goose would be unfrozen for a meal and its fat processed for use at Passover time. That is, if all goes well as expected. A further plan was to let the geese out of their coup to roam freely a day before the slaughter so that their muscles are relaxed and their blood circulation improved. This was meant to make the slaughter and feather plucking easier, also to improve the meat's taste.

As she thought of the plan, she realized that this is the first time in her life that she could afford to buy 20 geese at once, and eat a whole goose once a week.

She let the geese out of their coups in the evening and lay down to sleep, expecting pleasant dreams. In the morning, she rose early, thinking how blessed she was to be able to raise 20 geese.

[Page 233]

But, when she arrived in the barn she found the geese all dying, lying all over the floor. Eti cried; she could live with the loss of the geese and the disappointment. She could not live with the loss of the geese's feathers. Eti needed them to create feather beds and pillows for her daughter's future dowries. Eti went to her Rabbi to ask for permission to pluck the feathers of a dead bird. She hoped he would understand the need for such a dowry as is customary at every wedding. The Rabbi gave her he desired permission.

She and her daughters plucked the geese's feathers. They were thinking of the happiness a future wedding entails, and were consoled about the loss of the meat. When they finished plucking, they placed the geese on a pile and covered them with sacks to cover their shame. Eti waited for darkness to throw their bodies into the river, so that no one would know of her humiliation.

* * *

In the late afternoon, as the sun set, Eti was astounded to see the geese rise, quacking loudly, because they were cold.

The story ends with the following explanation: During the night when they were set free, the geese drank from the saucer that collected the liquor drippings. They became so drunk that they felt nothing as their feathers were plucked and their bodies thrown into a pile. Based on this story, believe it if a man tells you about "naked geese…."

4. How Idel Leibish Ideles Died

The image of a lit candle appeared at night in the famous swamps of Lanovits, located between the riverbeds that flowed near the houses of Moshe Kofitz, Zerach Feigeles, and Anton Habrod. No one knew what it was about, yet they were afraid of it. The candle appeared to guard their swamps. It was said that if a person dares to cross the swamps at night, the candle will blind and confuse him. The person will end up going in circles during the entire night. He will return home either dead or crazy.

[Page 234]

Most people chose to bypass the swamp, even if the alternate road was longer, to feel secure.

Idel Leibish Ideles was a man among men, a life-long wagoneer who knew the area's roads, also where dangers lurked. He was unafraid. One day he decided to no longer bypass the large swamp. He resolved instead to take the swamp road that shortens the distance to his house by one third. As he returned from a long day's journey to Volochysk, close to midnight, he directed his horses to the swamp path. The path was soft, as if carpeted. The cold air rising from the swamp refreshed him. He felt good. Suddenly, the lit candle approached his wagon, scaring the horses. Idel had difficulty controlling them. The struggle to control the horses continued all night.

The story ends with Idel returning home with broken bones, pain over his whole body, and difficulty breathing. Within a year he died. No doctor as able to help him.

[Page 235]

The Original Barons of Our Town

By the Editor

Translated by Joseph M. Voss z"l

1. Baron von Buelow

Baron von Buelow was a descendant of the famous von Buelow whom Czar Peter the Great brought to Russia to industrialize the country. One of the original von Buelow sons was named secretary of treasury, and another received the Osnick district as a present from the Czar. Our Baron was his great-grandson and heir. Over the generations, his origin and the circumstances of his arrival in Lanovits were forgotten. Regimes changed in the meantime. The Baron became a loyal Polish citizen. His life consisted of merrymaking in the style of the Polish nobility. He was careless, unfaithful to his wife and violated the rules of his Catholic religion whenever these conflicted with his needs or desires. Reb Uziel Rabin who leased his estates for many years, tried to guide him to become a decent person. The Baron listened to his mentor like a child to an adult, and was thankful for the guidance he provided.

* * *

Some traits of his German ancestry remained with him. He was always punctual and technically proficient in the tradition of his ancestors. His house was spacious, having several rooms dedicated to sports and study. Only a few rooms were meant for eating and drinking. His furniture was heavy, made of dark walnut wood. The image of an eagle with spread wings and claws was carved into the furniture to symbolize the family origin of the owner.

He regarded his furniture as sacred. Only a close friend or a person of his social standing was allowed to sit on a chair with an eagle emblem. His employees were allowed to sit only on kitchen stools or standard chairs.

Reb Uziel, a smart man, tried to persuade the Baron to sell him a couch that stood unused in the great hall. The Baron tried at first to hide his anger, then said: "My friend, Zilio [short for Uziel], you are dear to me, but you have forgotten that I am not a Jew. I will not sell my furniture, with our family emblem on it, for any price."

* * *

Years later, the Baron became heavily indebted when he borrowed money to support his mistresses. He appealed to Uziel to save him.

[Page 236]

Uziel replied: "I think I can find customers for your expensive and unique furniture." The Baron agreed to the proposal: "Sell all you can, just save me from bankruptcy." The Baron acted too late. His creditors came that very night and took whatever was available. The Baron, who owed money to Uziel as well, had previously filled a room with furniture and locked it. When the creditors left, the Baron approached Uziel and said: "You are the one I respect the most. Had I listened to you, I would not be in this financial state. The furniture is yours. I am moving to Poznan where the government has allocated me land, an estate and a house. Uziel entered the room, walked between the furniture items, and then asked the Baron for a hammer or an axe. When the tools were brought, Uziel proceeded to destroy the family symbols carved into the furniture. To the surprised Baron, he explained: "I am not a German Baron; I am a Jew, a person who is not allowed to have such symbols. I shall use your furniture but without these images."

* * *

2. Baron Roni Olishewsky

Roni Olishewsky was a Polish Baron. His grandfather received the title and local land because he betrayed the Polish insurrection of 1862. The men in the family were all over 2 meters tall and the women over 1.80 meters. His unusual height led to lechery. Russian princesses and Polish Baronesses came to his bed. Leaseholders offered their 16 and 18 year old daughters to satisfy his sexual desires for the generous payments they received in return.

When the Baron became entangled in debts, he approached Uziel, asking him to save him from his "shame". Each such discussion always ended with the remark, "Please understand, in my society, honor and religion are primary. You must save me. I will not spare cash, but I will guard my honor and my faith." Each time Uziel saved him financially until next year's crop was sold. In later years, the Baron lost his estate, no longer able to pay back his debts.

On a Friday night when, as he phrased it, "his Jewish creditors", prepared for the Sabbath, Roni appeared at Uziel's house, drunk as usual. He asked to speak to Uziel in confidence behind closed doors. As they sat in the room, Roni first hesitated, then took from his pocket a long velvet box and said:

[Page 237]

"This item has been in our family for generations. It is sacred, yet I have no choice but to pawn it for however much you can loan me." As he said that he collapsed into the von Buelow walnut couch and cried: "Please understand Zilio, I brought you an item that is dearest to me. I will not rest until I redeem it, and you will get your money back." Reb Uziel did not take the time to inspect the item. He took pity on the good-hearted Gentile, removing a packet of bills, he gave these to Roni.

At the end of the Sabbath, Uziel's wife Dina decided to investigate what happened between the two men the previous evening. She opened the velvet box and found a silk cross with stitched gold threads, covered with diamonds. On the short cross-arm was embossed the family coat of arms.

Dina, who was quite smart, said to herself: "This is the first time that the honor and faith of this noble Pole is worth the monetary value he received from a Jew."

[Page 238]

Experiences We Do Not Forget

By Israel Glazer

Translated by Joseph M. Voss z"l

There are experiences that cannot be forgotten. They come up in one's memory periodically even though they are not strictly personal. Inasmuch as these memories reflect something about the way of life of our town, they need to be told.

The Incident with "Bentzi Hudiah"

Benzion Gurewitch was a dreamer, as if functioning in another world. He was this way since childhood. When he reached adulthood, this characteristic persisted. There were times when others in the community doubted his sanity and degree of responsibility. Despite these liabilities, he married (the daughter of Aaron Mardeshicha) and led a normal family life. The youth of our town listened to him and always found him interesting.

Periodically, he would drift from reality, raise his head towards the sky and look yonder. When you tapped his shoulder to connect with him, he would look at you puzzled, expressing impromptu ideas that were beyond your comprehension. The worst aspect of his habit was his periodic aimless street wanderings. It is during these wanderings that he threw caution to the wind and ran into dangerous situations.

Once, on Christmas midnight 1924, Bentzi was returning from his aimless wanderings back to home and reality. The main street was empty. Suddenly, he encountered two Polish soldiers who had celebrated the holiday at a local tavern. When they saw a Jew on the street, they were reminded of Jesus and his crucifixion; it was time to take revenge.

What did they do? They beat up Bentzi until he stopped resisting. Next, they brought him to their headquarters. The local officers from the Polish nobility joined in to torture Bentzi systematically so as to force him to confess.

[Page 239]

They pulled his hair, and the hair of his mustache. They twisted his arms and pressed bullet cases under his fingernails. To make matters worse, they rubbed soap into his torn hair and fed him this mixture to cause him to vomit.

He confessed nothing and withstood the torture, a fact that angered the higher-rank officers at the headquarters.

Two soldiers were ordered to take him outside to finish the interrogation. The soldiers led him on the road to the village of Grobova. On the way to the village, the soldiers took him to a steep hill which had a sharp drop on the other side. They planned to kill him by throwing him downhill. Bentzi had, in the meantime, recovered from his torture and sensed the impending danger. He managed to flee from the two drunken soldiers. Rolling down the steep hill, he hid in one of its crevasses. The soldiers searched for him but failed to find him. Bentzi was saved.

The incident was brought up for debate in the Polish Seym (Parliament). The Jewish delegates demanded a formal investigation. As expected, the investigation ended without indictment of these officers.

* * *

The community was in despair for days after this incident. We teenagers realized that this incident was another convincing argument in our ongoing dialog with the older generation regarding our future in Lanovits. It was another reason for choosing the immigration route to Palestine.

[Page 240]

Calling Up 4th to the Torah

By Yitzak Meir Weitzman

Translated by Joseph M. Voss z"l

Shaya Nathans returned from America to his home, his family and wife. The connection with the community was renewed. He started his life anew as if America did not exist. Lanovits was worth more than 10 American communities.

On the Sabbath, he was called to the Torah and properly honored. He felt "at home". In Lanovits, he found warmth, friendship and honor. He found "Yiddishkeit". It was good that he returned. Here one can live; there is purpose to life. He began to enjoy his stay.

Except that he accepted the job of Gabbai [The person who selects congregants to come up to Torah reading]. His peace of mind was shattered. His days turned into nights. Life became gloomy. Here is how it all happened:

* * *

Shaya was touched by the reception he received at the synagogue. The service was followed by a Kiddush where, again, he was the honored guest. As he looked around, he noticed the darkness of the synagogue walls. He noticed a wet spot on the ceiling. All around there were signs of neglect. When he asked why the roof leak was not repaired, he was told, "We have no money for repairs."

Shaya decided to act. He took it upon himself to have the roof repaired, and the ceiling and walls painted. The synagogue looked festive again.

When congregants came to the synagogue on the Sabbath, they saw and appreciated the clean new appearance. All realized that these improvements were thanks to Shaya. He was elected to be the Gabbai of the synagogue.

He fulfilled this role in a manner not customary in Lanovits. He adopted the American approach to give out Aliyas [=being called up to Torah reading] in rotation in accordance with the honor and learning level of a congregant.

The Aliyas were divided up over the weeks to honor each congregant periodically while including Bar Mitzvas, Weddings, holidays and guests. This left the issue of the 4th Aliyah unresolved for obvious reasons.

[Page 241]

Offering the 4th Aliyah to a congregant is a form of contempt. It was a way to make light of him. There is, of course, an explanation that the reading of the Torah was commanded by G-d at Sinai, so each congregant needs to take part in the process. However, even this explanation was not convincing to those offered the 4th Aliyah.

Gedaliah, the water carrier, was asked to accept the 4th Aliyah. It was explained to him that he either accepts the honor or will get no Aliyah at all. The same was done with Hayim Rimer.

It was known that Hayim Rimer is not like Gedaliah. He was muscular, and anyone who tackled him risked a hospital visit. Rimer was ambitious; he expected to receive the same honors as any other congregant. He accepted the 4th Aliyah once, then twice. When he noticed that other congregants were whispering and secretly mocking him, he sought an explanation. Another person explained to him: "Being called up 4th to the Torah is something no one wants. It is depreciating to a person to accept it." After Hayim heard this, he went to Shaya, his neighbor, asking him to change the order of his Aliyah. Shaya, who regarded himself as responsible to G-d, and for synagogue decorum, would not even consider Hayim's request. Shaya regarded Hayim as a man who practices only a minor portion of the Ten Commandments, hence is not entitled to a "better" Aliyah. Reb Shaya felt that as a Gabbai he had a heavy responsibility, so he stood by his decision.

What shall Hayim do? To be called up to the Torah and not respond is clearly not allowed. If he responds, he will be ridiculed. What to do? Hayim would respond to the Aliyah, then, when finished, he would fold his Talis and leave the synagogue for home. There he would have a drink of hard liquor. As his blood rose to his head, he would wait and ambush Reb Shaya on his way home, throwing stones or mud at him. Reb Shaya returned home every second Sabbath with his clothes soiled, himself hurt or injured.

[Page 242]

One Sabbath, in the autumn, when it was very cold outside, Shaya put on his clean fur coat. He came home with his coat torn and dirty, as if returning from a pogrom. Frieda, his wife, always asked him why the dirt and injury. After she received an explanation from her husband she would say: "Shaya, offer him the 3rd Aliyah thereby ending this matter." His answer invariably was: "You demand that I give the 3rd Aliyah to this bastard, murderer and thief?" Next, he would enter my room - as a bachelor I was living with them - partly asking, partly shouting and laughing, "Mr. Weitzman, what do you say to a wife who wants me to give the 3rd Aliyah to Hayim Rimer?" I, who was their border, would agree with Reb Shaya. Having studied Torah I could not do otherwise.

As the attacks continued, Shaya's family life was disrupted. Frieda would cry and Shaya suffered both pain and anger. I, who enjoyed the company of these two quiet people, was affected by their depression, yet was unable to help.

What could Reb Shaya do? If he were to give in to Hayim, he would lose the confidence of the congregation. If he did not capitulate, how can he stop the continuous suffering? His life was peaceful only on the Sabbath when Gedaliah received the 4th Aliyah, and disturbed when Hayim received the "Honor". When his expensive coat was soiled and torn he felt like on "The 9th of Av" - the day of mourning, hurt and in pain. His wife pleaded with him to give Hayim Maftir [=the last part of the Torah reading] to end the misery. Reb Shaya answered her as always, asking me to mediate between them - "I should give Motil Melamed and Hayim Rimer Maftir? Where is her logic? Women do not think clearly."

This time, I decided to act. I felt that I must stop this hell that we suffer every second Sabbath. I decided that Hayim went overboard in his reaction. He threw stones and shattered Shaya's house windows. One stone fell into my room; I was lucky not to be hurt. I realized that my life was also in danger; that Hayim hates me as Shaya's tenant.

[Page 243]

I was now a party to this sad struggle.

There was another reason for my decision. From arguments on this subject I had overheard that there was no chance to offer 1st, 2nd, 3rd, 4th, 6th Aliyah or Maftir to a person such as Hayim, but it occurred to me that offering him the last (7th) Aliyah would be acceptable. On an autumn day, Frieda stood in front of the window, wrapped in a shawl, silent, and Shaya was in his room sad and alone. It is then that I proposed the aforementioned solution. Give him the last Aliyah, a less esteemed one, call him up for the 7th and settle the matter. I told him - "How long can one suffer?", and for emphasis I added - you suffered enough! I noted that my proposal was accepted. I next needed to have Hayim accept it, to settle the dispute. How to do this?

* * *

On Sunday morning I went out, resolved to put all business matters aside and focus on settling this sad matter that has turned our house into a house of mourning every two weeks (when Hayim Rimer was given an Aliyah). I had to find the right person to approach Hayim with the aforementioned solution.

As I stood outside thinking whom to ask, who do I see: Michli Itzik Shmueles. I said to myself: "This is a golden opportunity. He was a good friend of long standing. When I loaded grain on freight trains, I used to give him a portion to feed his horses." Ours was a true friendship.

> I asked Michli: "Where are you going?"
> He replied: "Nowhere."
> I said: "One does not go nowhere!"
> He replied: "I swear, what else is there to do?"

That moment Hayim joined us. He saw us from his window. He ignored me, regarding me as associated with his rival, Shaya. He approached Michli and asked him for a cigarette.

[Page 244]

While Michli took out cigarette paper to roll one, using tobacco, I left them for a moment and brought back a packet of cigarettes. I offered Hayim a cigarette. He looked at me, hesitated for a moment, then reached out to accept my offering, adding: "Let me have another one." I told him, I don't smoke, you may have another cigarette. He took the whole pack.

At that moment an idea occurred to me. I turned to Michli, asking him to honor me with a visit tomorrow, commemorating my grandmother's passing. I told him that I celebrate it like a birthday. I next turned to Hayim and asked him to honor me with his visit as well. He knew where I lived and where I was inviting him. Nonetheless he asked: "Where do you live?" He did come the next day.

* * *

I informed Frieda of my intent and asked her to prepare a festive buffet. The next evening both, whom I had invited, came dressed in holiday attire, and I in my Sabbath clothing. I asked Shaya to stay secluded in an adjacent room. After my guests ate enough and drank more than enough, I turned to Hayim and said: "I am a Cohen; as you know we are peace makers. You are in Shaya's house. You came to honor me. I ask you to do something in my honor and settle your dispute with Reb Shaya. Before I could finish my remarks he jumped up like a snake and said, "What? You want me to settle with this bastard, this thief?" I calmed him: "Reb Hayim, I ask you to do this in my honor; you know that we of the Cohen dynasty always try to make peace." I elaborated on my traditional role. Hayim interrupted: "If I settle, will he continue to offer me the 4th Aliyah?" Disregarding that he is in Shaya's house, he continued: "That thief, he has made my life miserable." In his anger, he turned to leave the house. I held his hand and said:

[Page 245]

"I promise that henceforth you will be offered the 7th Aliyah. I take responsibility for this change." We called Reb Shaya from his room to confirm the agreement. Hayim got the 7th Aliyah, Shaya was able to walk home in peace, and I was proud of my accomplishment.

* * *

One day, we were sitting down for a chat at the home of Dr. Joseph Zinberg. The atmosphere and company was pleasant as usual. Suddenly his Ukrainian maid came into our room pale and shaking. She turned to the host and said: "Reb Rimer is at the door, he wants to talk to Mr. Weitzman." I feared the agreement with Shaya had become unglued. I was afraid to meet him alone so I asked my friends to join me. We were all afraid of Hayim's anger. As we stood at the door, Hayim looked pale and angry. I asked him: "Were you again offered the 4th Aliya?" He looked bewildered and replied: "No, they offered me the 7th Aliyah, thanks to you. I came to hear from you if this event will distress me as much as getting the 4th Aliyah did?" I calmed him as a father calms his son, assuring him that the 7th is a respectable Aliyah.

Rabbi Shaya and his wife

[Page 246]

Yizkor for Lanovits's Martyrs

Ch. Rabin

Translated by Moshe Kutten

Edited by Karen Leon

Yizkor – may the remnants of Lanovits, residing in Zion, whom fate loaded mourning upon them, remember the diaspora's martyrs.

Yizkor – Lanovits's natives remember their native city, from the heights of the hills to the delight of the endless streams and playing meadows, where their youth blossomed and where the buds of the big dreams about a life in a homeland sprouted – a homeland of a hill, stream, freedom, and children at play.

Yizkor – we remember our parents, brothers, sisters, friends, and the neighbors in our alley, our schoolmates and playmates who perished at a young age before their time. Their dreams withered before they could taste life in their homeland.

Yizkor – we remember our dear ones, the victims of the human Satans who gave up their tortured souls with our names on their lips. Their last and only wish was for us not to forget.

Yizkor – we remember our dead friends with whom we dreamt and fought together and with whom we secured life and strength for our nation.

Yizkor – we remember all of the dear ones this book is dedicated to, and its pages serve as their memorial monument.

We will memorialize them every year on the first of Elul. May their soul be sealed within our souls and the soul of our descendants for eternity.

[Page 247]

Chapter 7:

Our Losses in Our Homeland

[Page 248] [Blank] [Page 249]

Feiga Roichman (Nechtelman)

By Ch. Rabin

Translated by Joseph M. Voss z"l

Feiga was born in Pikulski, a small village near Maryniker, north of Shumsk. Her father, Yeheskel Nechtelman, was known in the area as Yeheskel the Maryniker due to the fact that his cattle ranch was located between Maryinker and Pikulski.

In her youth, she experienced the loneliness as Jewess among Gentiles. She also experienced a great love within her family. It was thus natural that she would ponder over the fate of a lonely person and on ways of helping such people. She viewed society not as a large and abstract concept, but as a group where a person can do a good deed. She felt that as long as she was able to help a single person, she planted a positive seed in her society, above and beyond the help she provided to the needy person.

Her family was murdered by locals close to the time of her wedding, with her and her young sister, Sonia, the only survivors. The loss of her parents deepened her loneliness. Feiga took Sonia into her new household and raised her as if it was her child.

Her husband, Tsvi Roichman, loved his wife and admired her calm nature.

[Page 250]

He let her run the family household as she saw fit. He, who knew poverty as a child, appreciated her good nature and her tolerance. His patience was admirable. He tolerated his wife's charitable work even when their children were hungry. When Tsvi became wealthy in Poland as a general supplier to the regional army camps, he firmly believed that it was due to his wife's charity work. Feiga continued her work because she believed in the goodness of people.

She kept a leather glove in her house in Hadera, Israel, that had a thumb, but no fingers, similar to the ones found in a Ukrainian village household. The glove lay on a table at all times. When asked about it she explained that the glove was an inheritance from her father-in-law which he used to save one tenth of his income for needy people. It was her way of giving him credit for her charitable work. Every penny that was left over from the household budget went into this glove - a savings account for the needy.

Feiga carried out her charitable work avoiding all publicity. It was unimportant to her how much was distributed to needy people as long as she kept up the tradition of giving.

Lanovits, the home town of her husband, was the anchor for her good deeds. She did not plan to leave her town, and was glad that some of the needy she supported spoke of her glowingly.

It so happened that due to an incident, her husband had to leave his town hurriedly and chose to emigrate to Palestine. She joined him subsequently.

Here in Israel, where class differences did not exist, Feiga's charitable efforts were again fully recognized. She arrived in Hadera with the same positive attitude to others she had in the Diaspora. Her husband initially worked in the building trade. In addition, he worked for the Tepper Co. [from Shumsk] after regular work hours.

[Page 251]

By the time Feiga arrived with their sons, he had managed to save enough money to become a sewer and well-digging contractor together with his sons. The earning from this activity enabled him to return to his former occupation as a butcher. With his wife's encouragement, he rented a butcher shop. With the help of his sons, the business developed nicely. After a while it became clear that Feiga's encouragement to open a butcher shop was not in order to get rich. She realized that in the sewer business she would not be able to identify local financial needs. The aforementioned glove wandered with her to Israel and was again used to collect money for charity. In the butcher shop, the men served customers and she operated the cash register.

Tsvi Roichman of blessed memory

The successful business enabled her to offer cash to those she knew to be in need. In addition, she occasionally gave them meat that went unsold. For the recipient it was like a dream.

The butcher store business developed slowly at first. After Tsvi invested in his store, there was not enough money left to purchase cows. Feiga's "business" developed.

[Page 252]

She regularly packaged meat portions and brought these to needy locals during the noon hours when the store was closed.

After a while she became a known institution. "Witzo" leaders used to meet at her house secretly to find constructive solutions in an effort to help people who lost their livelihood, or ones who needed a loan to finance a wedding, or other cases where a family was about to disintegrate.

As time went on, Tsvi's butcher business developed in part due to the recognition given to Feiga's charitable work. Whoever knew Feiga recognized her warm heart and willingness to help others. She viewed her husband and sons as facilitators to allow her to do the desired good deeds.

When her son, Ya'acov was still a child he noticed that his mother would package meat portions and give these to certain customers in addition to the portions they just purchased. It angered him that he and his brothers, Mordechai and Eliezer worked hard in the store and she was so generous with the merchandise. At first, he did not dare protest. However, when a well-dressed woman customer received a double portion, he protested her action. Feiga calmed him and said: "There are people who save on food to maintain their appearance. Her dress proves nothing, except that she needs to be treated with extra care. I know this woman and know what I am doing."

Feiga did not question generally held opinions, but on issues dear to her she came to significant conclusions. She saw Zionism as a continuation of the Lanovits community culture as if to say: "If we do not carry with us this culture of sharing we will not succeed here. Let our leaders do what they need to do. We simple folks need to recognize that Zionism was meant to save and secure Jewish lives. We need to examine all our deeds to make sure his objective is met."

She saw in the Lanovits tradition her mission in life in Israel. Accordingly, she was ready to help and guide each Lanovits immigrant. Her house was available to her "Landsmen."

[Page 253]

They could sleep over, or stay until they could move into their own apartment. They all enjoyed her good cooking.

Feiga's character combined the simplicity of her village life and the good relations she found in Lanovits. She passed these two traits to her sons.

* * *

She died in 1951 after an illness that lasted one year. While she was ill, many of her friends cared and prayed for her. Her funeral was the largest Hadera experienced. Many cried secretly for they realized that their source of support died with her.

Lanovits residents followed her casket. They were proud of her and of her accomplishments.

Feiga's life included many satisfying moments but was not devoid of tragedies that depressed her. Her husband was murdered by a criminal. Immediately thereafter her son Avraham was killed accidently shortly before his scheduled wedding day.

Feiga was consoled by her efforts to raise her remaining three sons and by her continued charitable work. Yet, when alone, her sorrow increased leading to a fatal disease that attacked her body. "May her soul be bound up in the bond of everlasting life" [= a typical instruction on a Jewish grave.]

[Page 254]

Our First *Halutzah*, Feril Yishpa z"l

by Yisrael Glazer

Translated by Moshe Kutten

Edited by Karen Leon

I hardly knew Pearl Yishpa in Lanovits. I only knew that she was the daughter of Binyamin (Pawlichki). I also knew that she did not belong to any of the age-groups. She was not involved in any of the associations established in the town, and lived her life confined, isolated, and silent. I had no additional knowledge about her.

When we organized the "Hehalutz", we did not count on Pearl because of her older age and her isolating attributes.

Nobody knew what was going on in her mind, so when we got ready to make Aliya, we remembered that Pearl had already been settled in Eretz Israel for quite some time. . Her parents came to send regards to their distant daughter. They asked us to go and meet her and give her personal greetings from them and the town.

When I reached Eretz Israel, I went to see Pearl. She made Aliya in 1924 as our first *Halutzah* [pioneer]. I found her in Tel-Aviv working in a cardboard boxes factory owned by her uncle by the name of Bar [or Ber], a known family in little Tel-Aviv. Their house on Congress Street served as a meeting house for many of the first Tel Aviv residents.

She told me that she was attracted to agriculture.

I remembered that her home in Lanovits was the only Jewish home with a backyard of a dunam [about ¼ acre] or more. It was well cultivated and yielded sufficient amounts of flowers and vegetables for their needs and more.

We met according to the custom in those days - all of Lanovits's natives. There were only four or five of us then, and we met often.

Later on, she abandoned the factory and moved to Petakh Tikva. She worked in the citrus orchards like one of the men workers. She was a healthy woman – mentally and physically, happy in her work.

In 1927, Pearl met Gilboa, an immigrant from America. He was a Russian born man with all the good attributes usually associated with these men. He was among the settlers in the Moshav [cooperative agricultural settlement] Merkhavia. They married, and she moved to his home and farm.

I visited her occasionally in the Moshav. Her farm was exemplary. Her husband was proud of her and loved her tremendously. They were a couple that embodied happiness. When a daughter was born to them, their delight was limitless. It was a pleasure to visit them and enjoy their calmness and deep belief in the village's future. They were happy to work in agriculture with everything it brings to a Jewish person.

Pearl was tireless. Her hard work on the farm and at home was among the most famous in the Moshav. They loved her there and felt blessed having her with her mental integrity. Her status in the Moshav was one of the most respected.

When her daughter was six weeks old, Pearl came down to cover her, wearing sandals. The house was infested with snakes, and one of them bit her.

They transported Pearl to the hospital in Ein Kharod on the same night. The physicians did their best to save her. She died the next day. The whole village mourned her with a heavy heart.

[Page 255]

When her husband, Gilboa, entered the baby's room the next day he found a snake bound around one of the bedposts. He crushed the snake with his hoe. It turned out that it was a very rare poisonous snake.

Pearl's parents showed interest in adopting the girl. They wished to bring her to Lanovits. That did not materialize since the girl died.

Many of Lanovits's natives do not remember Pearl today. She was a unique woman who created her pioneering world for herself, a rare example among our town's young women. Her life in distant Eretz Israel brought honor and glory to our town. Her death severed the formation of a unique character.

May her name be preserved as the first complete and impeccable pioneer.

[Page 256]

The Late Zvi Rabin
(1913 – 1946)

by H.M. Ran

Translated by Moshe Kutten

Edited by Karen Leon

Zvi was one of the first halutzim [pioneers] of Lanovits. A deterrent hiatus in the Aliya progress transpired four years after our first pioneers, Israel Glazer, D. Gurewitch, and others, made Aliya. The news from Eretz Israel was depressing. The "Hekhalutz" branch underwent a state of stagnation, and cynicism raised its ugly head in town. Just then, Zvi, the youngest and the least active in the group, went out to a Hakhshara and then made Aliya.

Zvi came to Lanovits from Teofipol as an orphan whose parents were murdered there in what is known as Tchan Pogroms [Tchan was the town's name before the Bolsheviks changed it to Teofipol]. He was depressed and distanced himself from friends. He found a warm home with his uncle Shalom Weisman, a dear man, and began to recover. Not long after, he became a good friend to everybody, smiley and joyful. However, people felt that something was brewing in him. There were evenings when he disappeared and recused himself. Nobody knew his secret until he surprised everybody with his decision to go to the Hakhshara and to make Aliya. At the Hakhshara he endeared himself to everybody. He excelled in his ability to work hard and in his courage.

When Zvi arrived in Eretz Israel he tried living in Tel Aviv. There he became involved in the "Haganah's" activities. However, when he could not find work in Tel Aviv, he went south to Ba'yit VeGan, known today as Bat Yam. The place was desolate. The number of houses and Jews was small, and defense and security were most problematic there. [The Arab city of] Jaffa was located between Tel Aviv and Ba'yit VeGan. The trip from Tel Aviv to Ba'yit VeGan was dangerous on calm days and impossible on days of tension between us and our neighbors.

In Ba'yit VeGan, Zvi Rabin became known as a local. He worked, defended, and encouraged. Zvi did not let up on his efforts to attract settlers to the place. When a petition had to be brought to the governor, Zvi was chosen to talk to him to soften his anti-Israeli rigidity and motivate him to assist people in their lesser underground style of self-defense. He made the right impression on the governor with his smile, charm, and courage, and the governor relented.

Zvi left the police force in 1944 and planned to build his home and raise a family. He conceived of that dream at the peak of his power and vigor. However, in 1946 he underwent light surgery and died.

In his death, he left a dedicated wife and two little daughters. His wife, Dina, devoted her life to raising their daughters, and marrying them, carrying Zvi's memory in her heart.

May his memory be blessed.

[Page 257]

The Late Shoshana (Rozhya) Stein-Kwaitel

by B. Y. Haran

Translated by Moshe Kutten

Edited by Karen Leon

Shoshana came to us from Rivne [Rovno]. She was a lonely girl, orphaned from her father, murdered in the Ukrainian pogrom in Rivne, and deserted by her mother, who could not free herself from the widowhood depression. Her aunt, the good-hearted Elka Wolf-Koifsitz, who lost all of her sons, adopted her. Shoshana settled in Lanovits and interspersed in the life of the children and the youth like one of us.

Rozhya was gifted with charm, affability, and love of people. Her tragic childhood left its mark on her soul for the better. Her gentle face radiated understanding to every person and a desire to help.

We waited for her, every evening, to spread her calm among the querulous, straighten up arguments, and cast off from her forgiving spirit on those present. We loved Rozhya, her charm and understanding of human relations, and the seriousness of her destiny.

The Zionist Youth in Lanovits, 5692 [1931/2]
Standing third from the right - Rozhya Stein

In Eretz Israel, she integrated into the life of work and conquest, despite her health-related restrictions. She was happy with her husband and daughter and proud of the accomplishments of the "state in the making". A graceful smile never left her face.

In Eretz Israel, she was absolved of the blows in her life. She married, gave birth, and dreamt about family life without orphanhood or widowhood.

However, a light surgery put an end to her life. She died young and brought both widowhood and orphanhood to her family.

The funeral arranged for her by her town, Bat Yam, can testify to how much Shoshana was loved there. It is a pity that our comrade and others died in the spring of their life.

[Page 258]

Fotsi - Yizhak Gluzstein

by Moni

Translated by Moshe Kutten

Edited by Karen Leon

I came to know Yizhak in Lanovits by chance. He was seen walking around in the company of the young professional men in town. These young men were not from among our members. When we began to inquire about him, we found out that his father, a carpenter artisan from Matviivtsi, came to work with Azriel Rabin on constructing the new mill on the Zherd River, work that was scheduled to last months. The flame carpenter whose work "burnt under his hands" brought his son to Lanovits. His son wanted to stay in the town. He would remain in town during the Shabbats and make connections with his peers. He was attracted to little *Yiddiskeit*, not in a traditional moral sense but in a personal social sense. In other words, he was yearning less for *Yiddiskeit* itself than *Yiden*.

That was how we learned about that dark-looking youth who joined the landscape of Lanovits's youngsters in the alleys of a town, which was one colossal ally itself.

At one point, he stumbled alone into the "Hehalutz" without his companions. He carried with him a secret. It turned out that that self-conscious youth, who pulled his father away from his village and forced him to reside among Jews, was looking for a solution, not only for himself and his family from Matviivtsi but a solution that would be the answer to the entire Jewish question.

He elevated his image at the Hakhshara. His goal was Eretz Israel. However, his main objective was to establish a state based on labor, which meets the requirements of the working man. His dress style in town between the completion of the Hakhshara and his Aliya was nihilistic - an embroidered black shirt, puffed girdle belt on his waist, and black curly forelock on his forehead projecting an "I do not care about Lanovits" attitude. In his move from the village to the city, he left Lanovits far behind him.

So that was how he arrived in Eretz Israel - with a leftist-proletarian charge, and that was how I found him in 1945, in the "Argaman" hall during a general gathering where I appeared on behalf of the "Histadrut" [Israel's General Organization of Workers], held for the benefit of Berl Katznelson's fund. Later on, his views became more moderate. He accumulated some wealth. From a worker with extreme proletarian views, he became a profit-pursuing employer, and his life began to settle.

His satisfaction with his life was apparent in everything he did. He calmed down, called his acquaintances, mainly Lanovits's people, and participated in our memorial evenings, where he came accompanied by a small group. He hurried to help any Lanovits's native when needed. He was Lanovits's person with every inch of his body.

One morning we suddenly heard that he was gone. We could not believe it.

He was too young in his death. May his memory be blessed.

[Page 259]

The Late Avraham Roichman

by Ya'acov Walaizi

Translated by Moshe Kutten

Edited by Karen Leon

Avraham was born in 1914, the oldest to his parents, the late Zvi and Feiga.

He was recognized as talented from his childhood. He was dedicated and well-liked. While studying at the Yeshiva, he endeared himself to his rabbi R' Motil Speizman, who appreciated him as a boy who was respectful to adults. His rabbi also appreciated his infinite patience with his rivals and opponents among his peers.

During his studies, he was swept into the search for a solution for the Jewish youth. Upon finding that there was no salvation except for the individual youngsters taking on themselves the burden of the period, he rose and went to a *Hakhshara* to fulfill what he saw as the appropriate solution for his generation.

He was 17 when he went to the *Hakhshara* in Stanisławów and 24 when he boarded a rickety cargo ship to make *Aliya*. The seven years he spent in the *Hakhshara*, in Terniv [Ternov] and Chenstokhov, forged the attributes of patience and will of iron in him. The two characteristics combined to form far-sighted life wisdom. Lacking these attributes, who knows whether Avraham would have been able to withstand the tribulations of the *Hakhshara* and the disdained deceits of the British rejections of his *Aliya*.

In 1939, he sailed on the dangerous "nutshell" of a ship, ready in his heart for the biggest event of his life, which had a double meaning: Unification with his family after long years of detachment and loneliness and the fulfillment of his dream of reaching the homeland.

The trip was long. The ship was tossed around by malicious sea waves for 6 months, carried away by tidal surges, and slipping away from the prying eyes of the British Empire. In the end, when the ship reached the vicinity of the homeland's shores, it was wrecked, and its passengers were abandoned to the mercy of an angry sea. A miracle happened, and a cattle-carrying ship collected them all and brought them to the shore near Kfar Vitkin.

[Page 260]

In the Kfar [village], the members-residents took the rescued passengers to their homes. Avraham happened to be taken to the home of Mikhel Goldenberg from Bilozerka. Mikhel told him that his arrival was also the day of his father's funeral. Avraham hurried up to accompany his dear father on his last journey. Despite his haste, he arrived late at his father's home when the entire family was returning from the cemetery.

That day was etched in his heart in all of its sorrow. Joy never returned to his home, and he never smiled again. Avraham remained subdued and gloomy beyond his age for the rest of his life.

As the oldest son, he immersed himself in the family business and showed exceptional business acumen. Due to his good nature and earnestness he acquired many friends from among the merchants, who trusted his words. His business relations widened and spread over the entire hometown region.

It looked for a while that his heart calmed down and that his usefulness to his family brought him comfort. With a little more time, he would have begun to smile at his beloved mother and his loving brothers. However, his young life was cut short while he was still in his prime, and Avraham went down to his grave along with his grief.

He was killed in an accident on 26 of Adar II, 5705 [11 March 1945], opposite Ramat Gan's police building, two weeks before his planned marriage.

May his soul be bound to the bundle of life.

[Page 261]

The Late Y. Zingel

by Y. Glazer

Translated by Moshe Kutten

Edited by Karen Leon

Yizhak was born in Radzilov and came to Lanovits in 1918. His arrival brought a change to our group. He was full of life and vigor and thus different from other youths. He found something to do with every issue. We were depressed as we lacked prospects and opportunities, and we welcomed his appearance in town as an injection of new life.

Despite growing up while supporting his ailing mother, Yizhak did not possess the dreary seriousness typical of people busy making a living. He was always joyful, mischievous, and frivolous. However, his frivolousness was imbued by thoughtful reasoning and good judgment.

When Yizhak grew up he immersed himself in public service and Zionism. He began to somewhat neglect the support of his mother. His mother complained, but Yizhak, who loved her immensely, could not overcome his urge. He was attracted by the public service engagement despite his mother's pleas, complaints, and suffering.

He established our town's magnificent library, which acquired a name for itself over the entire district as a library rich in books and bustling with readers and book exchanges.

When the library was consolidated, he handed it over to others, and he concentrated on strengthening the national funds and heightening the Zionist publicity activity.

Yizhak was 20 when I, and several other members, established the "Hehalutz" branch. We were only 18 at the time and unknown. We treated him as the "Boss" of the Zionist influence in town, who could assist us in securing resources and people. Yizhak harnessed himself to our endeavor, and it did not take long before he devoted all of his energy to the "Hehalutz's" activity. We elected him immediately as the chairman of the branch. As a result, youths from classes we did expect to penetrate began to flock in. His image was divine in our town.

[Page 262]

When I made *Aliya*, our ways separated. The military arrested him in Warsaw. He was considered a deserter and was sentenced to jail time.

Years later, we met again in the organization for Lanovits natives. The people elevated him to the position at the head of the organization, just like in the past. Every year, he imparted his seriousness over our memorial and communion with our beloved town and its martyrs. His image was linked to us in the same way our pleasant past of our childhood town, Lanovits, linked to our hearts. His place [in our hearts] was always preserved. We knew that his heart disease drained him and limited his blessed activity. We tried to help him by ensuring he would not overwork at the memorial evenings. In the end, his disease overpowered him.

With his passing, we lost an able and accomplished figure. We lost a dear member of our organization.

We will remember him forever.

The library established by Yizhak

[Page 263]

The Late Yizhak Kirshon

by Y. Glazer

Translated by Moshe Kutten

Edited by Karen Leon

He was a single child of his parents and the pride of his family. He was always taken care of, but when the family lost its wealth, he began to work to make a living. When he reached enlistment age, he became the "breadwinner" for his family. Despite that, he decided his future was in Israel and made an *Aliya*.

It was 1925. Eretz Israel suffered from unemployment at that time, and the workers were subjected to the turbulence of having to jump from one job to another and from one place to another. Yizhak experienced all of that. He worked at the orchard, in construction, and as a porter at the train station. He suffered from unemployment between jobs, but he never complained.

In 1929 he was forced to leave Israel because he was besieged by pneumonia and malaria. He returned to our town for a period, and nobody knew how long it would last. Magically, Yizhak, who lost so much in Eretz Israel - reaching a desperate physical condition and experiencing a hopeless situation, did not complain, nor did he spread contempt and embarrassment. He stayed in our town like a guest without anchoring himself again in damned Poland. He dedicated his free time to Zionist activity and deepening awareness of Hebraic culture and pioneering values.

His stay in Lanovits was one of the most glorious in his life. We observed Yizhak Kirshon in that period demonstrating his full pioneering consciousness and personal honesty. He was active and talked about Eretz Israel, the moon-full evenings, and the barn. He spoke about the concealed light in suffering together, the *Horah* [?] [dance], and the romantic-heroic atmosphere. He enthused the youth to make *Aliya* and achieve fulfillment.

When his recovery commenced and his disease subsided, he did not hesitate for even a minute. He returned to Eretz Israel, back to a foggy personal future, the chances of unemployment, hard labor, and an unknown political future.

[Page 264]

Upon returning to Eretz Israel, Yizhak Kirshon began to build stability in his life. He established a family and settled in a job that suited his skill. However, he did not seclude himself in his own private life. He integrated himself fully into public service and carried loads of the "country in the making" - including participation in the "Haganah's" activities at night, assisting in enabling "illegal immigration", and involving in guarding duties.

He was a respected member of our organization and cherished the memorial for our martyrs.

He came to the last memorial directly from the sanatorium in Nazareth. As it turned out, he participated with the last of his strength. He died a few days after the annual memorial to Lanovits's martyrs.

We will remember him as a good member of our organization, a loyal friend, and a man who contributed to strengthening the pioneering awareness in our town.

[Page 265]

The Late Hava (Mirochnik) Teichman
(Born – 1901, Died 19 Tishrei 5725 [25 September 1964])

by R. Hadar

Translated by Moshe Kutten

Edited by Karen Leon

The late Hava lived through poverty and distress at her parents' home in Lanovits. Her home experienced the twists and turns of the generation's fate of the Gentiles' wars and pogroms against the Jews. As the eldest daughter, she stood out as a girl who carried the burden of livelihood for the family and as the caregiver for her parents.

She married at 18 and moved to live with her husband R' Avraham Teichman (may he live long), in the village of Vinnytsi.

She carried the load of providing for her family, standing alongside her husband at his small store and servicing customers while, at the same time, keeping the house in order, taking care of her children, and keeping the Jewish tradition as her family's way of life.

She would wake up early to bake cakes and other types of pastry for the gentiles' weddings, thus earning extra money for her household and help in raising her seven children.

The Teichmans immigrated to Argentina in 1935 under the auspice of J.C.A.'s [Baron Hirsch's Jewish Colonization Association]. She settled with her husband and children in an agricultural settlement where she quickly became a dedicated farmer. She worked the fields alongside her husband from sunrise to sunset for many days. As her health became frail due to surgeries she had to undergo, she developed that inner heroism - concealing her pains and physical suffering so as not to depress the spirit of her family and not to exhaust their staying power in the face of the physical and economic difficulties they endured.

Even in Israel, after she made *Aliya* and it was known that she suffered from pain and illness, she retained her kind and joyous face and always accepted everything willingly and lovingly.

[Page 266]

Her love was the most blessed of her attributes. She loved her husband, children, and the people around her. However, she bestowed her greatest love upon the homeland and its people.

She was religious to the point of zealotry but loved all Israeli people, and everyone was dear to her heart.

She integrated into the life of the country and the state wholeheartedly, began to listen and understand Hebrew, and even started to read its newspapers and literature.

She was reticent, smiley, and introverted. In her heart, she was open to what was happening to the nation and its people. She was willing to do anything to assist her country and needy individuals.

During her last two and a half years, she could no longer hide that a malignant disease was rolling through her body. Her immense pains burst forth, and she girded all her inner strengths to conceal the suffering from her beloved husband and those around her.

No one was aware that during her last days she experienced progressive blindness. Her appearance was always dignified, thoughtful, and quiet.

Death ended her life but did not overpower her. Her vitality did not cease until her last day.

Hava, a pure and proud daughter of Israel. May your memory be blessed.

[Page 267]

Hayya Fuchs

Translated by Moshe Kutten

Edited by Karen Leon

Hayya was born in [the nearby village of] Vizeshrodok in 1894, and at the age of 20, she moved to live with her husband in Krements. When things calmed down after the First World War, both moved to Matviivtsi, where her husband found a job as a carpenter.

In that village she worried about her children's education. She watched them playing with the Gentiles' children, concerned that their Jewishness would be impaired, so they moved to reside in Lanovits on the first opportunity.

Hayya was 42 years old in 1936, her husband was even older, and they were already considered to be at an advanced age. They made *Aliya* to Eretz Israel – the land of labor and respect for working people.

In Israel, she experienced suffering and financial ups and downs. However, toward the end of her life, she derived pleasure from her children and grandchildren. Her husband, a good-tempered man, saw happiness from the fruit of his labor, and this added to her satisfying feeling.

She died from old age in 1964, at the age of 70.

[Page 268]

The Late Hayya Feiga Fleishman

by Ya'acov Fialkow

Translated by Moshe Kutten

Edited by Karen Leon

Hayya Feiga returned her pure soul to her creator on the Holy Shabbat Shemot, 21 Tevet 5729 [11 January 1969].

She was born in Lanovits 74 years before to her father, the wise rabbi R' Aharon Yehuda, son of the late Rabbi Shneur Zalman Zingel, a descendant of "Baal Hatanya" [Rabbi Shneur Zalman of Liadi], a holy Tzadik [righteous] of blessed memory.

Her mother was Yente Mindel, the daughter of Rabbi Mikhel Halperin Tzadik of blessed memory, a descendant of the holy Maggid from Zloczow [Rabbi Yekhiel Mikhel], a holy Tzadik of blessed memory.

From her youth, anybody who came to know her knew he was standing before a noble figure with a pure soul, distinguished attributes, modesty, humility, and patience.

Hayya also possessed an enormous will to overcome life's obstacles through her Jewishness. The "daughter of a scholar" in her and the nursing from the roots of Hassidism were apparent in her thinking and her demeanor. She found her expression of quiet and modest deeds in public service. She never aspired to do too much at once. Hayya was satisfied with doing a little at the time. For her, every individual was the whole world, and she was happy when she could ease the suffering of one person, adopting and encouraging him.

Following the passing of her late father, she gave up on her young life and dedicated herself to helping her family. After a while, when she married and changed her name from Zingel to Fleishman, many remembered her former name, Yente Mikhel'es. She brought her good-hearted nature, manners, attributes, and graceful behavior toward others to her husband, R' Zekharia Fleishman's home, may he live long. When her mother passed away, they left Lanovits for Pinsk, where her husband served as a mohel and a Kosher slaughterer-inspector. Only a few months passed for her to make a name for herself as hospitable and charitable.

It did not last long for a wave of decrees and anguish of mind and body arrived and began

[Page 269]

to flood the Jewish diaspora. A decision ripened in Hayya's mind that they should make *Aliya*, and the Fleishman family made *Aliya* to the holy land.

She accepted the acclimatization pangs with love. During the first few months, when the family experienced hunger, bitterness filled her husband's heart, and hopelessness due to the lack of work penetrated and took hold, she would wipe the sadness from her husband's face and say: "We should not be grieving. Remember that, with G-d's help, we are in the holy land, and our blessed G-d will help us."

And G-d did help. Her husband accepted a position as a Kosher slaughterer inspector. Hayya opened her exemplary home in Tel Aviv. Family members, friends, and immigrants flocked to the house, along with her husband's friends who needed help, encouragement, and advice. She continued with her charitable deeds as long as she was able to and was interested in what was happening even after she became ill. She had a strong will to live, and by using it, she overcame her illness. She always tried to be involved in all the affairs of her family.

When I raise her image in front of me, the image, whose soul radiates through her beautiful eyes and her magical smile that even life's turbulences could not wipe away from her lips – I ask myself what was the source of her enormous power. The answer can be found in Isaiah's verse [Isaiah 40:31]: "…But they who trust in G-d shall renew their strength. As eagles grow new plumes. They shall run and not grow weary. They shall march and not grow faint". She was made of that precious substance since she trusted G-d and believed that only good comes from the heavens. Her innocent faith was the wellspring that flew in her endlessly. Therefore, she saw life through her shiny eyes.

May her soul be bound in the bundle of life.

[Page 270]

Rav Glazer

Translated by Moshe Kutten

Edited by Karen Leon

While preparing this book, Rabbi Glazer, a warm-hearted man, humble, modest, and G-d fearing, left us.

Rabbi Glazer was a rabbi who handled only affairs associated directly with his role. He, who knew the period of Rabbi Kook and had the chance to enjoy the poetry of Bialik, pinned the hope of Israel's independence on the working people. Rabbi Glazer wished that working people would improve their religious ways of life, but respected them and accompanied them with his spiritual blessing because he considered them the nation's soul. When he heard about the establishment of the Lanovits natives organization, he asked to allow him to participate in the memorial evenings for our martyrs, despite being a native of Tchan [Teofipol] and resident of Odessa, spending only a short period in Lanovits.

We considered it an enormous privilege, so we complied with his request. Since then, Rabbi Glazer has participated in every memorial service. He struggled to come even when his health became frail, and we would bring him back home.

To dispel every thought and remove every suspicion, we declare here that he did not request nor receive any compensation for his participation. He did not want his fulfillment of the Mitzvah of participation to harm any intention not associated with the memorial for the holy martyrs and praying for their souls.

I once visited him in his meager hut, where the wind howled through the cracks. Rabbi Glazer was sitting there, curled up with a blanket, and studied the daily portion with his younger son, also a rabbi. When I entered, he stopped his study and explained to his son that he was allowed to do that for Lanovits. When I asked him how he intended to improve his living conditions, he whispered his answer, accompanied by segments of loud laughter:

"In Odessa, I had a "*Bankeh*" (A heating pot made of casted iron). We used to put coals in it, and their whispering glowing warmed our cold house. I used it here for the first few years because I did not have a heater. Over time, the pot got damaged. It also became difficult to get coals. So what? Can't a person live without it or study?"

Rabbi Glazer, a member of our organization, was a Tzadik, honest, and modest.

May his image remain in front of us in all our memorial services.

[Page 271]

Yizhak Shemesh

by Ch. Rabin

Translated by Moshe Kutten

Edited by Karen Leon

Itzikle Shamoish's family was the poorest of the poor. His gracious father worried every day of every year. He worked and toiled in a profession allowed by his ancestry, that of a poor father and an impoverished grandfather. What can he do with an occupation that does not provide a sufficient living? The father suffers, and the mother is distressed.

In the meantime, class disparities break down in school. Children from all layers mingle at the Polish and Jewish schools and the Kherder, even as poverty expanded. Itzikle can compare himself to others during the school breaks when one child meets the other, each holding his lunch. Itzikle shows up in his greatness with a smile he was born with adorning his face. That smile serves as a shield against resentment in his world. Itzikle does not encounter resentment at home, on the street, in Kheder, or among his friends. He smiles, lowers his stature to fend against the blows of fate, and tilts his head sideway somewhat as if avoiding a hit. He makes up his mind to survive now, at this moment. There is no sense in worrying about things to come. "When I have a smile – I have everything, and I feel good now."

Itzikle is walking around among his happier friends, owning his happiness. He is not hurt by their envy and does not envy others. Izikle Shamoish weaves the secret of his life and the solution for his future alone. He knits them within himself and in his soul, the source of his redemption. And if his soul is smiling, so too would his fate.

That's how Itzikle arrived at the *Aliya*, fulfillment, and kibbutz. The latter was a way of life that loaded the nation's fate on its shoulders and won.

He fulfilled his dream.

Every day in his life is a step up the ladder of human spiritual elevation, and new steps are born daily. During the Hassidic period, his ascent would have bought a name for himself.

[Page 272]

Yitzkhak in the *Hakhshara* in Lanovits – second from the left

Only a few reach his level, modest, happy, rejoicing in his portion, and frugal.

When I saw Itzikle at his daughter's wedding in his kibbutz - his home, I saw him in all his glory. He stood like a person on the sideline as if he was happy to see other people being happy and enjoyed seeing other people having fun. Only a few among us elevated themselves from being a shoemaker in Lanovits to the superior standing of someone who fulfilled the pioneering dream. He was a man of perfection and forgiveness for his fate and the people who insulted him. He also forgave those lowly people who pretended to be his relatives.

With his death, a radiant, complete, and loyal figure left us. He was uprooted from us! We will adorn him on the pages of the book of Lanovits. We will remember him with love because he was himself a grace of love.

It was an honor for us for people like him to rise among us.

May his memory be blessed!

[Page 277]

Chapter 8:

Lanovits, History, People & Memories

[Page 278] [Blank] [Page 279]

Lanovits History and Memories
Lanovits, according to its historical sources and according to the "Lanovits Book"
(Historical survey)

By Ch. Rabin

Translated by Pamela Russ

Opening words:

As we see from the bibliography (that unfortunately exists in Hebrew only), the Polish king "Kazimierz Jagiellonczyk" gave Lanovits as a gift to prince Peshkov Wolowicki in the year 1444 for his patriotic service, and in "1583, Sava Yalowitcki increased the kingdom's taxes to fifteen orchards, fifteen --- [chimneys? not sure of this word], and two flour mills." "From the beginning of the 15th century Lanovits was famous with its large fortress-palace, whose description can be found in the Polish national archives."

In other words, as we see, Lanovits existed even before the Sephardi expulsion and the difference between the historical wells of information and the legends and the stories are too great, so we will not relate according to the "wells," but we will deal with it according to the encyclopedic sources, even though they are factually poor.

The Beginnings of the Jewish Lanovits

In the various encyclopedias, Lanovits is already described at the beginning of the 15th century as a "Jewish town," as a place of production, which was endowed with national heroes for their actions, and [was also known] as a stronghold city.

The orchard keepers and the --- [? repeated unknown word] flour mills indicate that it was already a town that buzzed with Jewish initiative, and was

[Page 280]

industrialized, something that was done in the entire Poland and Ukraine by the Jews from the beginning of the 10th century (see Dr. Y. Shipper, Story of the Jewish Economy, volume 2, page 532).

The "Geography Dictionary" of 1902, that is a pure Catholic organization and its tendencies lean to – Polish chauvinism, steadfastly states that Savo Yalowicki brought in a lot of money to the king, etc., and whoever knows the history of the Jews in Poland (Professor M. Balaban, and Mag. Y.Z. Trunk) knows that 15 chimneys means 15 factories, and according to those times – that was a huge industry, and industry means Jewish strong dependency in that place.

You can comfortably assume that in Lanovits, the Nazi vandals destroyed five to six hundred years of human creation, and for the Jews, a community of many hundreds of years old – a community that is already described in the "*Pinkus* of Four Countries," as a lively, Jewish administration fact.

Jewish Stability in Lanovits

Ukraine is famous as the least stable place in the entire Russo-Poland, the history of the Ukrainians is a history of enslaved masses whose dreams of national independence was always bathed in Jewish blood and Jewish possessions, until it became almost a fact that when there was talk of a Ukrainian uprising, there was also talk of Jewish pogroms. So, there is the question: Why did Chmielnicki's uprising in 1648, which is the only documented uprising, not shake up Lanovits, and it remained untouched, although we know that the main acts of that thug were concentrated around Lanovits and its surroundings. The villages Novodowka, Kozacek, Totorinec, Matowiewic (with Chmienicki's help, by the name of Matwei), were all marked by Senkewicz as centers of Ukrainian activity against Wiszniewski. Then why does history tell of Wisznewiec, Kremnic, Dubno, and Wiszogradek, that they were ruined, emptied, destroyed at the same time, and so on, by the Tatar Ukrainians, and so on, and not Lanovits?

The only answer is that Lanovits belonged to the Russian prince Yalowicki, and the Jews there benefitted from their situation as Russian subjects, not like the above-mentioned cities over which Polish earls ruled, and essentially identified with the objectives of the Ukrainian main enemy.

The family Yalowicki is the "black sheep" of the Russian monarchy family history, known for its liberal leanings which

[Page 281]

always looked for the nonconformity in Russian absolutism, loved all people, and … even supported the Kosciuszko uprising in 1863. The Yalowickis were the only enlightened ones, and it is almost clear that Lanovits was externally politically stable, and did not suffer from the Tatar Ukrainian uprisings which from time to time tore apart all the neighboring towns.

Internally, Lanovits, historically, was a stable community without harsh community disputes, rabbinic arguments, or criminal acts. The *Pinkus* [book of records] of the committee of four countries that envelops the era of the beginning of Lanovits, is also a *Pinkus* of Jewish justice – a society, or a judicial body, and according to royal decrees, it was the only institution that judged Jews and outlined the laws, and in that *Pinkus*, Lanovits was not brought even once to any legal court, even though it was always mentioned as a community (see *Pinkus*, section 1, Hilpern, page 530), it seems that Lanovits, as in our times, even then was a place that existed in an atmosphere of security of mind and livelihood concerns, and did not search for social outlooks in far out issues, which were the main goals of other cities (such as Shabtai Zvi discussions, Reb Jonathan Eybeschutz, and Yaakov Emden, and later *chassidic* themes, etc.).

It is written up as a stable Jewish settlement, without any spiritual areas and internal disputes, and without any external political-physical enhancement, until our century.

The century brought along all kinds of catastrophes, and Lanovits strongly felt all the political aftereffects. That's how it was after the czarist failure of 1905, when the Russian government wanted to refute the hatred of the masses towards the Jews and looked for traitors and Jewish deserters. Also, in Lanovits there were small pogroms of the "burghers" and larger pogroms, looting, and murder attempts of the Petlura camp of thugs. But at this point, Lanovits was already no exception, so we will not stop here, you can read about this in the martyr literature of the Ukrainian Jews.

Lanovits According to the Book of Lanovits

This is the last *Pinkus* book of the tragically destroyed Lanovits community, the only source of information about the town, and the editor did everything so that the material that was entered into the book should withstand the proof of fact and reality, so that the "Lanovits Book"

[Page 282]

would be the only historical source for Lanovits in its final period and final days.

According to the book, in the mid-20th century Lanovits was a city with a Jewish life pulse. The youth made its decision for the future and emigrated. The factor for this was specifically the Poles who conducted ruses among the Jews and Ukrainians as they [the Poles] took positions of power and pressured the Jews as they [the Poles] were the rulers in that part of Ukraine. Also, the Ukrainians helped in the immigration mood. Since they were hot, primitive, blood-thirsty people, they were always ready to incite a pogrom, looting, and killing. But in general, the Jews remained loyal to their stance, and remained in Lanovits with their philosophy: Everything disappeared in Lanovits, but remains in Lanovits.

Until the 1920s, the youth in Lanovits did not immigrate to Israel. At that time, Lanovits was dreaming about its *chassidic*, messianic illusions. You could go anywhere except for Israel. And at the same time, earning a living went on. Lanovits, that was deep in an area of many Ukrainian lively villages and Polish magnates, who drank and played away their property through prostitution and empty Polish pride, Lanovits benefitted from economic improvement, and a certain type of attitude was acquired that one had to "thank God that one is alive, one has livelihood, and there is nothing else for us to think about."

In the middle of these years, as they yeshiva of Reb Mottel Shpizman was put up, he was the beloved pedagogue and beloved scholar, the youth began to study in all three institutions – in Tarbut, Polish school, and in yeshiva, and it was here [in the yeshiva] that a strange thing happened. A group of passionate youth from Lanovits, the only ones who went to yeshiva, concluded that this was not an opening for the youth, it was not a well of studies, and it was not persuasive for beliefs, and the Talmud concretized the youth's negativity and raised the idea of immigration to Israel.

At that time, the first group of Lanovits *chalutzim* [immigrant pioneers] was organized (Y. Glakser, Y. Kirshon, D. Gurwitz, and M. Rosental), and also a hunched over shoemaker, who never had a place among those who knew him, he also went to Israel, an older unmarried girl who was loved in town, takes her leave saying Israel is a new world for those who want to start life anew, and Israel suddenly became the place that addresses general political Jewish questions as well as private problems.

The youth were active, and organized themselves with the drive for *Aliyah* during the time that their parents remained sunk in their day in and day out lives.

[Page 283]

Unfortunately, crazy fate hit Lanovits when the majority of the youth's yearning for *Aliyah* came to Lanovits, but there were no certificates and their dear parents waited for the Messiah, and were a helpless mass as sheep to the slaughter.

Lanovits was a city of learned and smart Jews, but sadly its learnings chased it from the dark realities and brought it into an inflated condition of waiting for miracles, and that miracle never happened.

Lanovits Culture and Yearning

[Page 284]

Unforgettable
or
Lanovits, a Spiritual Concept

By Yosef Warach (New York)

Translated by Pamela Russ

Lanovits had a spiritual quality fluttering in all its corners. They measured the town according to the holy entities.

There were: a scholarly rabbinic leader, two ritual slaughterers, Yoel and Yitzhok, and an immediate mention of places of prayer, the *kloizel* [small, informal place of prayer], a *kloiz*, a shul, a *Beis Midrash* and a small shul. Each shul had a *chazan* [leader in prayer], especially for the high holidays and for holy, festive holidays. And who of the congregants was not capable of leading the congregation in their prayer!

The congregants were proud of the fact that their main *chazan* was a religious person, a good scribe, well versed in writing Torah scrolls and *tefillin* [phylacteries], and immersed himself in the *mikva* [ritual bath] each time before writing out the name of God.

The High Holidays in the shuls were a busy time. It was a time of holy tremors, when each Jew reviewed his behavior towards his fellow man; it was time for inner reflection between man and man.

Immediately after Yom Kippur, they began to build a Succah, providing recollections about where the Jews came from. A long history: Egypt, the journey in the desert, becoming an independent nation through sacrifices,

[Page 285]

living in huts (*succos*) despite the inconvenience. It was a deep concept, that the Lanovits Jew had a source; that things did not actually begin in a small shop with a livelihood. And not to forget being a people with a Torah that looked down from the mountaintop of Sinai until today, and commands you: "Behave better than other nations such as the non-Jews." Everyone was celebrating with the Torah, that is Simchas Torah. It was almost even a greater joy than finding a marriage partner or earning a fine living. Everyone was eager to carry one of the heavy Torah scrolls, as they headed towards the *hakofos* [dancing with the Torah], dancing around and around with richness. The air was thick with joy. This was from the times that they still spoke Hebrew in the Holy Temple, when Torah was the flag whose fluttering was the power that accompanied the Jews in times of war.

The same can be said for days of mourning – a spiritually Hebrew Tisha b'Av [9th of Av]. The synagogue was illuminated with lanterns, the souls were dark. The world was going down. A small detail – there was once a Holy Temple, it was destroyed. So, how can you be calm, how can our hearts be quiet? There was a sadness, overall, prominent Jews, business people, suddenly left everything behind, removed their shoes, turned the benches upside down [not being permitted to sit on chairs comfortably on Tisha b'Av], and sat on the floor and cried while reading *Eicha* [Lamentations]. It was a spiritual cry. Only people who are so deeply spiritual can cry over what happened in the past.

One sensed the spiritual atmosphere of the town throughout the year, during freezing days and on Shabbaths.

It was a town that had its own rabbi, Reb Aharon Rabin, with his own little shul. The congregants sought his company, were eager to hear his sermons, and sat at his table, not for the sake of the served food, but mainly to hear his Torah commentaries. The Sabbath singing was important, removing you from the materialism and enabling you to feel closer to heaven. There was a *shalosh seudos* [third festive meal of

Shabbath], a *melave malka* [festive meal "escorting" the end of Shabbath], or a *yahrzeit* [memorial celebration] of a spiritual leader.

Periodically, other rabbis came to visit our town to spread the learning of Jewishness, chassidus, celebrate festive meals, spread Torah scholarship, deep songs, and awaken the spirit of the soul.

I remember in particular, the rabbis: from Trisk, Ustrog, Vizhnitz (he was called the Vizhnitzer Rav), and Shumsk, and other rebbes whom I do not remember who came to Lanovits periodically. My father was not satisfied celebrating a Shabbath only with one of the above-mentioned living rabbis. He celebrated the memorial *yahrzeit* of the Ruzhiner rebbe, the Chortkower rebbe, Usyatiner rebbe, and the Berdichever rebbe. He meant to commemorate them so as not to forget that they were more important than daily economic efforts. They worked hard for a week, a gray one, one with worries, in order to rise to the most important parts of human life - the Shabbaths and the *yahrzeit*s.

* * *

[Page 286]

Our youth sought alternate spiritual pleasures. They rebelled against the old forms of spirituality and searched for other forms. But their ultimate aim was the same. The question they posed was how best to reach their goal. They established a lending library, and promoted propaganda for literature, secular, technical, and artistic literature. They also established a school where children, whose parents could not afford the tuition, attended classes. They created a *Bikur Cholim* [helping and visiting the sick] society, whose members helped sick people as needed, and remained at people's bedside during a night of fever, until death.

The center point of the youths' activities was to provide help and brotherhood, to enrich a person with loftier feelings than their own egotistical ones, thus enriching the spirit of the person.

Lanovits had a reputation as a center for good deeds. When Yechiel Shamesh rose early in the morning, and went from house to house, knocking on windows, shouting: "It is time to get up for morning worship," his message was symbolic; saying in effect: "You've slept enough; now it's time to get to work. The body has rested, now it is time to nourish the soul, serving the Creator." And worship consisted not only of prayer, but it also encompassed good deeds and charity, all in an effort to do good deeds for the Creator of the World.

If a person did not have money to buy matzos for Passover, we were obligated to provide him with matzos so that he could fulfill the commandment to eat them on Passover. Should a young man be in difficulty, wishing to marry and carry out the deeds that were appropriate for his age, but not having the means, we were obligated to help him get married and provide bridal gifts and gifts for the groom and provide a dowry – then it becomes a couple. Then, a couple who would have little ones would facilitate the growth of the Jewish community.

Inasmuch as Lanovits merited to be a border town, and it had soldiers stationed in its barracks, and there were Jewish soldiers among the non-Jewish ones. It was a great *mitzva* to invite them into Jewish homes for the Sabbath and holidays, to let them enjoy a *kiddush*, a prayer, a blessing on the food - to reduce the frequency of eating non-kosher food and the defilement of the Shabbath and the Jewish holidays.

* * *

From a distance of years and oceans, Lanovits appears as a huge barrel of small, buzzing people, who are busy, buzzing, and do not rest. They are always rushing to do good deeds, help with charity, a Jewish event, a *mitzva*.

[Page 287]

It was a laboratory for spirituality, warmth, and communion among the residents. The Gentile neighbors could not understand this spirit. But how could they understand the taste of the Lanovits spirit?

* * *

It was an unforgettable town.

The more we lived with Gentiles, the more the spirit and pride of Lanovits was raised. It was a kind of mountain peak of highly spiritual people. Today, it is hard to believe that we are no different, thanks to communities like Lanovits, and it is hoped that the Jewish state will be different than other nations thanks to Lanovits.

It is a community that should not be forgotten.

A new generation, new spiritual deeds

[Page 288]

Lanovits - Types and Customs

By Abraham Teichman

Translated by Pamela Russ

It is not easy for me to take my pen and describe my recollections of Lanovits and the dear Jews who are no longer among the living, who left the living world not because of the sin of Adam and Eve, but because of the deeds of animals in human form.

I shall remember forever the various classes of Jews with their good values and their pride, without any sign of arrogance. They were loyal and good to everyone without exception, wherever one met another, just as well in the street as in the *Beis Midrash*, and in contrast, even in the bath house. At a joyous event, their wishes, which came after a few drops of a bitter drink or a piece of homemade cake or pie, came from their purest heart. If, heaven forbid, a person became ill, everyone felt the pain as if the ill person was part of his household. One could see the sorrow on each person's face.

The whole town of Lanovits was like one devoted family. A family's joyous occasion was an occasion for everyone, and heaven forbid, a misfortune was also felt by all, without exception, rich or poor.

The town was slumbering

[Page 289]

I had the opportunity to know many towns around the world. I did not meet Jews who were as warm-hearted, welcoming, even to those whom no one had ever seen nor heard about, and good to one another as to those in Lanovits.

When the Austrian prisoners of war were stationed in Lanovits, the Jews went out to take care of them with all kinds of food. Everyone knew, for instance, that Jews who sold quick lime were not wealthy, yet they hosted five of these POWs. I remember well that a Jew from Buchach, Galicia, with the name of Yidel Geltner, stayed in my home. He wrote to his wife and children how well he was treated. We received a thank you letter from her. We never demanded a payment reward nor any thanks. This hospitality custom was in the blood of every Lanovits Jew.

* * *

Once, on the day before Passover, I went to Yekil Yisrael, son of Wolf, to bake matzos. He had a machine for baking matzos. I don't remember his family name. On that occasion I met a 15-year-old lad, a grandson of Lipeche. I noticed, as he moved, that he was only using one of his hands. The other was wrapped in rags. I asked him what was the matter with his hand. He replied that his hand had broken while he was working picking apples in the orchard of Eli Kuziel. He fell off a tree and broke his hand. I asked" "Did you go see a doctor?" He replied that his hand was looked at by Bakshe, the country doctor. I asked him: "When did this happen?" He replied: "When we were picking apples. So, you know what happens when you pick apples or bake matzos!" I told the story to Yidel Kiskiwitzer, also known as Greenblat, who lost no time looking into this matter because Bashke said that it was necessary to amputate the hand. The case immediately came before Asher Brilant, of blessed memory, and he took the lead to Lemberg to try and save the hand. And if not, at least he would be left with one hand. The injured hand was already black, and the young boy was now in overall danger.

In the end, he was able to go home with both hands intact. When I spoke to him and asked him if his family knew about the matter, he replied that he told no one. He had visited Bashke only once; that Asher Brilant had paid on his own for the treatment in the Lemberg hospital, and had visited him often to track his recovery.

The town of Lanovits had no heroes, but the virtue of kindness and mercy

[Page 290]

could be seen in everyone at all times and in all circumstances.

* * *

Flowers from Polish Ornaments

When Poland, may its name be erased, annexed Lanovits, the local Jews could not benefit in any way from the new regime. The Poles imported with them Jew hatred.

When the first Poles came, with the assistance of French officers, we three,

I, Asher Brilant, and Yisrael Katz, left to the house of Leah Chana Etty, and honored the entering army with bread and salt. I predicted then that we were likely to regret their arrival. To our sorrow, this ended up being the case.

The Polish occupiers of Lanovits very soon displayed their poison. They settled Polish hooligans from the Warsaw area into the entire area, and they were called "*Osadnikes*" [settlers], may their names be erased. One fine day (fine for the newly-arrived Poles, but not for us Jews), three *Osadnikes* stood in the middle of the street. One of them, named Ogurek, may his name be erased, was from Napadowka [NW of Lanovits]. They stood across from Shmuel Moshe Luzer's house. As his son Toleh left the house just at that minute, one of them, apparently Ogurek, called him over and slapped his face, without any reason. The second Pole urged Toleh to hit him back. All of this was just a taunt because everyone knew that we Jews were powerless.

* * *

A few days later, while in my shop, I was visited by Moshe Tepper from Itzkowitz [Juskowcy]. And just standing there, caught up in the busyness of the shop, thinking about the greater situation and the details thereof, Uziel Chaim Mordechai's comes in, also known as Rabin, and he asked me: "Why are you so pensive today? Have your ships sunk?" I replied : "I never thought about being wealthy, I am only thinking about what will be tomorrow. I do not see that our new neighbors that have been transplanted to our region from the Warsaw and Poznan region are likely to improve our lives." He next asked what I had observed to lead me to this opinion. I told him what had happened to Toleh, Moshe Luzer's son, a few days earlier. Uziel proceeded to say: "If only you would have seen what just happened to me." He recounted: He has for a long time, as everyone knew, had business relations with estate owner Ladiniuk, may his name be erased. Recently, he went to see him regarding a business matter, as usual, and there was no shortage there of four-legged dogs, even two-legged ones. One of the dogs ran forward and attacked him. Miraculously, Uziel had a stick which he used to protect himself. When Ladiniuk came out of his house to greet him, he said,

[Page 291]

"You are lucky that I don't have a gun on me, otherwise I would have shot you on the spot for hitting my dog."

It was under such conditions that our Lanovits community lived and hoped with a pure belief in God and in a better future.

* * *

Monish Riba, son of Yosel Moshe, of blessed memory, was a decent young man, good looking, and honest. He ran a small business of buying eggs from farmers in the surrounding area and selling these in Zbarazh. He would return early in the evening, taking a route distant from the Soviet border so as to avoid the danger of being arrested by a Polish border patrol, as was their usual behavior. But this time, one or two young thugs from that same village came out and murdered him. It was not difficult to find out who the murderers were, because the next day a blood-soaked garment was found on one of the murderers. But Jewish blood was expendable, so the local authorities were not interested in indicting the murderer. Instead, they encouraged the Gentile communities to distance themselves even more so from Jews.

* * *

To enter or leave after sundown to or from Shumsk [Szumsk], Kremenec, or Vishnevitz [Wisniewski, Wiszniew] to Lanovits was like an inquisition. It was particularly dangerous in the winter period when, for example, transporting coal to a storage place made of earth, in order to warm the houses. The following happened to Yitzchak Borg's son-in-law Shmuel Karshenboim. He traveled to Shumsk to trade in flour as was his custom. It happened that on the way, his wagon broke down in the middle of a field. Because they could not reach Shumsk in time by nightfall, they decided to stay put in the field until daylight fearing the Polish bullies. The night was freezing and long. Due to this accident and exposure, Yitzchak died several weeks later, long before his time. The village Poles, may their names be cursed, did not hesitate, even on these freezing nights, to snatch up innocent Jews and do some kind of trickery.

* * *

Bentzi Gurewitch, or as we called him, Bentzi Itzik Hirsh, of blessed memory, was engaged to the daughter of Aharon Marczich. As was our custom, the groom went to his bride's house on a Friday night. On Shabbath evening, one can stay a bit longer, so as he left their house at 11 o'clock at night. As he left the house, he was attacked by a group of Poles, may their names be erased, who beat him until he collapsed. Next, they picked him up and placed him on a bench and cut his hair off at the front of his head.

[Page 292]

Afterwards, they smeared the hair with soap and forced him to eat the mixture while fiercely continuing to beat him. When they saw that he was already severely tortured, they led him to the village of Novosilkes. There, on a high hill, which was a gravel pit, from which they used to dig up gravel to repair the roads, they threw him down while he was semi-conscious, quiet as a wall. He remained like that until morning, when he regained consciousness. He would have died there and no one would have known, but luckily a well was nearby which they called Loicziche's well. A Christian woman went to this well to fetch some water and she heard moaning from nearby, and noticed him lying near there. That is how he was saved. This episode did not happen during Hitler's times, but a lot earlier when one still hoped that you could live in peace with the Poles. We thought (mistakenly) that they would get used to living with us and with time, we would learn how to deal with them.

* * *

I once happened to visit my brother-in-law, Moshe Tepper, in his village, Iskevitz. A policeman by the name of Tomzhik positioned himself at Tepper's door and proceeded to address the assembled crowd of Christians. The policeman implored them to stop selling any of their produce to Jews. He added, "Note that the Jew has a big belly. It is due to the butter and chickens you sell him and do not eat yourselves, so the Jew acquires a fat stomach. Afterwards he travels to a spa to reduce his excess weight. To carry out your hard labor you need a pair of boots. So, you go to a Jew and ask him to loan you a few zlotys to buy the boots. He takes three times the amount from you, and you are ignorant of the debt details, and believe his Jewish face." At the same time, he instructs the crowd that there are already Gentile buyers at the train station who will buy their grain, eggs, and poultry. Those Gentiles who persisted to sell their goods to Jewish merchants became afraid to leave their homes at night for fear of a beating. The Poles came to realize that such threats were an effective tool since almost no peasant had indoor bathrooms. Even many Jews did not have such a luxury. As a result of these threats, many Gentiles succumbed to these threats against their own comforts and so had to meet the demands. Selling to a Jewish merchant normally fetched a better price because of the fierce competition amongst Jewish merchants. Jews sharply shaved their profit in order to make a living.

* * *

Opposite our home lived Asher Leib Melamed. His niece and her eight-year-old son lived with them.

[Page 293]

She supported herself by selling kvass [low alcohol drink] and sunflowers on Fridays for the Shabbath. During her free time, she used to drop in to visit us. One night, after we were already asleep, she came to our house with her child. She told us that the aforementioned policeman, Tomzhik was on duty that night. Instead of patrolling the town, he chased her out of her bed and went to sleep there. We stayed awake with her for the rest of the night.

* * *

When the forces of Petlura's army (1917) bombarded Lanovits, most of us fled, just a few stayed behind. My late wife also fled with a child only several weeks old. She did not know where to flee and I did not know where she fled to. I escaped to Lieber, behind the mountain, and hid in a Gentile cemetery. While I was hiding there, a Pole from my town, Woznikevich, approached me. He tried to console me, saying, "Notice what hooligans these Ukrainians are? I don't understand what they have against Jews." I thought then that the Poles were our allies. However, as later events showed, once the Poles were "in the saddle," his son went around town with a whip in hand. Woe to the Jew who came under his hand. He wanted to test his whip, regardless on whom, old or young, small or big.

Once, I, with my brother-in-law, Eli, may his memory be blessed, had to go see him in his courtyard. At the time, Eli had a tile business. He needed a machine with which to mix the lime. In those days, no one walked bareheaded. Eli and I went to this Pole's smith shop, where he worked, located 30 meters down a path with a gate. We entered his property wearing our hats. The fact that we did not remove our hats the Pole found insulting. As a result, he demanded a much higher price for the desired machine than it would have cost in a Kremenitz store. Eli remarked: "That's a lot of money." The Pole replied: "Money is of no consequence for you. If it were not for your wealth, you would have removed your hat at my door and not dared to walk with your head covered until you approached me."

* * *

One day, our district chief of the area, a resident of one of the villages, received a letter from the Warsaw magistrate to arrange a collection for poor Poles, not, heaven forbid, including any Jews. This collection was probably destined to support the very hooligans, the *"piketchikes"* [picketers] who used to stand in front of Jewish stores not allowing entry of any potential customers. The locals that organized the collection were the district chief, the local *Kommandant* [police chief] and the local town physician, a Jew, Dr. Litwak by name. Everyone had to contribute, whether they were able to or not. First, everyone was afraid of the *Kommandant*. We knew from experience that to refuse would risk the anger of the local *Kommandant* who could easily concoct an infraction that would cost us dearly.

[Page 294]

The aforementioned commission addressed our community, and Dr. Litwak explained the purpose of this important meeting. At that time, there were a few *Asadnikes* [Polish settlers], our "new neighbors." One of them rose to complain in a loud voice asking why a Jew was allowed to speak on behalf of "our cause." The district chief replied that he is a respected physician, implying a high local status. To this, the complainer retorted that he prefers to hear Stasik than the doctor.

Do you realize who Stasik was? He was a dirty Polish drunkard who never earned a penny in his life, always begging for bread.

* * *

Avraham Eliezer, Chava's son, also known by the name Graffen, had a brother-in-law named Yaakov *chazan*, who was a very poor man. He barely made a living from selling goods at the weekly fairs, both in the summer heat and winter frost. His livelihood was made from selling odds and ends from manufactured merchandise, and he never had money to buy these goods, so he depended on interest-free loans from such local benefactors as Mordechai Guberman, Kahas Kaufman, Eli Mirochnik, or Zelig Rofeh. One day, the late Hirsh Starosty [district chief], of blessed memory, came to the *chazan's* house warning him to hide his goods for sale at the market because the "Executor" [tax collector] was due to visit soon.

As usual, such a warning, that is for wanting to bring harm to the Polish authorities, is subject to a significant fine. However, his good heart and love for the poor among his brethren did not scare off Hirsh.

The end of this story was that the tax collectors did come, but found nothing except for a small parcel. That same week, as Hazan prepared on the next day to attend the trade fair in Viszgorodek, the tax collector came to him again unannounced and found the parcel of goods. He ordered *chazan* to follow him to the *Gmina* [Town Hall], in order to confiscate his goods. *chazan's* wife, crying, asked the tax collector what he expected her to feed her children with. He replied: "Feed them stones."

When *chazan's* creditors heard about the confiscation, they immediately provided him with funds to buy additional goods. Several other locals contributed funds in addition to the original creditors: Shmuel Poliak, Usher Brilant, Shlomo Kesil, Benzion Wohl, Eliezer Kiwes, and others. We also need to praise the good heart of Hirsh Starosty, also known as Hirsh Meilman, of blessed memory.

Hirsh was afraid that this tax collector, this robber, wanted to repeat the procedure that was done before. He, therefore, spoke to the tax collector and said:

"In my opinion, this man deserves to be free of tax. Come with me and I will show you what his family lives on, what they eat."

[Page 295]

While sitting in the Starosty's house, the tax collector told Hirsh: "You are lucky that your daughter is here today. Otherwise, I would have had you in chains and sent away, and you would have never seen your home or your Jews again." Hirsh Starosty, the son of Leah Hind, as he was called, was a *mentch* [polite person], who never failed to greet another person with a "good morning." He greeted everyone, from young and old, always there first. He shouldered all the town's troubles and helped the locals of the community whenever possible.

One day, Hirsh came with the tax collector to Lipekh's son-in-law at home to collect taxes. The son-in-law made his living collecting old rags with the help of a wagon pulled by two old mares. When Hirsh and the collector entered his home, they saw his wife standing at the *pripitchek* [firewood stove] trying to boil some potatoes. The wood she used refused to ignite because it was wet. Dry wood was expensive, and this wood was the cheapest, and was wet. The wood would not ignite and the potatoes would not boil. The children were crying and wanted to eat. She tried to ignite the wood by persistently blowing on the lit twigs. Even though she was thin and pale, with each puff, her face reddened as the twigs burned.

When the two visitors arrived, she ran over and asked the Starosty what the collector wanted. Hirsh replied that he came to collect taxes. She began to cry, pleading that she does not have enough funds even to feed her children. The collector yelled at her, asking her why she had such healthy-looking red cheeks. "Do you eat everything yourself and give nothing to your children." He added: "I now realize that the state of deficit is primarily due to the fact that Jewesses refuse to pay taxes. Of this, you, Hirsh, are the primary culprit!"

* * *

Mechel Yekil Efroim's, also known as Leider, trained himself as a cobbler. However, he failed to earn a living in his profession. He turned to Bunim Brimmer, of blessed memory, and Bentzi Reichman for help. These two bought him a horse and wagon to use for his livelihood. He was not lazy. He used his wagon under all rainy and muddy weather conditions, and the horse was not very strong. Sometimes, when his horse could not pull the wagon's load, he acted as a "second horse."

One day, he traveled with his wagon to the village of Wolica (southwest of Lanovits). It was a cold, autumn day. His wagon landed in a puddle and got stuck. No one in the village came out to help him. Only a few gathered and helped him scream "whoa!" and nothing more. No one wanted to get their boots wet.

Mechel hit his horse to urge it to attempt another pull-out, and just at that moment, a Polish policeman, who saw him do it, showed up. The policeman slapped his face three times for hurting the horse.

[Page 296]

He could not stand seeing the merciful horse who was being whipped by a Jew. The incident did not end there.

This same policeman reported Mechel to the above-mentioned executor for avoiding payment of taxes. The executor asked the policeman who was that Jew and where did he live. The policeman replied that he did not know where Mechel lived but that Hirsh the Starosty would know.

The executor called on Hirsh and asked: "Do you know this man?"

"Yes."

"How does he support himself?"

While he knew the answer already, he said: "He travels around trading needles, thimbles, thread, thimbles, for old rags." It was actually the whole truth.

Then he asks: "When can I meet him at home?"

He answers: "At night."

He says: "Meet me at the evening hour so we both can go over to this thief who hides so that he does not have to pay tax."

When Mechel Fellig, as he was called, returned from his days travel, his wife met him, and told him that Hirsh Starosty had been there and, so that he should know what to do, she related that the authorities planned to confiscate his horse and wagon. Having heard the terrible news, Michel turned around, though he had not eaten all day, he left quickly, with the horse, to hide in a nearby village for several weeks. In the end, he was caught; his horse and wagon were confiscated and auctioned off at the Lanovits fair. His mother-in-law lived next to the bathhouse. With no job alternative, she helped him get a job as a bath attendant in that bathhouse.

* * *

The family Itzi Tzop, whose real family name was: the father Yitzchak Gershom. There were three sons: Yaakov, Moshe, and Uziel Gershom. Theirs was one of the finest, most honorable families. Their livelihood was a leased flour mill in Gribova [three kilometers northeast of Lanovits].

The father, Yitzhak, of blessed memory, preferred to pray in the *kloiz* [small chassidic shul] located next to his house. It was his custom after the prayers to sit and learn *gemara* until noontime. His eyesight was not so good, but he knew many *gemara* parts by heart. When he returned home midday from the *kloiz*, his wife, having prepared his meal, greeted him and asked him to go and wash his hands. As he turned to wash, he suddenly remembered that the miller at his flourmill may not remember where the grain pail was located. He, therefore, turned to this wife and said, "You can serve my food, I shall return shortly." She asked him, "Where are you going?" He replied, "I need to go to Gribova, to our mill!" He ran on foot for the three kilometers and returned shortly thereafter. His soup was still warm.

[Page 297]

On Rosh Hashanah, Reb Yitzhak used to recite the entire prayer by heart, likewise on Yom Kippur.

His oldest son, Moshe, was a Torah scholar. When one person had a case against another, he often acted as a mediator and both parties felt satisfied.

He showed humility with everyone equally. He was interested to know how the other person was faring, if anyone needed anything, and no discussion about whatever was possible. He always helped everyone. The word "impossible" was not in his vocabulary. He intervened in things that were actually impossible for him, and went to the place where his intervention would actually make things work.

I became acquainted with his deeds because I lived in their house for a period of time.

The second son, nicknamed Yekel, as he was called, was also a scholar, a learned man who excelled in learning Gemara. He was never angry, nor did he ever speak badly about others. He was a very respectable man. He spent the entire week at the Borsikowitzer mill, a mill his family leased for many years, returning home for Shabbath only. His wife Rachel, a great woman, was the daughter of the Lanovits Rav [chief rabbi].

The third son, Uziel Tzop, was a scholar with a good heart who celebrated at weddings and bemoaned the situation at funerals. He attended many weddings regardless of how closely he was related to the couple. His presence always added to the festivity of the celebration. And he attended many of the weddings uninvited and always brought a gift as was the local custom. He never had money because the family income from the mills went into one hand, and everyone his older brother Moshe, of blessed memory, and everyone received funding for their needs. And not looking at the income, if someone said that his shoes were too tight, Moshe saw to it immediately that the "shoes were loosened."

With the demise of the Tzop family, we lost a respectable, Jewish component of our community.

* * *

Kehos Kaufman, the son of Bubbe Uziel, always had a great sense of humor. He loved to make jokes on order to temporarily forget our bitter fate.

The buyers and sellers of these stories were Aharon Maharshak, Mordechai Guberman, Avraham Teichman, and Akiva Leibish's.

Kehos's first question one day was: "When will Poland suffer a defeat? Whoever has the answer will receive from me a good piece of smaltz herring for 10 groshen." [The herring actually sold for this price at the time.] Mordechai Guberman replies

[Page 298]

that only Avraham Leizer, son of Chava, could solve this riddle. At that moment Avraham Leizer arrived and we all had a good laugh. Puzzled, he asked: "What are you laughing about?" Kehos replied that everyone wanted to know when Poland would suffer a defeat. Avraham replied that when Jews can afford to make jokes at Poland's expense, it is a sign that our state is in decline, and he is however afraid that the state would drag the Jews down with it.

Then there was a love (consideration) for one another, which had no bounds. When, in a turn of fate, one such person approached one of us merchants for an interest-free short-term loan, we would ask one another who amongst us had some extra funds to lend for several days. Quickly comes the answer: Guberman replied that he could spare the funds for eight days. He then turned to us and said: "Can one of you mind the store for a few minutes until my return?" So it always was. Such loan-need episodes were an almost daily occurrence. When a creditor was not found at his home, one looked for him on the street or in the *Beis Midrash* or one visited him the next day early in the morning while the person was likely to still be in bed.

I remember one such episode when Eli Mirochnik, Eli Yidelich's, received a wagonload of lime from Podwysokie. The factory's owner was Mr. Shmarak, now living in Israel. Eli needed to pay for the load before Shabbath but he had no money. And it was Friday. If he couldn't find the funds to pay for the loan then it would have to stand for three days and then it also risked being stolen. But since it was Friday, Eli's mother figured that very likely she would receive an interest-free loan from Bunim Brimmer. She furthermore anticipated that Bunim's wife, Chaya, was likely to have arisen early that Friday morning to prepare the *challah* for Shabbath. In order to lose no time, Eli's mother walked over towards the Brimmer house and met Chaya carrying a pail of water from the well that was near the shul, not far from her house. She said her good mornings as usual, and asked her if her husband, Reb Bunim, was already up. Chaya replied, "He's still in bed and I have to knead the *challah* on Friday mornings, not him. What do you want?" Chaya asked, "and how much do you need?" Bunim overheard the conversation between the two women from his bedroom. When his wife entered their bedroom, he said to Chaya, "Chaya, see how much money is in the drawer, and the key is in my jacket."

Bunim Brimmer was a tall, good-looking, man with a beautifully expressive, intelligent face. He never spoke idly; his sentences were well thought out before he spoke a single word.

* * *

When I first came to Lanovits in 1912, I noticed the warm, joyous reception that everyone received daily, either a beautiful "good morning" or "with God's help," regardless of one's professional or financial standing. I remember these warm feelings to this day. I never encountered such warm greetings in any other place.

* * *

[Page 299]

Moshe (Rynkowiczer) Gurewitch was a Jew who once lived in the village of Rynkowicz. I once had the task, together with a colleague, to fix the baths. An order had come from the Kremenets [Krzemieniec] Starosty [district executive] that within six weeks the community bathhouse had to be brought up to specific hygiene standards as was written in the papers.

Shalom Wiesman was the community head at the time. The usual procedure in such a case was to convene a meeting on Shabbath in shul, at which experts came up with an estimate of the upgrading costs. Next, several of us fanned out into the community to collect the needed funds. When we came to Moshe Rynkowiczer he asked me: "How much have you already collected?" I replied: "We have yet to collect from such and such places." He then volunteered, "When you will finish your collection process, I will match the highest single contribution." And so it was, even though he was not a wealthy man.

The arrival of beggars in Lanovits was an almost daily phenomenon, asking for donations. Besides the small change they received they also needed to eat a meal. It was general knowledge that beggars could get a meal at the house of Moshe Rynkowiczer.

* * *

Dovid Lipa, also known as Zaborsky, an honest person, traded horses and was a contractor.

One day Leibzi Shziagel came to my shop. He lived next to Chaim Yisroel who processed oats and made groats. He told me that he recently transported tobacco from Zbarazh to Lanovits. Someone reported him to the police, and they confiscated his merchandise. He was not wealthy, nor was he a beggar. He asked my advice as to what to do. I knew the police chief was a big hooligan, but I also knew that he loved to ride horses. Knowing that Dovid Lipa always had a few beautiful horses in his stable, I immediately left the shop to visit him. I did not visit Dovid Lipa often because I had no need for horses. Besides, my brother-in-law, of blessed memory, also traded in horses. I arrived at his house as he was eating his noon meal, consisting of a beautiful, red borscht. When he saw me, he said: "Your brother-in-law should live to 120." I thanked him for his good wishes. He then asked me to sit down and his wife immediately offered me some of the borscht soup she had prepared that day, to honor my visit. I thanked her and added that since I wanted to earn a *mitzva*, I did not want to trade it for some borscht, but would better want someone to help in my important mission.

I next told him why I came to see him. He replied that only an hour ago the chief of police came to him to borrow a horse,

[Page 300]

to ride to Borsekowitz [Borszczewka]. He agreed to speak to the police chief when he returned with the horse.

The same night Dovid Lipa returned my visit and told me that the entire merchandise was now in his house. I knew that this favor, as were other such favors, came out of his own pocket. Dovid Lipa never asked for any monetary compensation. He was a simple man, yet a good, brotherly person.

* * *

In Iskewic [Juskewice] lived a couple, Moshe and Hinda Tepper. Hinda used to drive to town with a red horse who had the good fortune to be with them for twenty years. Day in and day out she used her wagon to transport potatoes, beans, barley, and flour for bread, and even a chicken for Shabbath for well-known beggars who knew that Hinda would come from Iskewic and would bring some things for them.

Moshe Tepper's father lived in town. He was a good-looking and respected person, knowing how to read the fine print, intelligent, and a particularly good accountant.

I think he seldom made accounting mistakes because he was very careful with his duties, very patient. He felt similarly that one should eat leisurely, that slow eating was like eating two meals. He was a refined Jew, able to lead a congregation in prayer, but he never accepted the honor of leading the prayers, except on his day of *yahrzeit* [anniversary of a parent's death]. He also maintained that if others derived joy from leading prayer, he preferred to let them do the job. He never angered another person nor uttered any offensive words about anyone. Modest in all respects, may his memory be blessed.

* * *

Moshe Tepper's brother-in-law, Yitzchak Barg, whose wife was Minda Tepper's sister, spent WWI in captivity as a POW in Austria under the worst conditions. He and his wife moved to Lanovits after the war and ran a store selling flour. Yitzchok always loved to polish his boots even when he had to go through muddy swamps. He even liked to lead the prayers and loved to do *mitzvos* [good deeds], and never declined providing an interest-free loan. His late wife, Toba, was duly proud of him when they came to ask him for a loan.

* * *

Yitzchok Melamed and his wife, were satisfied with their lot. They envied no one. They only strived to have enough money to be able to celebrate Shabbath with *challah*, wine, and fish. They never envied others who had more or greater conveniences. Their greatest striving was to provide their two daughters with an education.

* * *

Leizer der Griener. Leizer did not know even a page of Gemara, nor did he speak a decent Polish, yet he was a Jew with a "Jewish heart," never refusing

[Page 301]

… to do a favor, either monetarily or to fulfill a task. When a person ran into difficulties with the authorities [the Komandant or the Inspector], they immediately ran to *Leizer der Griener*, as they called him, to ask for help. He did not lose himself in his words, despite the fact that they were a mixture of Polish, Ukrainian, and in the middle of all that, even a little Yiddish. Those whom he had to persuade of his particular case somehow understood him because his arguments were smart and a product of a sharp mind and profound thoughts. He never had to go look for that extra word in his pocket. All those who handled the cases of the Jews in town, knew that he was not a trained lawyer, that meant that this was out of his goodness and willingness to help others while not expecting anything in return. So, they gave in.

[Page 302]

A Visit to Lanovits

By Yosef Warach (New York)

Translated by Pamela Russ

After having lived for several years in America, my heart yearned for my dear hometown, Lanovits. I yearned for my family and my friends. In reality, though, I wanted to feel a little of the warm atmosphere of the good Lanovits Jews.

I saved some money and traveled to Lanovits in the year 1913. The trip left a deep impression on me so that I remember it to this day.

I arrived on a Thursday evening. The town was wrapped in an odd quiet. The workday atmosphere of the day was over and was replaced by a spiritual calm. The stores were now manned only by women. The men of the community were washing their hands, combing out their beards, putting on their black clothes, and preparing to go to the *Beis Midrash* [study hall, part of the shul] for the *mincha* and *maariv* prayers.

I stood in the middle of the street feeling like a stranger. After experiencing the hub-hub of New York, the quiet atmosphere of Lanovits dulled me. My heart beat with doubts: Who knows what is more important for mankind, and particularly for Jews? Maybe only Lanovits?

Before visiting my only sister, Tobe Katz and her dear husband Leizer Kibes, I went to the *Beis Midrash*.

When I arrived, I was immediately surrounded from all sides by warm handshakes and greetings. Yoel Shokhet [ritual slaughterer] was leading a hearty *mincha* and *maariv* prayer. After the prayer session I contributed a bottle of liquor and a snack and everyone drank *le'chaim*, celebrating my return visit.

All those present drank a *le'chaim* and moved to the table, wishing everyone well. I was the center – a Lanovits son, a person who did not forget Lanovits. Only after that did I go visit my sister and brother-in-law.

Before I left the *Beis Midrash*, I told the congregants that whoever would like to hear greetings from the Lanovits emigrants in America should come to Leizer Katz's, of blessed memory, house. At the time there were only a few Lanovits young men who had left their wives and children to seek work in America in order to provide for their families. I knew them all and met them all in America, since they all lived almost in the same New York neighborhood.

On Friday and Sunday, my brother-in-law's house was full of visitors. People came to ask questions, to accept greetings, to find out how their relatives were doing health-wise and economically. They had a drink, a snack, they shed tears, and hoped for a better future.

[Page 303]

On Shabbath, after the prayers, the whole community came to my sister and brother-in-law's house for *kiddush*. Almost every family had delivered a *kugel* to their house for the occasion. After the *kiddush*, we sang *zemiros* [songs for Shabbath] and said the special grace after meals.

Later in the afternoon, I went to shul for *mincha*, had the third Shabbath meal, sang the special songs for the end of Shabbath [*askino seudoso*], and then recited the *maariv* prayers.

At the end of Shabbath, the congregants and I all went again to Leizer Katz's house to celebrate an evening of beautiful singing until the late hours of the night.

This was a great Shabbath, a spiritual rest, something to remember for years thereafter.

On Sunday, I was invited to the home of Rebbe Aharele. We had a wide-ranging discussion regarding *yiddishkeit* [Jewish life] in the distant country. I believe I gave him an accurate account of the subjects that interested him. Even simple folks of our community asked me questions, not only about golden dreams, but about the *yiddishkeit* in New York.

From Lanovits, I traveled to Zbarazh [near Tarnopil] to visit my parents. The whole community came out to say goodbye and wish me a successful journey.

* * *

Many events have happened in the world since then. The world gave a shiver, maybe two, maybe three. Many terrible things have happened. Everything became confused and shaken. However, my days in Lanovits during my 1913 visit have left a deep impression in my memory. I cannot and will not forget those warmhearted Jews, brothers of Lanovits. The best example of a person that the world can present, cannot compare to them.

[Page 304]

A Few Family Remembrances

By Byya Goldenberg

Translated by Pamela Russ

Editor's remarks

The Yizkor books, which are being written in order not to forget the horrors of the Nazi regime, with its expression of Jew hatred as it wanted to rule the world, while during this time we are paying a bloody price for this – these books are being written in an epoch where an anti-Semitic regime exists, which along with the voice of Marxism, wants to destroy Jewishness and rule the entire world. In all this, the story of Byya Goldenberg has a special meaning. It tells that during the Czarist black regime, the government and the police still defended the Jews.

Therefore, the story is still real now.

My father was a Pankiewicz "citizen" (previously registered citizen), and therefore we had no citizen rights in Poland and did not have a Polish passport, only a "*karta pobitu*" (interim resident rights), and were suspicious as people from whom the Polish regime had to carefully protect themselves.

Pankiewicz was a very large town that passed from hand to hand when the Polish-Russian borders stabilized. In 1920, when the Russians entered Poland, and the borders changed, and went from Zbarazh to Horin, then Pankiewicz, with its wealth, remained in Russian hands.

[Page 305]

Generations thought that Pankiewicz was famous. We remembered the big river with the big lake and the giant mill with the fish catchers, which Dovid Berman, with his genius mind, got for nothing and thought he would become rich, earning enough for his children's children. But just then Poland lost it [the city], and Pankiewicz left and distanced itself from Dovid, but it became an obsessive idea for him, pushed him out of his mind, and brought him to endless trips to Prince Zamoiski and to writing memorandums to Piłsudski.

For us, the Goldenbergs, however, Pankiewicz was a well of family pride and problems, from the talks at the fireplace and arguments with the Polish regime that was hostile to us.

My father left the village as a child and could have forgotten about it. Every child who was born from him in Poland and its regime, was written off as a foreigner. In his metrics [documents] was written: To the father who was a ground worker from Pankiewicz, a child was born, and the name given is …

The reason for this is: Czar Alexander II would often dress as a regular citizen and go among the people, go around in all the far corners of his country, and listen to what the people were saying.

When he went like that to Pankiewicz, a village of thousands of non-Jews, and learned that among them there was one single Jew, he was very interested in seeing this wonder. He wanted to see this remarkable family with his own eyes, who maintained its Jewish life in their great loneliness, in an ocean of non-Jews. He also wanted selfishly to see the type of person about whom it was said that he only had money in mind and people were inferior.

He himself came to our door, knocked – this is what my grandfather recounted – and asked if he could come in. When he came into the house, he said that he had come from a distance and he did not have a penny to his soul and no money for food.

My grandmother had just finished cooking her gefilte fish for Shabbath, so she fed him with all the tasty food and gave him Russian hot tea to drink.

When the Czar finished his meal, he got up from the table and said:

"Dear Babushka, what would you like me to give you so that you remember me forever?" So, she asked who was he that he could give her such a gift. Then he told her his secret.

[Page 306]

She pleaded: "None of my children or my children's children should be drafted into the military and not have to eat *treifus* [non-kosher]."

He replied: "Even I cannot promise this. Military is military."

"If so," she said, "then give me a certificate showing that my family and I have permission for generations to remain in the villages of your country."

As was known, no Jew was allowed to live in Russia in the villages. He promised her and left.

Within a week, land surveyors looked at the maps and plans, measured and measured, and left.

Sometime later, a messenger from the Czar came to my grandmother and brought her a property certificate of 24 tithes [approx. 2.7 acres per tithe] of grain fields and 18 tithes of --- [?]. That means, swamp pools that provided green fodder for the animals and hay. Also, a certificate for the rights to live in that village, or a different one, forever.

This property owner's certificate had large script, written completely in gold, and the two-headed eagle of the Ramanoffs had gold right across it.

The letter gave her two things: an atmosphere of legends and high standing in the family's talks, and … endless problems.

As mentioned, the Czar Alexander did not exempt the son from military service, and when my oldest brother Shlomo had to register in the army, and he was small, thin, and frail, he decided to cross the border near Zbarazh and go from there to America.

Along with five other boys, he left, and arrived in a certain town, where a certain Christian lived, one who was known to be a border smuggler. They hired him and quickly left right away. That night, in the dark, the Christian led them into a deep valley where the darkness was thicker and deeper. Suddenly he gave a cry with a strong voice: "Tfrrr!" That means "stop" in horse language.

One person of the group said that it was forbidden to scream at the border, and he wondered how this Christian, a well-known smuggler, did not know this. But it was already too late.

Because of the scream, soon noise was heard around them along with the sound of clogging shoes in the deep, sticky mud of the dark valley.

[Page 307]

The "children" understood that they had fallen [were in trouble]. Out of great fear, my brother Shlomo ran into the nearby bushes, and Moishke, the bathkeeper, ran and disappeared. The remaining four were in trouble.

The two tried to find each other but did not. So, Shlomo remained alone, filled with fear and edginess. Suddenly he heard one person saying to another: "Vladimir, cut it! What are you waiting for!" And the second person answered: "But you're not allowed! The two ran away and we can also get into trouble!"

After that, Shlomo decided to run, and they heard his movements. One of them said: "I hear them close by!"

As he was speaking, he threw a piece of steel, and it hit Shlomo on the foot. Shlomo began to moan in pain. The bandit heard, went to grab him by his pants, and tore off a piece.

There was gold sewn into the pants - gold that his father had given him so that he should have what to live from for those first few days. That is why the seam was done by hand and was a weak one.

When the bandit felt the treasure, he forgot about my brother and shouted for joy. But in the meantime, my brother moved away and used his last energies to run.

Beaten and in pain, he went into the first lit house in the village near Wyzheradyk. That was the only Jewish house.

The Jew [who was living there] became frightened when he saw a dirty person, dressed in black and white, but when he heard Yiddish and heard the story, he let him into the house and figured he would take him home the following morning.

Meanwhile, Moishke, as he was running away, came to the police and frantically told them what happened and took them to the place [where it happened].

Shlomo was my brother from my father. His mother died during his birth. My father did not want him to suffer from a stepmother, so he married his wife's sister, afterwards my mother.

That night, my mother woke up from her sleep with a terror and a scream … and she told us about her terrible dream.

In her dream, her dead sister came to her and said:

"My one and only son is in great danger, surrounded by bandits who want to kill him, and you don't seem to care. I am running to save him. You have other children and you do not worry about him. I am running to him and am going to save him."

[Page 308]

My father laughed this off, calmed her down, and told her to go back to sleep.

But soon, once again she woke up and disturbed my father's sleep. Now he became angry. "Why are you so preoccupied with silly dreams. Let me sleep!"

But my mother did not leave him alone. "She came to me again from her grave, but this time she said:

"The child is saved, go bring him home. If you think this is a dream, then I will stop your double-guarding [?] clock.""

Here my father wanted to show her the nonsense of her dreams. He angrily got up from his bed, turned on the lamp, held it in front of the clock, lit it up, and … it actually had stopped.

My father broke out in a deep sweat. His legs and hands began trembling. He quickly dressed, and went to Dusi, his best non-Jewish friend, and begged him to quickly ride him over to the Rav in Lanovits.

It was Wednesday, the day of the fair in Lanovits. It was too early to go see the Rav. So, my father went an inn. He overheard a Jew, who was sitting there, telling people that the night before, a young boy came into his house absolutely terrified, then he told the police about six young boys, and so on. He finished by saying that four boys were in the hands of the bandits, but the sixth, the small one, had disappeared.

My father fainted. Everything was true.

When he revived, he asked Itzik Shmuel to take him to Wyzheradyk, and that's how he brought Shloime home.

* * *

In the trial against the thugs the complete story came out:

Moishke notified the police commissioner and the police. In the morning, when they came to the place where everything happened, they found the piece of black material from the pants, and the piece of steel. When they went into the village they asked about Vladimir, who was considered a bandit in the village, and a "murderer for hire."

In his home, there was a five-year-old child and an old lady who was still lying on the stove and sleeping. The commissioner placed the steel on top of the oven and asked the child:

"Where is your father?"

The child said that the father had come very early and threw a pile of gold coins onto the table, and shouted: "We became rich!"

[Page 309]

The mother told him to leave with the money and he left to put away the money, because the mother had argued with him.

At this point the old lady woke up and the commissioner turned to her:

"I see a piece of steel on top of the stove. Can you lend it to me? You see, my wagon broke, it sank on the way to the village, etc.…"

The old lady shivered.

"No, no, my dear. I am not allowed. Vladimir will kill me if he does not find his steel bar."

The steel bar and the piece of black pants and the mud from the valley on the pants were the obvious pieces of evidence against the bandits, the murderers, in the courts. The judge sentenced them to lifelong expulsion to Siberia with hard labor.

[Page 311]

Chapter 9:

Death and Horrors

[Page 312] [Blank] [Pages 313-328]

In the Lanovits Ghetto, from the Beginning until its Liquidation

By Moshe Rosenberg

See: In the Lanovits Ghetto- From the Beginning until its Liquidation – Page 39

[Pages 329-338]

My Escape from the Lanovits Ghetto

Meir Beker

See: The Lanovits Ghetto and my Escape from it – Page 49

[Pages 339-340]

How Our Rabbis Perished

Byya Goldenberg

See: Horror Details - Page 72

[Page 341]

In Our Shtetl and Far Away

Yaacov Kagan

Translated by Pamela Russ

Our town Lanovits is etched deeply in our souls. If we want to know why, we only need to look backwards. There we discover a familiar world, a *shtetl* that has all the attributes to provide everlasting happiness. There are a number of such small places and locations.

At first glance, from Shalom Aleichem's perspective, it was a dirty town. Yet it had an honest society, pleasant summer days, and fragrant wildlife places, such as the "*Zeide's shtikel*" ["grandfather's piece of land"], the "*blote*" [the mud], the "*Zwinterberg*" [the hills with the non-Jewish cemetery], the seven wells, the ponds around the town and other places, all of which lifted the spirits and provided freshness and dreams.

*

Lanovits appealed to the older residents with its small synagogues and *shtiebels*, and with the *Beis Midrash* [study hall]. They had great pleasure as they ran at dawn's hours to meet with fellow believers, and then together have a discussion with the Creator of the Universe.

For us children, the holy places had a special meaning on the Jewish holidays, and particularly on the high holidays and on *Simchas Torah*. There was a feeling of being uplifted, great joy, and huge days with deep awe and judgment. On days like that, a nation grows in depth and in size.

Lanovits had a tendency to strive for spiritual greatness. The library, for example, was the largest in the surrounding area. Whatever we gained from there came from the great literary, cultural movement. We strove through that library to reach a greater and higher niveau, and tried to attain a broader horizon.

We had, I feel, a Tarbut school and *cheders*, unlike other places, with good teachers, open tasks, and an open social life. When I think of Motel Melamed, I know that it is hard to find a pedagogue of his caliber.

[Page 342]

He had a special level of understanding and an open heart for his students. We need not forget the other *cheders* and good teachers that we had. I remember them well as better than the typical angry teachers with clubs in their hands that I encountered elsewhere. There was a loving atmosphere in our *cheders*. Our *rebbes* [teachers] were *tzadikim* [like saints] as they tolerated us troublemakers.

Our town had no shortage of pious men and women, who did good deeds and tried hard to minimize the suffering of others.

We had no beggars in Lanovits, nor beggars in the corners. It was a town of respect and self-care, a town of happy people, who saw the good fortune in every situation.

This was so until 1940…

In 1940, the Soviets arrived, introducing their concept of "order" and spirit, with their understanding of good morale and joy, Christian, foreign, murderous, as the human being and human values became unnecessary, and fear and worry became the primary values of society.

During the Soviet period I came to appreciate what was Shabbath and what it meant to be a person, heartfelt and feeling. Everything disappeared and Lanovits Jewry became deeply depressed. They waited with clenched teeth hoping that this too would disappear, along with the regime.

* * *

I spent the war years in Russia. Part of the time I spent with Pessy Weitzman, Yosel Weiner and Yisrael and Yaffa Kusiles. We were together for some time. Later, we separated.

While in the Red Army we experienced strong anti-Semitism. From time to time, they spread rumors that Jews occupied Tashkent (Uzbekistan), that Jews were responsible for the war, etc. When the Soviet radio broadcast the horrible murderous anti-Semitic statements, that the Jews supported the Nazis, our Ukrainian-Russian "fate brothers" enjoyed the remarks.

At times the going was difficult, but the thought that this would end soon, and I would meet my dear ones, with my fellow Lanovitsers and Lanovits itself, gave me courage. I fought, lived, and hoped.

In 1944 the Soviet radio indicated that the enemy was vanquished, and the Russian army was coming forward and liberating one town after another, among them Lanovits, our town, and my heart gave a leap.

I soon wrote a letter to my family but received no reply. Several months later I received a reply from Ita Kreper. She wrote that she was the only (Jewish) survivor in Lanovits.

I wrestled with impatience until 1946. When I was demobilized,

[Page 343]

I resolved to return to Lanovits, in the hope that maybe [some of my relatives survived].

On the train from Moscow I met Chaim Nosson Gitelman and Shalom Segal.

Upon nearing Lanovits, I could see from afar the destruction of our town. Local Gentiles met me, expressing wonder that I survived, as if I had no right to remain alive. They told me everything, with a cold-bloodedness, that my mother Faiga Sile and Laizer Katz (Charne's father) were found in a cellar a few nights after the ghetto's liquidation. Both were shot. Of the last ones to be liquidated were Tuvia and Aharon Milman, Chaim Pinchas, and Avraham Mates's.

I went to our cemetery and found it also in disarray with gravestones turned over and laid in ruin. Cattle had been grazing there, also soiling the cemetery ground.

In the meantime, Yosel Marder, Mendel Brimmer, and Tzvi Meil also arrived. We sobbed together, and worked together to put a fence around the cemetery.

This was the only thing we could do for our dear ones in our lives.

Ours was a wonderful *shtetl*, what remains is a cemetery. And who knows what will become of the cemetery in the future.

[Pages 344-351]

From Lanovits to the Soviet Union

Aryeh Ginzburg

See: From Lanovits to the Soviet Union – Page 79

[Pages 352-359]

This is How We Lived in Russia

Batya (Melamed) Taitel

See: This is How We Lived in Russia – Page 84

[Pages 360-361]

An Addendum to Batya's Report

Shlomo Taitel (Tamari)

See: An Addendum to Batya's Report – Page 88

[Pages 362-367]

My Experience Under the Soviet Regime

Joseph Weiner

See: My Experience Under the Soviet Regime – Page 89

[Page 368]

It Pulled Me….

By Yitzhak Weinstein (Itzikel Benye's)

Translated by Pamela Russ

In 1941, I was in Stanislavov when the German-Soviet war started. I was sent there by the Soviet authorities to recruit workers, especially Ukrainians, to work in the oil fields of Baku, Kavkaz [Caucasus].

After that, as part of the powerful flow from the bloody catastrophe, I was dragged into many fronts with the Red Army, in the first and second Ukrainian general front.

In 1943, when Vanda Wasilewskaya formed her Polish legions, I was assigned to the first Polish army named after Tadeus Kosciuszko. With them, I entered Poland via Volynia.

While I was stationed in Kiverts, near Lutzk, I decided to try to go to Lanovits and visit my hometown.

I had no concrete information regarding the extent of the catastrophe that occurred. Polish theaters performed shows of burning towns and villages, street murders, and specifically, of murdering Jewish victims. Soviet newspapers described harrowing facts of the German occupation in their typical Russian exaggerated and bombastic style. I believed some of it and disbelieved some of it. I could not imagine the terrible truth because I probably did not want to believe it.

I just did not have the proper background facts to have a real idea about all this.

It was a summer day. The black earth of Volynia carried its smell which reminded me of my home region. My heart longed for my hometown of Lanovits.

* * *

I was an officer in the Red Army. I knew that it would be difficult for me to obtain army leave from my responsibilities. But I went to my superior commander and told him what was going on in my heart. I begged him to permit me to go to my hometown to find out who of my family and friends survived. Perhaps they needed help or protection. Maybe their lives were in danger or they were starving.

To my surprise, he not only granted my leave request, but he also

[Page 369]

selected two armed soldiers as guards. The war was still waging here and there, and you could not know exactly where the danger was.

I left from Skiverts to Lutzk, from there through Rovno, Kremenec to Lanovits, all by horse and wagon.

* * *

While in Lutzk I ran around unhindered through the town looking for Jews. The town was in ruins. I saw no civilians on the streets. Other than the Red Army and Polish soldiers, who were stationed around the city in the woods and suburbs, there was no living soul in the city and the surrounding areas.

* * *

But I had met someone on the train, an older, lonely looking man, who was totally enveloped in dense fear. I recognized him as a Jew. He told me he was Yosef Kaplan from Pomieruwka region of Poznan. With the first occupation of the Germans, he escaped to Volyn and survived the entire occupation period in Lutzk. A Polish family dug a shelter for him in their yard, near a path, and fed him there throughout the war period. A few days ago, the local Ukrainian authorities slaughtered this Polish family. He was now alone, waiting for an opportunity to return to his hometown and search for some remnants of his past. He knew nothing of the extermination. But as we walked the streets of Lutzk, he came to realize that the town was no more: neither its houses nor its Jews.

We did not see Rovno nor Kremenec. We rode with captured vehicles, and people passed without stopping. The sounds and noises of war were still clearly heard. No one was allowed to stop.

I arrived in Lanovits at about one in the afternoon. The Red Army trucks in our group continued to Jampol while we left them at Wolica near the train to Lanovits.

As I walked into town I met Theodora Godamsky, the sister-in-law of Korczaczikh. She recognized me immediately and fell faint. Her husband arrived, saved her, and we were asked to come to their house. The house was still standing next to the house of Itzik Eliyahu in the *blote* [area of the muddied lake].

Godamsky warned us to be extra careful because Ukrainian bandits roamed around the area killing Russian and Polish officers.

We spent the night in their house. The woman took extra precautions to ensure that our visit not be known to her Ukrainian neighbors. She feared arson. This was true for the entire Lanovits that remained standing and was tightly occupied by the local Soviet authorities.

[Page 370]

Itzik Eliyahu's house was completely overgrown with grass. The rest of the houses on the street were destroyed. Ruin lay everywhere, and we remember that here there was once plentitude.

The next morning, I went to the office of the Soviet commander, located in the old school. I asked the commander for an additional guard. They did not want to hear about it. And at the same time, they also suggested I not "crawl" anywhere. I must get out of here. The main thing was, they were not responsible for us.

Despite his warning I went into the town.

From Godamsky, I learned that the Ukrainian families: Horutz, Primas, Somolitsky, and Butenko served in the local German-led police force and were at the head of the Ukrainian extermination bandits who slaughtered Jews. The local police force consisted of only two German gendarmes, and the killing was largely done by the Ukrainians. (It is interesting that Butenko is now a priest in Wyszehradzka, and the main bandit, Mishka Horutz, tried to escape, and was not even tried in the courts for his crimes.)

* * *

I first visited the town's mass grave. It was dangerous to do so. That same night, the Ukrainians in nearby Kozatsky murdered a Russian officer. I went to the mass grave regardless, to be with my dear relatives and friends who perished there.

Alexander "the blind one" was still alive, and he recognized me. He cried bitterly and begged me to leave the area. I approached the graves. The earth beneath me was still rumbling, as if the dead had not yet settled in and the Jews still wanted to live. There were lives of young children and girls and women and men. I became hysterical, and prostrated myself on this "warm" earth, then fainted and … I later revived in Godamsky's house. No one told me who had brought me back here.

* * *

In the meantime, I heard that a Jewish young woman lived in the area, and Pawlushe's son, and a local Russian officer, who had come to Lanovits, told me about her. I visited Mikita Diduch, and he told me that the young woman was from Wyszehradzka, presently living in the house of Ilka Diduch.

I went there and found her sitting on a couch, thin, exhausted. She was frightened by me, because she did not recognize me. She spoke Ukrainian, spoke haltingly, and continuously claimed to be Ukrainian.

[Page 371]

When I calmed her, and she felt comfortable with me, she admitted that her name was actually Sobol, and she lived near my aunt's house in Wyszehradzka. (She now lives with her husband, Moshe Fuchs, in Israel.)

We sat and talked for a long time. She told me that she recently arrived from Vishnevets, where she was hiding during the entire time of the extermination. She told me of the tragedy of the Vishnevets and Wyszehradzka Jews who all perished in the Vishnevets ghetto.

I left the Diduch house to visit Boshke, the "*felsher*" [country doctor]. He told me that all the Jews were led to their death through a field next to his house. As they passed his house, these Jews threw their money into his garden so the murderers would not get it. He told me that he regarded this money as "holy" and donated it to the Red Army to "fight the Nazi beast."

Boshke added that from the grave, in the final minutes before the shooting, Yoelik Korolki succeeded in escaping the shooting area by quickly jumping the fence. However, the Ukrainian guards noticed his escape, laughed, and cried out: "You had the audacity to escape!" and then they shot him. (Boshke's wife told me that weeks later she found a number of gold rings in her yard. She told me, "These are stained with blood. I don't want them, take them." I did not accept them because of the blood.)

Lanovits was a simple town surrounded by hills and greenery that were witness to a Jewish tragedy. Now, Lanovits was no longer. There was no one to turn to. I went to visit Zuber, the *felsher* [country doctor] who used to live under the same roof as Chaim Nosson. He was no longer alive. His 24-year-old daughter, a local teacher, told me that she noticed that the Ukrainian students in her school often wore blouses, dresses, and slacks that used to be worn by Jewish children. When Mishka Horutz's non-Jewish daughter appeared in school in a blouse, the teacher recognized it as having been worn previously by Necha'le, Chaim Nosson's daughter. The teacher asked the student where she got the blouse. The student answered, "My father bought it for me."

Zuber's wife told me details, as she cried about the Lanovits tragedy. She described how hard the Jews had to labor, unloading coal and clearing snow, and how Richter, the local German murderer, beat the Jews for every small infraction, tortured them to death, those who were already depleted and destined to be executed. She insisted that I go with her to the nearby well to witness with my own eyes where Ukrainians threw live Polish children into the well only a few days earlier.

[Page 372]

A terrible smell rose from the depth of the well. The air was filled with the smell of decay and death. Among the bodies were Wodos's six children. All six drowned together. It was said that the Ukrainians, at the urging of the Germans, attacked the Poles and did their duties: burned the veterans alive, shot, killed, raped their wives. They even ruined and uprooted their cemeteries.

Zuber's wife pointed out the most important fact. As soon as the Germans left the area, the Ukrainian authorities let it be known that Jews were now free to come out from their hiding places. These Jews, tragically beaten and distraught, allowed themselves to be convinced and left their hideouts. These survivors were soon murdered by the Ukrainians so that there would be no witness to Ukrainian collaboration with the Germans. Mordechai Liverant's sister, David Lipe's daughter, and others whose names I do not know, were all killed by them.

The hunched cobbler Lewitsky, a passionate Communist under Soviet rule, became a serious German collaborator, who, with his own hands, murdered many Jews.

When the ghetto was liquidated, Chana'le, Chaim Nosson's, was able to hide herself. She remained alive, and went to Lewitsky, their neighbor and her father's good friend, and begged him to help her find a hiding place. He threw her out of his house and informed the thugs of her whereabouts. They killed her on the *blote* [muddy lake area] near Godamsky's house.

Lewitsky now lives in Lanovits, and goes about freely.

I next visited Fenin, the Soviet district chief who served here in 1939. I asked him to arrest these bandits. I gave him names and addresses. He replied, "At the moment we are still weak. They are still killing our people. We will deal with them in due time."

He next took me to the old school now in a prison and showed me that the place was filled with many bandits. It seems that they had already started to take care of the situation.

On the third day, I went to our house which we had previously been sold to Khilos. The house was intact. Mindel's house next door was torn down. That house was in Ukrainian possession and so was left standing. At Khilo's restaurant, I met the hunched Ukrainian tailor. He came over to me and screamed:

"Too bad you left town, otherwise we would have shot you, like a dog."

[Page 373]

I grabbed my revolver ready to shoot him, but those present stopped me. But he was arrested very soon. On my return to Poland, I wrote to the Lanovits Russian authorities the facts of this case. I was called as a witness to his trial. He was sentenced to eight years in prison.

I was about to leave Lanovits, when, by chance, I met Uliana, the domestic that had previously worked for Golda Berenstein. She cried bitter tears as she told me the following details, that in June 1941, when the Soviets left Lanovits but the Germans had not yet arrived, the Ukrainians established their own local authority and forced thirty-four Jews out of their homes, took them outside of the town, and murdered them. She remembered some of the names: Zalman Parnas, Uziel Rabin, Yisroel Katz, Yitzhok Buchstein, Pesach Buchstein, Yosel Margaliot and Burhe, Nachum Weiner, Uziel Reichman, Yitzchak Melamed, Nachum

Kerper, Bentzia Katz (Luzek Betzak's), his nephews Yosel and Yoelik, Benyik Gurewitch, and Berchik Dawidson.

They broke the hands and legs of Berchik Dawidson and left him lying in the field. Uliana found him, took him into her house and tried to care for him. But the following day the attackers returned to her house, dragged him out, and shot him at her door.

She, with her own hands, dragged him to the Jewish cemetery, and with the help of a few Jews, gave him a Jewish burial.

I left Lanovits broken spirited. I had to sneak out of town like a thief. My life was in danger.

Later, I visited my tragic hometown twice more because I was drawn to it. But I believe I reported all that happened to me and all those whom I met there.

[Page 374]

Together with gentile youth - perhaps these are the future murderers of our youth

Lanovits - One cemetery
(Hershel Meil, Joseph Marder and Mendel Brimmer who set up the park in front of the cemetery)

[Page 375]

Chapter 10:

Dr. Yisroel Zinberg

[Page 376]

Zinberg Pages [and his archive]

By Hillel Alexandow

Translated by Pamela Russ

Yisroel Zinberg

Editor's comments:[1]

Alexandow's article is an exact reprint of Noach Prilutzki's discourse of Yisroel Zinberg, and in order to "make him kosher" for the Jewish extremist newspaper, at the same time he polished it with a few quotations of Marx-Lenin.

The value, therefore, of this article, is almost a historical, heroic one, showing how the Jews would self-sacrifice for Jewish literacy in a place of spiritual destruction, but the value is also to bring out details about Dr. Zinberg.

Reading this, the world learns that in small Lanovits there lived and grew up a brilliant person of the generation, and the phenomenon that his largesse was not only in his greatness and geniality, but particularly in that he used his skills to serve the people and his students and judges. And at the same time, all his life, he was involved in various political-economic circumstances.

So, I suggest that we should abstract from the Stalinist need of approval and read this article as a well to acknowledge our Dr. Zinberg, and also our Lanovits Zinberg, and the refinement and inclusion of his work.

Yisroel Zinberg has long been the protector of the entire Jewish nation and its pride, but he is still ours, because if a person is a product of his environment and his societal circle, then Dr. Zinberg is actually a product of Lanovits, and as such, he suddenly becomes a worthy asset for our small town, with his dear character and company, and this book about Lanovits could not be complete without Dr. Zinberg's chapters.

Ch. Rabin

[Page 377]

Regardless of the fact that Y. Zinberg left behind a great literary legacy, his name in the wide reading circles was not well known. But therefore, in the small circle of critics and researchers of Yiddish literature, it was known that in Peterburg (later in Leningrad) there was an engineer Sergei Lazarovitch (Yisroel) Zinberg, who was a great genius in Yiddish literature. You could turn to him for a literary "investigation," and he would give, very quickly, an exact answer which you could totally rely on.

Yisroel Zinberg was born in the town of Lanovits, in the province of Volhyn, in the year 1873, into a family of wealthy farmers of wolvarken [pig wool workers]. His education happened in the same place. He did not go to cheder, he did not study in a yeshiva. His father brought him from Odessa (I think under the recommendation of Mendele Mocher Sfarim), a former teacher in the Zhitomir rabbinic school. In his younger years, Zinberg already demonstrated his capacities and work abilities. You did not have to be a deep observer or someone who understands people, to see in the young Zinberg a "book devourer," a "genius," and a "*masmid*"[2] [diligent student of Torah studies].

Y. Zinberg received a high education outside of the country: In Karlsruhe, he completed the polytechnic school as a chemical engineer, and in Basil, he completed a dissertation and received the title of Doctor of Philosophy. A chemist and a humanitarian intellect – that's how he returned home from outside of the country. In the year 1898, he settled in Peterburg, and received a position as representative of the chemistry laboratory in the large Putilov-Factory (now Kirow).

* * *

In the year 1900, the first two works of Y. Zinberg were published: 1) in Yiddish – "*Vos tut zich oif der velt*" ["What is going on in the world"], Warsaw, p. 73; a popular scientific book about the science of nature; 2) in Russian – "Yitzchok Ber Lewinson," Peterburg, p. 75; a monograph about one of the most distinguished representatives of the bourgeois enlightenment. The interest in Lewinson

[Page 378]

also appeared later in the article "Yitzchok Ber Lewinson and His Times" ("*Yevreiskoye* Starina" [the Jewish community of Starina], 1910).

In the year 1901, Y. Zinberg began working at the Yiddish-Russian *Voschod* ["Sunrise"], and from that year on (until 1918) he was a permanent co-worker in the Yiddish/Russian press (weekly newspaper – *Svoboda i Ravenstvo* [Freedom and Equality], *Yevreiskii Mir* [Jewish Peace], *Yevreiskoye Obrazovanye* [Jewish Education], *Noviy Voschod* [New Sunrise], *Yevreiskoye Niedeliye* [Jewish Week], and so on. There, he managed a constant section "Overview of the Jewish Press," (under the pseudonym -- -------). At the same time, he wrote great investigative works, which he published in *Voschod* ("Shylock's Roots," "Two Streams in Jewish Life"), and the historical collections in: "*Perezhitoye*," ["Repetitions"] ("The first socialist organizations in Jewish literature." B1. "The Writing Inns in Jewish Literature." B2. "The Foremen of Jewish journalism in Russia." B4. and so on, in the historical journal "*Yevreiskoye Starina*." Y. Zinberg had great input into the major work of the sixteen volume *Yevreiskoye Encyclopedia* [Jewish encyclopedia] (1913-1908), in which he edited the section of "New Hebrew and Yiddish Literature." He was not only an editor, but he also wrote major articles, in which several are almost like monographs ("The New Hebrew Literature," "The Yiddish Literature," "Periodical Press," "Haskalah" ["Enlightenment"], and so on. There were articles about individual writers and publicists (Abramovitch, Peretz, Shalom Aleichem, Mendelson, Achad Haam, Lilienblum, Lewinson, etc.), about middle-aged poets (Yehuda Halevi, Emanuel Haromi). Other than that, he also wrote important articles that, at the same time, were not tied to literary history (assimilation – together with D. Pasmanik; Yeshiweye from Volozhyn; English socialist missionaries; censors of Yiddish books in Russia – together with Y. Hessen, and so on). Y. Zinberg wrote several tens of these types of major articles. He also wrote lesser articles which were entered into the encyclopedia under the number 7.

In the major collection "The History of Jews in Russia" (in Russian, the publication "*Mir*" [Peace], 1914), Y. Zinberg wrote the following chapters: "The Evolution of the Rabbinic literature," "Folk Literature," "Mystical Currents."

In the post-revolutionary years, Y. Zinberg presented his works in various Yiddish-Russian collections ("*Yevreiskoye Missel*," [Jewish Assignment], "*Yevreisky Almanakh*" [Jewish Almanac], "*Yevreiskoye Liyetofus*" [Jewish Chronicle], and so on. In the Jewish science publications ("*Zeitschrift*" [magazines]) and so on, he published a series of literary, historical material.

[Page 379]

One has to mention exceptionally the works of Y. Zinberg in Russian, that is his great monograph, "The History of the Jewish Press in Russia, and Ties with the Socialist Currents" (1916, volume 3, page 264), which received the award from the "Society to Spread Education between Jews in Russia" ("*EPE*"). The history of the press was brought to the year 1881, and includes the "Press for the Jews" in three languages: Yiddish, Hebrew, and Russian.

Reviewing Y. Zinberg's works in Yiddish, first you have to point out for all of it, that his relationship with Yiddish was always a positive one. He began working with the Russian "*Voskhod*" ["Rise" of the sun or moon], at the time when there was a negative relationship with the folk language. Mordche Spektor recounts, that when he came to the editor and publisher of the "*Voskhod*" in the year 1883, Adolph Landau, and presented a review of two books, his and Shalom Aleichem's, which were published at that time, the editor replied: "Jargon is not literature. Therefore, I cannot publish a review in my newspaper." That same spirit, almost without change, ruled in the paper about 18-20 years later, when Y. Zinberg began working there.

In the year 1903, he printed in the "*Voskhod*" (March-April) a piece that was called "Jargony Literature and Its Readers." This was one of the first attempts in the area of Yiddish literary stories. In the years 1903-1905, he was an active person in the evolvement of "the new library." Here, there were translations done from Russian and Hebrew into Yiddish (Karalenka – "The Legend about the Flohr, Agripa, and Menachem ben Yehuda"; Giovannielli – "*Sportok*"; Feierberg – "Stories"; and so on). He takes part in the first daily Yiddish newspaper "*Der Friend*" ["The Friend"] (first published in 1903 in Peterburg under the editor Sh. Ginzburg). In that newspaper, as well as in the Hebrew newspaper "*HaZman*" ("The Time"), he argues with the opponents of the Yiddish language, and underscores its national, cultural meaning. In the later years, his connection with the Yiddish writers and culture activists became narrower. In 1912, he became a member of the editorial board of journal "*Di Yiddishe Velt*" ["The Yiddish World"]. In the years of World War One, when the Tzarist government placed the Jewish people in a terrible situation, expelling them from the front and bordering areas, carried out pogroms there, Y. Zinberg did not limit himself to literary judges and critical works. In various journals, which in those days, often changed their names because of censorship,

[Page 380]

he published a series of articles about Peretz in relation to his death, about Bialik, about all kinds of facts of literary-socialist life in those times; once, he wrote publicity articles ("Thoughts of an Insane Man," "The World Judges," and so on). After Shalom Aleichem's death, he compiled, along with Sh. Nigeren, a collection, dedicated to his memory.[3]

In the year 1915, Y. Zinberg goes back to his fundamental work – "History of Literature of the Jews." The title alone demonstrates that he put before him a task that was a lot more difficult and expansive than writing only "History of Hebrew Literature" and "History of Yiddish Literature."[4] This undertaking resulted in the literatures became as separated as if with the Wall of China, one from the other. The language of the literary work moved into very Judeo-political content. Because of that, in our literary historical research, the history of Jewish Russian literature, which in its time filled a distinct socialist function, almost completely disappeared.

In his large, main work, Y. Zinberg proceeded to use the introduction of his former monograph "The History of the Jewish Press in Russia in Connection with the Socialist Waves," but the scale was, understandably, much larger.

Y. Zinberg well understood that writing a scientifically independent work about the essence of the first sources and to add how his own judgments, which would encompass the entire literary creations of the Jewish people for the very long duration, this would be almost impossible for a single person to do. He therefore put chronological limits onto his work, and began, from that moment on, since from an Asiatic people we became European, and the hegemony of the Yiddish culture moved from *Foder* [?] Asia to Western and Southern Europe, up to the *Haskalah* ["Enlightenment"] era.

[Page 381]

The material was divided into six volumes (8 parts) in the following order:

Volume 1 – the Arabic-Spanish era (part 1)
Volume 2 – the German-French kibbutz (second part); the Jewish kibbutz in Italy (part 3)
Volume 3 – the conflict between Kabbalah [mysticism] and "*mesoira*" [tradition] against rationalist philosophy (part 4)
Volume 4 – The Italian Jewish population in the Renaissance period (part 5). The Yiddish culture center in the Ottoman regime (part 6).
Volume 5 – The German Polish culture center (part 7).
Volume 6 – Old Yiddish literature from the earliest times until the *Haskalah* [Enlightenment] era. (part 8).
Leading his work until the *Haskalah* era, Y. Zinberg did not stop there. In the published volumes 7 and 8 (which contain "*Chochmas Yisrael*" [Wisdom of Israel], the Galician enlightenment, the beginnings of the *Haskalah* movement in Russia, and so on), he presents his historical excursion until the 50s of the 19th century. As he writes in his introduction in volume 1 (December 1927), he wrote the first four volumes initially in Russian, and was not working them over in Yiddish (not a simple task). Only the first five chapters of the Russian text were published in Kiev in the year 1919.

In the time that Y. Zinberg began to busy himself with the literary research, in that same area, the characteristics of the cultural history took a prominent position, which contained its own authoritative representatives (Hettner and Sherer in Germany, then in France, Brandes in Denmark, Pepin, Wingerow, and so on, in Russia). The attitude of this school was carried by Y. Zinberg into the research of "Literature of the Jews." Today, we take from the cultural-historical school not its methodological principles, but the great, factual material that it brought into its works. The same is relevant in Y. Zinberg's literary history.

Y. Zinberg was not satisfied only with the history of the so-called nice literature. "The development of the poetic forms will be investigated here for the source of the entire cultural Jewish environment, with its spiritual and socialist waves, tightly connected with the general European culture of that period." That is

[Page 382]

characteristic for the cultural historical school, which, in its research, gave attention to the socialist waves of that era. But Lenin's attitude towards that was foreign to him, saying that "in every nationalist culture there are undeveloped elements of the democratic and socialist culture, since in every nation there are working and exploitive masses in whom the conditions of their lives create a democratic and socialist ideology."[5]

His credo regarding the methodology of history of literature of the Jews is explained by Y. Zinberg in his introduction ("from the author") in the first volume of his work:

"The eras of rising and falling, from beautiful growth to tragic failing and waning, happened in an entirely different manner (in Yiddish – H.A.) than in the other European countries. The Jewish cultural history has its own style, evolved on its own level, experienced completely different stages…" And then facts are brought here, which, according to Y. Zinberg, have to validate the above-mentioned founding thoughts. At the end of the 15th century, there was a spiritual upheaval in Europe – discovery of America, of book publication, religious reformation – and Jews were expelled from Spain; in the 17th century – in European Descartes, for Jews – there was the destruction of "*Gezeiras Takh*."[6] It is enough to present these two examples so that it should become clear that we are dealing with a purely ideological concept of the history; other than that, there are many confused historical facts which do not allow themselves to be compared, and which happened in many different countries, under different circumstances. This relates to the old Spanish Jews' concept formulated upon the old phrase, "*Lo kekhol goyim beis Yisrael*" (Jews are not like any other nation).

If we are already taking historical parallels and similarities, then we have to accept these facts that lie, if we can say this, in one line and which happened in one and the same time. We can take as an example religious reformation, the efforts that were put forward in various Western European countries, that the religious books should be translated from the incomprehensible Latin for the broader people, to the people's language, and then demonstrate, that at the same time (1544)

[Page 383]

the *siddur* [prayer book] was translated into Yiddish, and the translator, Yosef ben Yakir, says in the introduction: "I hold that these are real fools, those who wish to pray in the holy language even though they do not understand a single word. I would like to know how someone who prays like that can have real concentration. So, we decided to print the prayers in a translated form." Remembering that they herded the Jews out of Spain, we cannot forget that in that same time they also expelled the Muslims. And if we are already speaking about Descartes, and you want to compare what happened at that time to the Jews, then we have to mention that at that same time Boruch Spinoza appeared in Holland, who, about thirteen years after Decartes' death, published a book where he polemicizes with Decartes ("The Philosophical Principles of Decartes," 1663). You can find many such comparisons in Jewish history because the history of the Jews in various countries somehow crosses lines with the history of that country, and Jews "unintentionally protected their own history for themselves" (Marx).[7]

Y. Zinberg's history, as we explained, encaptures, other than artistic literature, the history of Middle-Ages' religious philosophy (in the first publications), history of the so-called "*Chochmas Yisrael*" (in the later publications). The great scope was, as one of the reasons states, that until that time, there was no critical appraisal of this work. This, Y. Opatoshu showed in one of his enclosed letters. Only a team of specialists can take on such a work. Meanwhile, we can earmark the surprising erudition that Y. Zinberg demonstrated, and that which can and must serve us and be used in the research work in the area of "literature of the Jews."

It seems that Y. Zinberg did not complete his great work. His fate was: They did not write much about him while he was still alive, and even after his death, there was no real necrology, because he died in the Stalin cult (1939). Now, after the 20th assembly of our party, when Y. Zinberg had a full recovery, it is our obligation to remember the great researcher of "Literature by the Jews" and critically analyze his literary heritage.

Original footnotes:

1. For the 30-year jubilee of Y. Zinberg's literary activities, Tzvi Prilutzki wrote an article in "*Moment*" about "Dr. Yisroel Zinberg," ("*A bintel zichronos*"; "A collection of memories"). From this article, we used the material for the young Zinberg, until the beginning of his literary works.
2. *Ilui* (from the Hebrew; def: young Talmudic prodigy), that is what this phenomenal young man was called, who would share his thoughts and sharp mind. *masmid* (from the Hebrew; def: a diligent student of the Torah); that is what the bright students in the yeshivos were called.
3. Collection, "In Memory of Shalom Aleichem." Volume 3, 1917.

4. In Reisin's "Lexicon," the title of the book "The History of the Hebrew and Yiddish Literature," was incorrect. For our work, we used: Dr. Yisrael Zinberg, "The History of the Literature of the Jews, European era." Publisher, Moshe Shmuel Skliarski, New York, 1943. The publication is a photographic printing of the second filing of the publication "Tamar," Vilna, 1933 (in eight volumes).
5. V. A. Lenin. Fifth file, vol 2. p. 120
6. *Gezeiras Takh*. In Hebrew literature, this was how they referred to the Jewish pogroms that took place in Ukraine, 1648.
7. The first volume of the first publication "Works by Marx and Engels," p. 381.

[Page 384]

Zinberg's Archives

Translated by Pamela Russ

Zinberg's fund, which is found in the archives of the Leningrad section of the Institute of the nations of Asia in the Science academy, and is marked under number 86, is divided into three lists. List #1. There are 87 numbers; # 2, there are 367 numbers; #3, 167 numbers; total 630 "archival units." This technical term is very broad, according to its style, and also is on a card on which one line is written. Also, an original from a large work that holds 1,000 pages and more. The greatest position (according to the number of pages) is held by Zinberg's original work, articles, lectures on various historical and literary themes; other than these originals, that were given in completed form, there is a great number of archival entries that present raw material, arrangements ("*zagadavkes*" [enigmas]) of all kinds of works. There are originals of all eight published volumes of "The History of Literature by the Jews." Completely ready for print is the manuscript of the ninth volume, which was rewritten by Zinberg's wife Rosa Vladimirovna. This volume encompasses the literature of the 50s and 60s in Russia. As is known from the correspondence with various American writers and journalists, Zineberg had in mind to write a tenth volume, of which a large place was to be taken by Yiddish literature in America (see, for example, Opatoshu's letter of March 14, 1938). Unfortunately, Zinberg was not able to fulfill this plan.

From the so-called "*zagadavkes*," the following can be indicated: 1) material for the lectures about the history of Yiddish literature (partly in Yiddish, partly in Russian); 2) or the history of the Yiddish socialist press; 3) or the history of the Yiddish language; 4) or the cultural history of the Jews in Russia; 5) of the Middle- Ages rationalists; and so on.

Other than originals from Zinberg's works and "*zagadavkes*," which have a connection to his research works, there are various other materials in his fund, that are connected to other authors. There is a mathematical work (in Hebrew) from an unknown author; there is a "*kolbo*" package [random collection], which was not yet figured out, and some which are marked under the title "excerpts from various letters,

[Page 385]

literary works, songs, various manuscripts in Russian, Yiddish, and Hebrew"; we also find here "satirical songs from unknown authors" (unedited). In particular, a list from Sh. Ansky's literary heritage should be noted, which was compiled by Y. Zinberg.

Y. Zinberg preserved in his archives not only literary material, but also historical documents which were connected to the works of various Yiddish cultural societies, political parties, and organizations. In particular, we can note those materials that are related to the treatment of the Jewish question in the "*gosudarstvo dome*" ["state house"].

A large section of Zinberg's archives is given to his correspondence with Yiddish writers from different countries – without exaggeration, you can say – that there was no Yiddish writer and publicist, who wrote in Yiddish or Hebrew, who was not in communication with Zinberg. There are no less than 500 letters in the archives, among them – from Shalom Aleichem, Peretz, Bialik, Sholem Asch, Opatoshu, Winchewsky, Niger, Bergelson, Breinin, Sh. Ansky, Achad Haam, Klausner, Hillel Zeitlin, and so on. The final count of the number of letters is not yet determined because there are packages under the title of "letters from unknown people to Zinberg." There are also many randomly collected letters which Zinberg kept, placed on the list of the archives of "the society to spread education between Jews in Russia" ["AFE"]. Letters in this category belong to Sh. Ansky, Shaul Ginzburg, and so on.

Among the letters addressed to Zinberg, there are many that have an autobiographical character. As one of the editors of the 16-volume "*Yevraiskaya Encyclopedia*" ["Jewish Encyclopedia"], and the director of section of "New Hebrew and Yiddish Literature," Zinberg approached the writers of that time with the request that they also submit their autobiographies; the responses are in the archives. Many of them are brief, with questions (such as Sholom Asch's). Other writers used this opportunity and submitted detailed autobiography material, saying also that the editor can use it all, as he alone understands. Dinezan, Spektor, Weisenberg, Yitzchok Katznelson, and many others, gave these detailed replies.

Other than the autobiographical letters, the others were connected to all kinds of literary and social issues of the time.

[Page 386]

A large number of letters are connected to the works of many various newspapers and journals, in the first column of "*Der Yiddishe Velt*" ["The Yiddish World"], where Zinberg was one of the closest co-workers.

From Zinberg's answers, only a small number of "*chernovikes*" ["rough drafts"] remain. It is now hard to say if these rough drafts have factual answers, which were sent to the correspondent, or maybe they were fabricated by Zinberg himself.

I am using this opportunity to thank the representative of the archives, Dimitri Yevgenyevitch Bertels, for his careful instruction and his assistance in my work.

[Page 387]

The Rich Archives of Y. Zinberg in Leningrad

From Avraham Belov, Moscow (press agency "*Novosty*" [news]

Sunday, April 26, 1964. "*Novosty*" ["Morning Freedom"]

Translated by Pamela Russ

From the editor: Along with the very important article about the representative of Yiddish literature Y. Zinberg, the press agency *Novosty* sent us the following information: Y. Zinberg was a fallen victim of the Stalin cult in the year 1939. After the 20th Congress of the Soviet Communist Party, in 1956, he was rehabilitated. His rich scientific heritage is now being studied everywhere, as Avraham tells here. Y. Zinberg's wife, Rosa, at 80 years old, lives in Leningrad, very respectably. Also, Zinberg's grandchild lives there, an engineer, along with his family.

The docent from Leningrad university, Hilel Alexandow, is currently studying the archive of the famous Yiddish historian Sergei (Yisroel) Zinberg, located in the Leningrad department of the Institute of Asian Nations in the *Alfarband* [union wide, Soviet Union] Science Academy. The correspondent from the press agency *Novosty* asked the learned person to present information about this archive. "My work is still very far from complete, because the archive is a large one. But now, I can tell you about the first results. In the archive, there were hundreds of letters from famous writers, philologists, historians, publicists. Among them, letters from Shalom Aleichem, Chaim Nachman Bialik, Yitzchak Leib Peretz, Achad Haam, Ber Borochow, Shimon Dubnow, Sholom Ash, Morris Winchewsky, Yakov Fichman, and others.

What can you say about Zinberg himself? Yisroel Zinberg was born in 1873 in the town of Lanovits (province of Volyn). He was a very talented and timeless, educated chemist. In his upper thirties, he managed a chemistry laboratory from Putilov, later Kirov, a factory in Leningrad. Zinberg is the author of many works about chemistry, particularly of the educational book "How to Do Chemical Analyses," which went through two publications (in 1921 and 1929). But Zinberg only yearned for literary knowledge. In 1900, he debuted with monographs about the Yiddish writer Yitzchok Ber Lewinson. In 1901, he published a book "Shylock's Ancestry." He is also the author of the works: "Two Aspirations in Jewish Life," "The Forerunners of the Yiddish Journalist,"

[Page 388]

and a list of others. In 1911-1913, I also attended a cycle of his lectures of the higher courses of Eastern knowledge, extended and completed, taken as a source from his nine-volume "History of the Literature of the Jewish People." For us students, there actually remained a question, where does our lecturer have the time to prepare his lectures for us? He would come directly to give us the lectures, straight from the Putilov factory…

What do the letters discuss, those that you have already read?

The great majority of the letters are written in Yiddish, Hebrew, or Russian. There are also letters in western European languages. A separate group of letters present an autobiographical character. Being one of the editors of the sixteen-volume "Yiddish Encyclopedia" (1913-1908), Zinberg, it appears, approached the writers of those times with the request that they send in their autobiographies. In Zinberg's archives, the replies are there, which he received from these authors: Sholom Ash, Yakov Dinezon, Yosef Kloizner, Dovid Frishman, Zalman Schneur, and others.

The prosaic Yitzchak Meyer Weisenberg and Mordechai Spektor wrote with a lot of details and poetical writing. The letter written by the classic Yitzchak Leib Peretz in Yiddish, dated December 11, 1911, presents great interest. The author of the famous stories "Chassidish" – Y.L. Peretz, shares that he himself was never a chassid, he never had any connection to chassidim, and did not really know the Chassidic rabbis. Y.L. Peretz also informs that he began to write in Polish, but burned all his manuscripts. After that, he began to write in Hebrew. But in this case too, his first literary proofs did not satisfy him. Then he started to write in Yiddish. This was about 35-40 years ago, comments Y. L. Peretz, as he describes how he acquired his world view. It seems that the literature of the prophets had an effect on him, and his first songs were written under the influence of Heine and Berne.

Letter from Bialik. There are letters that address all kinds of literary problems, or they are related to the published or other works. The six letters of Chaim Nachman Bialik, for example, written in the years 1921-1927, belong to this category. They mainly discuss the scientific result of the work of the famous Yiddish writer of the Middle Ages, Shlomo Ibn Gabirol,

[Page 389]

which Ch. N. Bialik prepared for publication. The valuable lists of Ibn Gabirol's songs are found in Leningrad in the open library. Bialik asked Zinberg to help him get the necessary material in order to clarify certain questions which arose during his work with Achad Ha'am's four letters, sent from London, which are connected with the journalist Uri Kowner and also to Shmuel Bukh ("*Sefer Shmuel*"), which is very valuable, and is located in the British museum.

The five letters of Yosef Opatoshu, sent from New York (during the years 1937-1938), address the question about the oppositional relationships between the Yiddish and Hebrew authors.

In Ber Borochow's letter from Vienna (January 4, 1914), the main topic is about his potential participation in the Yiddish encyclopedia.

The letter from the founder of the Yiddish proletariat poetry, Morris Winchewsky (sent from New York, September 20, 1909), touches on the question of the history of the newspaper "*Vahrheit*" ["Truth"].

Zinberg had many correspondents – around 400. It is quite impossible to describe all of them. I would like to mention just a few. Zinberg's archives contain letters from critics and publicists: Shmuel Niger, Reuven Brinen, Hilel Zeitlin. From the dramatists: Peretz Hirschbein, Ansky (Rapaport). From the prose writer: Uri Gnesin. Lexicographer: Zalman Reisin. Historian of Chassidism: Shmuel Abba Gorodetsky. From the well-known publisher and publicist: Shaul Yakov Horowitz…

Shalom Aleichem's letters. Finally, I will discuss Shalom Aleichem's two letters. The first letter, dated October 24, 1909, written in Switzerland, is dedicated to the Yiddish folk-writer and composer Mark Warshawsky (1848-1907), on two pages, written in a calligraphic, pearly handwriting. The Yiddish classic writer, with great spirit, wrote about the people's talent, which he spoke about, and which he himself described and which he too "put forth for the people."

In the second letter, written on November 3 of that same year, in Italy (written in Russian), there is discussion about the same Warshawsky, Shalom Aleichem declines any honor for the article about Warshawsky and requests an improvement on his first letter: "I ask you to review once again my letter to you about Warshawsky. In one place there, where it discusses his declamation of his own songs, I think you will find a phrase that while performing with the deceased poet in the province, we had a great success.

The word "we" (if

[Page 390]

it is in there), I ask that it be removed and changed to the word "he." It is not civil and not comfortable to speak like that of one's own success."

This is a demonstration of the humility of the great writer, because it is well known that he was greeted with huge enthusiasm in every single auditorium.

H. Aleksandrov said that in Zinberg's archive, there is also material that is related to the history of the Yiddish socialist press, of the Yiddish theater, of the Middle-Ages rationalists, and others. A precise catalogue of Zinberg's archives will be presented in the "Bulletin," which the archives publish from the Institute of Asia-Nations.

[Page 391]

Chapter 11:

People and Types

[Page 392] [Blank] [Page 393]

Dina Kawkes

by Muni

Translated by Pamela Russ

You were dark, and unforgettably beautiful,
My mother, Dina Kawkes, my longing for you,
Oh smart, proud, princess of charm,
You were the Shabbath during the weekdays. Beard and sidelocks, old Jews
Smart, strong masters of the house,
Came to seek advice
And your wisdom was seen as the best. At all the times in our lives
Good, bad, difficult, simple,
Your spirit gave us strength
And your wisdom supported it. I remember when in 1920, naked,
Russia left us and went away
Then you sewed clothing and suits
For us from old jackets.

[Page 394]

But you did not make shoes from old ones
Because leather does not allow for it to be done so well,
But our feet, barefoot and cold,
With love and warmth, healed and smoothed. We went to cheder barefooted,
Frozen on ice, walked carefully,
And never caught cold as everyone else always did,
Because with your warmth you fed our bodies. I see your last minutes, my mother,
I see how you stand naked in front of the open grave
And at a distance stands Shay'ke, and you are looking at each other
And search, where is Muni? He has left the house. It's fine that he left for the good,
My Munye remembers me – do you think – so likely that
For me it's all the same, I already made my trouble
As a Jewish daughter, as a Jewish mother. I already put my brick in the wall,
It's all the same for me, I can already go.
When a person dies, it's not so tragic
It's important for the nation to remain strong. You were large as a mother
A giant as a person,
For me you are still so big, I tremble
When I pray or say blessings for your name.

[Page 395]

Uziel Chaim Mordche's

by Muni

Translated by Pamela Russ

Lanovits grew you up until adulthood
Your dark green eyes reflect distance,
Have seen the past and see the future.
You were her son of loyalty. You were her sage, beard,
Sexton, chassid, and main provider.
You shared her fear
And knew her fate of secrecy. From the Jew's clouds of history
From the doubts of the ocean's depths
You provided her with joy,
Comfort, faith, and fiery closeness to God. Because of that, the murderers of Jewish history
Took you first as a sacrifice
Because you were the sky-earth
You acquired God for the people. Uziel Chaim Mordche's gracious father!
You gave us children everything!
But you knocked it into our branches [growth]
That our ways should grow [like branches]. You worked hard until there was no more energy,
Smeared our bread with pride and depth
You planted into us our hearts and minds
Prepared for distant heights. You burned with planted pain,
You chased to find God,
So that the god's of other nations
Should not poison your thoughts. No one can know how great you were
Except for the person who painfully felt your fire.
I saw how my father understood you,
You are wrapped into my heart for eternity.

[Page 396]

Uziel and Dina are people's Jews
That's what my nation is, in general and in detail
You are its symbol substantive as a duo,
That is why the other nations hate us. But thanks to you to others like you
My nation will yet know of joy and beauty
And all those who are rich from the Russian and German
Will fall and thrash and stop existing.

[Page 397]

Shalom Weisman

Sarah Fiks

(By Sara'ke Kavkes)

Translated by Pamela Russ

Aside from my family in Lanovits, Yisroel Berenstein and Dina Kavkes (Rabin), as they called her, I have the face of Shalom Weisman, a person with a kind soul, etched in my memory.

Shalom Weisman, of blessed memory, was a learned and well-read person who spent all of his free time reading books or as bookkeeper at his place of work. Sh. Weisman, of blessed memory, did not bother to deal with *kehilah* (community) matters, never offended anyone or criticized anyone, always sought only to interpret everything for the good.

Genesia, his neighbor, visited him regularly and sat comfortably at his table to update him on the goings on in their town. She reported the good and the bad, including lots of gossip. When I once asked him what he thought of Genesia's stories, he replied quietly and humbly, as he usually did: "I did not hear what she said." I am sure he told me the truth.

Weisman worked for Yisroel Berenstein who at the time had a Polish partner named Nartowski. Yisroel told me that he used to give Berenstein large sums of money to settle accounts with the wheat traders.

"As my uncle's part-time bookkeeper, I sometimes made a mistake and entered a lower than correct figure in our books. Once I became very agitated about the mistake I made, and each error had to be corrected by underlining the error using red ink. I begged Shalom Weisman: "Do me a favor, take what you need from the till and enter the amount in our books." From then on, I had no more problems with our account books."

[Page 398]

Sh. Weisman worked for many years as an employee of Countess Kosakowski. She was a devout Catholic, prayed twice a day, accepted money only using a handkerchief so as not to touch a male's hands. Once, the Countess asked:

"So, Sholom'ke (as she used to call him), do you want to manage my entire estate?"

Shalom related that he thanked her for the trust she placed in him but said that one should not take away another man's livelihood. She employed a Polish Christian, and he would continue working his post.

There was never a shortage of anti-Semitism. One day, the director approached the Countess and asked her:

"Why is it that the prominent Polish Countess employs a Jew? It is well known that Jews are exploiters and swindlers, all the way back to the times of Jesus."

Six weeks later, Shalom received a letter from the Countess asking him to accept the post of estate director (manager) of her entire estate.

Two days after he received the letter the Polish estate director came to Shalom demanding to know why he, Shalom, was taking his livelihood away.

* * *

I read the Countess' letter which for me was a surprise. It said that I had decided to do what I could to see to it that the Polish director kept his post. I had a thirty-minute audience with the Countess. A side door suddenly opened and the director appeared. She asked the director to enter the room and she told him of my appeal. He remained quiet. Hearing of my appeal he turned pale. I was sitting. He remained quiet for a few minutes. Then, the Countess turned to him and said:

"You are a Pole, yet you do not follow Jesus' teaching of 'forgive men their sins, help the needy, and love thy neighbor as you love thyself.' Remember what you said about Jews? This Jew, with his kind soul, good heart, is begging me to keep you in your present job. He argues that you have four children who are in the middle of their studies, and so on. I feel sorry for you, but you have lost my trust."

And Shalom Weisman, of blessed memory, became the director of her entire estate. However, he told me during our conversation that this episode caused him a great deal of aggravation.

I had a chance to read several of the Countess' letters to Weisman. They included the most beautiful epithets with great respect: "I have the honor of addressing Mr. Weisman, a wise and respectable man, who is filled like a pomegranate, with wisdom of all our old treasures [culture]," and so on.

[Page 399]

We also must mention the esteemed wife of Sh. Einstein – Chana. She was a symbol of goodness and politeness. I distinctly remember an episode that I myself witnessed. It occurred on a winter day. The esteemed Chana was sitting on a stool next to the oven. Sh. Weisman came into the room, took off his sheepskin coat, and warmed his hands from a distance (he generally did not sit near the oven). He noticed that his wife was crying. She proceeded to tell her husband that someone (I don't remember who it was) told her that for three days his house had been without heat because he has no firewood and no money to purchase any. His children were freezing and the family was suffering. Shalom said that she should have given them some of their firewood.

Chana replied: "I know, but I did not want to do that without you."

Shalom agreed and said: "You're right. I would have divorced you immediately."

Hannah wrapped herself in a big shawl and immediately brought money to the needy family.

Oh, I spent many days and nights in the Weisman house in the company of their daughter, Sara'ke Weisman. She had a lovely, moving, sweet alto voice and a beautiful face like a madonna. And she was as good-hearted as her mother Chana. In general, this was a quiet, cultured, and modest family of discreet doves, rich in spirit. It is hard to imagine that despite the difficult life conditions of Jews in these small towns, such quiet and good-natured families existed.

Chana Weisman

[Page 400]

My Three Sisters

By Shalom Kwaitel (Avital)

Translated by Pamela Russ

My mother, Sarah Shiye Nosson's, as she was called in our *shtetl*, gave birth to four children: me, her only son, and my three sisters: Breindel, Baila, and Dora. When I immigrated to Israel, and my older sister Breindel married and built her own family life, Baila and Dora, my two beautiful, blossoming younger sisters remained at home. They strove to join me in Israel to fulfill their dream of becoming *chalutzim* [pioneers] and change their lives to participate in the building of our homeland. They were raised with the Zionist spirit, and that was their goal. Their letters to me were soaked with love and heartfelt feelings for their ideals and fulfillment thereof. They waited for years and wanted to know from me what life in Israel was like. Life for them on a kibbutz was the most beautiful and the best, giving a person whatever he could possibly yearn for. But as they say, a person plans and God laughs. The deluge of World War Two that befell the Jews killed their life's hopes, efforts, and dreams. The Nazi thugs destroyed everything. My three sisters perished, disappeared together with our other brethren from our *shtetl*.

A short time ago one of the survivors visited Israel, and told us the following story: "When the Jews from our town stood in front of the open mass-grave in the last minutes of their lives, your sister Baila, that little girl whom I left back home, held a short speech for the tormented, tragic living dead: "

"Jews, we go on our last way with pride and strength. We are the victims of a huge tragedy that befell our people. Wild beasts are roaring while the big world remains silent in the distance. (Jews:) Take revenge! Take revenge! The Jewish nation in the rest of the world will not remain silent. "

[Page 401]

"We are the martyrs and victims that are sacrificing in the name of God. Our comfort and last wish before death is that the land of Israel will rise and be built for the next generation. Let the people of Israel live!'"

Beaten, tortured, broken spiritually and physically, the Jews of our *shtetl* were all murdered. Their blood boiled and poured for many days until their holy souls were appeased and found their eternal rest.

The above-mentioned words of my sister Baila shall be remembered forever, and the memory of my three sisters should be eternal. As well, Baila spoke for them and for everyone. Her words spoke for all of us.

[Page 402]

Regarding Zunye (Azriel) Rabin

By Yitzchak Weinstein

Translated by Pamela Russ

I found out that a book is being written about the righteous people of Lanovits. I thought: The image of our *shtetl* would not be complete without the richly spiritual contribution of Zunye.

I grew up in his house and got to know him better than his closest ones. I saw in him a great personality of a young man who had a wonderful future waiting for him as a promising leader and director, organizer, and developer of ideas.

From an early age, Zunye was brought up to think independently, to understand social issues, with broad and deep horizons. Together with Shalom Maharshak, he led the "*Ha'noar Hatzioni*" youth group. He himself was very left-leaning in his thoughts but he knew that his leftist leanings were not for this generation nor for these times. First, the devoted Lanovits young children must be freed from their narrow thoughts, and then they would find the road to freedom as individual members of a free people.

Zunye used to read and study for hours. In the evenings, he would deliver his "lectures," these were not ordinary speeches. Each lecture addressed an answer to a question people did not immediately think about. He clarified life's problems to the lost, confused youth.

Every evening, Zunye gathered his friends, his dear Lanovits children, and connected them to thoughts, brought them to dreams, and awoke them to be daring.

His historical views, as his actual ones, were popular scientific comments of people's ways, no matter how deep and how much he deviated from the standard.

Zunye did not have an easy life. His respectable and rich parents, Uziel and Dina Rabin, became poor. He had to work hard to help his parents in their difficult circumstances. Internally, he was angry, and worried about the catastrophes that awaited the world, his people, and the individuals of his tragic generation. His soul was filled with the "world's pain," yet he always shined. His beautiful face was always lit up, and his tall, tall presence made him always stand out,

[Page 403]

Zunye Rabin - seated on the far left

[Page 404]

with his head of curly hair, raised high, high, up. Nobody knew where he got such amazing strength to overcome everything.

He once left for Lemberg [Lvov] for a while and became a certified teacher. He worked, supported himself, and studied hard.

He had unusual talent and was an exceptionally hard worker, yet always humble with himself and friendly with everyone else as well.

He left Lanovits with the Russians and went to a distant place. He left with a heavy heart but survived his ordeals. At the end of the world's catastrophe, he returned to Poland with the Polish Army.

In Poland, when the war was still ongoing, I found out that he was in Kamieniec Mazowiecki. I quickly went to see him. Zunye sounded confident and with his characteristic humor said, "Itzikel, we are alive! We shall take our revenge. The days are numbered, and I will see my ideas fulfilled. You understand what I mean?" He meant living in Israel. Unfortunately, this was not to be.

On the day of victory, he fell in a battle with the murderers. He lived an active life and was an example for our Lanovits youth.

We cannot forget Zunye.

[Page 405]

Elazar (Luzer) Meil

By Muni

Translated by Pamela Russ

Lanovits was an odd *shtetl*. Its butchers were learners and humble Jews, its cobblers were honest and the tailors were peaceful workers who were not embarrassed by their scissors and irons, but they wanted to be rid of these things and get to business, meaning to serve in the *shul*, to address community issues, to arrange beautiful marriages for their children, and become equal with all people.

Luzer son of Senek was an artisan who found an esthetic satisfaction in creating beautiful clothing for others in his workshop. He also had a deep respect for the worth of manual labor.

We youngsters were drawn to him. We wanted him to make us beautiful in his clothes. We were eager to hear his opinion about our figure, our appearance, and our esthetic look.

Luzer was a deeply quiet man, a devoted father, a hard worker, and a pleasant and sociable person.

When I was young, I did not understand why he treated me, and perhaps other youngsters among my friends, with such respect. I wondered why he sought to talk to me occasionally, and our discussions were never idle. We always talked about lineage, beauty, the outlines of a figure, and their cultural contribution to social relations. Over the years, I suddenly saw Luzer not in his milieu, and I understood him. I had tried to fit him into a conventional mold, but his personality became clear to me.

[Page 406]

He simply was a man who did not fit his time nor his place. There were many such people among us. He solved his problem by creating a lifestyle where he found satisfaction in his professional work, with creative joy, with all kinds of struggles for earning a livelihood, all as a basis for the highest level of human culture.

He was simply a Jew who saw many shortcomings in the diaspora concept of *yiddishkeit* where false concepts of morality ruled and had shortcomings in what is important to people. He did not want to share that outlook.

He was simply a proletarian Jew who did not realize that his work was his lot and that it also shaped his character.

He was simply a good Jew, but one who was unwilling to share some of the generally accepted conceptions of the Jewish character.

He was simply an "expression." A person who could not express his criticism of his environment, nor express in words his life's credo. Instead, he expressed his credo in his attitude in his home, on the street, to his family and within the community. He expressed goodness as he visualized it.

I had a warm feeling in my heart for him when I went on a date with a girl, dressed in his well-tailored suit under his finely tailored winter jacket on a starlit night in the winter frost. On these occasions I remember Luzer Meil, the unique and charming person and tailor, who, as all the others, ended his life in our warm-hearted *shtetl* of Lanovits.

I must remember him.

[Page 407]

My Grandfather Akiva

By Z. Katz (Rabin)

Translated by Pamela Russ

My grandfather Akiva Weirach stood out among Lanovits Jews, not because he was the greatest Torah scholar, not because he was the richest Jew, but because he had a beautiful face and was a good Jew. The Lanovits Jews remembered his good deeds and revered him for them. Those who remember Akiva the "pleasing one" (that's what they called him), remember his tall build, his snow-white beard, and pleasant face, all reflecting his goodness, and the kindness just came out of him, and he was always clean. I remember his Sabbath clothes, his neatly pressed black pants, with his beautiful black frock, and the always shiny black polished shoes, and his shirt smelling of cleanliness.

He was good to all: to his wife, to the children, the grandchildren, and to all others. I remember as a child that we children used to play in our house on a Shabbath afternoon while the rest of the family took a nap. On these occasions my grandfather would get out of his bed quietly so as not to awaken anyone, then come and ask us children if we wanted anything. We were so busy playing that we did not think of having any food. Not waiting for our answer, he would bring out the best that was available in the house. We were so happy with that. Not only I, but all my friends loved my grandfather Akiva.

The Lanovits Jews remembered my grandfather's good deeds while he and his wife lived in Zbarazh. He originated from Galicia, and it was difficult for him to get used to life in Lanovits. After some time in Lanovits, however, they moved back to Zbarazh

[Page 408]

where my grandfather felt at home.

It was wartime, and there was a border between Lanovits and Zbarazh. Nonetheless, trade continued across this border. Some Lanovits Jews traded regularly with traders in Zbarazh. But it was difficult in those days. The entire Akiva Weirach family was always there to offer support to others, whether someone's business was good or bad, or if the trader had problems with the government, or at the border, the person invariably went to Akiva for help. The latter never refused him. Akiva did whatever he could to solve their problems. He was also a great host as was his wife, no less than he was. She too came from Lanovits. Their house was like a private hotel for Lanovits Jews.

Akiva Weirach helped both Jews and Gentiles with formalities connected to immigration to America. These immigrants stayed at his house until their departure. All, including Gentiles, were grateful for his help and hospitality. And after they left to America, they all missed "Akiva the Zbarazher's house." When after a few years they returned to Lanovits, because his wife could not adjust to the "big land," they were received with great joy. The Lanovitsers remembered what my grandfather had done for them.

My grandfather was a wonderful and good type.

May his memory be blessed.

[Page 409]

My Family

By Moshe Zak (Mexico)

Translated by Pamela Russ

My father, Manus Zak, was a Jew who thought only about the love of one Jew for the other. He was deeply religious but never made a comment about another Jew who was not so Jewish in his behavior. He loved him as he was.

My mother Zelda was good-natured. She welcomed everyone with a smile. People who lived in her house were as if in their own home. That's also how she accepted her life, with goodness and a good feeling, since we could not change anything. It was likely God's wish to be that way, and we had to accept it for the good.

They gave over these good characteristics as inheritance, and in the worst of times of my life in a strange place, when I would remember the good views of my parents, then I felt better in my heart, and then I too became a better person, less ambitious, more generous and filled with faith.

Our home was dipped in greenery, and the encircling trees eased the edgy prayers into the earth itself. On Shabbath in the summer, we spent daytime under the trees and drank cold water from the well, which was near the rabbi, Reb Ahara'le. The water would intoxicate me with its freshness. For years now, I drink all kinds of drinks, but of the thousand flavors from the tasty tap water I was never able to feel the same way.

My father merited to die a natural death, but my mother and my two sisters and their husbands and children died along with all the other dear Jews of Lanovits. According to Jewish tradition, I would like to ceremoniously elevate their souls, and I believe that the only way to do this is to write a book. Also, I think we have to remember for always our dear, good Jewish parents, because all the good things that we have comes from them.

Let us also not forget that because we merited to remain alive, we have a particular obligation to remember them and us as their descendants.

May their souls be bound up in the bond of eternal life.

[Page 410]

Manus-Zak's, and his daughters, son-in-law, and grandchildren

[Page 411]

Farmers

By Yechezkel Shmukler (Beis Yitzchak)

Translated by Pamela Russ

The village Jews, *arendares* [farmers], as they used to be called, did not merit to be written about nor to be mentioned in the Yizkor books, among all the martyrs whose names were mentioned. Not with them, and not on their own. They simply are not mentioned, likely because they were not in this category.

And it was specifically these Jews who were exceptionally and tragically devoted Jews.

All the Jews in the small towns were dominated by the Christians, but there was still some kind of unity among them [the Jews], who were protected from a sudden catastrophe, or daily personal vengeance from Christians. But the village Jews were separated, lonely, alone, despondent, and dangers were upon them every minute, not having any protection or help from anyone. They had to protect themselves. Nonetheless, they took upon themselves the yoke of "an exile within an exile," and they did not budge from their Jewishness, not even one hair.

In the towns, you could have made jokes at the expense of the farmers, maybe that he is hunched over a little when he reads "Hebrew" [trying to figure out the text since he is not so educated]; that he confuses "*bnei adam*" [recited when one swings the *kapparot* chicken over one's head before Yom Kippur] with "*kol nidrei*" [recited on the eve of Yom Kippur]; and other things. But whatever was connected to Jewishness, and bearing the full yoke of Jewishness, they bore all as permanent for the sake of the Holy Name. It was not easy, nor was it comfortable, not physically nor spiritually. For them, in this aspect, there was no one to compare.

I myself was the son of a farmer - my father, Moshe Kiskiwitzer, and my mother, Yehudis. We were eight children of my parents. And our parents raised us with a deep Judaism, in an environment of Christians filled with hate towards us, and primitive in their expressions of hatred.

The village was large, wide, filled with Christians, fanatics, whose entire culture they sapped from their visits to the churches every Sunday, and all their expressions of humanity and society were tied to religion and fanaticism.

There were two other Jewish families living with us in the village: Moshe Tepper and Meyer Fishman. All three families lived by renting the mill from the landowner Poplowski. He was a businessman, and later was elected as

[Page 412]

wojt [village head, later chief administrator] of the region that surrounded Lanovits in the vicinity. That is why he was happy to hand over the maintenance of the mill to the Jews, and they promised him a monthly income, a comfortable and guaranteed one.

* * *

The issue of income was not always straightforward. We had good and bad years. The insecurity in the economic situation unsettled the Jewish families from time to time and brought many problems that pressured and lowered the spirit. But this did not unsettle the Jews in the village. They comforted themselves by saying this was their fate, luck, and they did not stop believing in better times, and that better fortune was yet to come.

What was worse for the parents was to raise their children in Jewish ways. No one spoke of the Torah, good deeds, or great scholars – there was only talk of behaving a little in the Jewish manner. And how do you do that in a sea of Christians that are all around? And my parents' opportunities were so restricted, and concerns for a livelihood exhausted them.

We loved our parents and surrounded them with our love, and worried along with them about how to guard the specifics of our Jewishness. It was good for us when the family held solutions of how to maintain the little Jewishness. Then we suddenly saw ourselves as "the great ones" that were guarding a great secret along with them. We went into the streets, and on our faces was a great seriousness, which created a sadness and heaviness. When we encountered the young Christian boys, we ran away from them and separated ourselves as if from those who were lower and others – but in about a minute, we saw them playing happily, whole-heartedly, and fine, just as other children. Our hearts would soften, and we were drawn to them. In a second, when "the ice melted," our stiffness left. The child in us, our gentle shoving, summoned us, and our feet pulled us towards the children, the Christian children, and in a second – we were among them, and all the separations of our Jewishness disappeared. Ordinary children with children.

We had a difficult childhood, our parents had a difficult life – these good and pure Jews. We loved the environment, and separating us from there was difficult for us, and the strength of our parents to give us that Jewishness was limited. There were

[Page 413]

few teachers who wanted to settle in the village. Driving into the city was also tied to challenges, but then it was very difficult. We happily connected ourselves to the Christian children who drew us over, disregarding the fact that our parents did not allow this, and we loved them so much. We simply did not know how we were sinning, why we were sentenced to such complications among people and societies.

Meanwhile, other winds began to blow among the Ukrainian people. Added to the religious fanaticism was now the nationalist propaganda, a Ukrainian one, that was based on terror against the Polish regime and against Jews, and the situation became very difficult. Until this day, I do not know how the scattered, separated Jews, the warm-hearted farmers, found the strength to remain in their villages.

Still, they remained. They used to travel to Lanovits each week, coming back from there with the aura of the brotherhood of the city and also … with the challenges from there – yet they still remained in the villages.

* * *

We had a great experience before a Jewish holiday, and in particular before the High Holidays. When the farmers, our parents, went to the city, the families in the village would get themselves together and discuss how they would go, who would go, whose horse and buggy they would use, how they would organize the homes, when they would all go, and many other things.

A sense of unity flourished everywhere. Preparing for the holidays was an act of unification that was felt by everyone.

The issue of livelihood was put aside, and at the center of everything was the question of going to the city for the High Holidays and the Jewish holidays. The greatest experience for us was to assemble all the details: bedcovers, pillows, pots, kettles, clothing, coats – and every Jew in the village stood between the wagon and his house. People were running back and forth, dragging things, while the men stood and loaded up, putting everything in its place, making sure there would be place for the passengers.

The act of self-sacrifice and straining for creating memories, was a thought that was hardly there, whose details and roots were not

[Page 414]

even clear! And these people were honest, dried out economically, bearded – our parents. And the Christians surrounded us and winked with their eyes, standing still and wondering what sort of festivity did the Jews suddenly have in the middle of a clear weekday?

Who can describe the grandeur of the Jewish souls of those village Jews? Who can stand in their spaces?

* * *

In the city, we arrived as strangers to strangers. There was some sort of separation between us. Not the same expressions, not the same traditions. We children were also the target of mockery and distancing themselves from us. Here too, among the Jews, we children suffered terribly when we came into the city.

The household of our uncle, Yidel Kiskiwitzer, gave us a warm welcome, as family. They, who moved from the village into the city, understood us. A special attraction awaited us at our uncle's. The Chortkover Rebbe was there. The level of joy and the loftiness of seeing the Rebbe up close, from counting all his wrinkles, this Jewish joy, all of it, etched itself deeply into our souls.

The prayers in shul, the concentration of the Jews with their Creator, for hours, the loftiness of the day of our personal national religion that was shown only to oneself, all this gave us the power, for the full year, of tolerating the pressure of the village.

Going into the city was a type of exodus from Egypt for the Jews, with real challenges. Life in the village passed before our eyes with its purpose and doubts. Going back to the village, to the nest of the enemy, hatred, and all its discomfort, deepened our anguish and loneliness. But we pushed forward and continued to live in the village. We – that means not our parents, because all these doubts grated on us. We left behind our unfortunate parents, the great, simple souls, to their tragic fate.

We did not remain in the trenches of Judaism, in exile, in the village. We left on *Hachshara* [training for agricultural work in Israel], and to Israel. That was our goal. Of course, we dreamed of bringing them over to us from that hell, but sadly we were not successful.

[Page 415]

When we wrote the Lanovits book, I thought that it would be good to mention, along with the Lanovits Jews, the farmers, the good Jews who together bore the yoke and pain for Judaism, and together fell as one victim of their deep, heartfelt faith.

We went on *Hachshara* and then to Israel

[Page 416]

Shmuel Fisher, of blessed memory

By Ch. R.

Translated by Pamela Russ

Fisher was born in Bessarabia, and from there he absorbed his warmth, his humanitarianism, and his pleasure in giving charity.

He belongs to us from Lanovits because of his wife Esther Mutel, the American, but also because he united himself with our small town as his second motherland.

He came to America as a young boy and very soon comfortably fit himself into its tempo and business rhythm, but his soul was far away from that. Fisher also searched for Jewishness in that country, too [America], where the dollar swallows the spirit and soul and turns the person into a foolish money devourer, and he found the Jewishness – both traditional and the religious – with his Lanovits friends and our respected friend, Yosel Weirach Berosh.

Fisher knew all the Lanovits tales, knew all the charming nuances, and lived with all the Lanovits memories.

In 1956, Fisher and his nice Esther visited Israel, and enjoyed it immensely. He felt that here he would be able to regain everything that he had lost in America with the business stresses, here in the Israeli neighborhood he would be able to regain his lost dollars from the past. Fisher wanted once again to become Fisher, this time in Israel. He fell in love with the country and with the people and with those from Lanovits, with whom he spent most of his time.

[Page 417]

His plan was overall to live out his life in Israel. And when his wife opposed his plan, he planned to come here without her with the intention that she would come later.

In America, Fisher gave his children a Zionist education and involved them with Zionist activities, and when he saw that he was not successful with all this he lost all his good fortune, and he was broken-hearted.

In the year 1962, as he was boarding the plane to Israel once again, he tripped on a step and exhaled his deep, Jewish soul. According to his will, he was buried in Israel on *Har Hamenuchos*, just as he demanded.

Before his passing, he tried to convince his grandson, a prominent atomic scientist, to switch a year of science for Israel, and the professor [the grandson] now fulfilled his wish in Rechovot.

Shmuel Fisher, who with this $100 laid the foundation of our loan account, and lived through experiences together with us, is engraved into our organization and entrenched into its memory of facts.

We will remember him.

Esther, wife of Fisher, beside his gravesite on Har Hamenuchos

[Page 418]

Spring – Youth in Lanovits

On the grandfather's small piece [of land]

[Pages 421-435]

Alphabetical List of those Who Perished

Transliterated by Shalom Bronstein

Family name(s)	First name(s)	Sex	Marital status	Father's name	Mother's name	Name of spouse	Remarks and additional family	Page
ADLER	Esther Mentsh	F					On the list next to her name Esther (Mentsh) is written. And 2 children	421
ADLER		F			Esther			421
ADLER		F			Esther			421
ADLER	Baruch Daniel		married			Yenta		421
ADLER	Yenta	F	married		Roni	Baruch Daniel		421
	Roni	F	married					421
	Odas	F			Roni		On the list it states 'the sister of Roni ADLER'	421
	Tzizi	F			Roni			421
ADLER	Chaim Shlomo		married					421
ADLER		F	married			Chaim Shlomo		421
ADLER	Simcha	M	married		Esther Mentsh		Lived in Michalowka, Krzemieniec, Wolyn before war; during war lived in Lanowce. And children	421
ADLER		F	married			Simcha		421
OFEH	Eliyahu	M	married				And children	421
OFEH		F	married			Eliyahu		421
	Yisrael	M					On the list it states that he was a soldier killed in the war	421
OFEH	Chana	F						421

Surname	First Name	Sex	Marital Status	Father	Mother	Spouse	Notes	Page
OFEH	Meika	F	married				And husband & children	421
ISAACS	Sheindel	F						421
ITZKOWITZ	Fishel	M	married				On the list it states 'the son-in-law of the (Bozhenitz') in parenthesis. . And children	421
ITZKOWITZ		F	married			Fishel	And children	421
AKERMAN	Mordecai	M	married			Susiya		421
AKERMAN	Susiya	F	married			Mordecai	On the list her maiden name BUCHSTEIN is written next to her name	421
AKERMAN		F		Mordecai	Susiya			421
EHRLICH	Moshe	M					And his family	421
BUCHSTEIN	Yehuda Yidel	M	married			Devorah	On the list after his name the name (Yidel) appears in parenthesis	421
BUCHSTEIN	Devorah	F	married			Yehuda Yidel		421
BUCHSTEIN	Motel	M						421
BUCHSTEIN	Brandel	F						421
BUCHSTEIN	Yitzhak	M	married			Bina		421
BUCHSTEIN	Bina	F	married			Yitzhak		421
BUCHSTEIN		M		Yitzhak	Bina			421
BUCHSTEIN	Paysi	M	married			Bat Sheva		421
BUCHSTEIN	Bat Sheva	F	married			Paysi		421
BUCHSTEIN	Chana	F		Paysi				421
BUCHSTEIN	Shmuel	M						421
BAZLINSKY	Yoel	M	married				On the list it states that he was a soldier who fell in battle. And 4 children	421
BAZLINSKY		F	married			Yoel	And 4 children	421
BAZLINSKY	Ita	F		Yoel				421
BAZLINSKY	Lipa	M		Yoel				421

BAZLINSKY	Moshe	M		Yoel					421
BEIMBLATT	Zvi	M	married					He was the town's pharmacist	421
BEIMBLATT		F	married			Zvi			421
BEIMBLATT		M		Zvi					421
BECHTEL	Shmuel	M	married						421
BECHTEL		F	married			Shmuel			421
BECHTEL	Pinchas	M							421
BECHTEL	Chaim	M							421
BLUMENFELD	Avraham	M	married			Devorah			421
BLUMENFELD	Devorah	F	married			Avraham			421
BLUMENFELD		M		Avraham	Devorah				421
BLUMENFELD		F		Avraham	Devorah				421
BLUMENFELD		F		Avraham	Devorah				421
BLUMENFELD	Zecharia	M	married					And 11 children	421
BLUMENFELD		F	married			Zecharia			421
BLANK	Tova	F							421
BLANK	Zeidel	M						His profession is listed as a pharmacist	421
BLANK	Leiber	M							421
BLANK		F		Leiber					421
BEKER	Yisrael	M	married			Hinda		And children	421
BEKER	Hinda	F	married			Yisrael			421
BERG	Baila	F	married					And husband & child	421
BERG	Yitzhak	M	married			Tova			421
BERG	Tova	F	married			Yitzhak			421
BRONSTEIN	Leiber	M	married						421
BRONSTEIN		F	married			Leiber			421
BRONSTEIN	Rachel	F							421
BRONSTEIN	Esther	F							421
BRONSTEIN	Sarah	F			Esther			And her family	421
BRODSKY	Zalman	M	married			Sarah		And 9 children	421
BRODSKY	Sarah	F	married			Zalman		And 9 children	422

FORMAN	Sarah	F			Shimshon	Maiden name BRODSKY	422
BARI	Eidel	F			Moti	And 2 children	422
BRILANT	Chava	F					422
BRILANT		F		Chava			422
BRILANT		M		Chava			422
BRIMMER	Bunim	M	married		Chaika		422
BRIMMER	Chaika	F	married		Bunim		422
BRIMMER	Gittel	F					422
BRIMMER	Leah	F					422
BERMAN						On the list the name (MARISHKEWITZ) appears after his name; it is not clear if it refers to an individual or to a family	422
BERMAN	Etel	F					422
BERMAN	Chaim	M					422
BERMAN	Yeshaya	M					422
BERNESTEIN	Golda	F					422
BERENSTEIN	Rachel	F					422
BERENSTEIN	Avraham	M	married				422
BERENSTEIN		F	married		Avraham		422
BRATZ	Avraham	M	married		Sonia	His profession is listed as a shochet; the list states that he was murdered along with his 11 children	422
BRATZ	Sonia	F	married		Avraham		422
GUBERMAN	Yosef	M	married		Sheintzi		422
GUBERMAN	Sheintzi	F	married		Yosef		422
GUBERMAN	Mendel	M					422
GUBERMAN	Mordecai	M	married		Esther		422
GUBERMAN	Esther	F	married		Mordecai		422
GUBERMAN	Tzipa	F					422

Surname	First Name	Sex					Page
GOCHMAN	Ya'akov	M				On the list it states 'Yankel from the Matzot' in Yiddish	422
GOCHMAN	Hinda	F					422
GOCHMAN	Bavla	F					422
GOCHMAN	Cheina	F					422
GOCHMAN	Leib	M		Srul Wolf		On the list after his name it states in parenthesis (Srul Wolf's) indicating a connection with him	422
GOLDBERG	David	M	married				422
GOLDBERG		F	married		David		422
GOLDBERG		F		David			422
GOLDBERG		F		David			422
GOLDBERG	Mirel	F					422
		M				And children	422
GOLDBERG	Sonia	F			Beye		422
GOLDBERG		M		Beye	Sonia		422
GOLDBERG		M		Beye	Sonia		422
GOLDMAN	Moshe	M	married		Tzivia	And children	422
GOLDMAN	Tzivia	F	married		Moshe	And children	422
GOLDMAN	Yisrael	M		Moshe	Tzivia		422
GOLDMAN	Meir	M		Moshe	Tzivia		422
GOLDMAN	Binyamin	M		Moshe	Tzivia		422
GONN	Ya'akov	M	married			On the list it states the son-in-law of ZAK	422
GONN		F	married		Ya'akov		422
GONN		M		Ya'akov			422
GOFMAN	Yosef	M	married		Miriam		422
GOFMAN	Miriam	F	married		Yosef		422
GOFMAN	Feiga	F					422
GOFMAN	Sarah	F					422
GOLDZAKER	Yona	M	married		Zunya	And child	422

Surname	First name	Sex	Status	Father	Mother	Spouse	Notes	Page
GOLDZAKER	Zunya	F	married			Yona	Maiden name KIGEL. And a child.	422
GOLDZAKER		F		Yona	Zunya			422
GOLDZAKER		M	married					422
GOLDZAKER		F	married					422
		M	married			Sima		422
	Sima	F	married				Maiden name BRIMMER	422
GOLDZAKER	Ya'akov	M						422
GUREWITCH	Benik	F					And 2 children	422
GUREWITCH		F		Benik				422
GUREWITCH		M		Benik				422
GUREWITCH	Ben-Zion Bentzi	M	married			Reiza	Next to his name on the list it states (Bentzi CHADIA) in parenthesis	422
GUREWITCH	Reiza	F	married			Ben-Zion Bentzi		422
GUREWITCH		F		Ben-Zion Bentzi	Reiza			422
GUREWITCH		F		Ben-Zion Bentzi	Reiza			422
GUREWITCH	Moshe	M	married			Esther	On the list after his name it states (Rinkiwitzer) indicating that he was from the town of Rinkivitz	422
GUREWITCH	Esther	F	married			Moshe	She is the sister of Mordecai (Muni) WEISSING	422
GUREWITCH	Azriel	M						422
GITELMAN	Avraham	M	married				And child	422
GITELMAN		F	married			Avraham	And child	422
GITELMAN	Aharon	M	married			Chaya	And 2 children	422
GITELMAN	Chaya	F	married			Aharon	And 2 children	422
GITELMAN	Yerachmiel	M	married			Yokel		422
GITELMAN	Yokel	F	married			Yerachmiel		423

GITELMAN		F		Yerachmiel	Yokel			423
GAYLIKHEN	Avraham	M	married			Bilah		423
GAYLIKHEN	Bilah	F	married			Avraham		423
GAYLIKHEN	Eliezer	M						423
GAYLIKHEN		F					She is the daughter of Eliezer GAYLIKHEN; her personal name does not appear	423
GAYLIKHEN	Genendel	F						423
GAYLER	Ayzik	M	married					423
GAYLER		F	married			Isaac		423
GAYLER	Bat Sheva	F						423
GAYLER	Avraham	M						423
GAYLER	Machli	F						423
GAYLER	Zvi	M	married					423
GAYLER		F	married			Zvi		423
GAYLER	Yitzhak	M						423
GINZBURG	Riva	F				Yosel Moshe	On the list it states after her name 'Yosel Moshe's the mother of Atzi	423
GOLDIN	Hirsh Mendel	M	married			Brandel		423
GOLDIN	Brandel	F	married			Hirsh Mendel		423
GLUZMAN	Efraim	M	married					423
GLUZMAN		F	married	Yudil		Efraim	Maiden name KIGEL	423
GLUZMAN	Ya'akov	M	married			Malka		423
GLUZMAN	Malka	F	married			Ya'akov		423
GLUZMAN	Rivkah	F						423
GLUZMAN	Batya	F						423
GLUZMAN	Paltiel	M						423
GLUZMAN	Zvi	M						423
GLUZSTEIN	Yosef	M	married					423
GLUZSTEIN		F	married			Yosef		423

Surname	First Name	Sex	Status	Related	Spouse/Parent	Notes	Page
GLUZSTEIN		F		Yosef			423
GLUZSTEIN	Sima	F					423
GLINIK	Leah	F					423
GLINIK	Shimon	M	married		Hinda	And 2 children	423
GLINIK	Hinda	F	married		Shimon		423
GLAKIL	Beirel	M					423
GELLER		F			Chaim		423
MAZOR	Miriam	F			Hersh Ber	Maiden name GLUZSTEIN	423
GRUBER	Brandel	F				The name (KWAITEL) appears after her name in the list. And 2 children	423
GRUFFEN	Avraham	M	married		Chaya Sarah		423
GRUFFEN	Chaya Sarah	F	married		Avraham		423
GRUFFEN	Yosef	M					423
GRUFFEN	Sanya	M	married		Rivkah		423
GRUFFEN	Rivkah	F	married		Sanya		423
GRUFFEN	Yisrael	M					423
GRUFFEN	Yitzhak	M					423
GRUFFEN	David	M					423
GRUFFEN		F		David			423
GREENBLATT	Yidel	M					423
GREENBLATT	Frayda	F					423
GREENBLATT	Ozer	M	married				423
GREENBLATT		F	married		Ozer		423
GREENBLATT	Yitzhak	M					423
GREENBLATT	Zeida	M					423
GREENBLATT		F		Zeida			423
GREENBERG	Avraham	M	married		Feiga		423
GREENBERG	Feiga	F	married		Avraham		423
GREENBERG	Ya'akov	M					423
GREENBERG	Aharon	M					423

Surname	Given name	Sex	Status	Father	Mother	Spouse	Notes	Page
GREENSPAN	Avraham Hersh	M						423
GREENSPAN	Moshe	M						423
GREENSPAN		F		Moshe				423
GREENSPAN		F		Moshe				423
GORMAN	Chaim	M						423
GORMAN		F		Chaim				423
GORMAN		F		Chaim				423
GORMAN		F		Chaim				423
GORMAN	Chaim	M	married			Chaika		423
GORMAN	Chaika	F	married			Chaim		423
GORMAN	Leosik	M						423
GERSTEIN	Eliyahu	M	married				And 4 children	423
GERSTEIN		F	married			Eliyahu	And 4 children	423
GERSTEIN	Elyakim	M	married			Chana Zelda		423
GERSTEIN	Chana Zelda	F	married			Elyakim		424
	Feirl	F	married	Elyakim	Chana Zelda	Aharon	Maiden name GLUZSTEIN	424
	Aharon	M	married			Feirl		424
GERSTEIN	Ya'akov	M	married				And 4 children	424
GERSTEIN		F	married			Ya'akov	And 4 children	424
GERSTEIN	Pesia	F						424
GERSHOM	Ya'akov	M	married					424
GERSHOM		F	married			Ya'akov		424
	Feirl	F		Ya'akov			Maiden name BRIMMER	424
		M		Feirl				424
		M		Feirl				424
GERSHOM	Moshe	M	married			Dvosi		424
GERSHOM	Dvosi	F	married			Moshe		424
GERSHOM	Uziel	M	married					424
GERSHOM		F	married			Uziel		424

DLUGATZ	Shmuel	M	married		Bluma	And children	424
DLUGATZ	Bluma	F	married		Shmuel	And children	424
HOROWITZ	Golda	F				On the list next to her name in parenthesis it states 'Itzik Hirsch's,' indicating a connection with him	424
	Motka	M	married		Brandel	His mother's maiden name was GLUZMAN;	424
	Brandel	F	married		Moska	Maiden name BRIMMER	424
WASHIN	Efraim	M	married		Feirl		424
WASHIN	Feirl	F	married		Efraim		424
BRODSKY	Cheitzi	F			Yisrael	Maiden name BRIMMER	424
WASHIN	Michael	M	married			And 2 children	424
WASHIN		F	married		Michael		424
WALL	Ben Zion	M					424
WALL	Roiza	F		Ben Zion			424
WALL	Pesach	M	married		Malka		424
WALL	Malka	F	married		Pesach		424
WALL		M		Pesach			424
WALL		F		Pesach			424
WITELSTEIN	Chaika	F					424
WITELSTEIN	Yosef	M	married		Dina		424
WITELSTEIN	Dina	F	married		Yosef		424
WITELSTEIN	Paltiel	M					424
WITELSTEIN	Yishayahu	M	married		Feiga		424
WITELSTEIN	Feiga	F	married		Yishayahu		424
WITELSTEIN	Yisrael	M					424
WITELSTEIN	Leib	M	married		Henya		424
WITELSTEIN	Henya	F	married		Leib		424
WITELSTEIN	Natan	M	married				424
WITELSTEIN		F	married		Natan		424

Surname	Given Name	Sex	Status	Spouse 1	Spouse 2	Notes	Page
WITELSTEIN	Sarah	F					424
WITELSTEIN	Paltiel	M					424
WEINER	Grina	F					424
WEINER	Yosef	M					424
WEINER	Feirhali	F					424
WEINSHEL	Moshe	M	married		Rachel	The list states that he was from the village of Borskovitz and that he was murdered in the Borshtshivki forest	424
WEINSHEL	Rachel	F	married		Moshe	On the list it states that they were murdered in the Borshtshivki forest	424
WEINSTEIN	Benya	M					424
	Zuzi	F	married	Benya		Maiden name BRIMMER	424
		M	married		Zuzi		424
WEISS	Zelig	M	married		Reiza	On the list it states 'the doctor' in Yiddish	424
WEISS	Reiza	F	married		Zelig		424
WEISS	Fruma	F					424
WEISS	Feiga	F					424
WEISS	Leibka	M					424
WEISS	Malka	F					424
WEISS	Yitzhak	M	married		Yocheved		424
WEISS	Yocheved	F	married		Yitzhak	Maiden name BUCHSTEIN	424
WEISS		F		Yitzhak	Yocheved		424
WEISS	Zvi	M	married		Feiga	And child	424
WEISS	Feiga	F	married		Zvi	And child	424
WEISSING	Mordecai Muni	M				He is the brother of Rachel Leah WEISSING	424
WEISSING	Rachel Leah	F					424
WIESMAN	Shalom	M					425

Surname	Given Name	Sex	Status		Spouse	Notes	Page
WEITZMAN	Avraham	M	married			The name (Panitch) appears in parenthesis after his name on the list	425
WEITZMAN		F	married		Avraham		425
WEITZMAN	Avraham	M	married		Yenti	The name (Panitch) appears in parenthesis after his name on the list. And 2 children	425
WEITZMAN	Yenti	F	married		Avraham		425
WEITZMAN	Yerachmiel	M	married		Mishka	And 2 children	425
WEITZMAN	Mishka	F	married		Yerachmiel	Maiden name KIGEL. And 2 children	425
WEITZMAN	Yisrael	M	married		Chaya		425
WEITZMAN	Chaya	F	married		Yisrael		425
WEITZMAN	Rachel	F					425
WEITZMAN	Shlomo	M					425
WEITZMAN	Keila	F					425
WEITZMAN	Pesach	M					424
WEITZMAN	Leib	M					425
WEITZMAN	Meika	F					425
WEITZMAN	Shlomo	M	married		Bela		425
WEITZMAN	Bela	F	married		Shlomo		425
WEITZMAN	Yehezkel	M					425
WEITZMAN	Pesach	M					425
WEITZMAN	Idel						425
WEITZMAN	Esther	F					425
WEITZMAN	Sarah	F				After her name (Baruch PARTZIS) is recorded in parenthesis	425
WEINER	Aharon	M	married				425
WEINER		F	married		Aharon		425
WEINER	Mordecai	M					425
WEINER	Shulka	F					425
WEINER	Binyamin	M					425

WEINER	David	M	married				425
WEINER		F	married		David		425
WEINER		F		David			425
WEINER		F		David			425
WEINER	Zisa	M	married		Tzvia	And 2 children	425
WEINER	Tzvia	F	married		Zisa		425
WEINER	Ya'akov	M	married			And 2 children	425
WEINER		F	married		Ya'akov	And 2 children	425
WEINER	Ruchtzi	F					425
WEINER	Naftali	M					425
WEINER	Eliezer	M					425
WEINER	Moshe	M					425
WEINER	Yitzhak	M					425
WARCHMAN	Miriam	F					425
WARCHMAN	Ayzik	M					425
WARCHMAN	Leah	F					425
WARTZMAN	Yosef	M	marricd				425
WARTZMAN		F	married		Yosef		425
ZEIGER	David	M	married				425
ZEIGER		F	married		David		425
ZEIGER	Ya'akov	M					425
ZEID	Ya'akov	M	married		Ita		425
ZEID	Ita	F	married		Ya'akov		425
ZEID	Shimshon	M					425
ZALZNIK		F			Eliezer	And 4 children	425
ZALZNIK		F		Ya'akov			425
ZALZNIK		F		Ya'akov			425
ZALZNIK	Shlomo	M	married		Gisa		425
ZALZNIK	Gisa	F	married		Shlomo		425
ZALZNIK	Mika	F					425
ZALZNIK	Frieda	F					425
ZALZNIK	Esther	F					425

Surname	First Name	Sex	Status		Spouse	Notes	Page
ZALZNIK		M		Esther			425
ZALZNIK		M		Esther			425
ZELNER	Muni	M	married		Dovtzi	The name of the town Zahoritz appears after his name in parenthesis. And 2 children	425
ZELNER	Dovtzi	F	married		Muni		425
ZELNER	Rephael	M	married			The family name (MAZHORITZ) appears after the listing of his name	425
ZELNER		F	married		Rephael		425
ZELNER	Rachel	F					425
ZELNER	Ya'akov	M					425
ZELNER	Shimshon	M					425
ZALTZMAN	Tzipora	F					426
ZALTZMAN	Chava	F		Tzipora			426
ZALTZMAN	Shmuel	M	married			On the list the name (NIOSKIS) appears in parenthesis after his name	426
ZALTZMAN		F	married		Shmuel		426
ZALTZMAN		F	Shmuel				426
ZASLAWSKI	Beirel	M	married			And 2 children	426
ZASLAWSKI		F	married		Beirel	And 2 children	426
ZASLAWSKI	Shmuel	M	married				426
ZASLAWSKI		F	married		Shmuel		426
ZASLAWSKI		M	Shmuel				426
ZASLAWSKI	Bluma	F				On the list it states that she is the sister of Shmuel & Beirel ZASLAWSKI	426
ZASLAWSKI	Eli	M				On the list it states that he is the brother of Shmuel & Beirel ZASLAWSKI	426
ZASLAWSKI	Shmuel	M	married			And 2 children	426
ZASLAWSKI		F	married		Shmuel		426

Lanowce: Memorial Book of the Martyrs of Lanowce Who Perished During the Holocaust

Surname	Given Name	Sex	Status	Father	Mother	Spouse	Notes	Page
ZASLAWSKI	Sarah Rivkah	F						426
ZAK	Zelda	F					On the list after her name it states (MANOSES) in parenthesis	426
CHAZAN	Ya'akov	M	married			Devorah		426
CHAZAN	Devorah	F	married			Ya'akov		426
CHAZAN		F		Ya'akov	Devorah			426
CHAZAN	Yitzhak	M	married				And 2 children	426
CHAZAN		F	married			Yitzhak		426
CHAIKES	Yitzhak	M						426
CHAIKES	Butzi	F						426
CHAIKES	Hershel	M						426
CHAIKES	Feirl	F						426
CHALAMISH	Shlomo	M	married			Sarah	And children	426
CHALAMISH	Sarah	F	married			Shlomo	On the list after her name the name (Yitzhak Hersh) appears in parenthesis. And children	426
CHISDA	Michael	M	married			Rivkah		426
CHISDA	Rivkah	F	married			Michael		426
CHISDA	Devorah	F						426
CHISDA	Zisel							426
CHISDA	Eidel	F						426
CHASKALSON	Bartzik	M	married			Dina		426
CHASKALSON	Dina	F	married			Bartzik		426
CHASKALSON		F		Bartzik	Dina			426
TABERMAN	Yosef	M	married					426
TABERMAN		F	married			Yosef		426
TABERMAN		F		Yosef				426
TABERMAN		F		Yosef				426
TAITEL	Malka	F						426
TAITEL	Ya'akov	M						426

TEICHMAN	Chona Reuven	M	married					426
TEICHMAN		F	married			Chona Reuven		426
TEICHMAN	Zeida	M						426
TEICHMAN		F		Zeida				426
TEPPER	Yosef	M						426
TEPPER	Moshe	M	married			Hinda		426
TEPPER	Hinda	F	married			Moshe		426
TARLO	Zvi	M	married			Mindel		426
TARLO	Mindel	F	married			Zvi		426
TARLO		M		Zvi	Mindel		On the list it states that his personal name did not appear	426
YISHPA	Aharon	M						426
YISHPA	Reizi	F						426
YISHPA	Sarah	F						426
YISHPA	Henya	F					On the list after her name it states (Shmulichis) in parenthesis	426
KATZ	Avraham	M	married				And children	426
KATZ		F	married			Avraham		426
KATZ	Eliezer	M	married				He is the brother of Moshe. And children	426
KATZ		F	married			Eliezer		426
KATZ	Eliezer	M	married			Hinda	He is the brother of Moshe	426
KATZ	Hinda	F	married			Eliezer		426
KATZ	Elka	F						426
KATZ	Ben Zion	M	married			Rachel		427
KATZ	Rachel	F	married			Ben Zion		427
KATZ	Yoel	M						427
KATZ	Chana	F						427
KATZ	Yehudit	F						427

KATZ	Gershon	M	married		Brantzi	And children	427
KATZ	Brantzi	F	married		Gershon		427
KATZ		F		Gershon			427
KATZ		F		Gershon			427
KATZ	Dov	M	married		Chana	And 5 children	427
KATZ	Chana	F	married		Dov	And 5 children	427
KATZ	Yosef	M	married		Bluma		427
KATZ	Bluma	F	married		Yosef	She is the sister of Michael CHISDA	427
KATZ	Eliezer	M				He is the brother of Moshe	427
KATZ	Chava	F					427
KATZ	Ya'akov	M	married				427
KATZ		F	married		Ya'akov		427
KATZ	Bilah	F					427
KATZ	Devorah	F					427
KATZ	Yisrael	M				On the list after his name (Baruch Peretz) appears in parenthesis; there are 3 people on the list with the name Yisrael KATZ	427
KATZ	Yisrael	M	married		Chana	On the list after his name (Baruch Peretz) appears in parenthesis; there are 3 people on the list with the name Yisrael KATZ	427
KATZ	Chana	F	married		Yisrael		427
KATZ	David	M					427
KATZ	Yisrael	M	married		Rivkah	On the list after his name (Baruch Peretz) appears in parenthesis; there are 3 people on the list with the name Yisrael KATZ	427

KATZ	Rivkah	F	married		Yisrael	She is the third of the three wives of Yisrael KATZ	427
KATZ	Yoel	M					427
KATZ	Yitzhak	M					427
KATZ	Moshe	M					427
KATZ	Mordecai	M					427
KATZ	Esther	F					427
KATZ	Ziama	M					427
LOPATIN	Meir	M	married		Neski		427
LOPATIN	Neski	F	married		Meir		427
LOPATIN	Meir	M	married		Sarah		427
LOPATIN	Sarah	F	married		Meir		427
LOPATIN	Ozer	M					427
LOPATIN	Ratziye	F					427
LOPATIN	Shlomo	M					427
LIBERGAL	Moshe	M	married				427
LIBERGAL		F	married		Moshe		427
LIBERGAL	Yisrael	M		Moshe			427
LEIDER	Ya'akov Efraim	M	married		Feiga		427
LEIDER	Feiga	F	married		Ya'akov Efraim		427
LEIDER	Leizi	M	married			On the list it states that he was from Belozerka. And children	427
LEIDER		F	married		Leizi	She is the sister of Reiza MIROCHNIK	427
LEIDER	Manus Leib	M				On the list it states that he was from Belozerka. And his family	427
LEIDER	Michael	M	married		Yocheved	The name (Michal Peleg) appears after his listing	427

LEIDER	Yocheved	F	married			Michael		427
LEIDER		F		Michael	Yocheved		She is the sister of Reiza MIROCHNIK	427
LAMSIDER	Mendel	M	married			Yocheved		427
LAMSIDER	Yocheved	F	married	Kehat		Mendel	Maiden name PARNAS	427
KISHKRONIK	Mendel	M						427
LANGBERG	Shalom	M	married			Rachel	And 2 children	427
LANGBERG	Rachel	F	married			Shalom		427
LANDER	Meir	M	married					427
LANDER		F	married			Meir		427
LANDER		F		Meir				427
LANDER		F		Meir				427
LANDER	Reuven	M						427
LANDER	David Hirsh	M						427
LANDER	Manya	F						427
LANDER	Zeilik	M	married			Rivkah		427
LANDER	Rivkah	F	married			Zeilik		427
LANDER	Yosef	M	married			Gisa		427
LANDER	Gisa	F	married			Yosef		427
LANDER	Zalman	M	married			Etel		427
LANDER	Etel	F	married			Zalman	On the list the name (GLUZSTEIN) appears after her name in parenthesis	427
LAFTIN	Chaim Yisrael	M	married			Pesia		427
LAFTIN	Pesia	F	married			Chaim Yisrael		427
LAFTIN	Sarah	F						428
LERNER	Elka	F						428
MADD	Ya'akov	M	married				And 2 children	428

Surname	Given name	Sex	Status	Father	Mother	Spouse	Notes	Page
MADD		F	married			Ya'akov	Maiden name GERSTEIN. And 2 children	428
MADWED	Avraham	M	married					428
MADWED		F	married			Avraham		428
MADWED	Yosef	M	married			Sarah		428
MADWED	Sarah	F	married			Yosef		428
MADWED	Meika	F						428
MADWED	Simcha	M						428
MADWED	Meir	M	married			Chaya		428
MADWED	Chaya	F	married			Meir		428
MADWED	Manya	F	married				And husband	428
MADWED	Zvi	M						428
MIRATSHNIK	Reiza	F	married				She is the sister of Esther Malka; on the list it states (BORKOWITZER); it is likely that the surname is different. . And husband & 2 children	428
	Sarah Malka	F						428
MAHARSHAK	Aharon	M	married					428
MAHARSHAK		F	married			Aharon		428
MAHARSHAK	Shalom	M						428
MOSHLIN	Zvi	M	married			Yenta		428
MOSHLIN	Yenta	F	married			Zvi		428
MOSHLIN	Chaya	F		Zvi	Yenta			428
MOSHLIN		F		Zvi	Yenta			428
MEIL	Eliezer	M	married			Miriam		428
MEIL	Miriam	F	married			Eliezer		428
MEIL	Chaim	M						428
MEIL	Pinchas	M						428
MEIL	Feiga	F						428

MALL	Yehudit	F						428
MEILIKER	Avraham	M	married			Sarah		428
MEILIKER	Sarah	F	married			Avraham		428
MEILIKER	Yosef	M		Avraham	Sarah			428
MEILIKER	Nachman	M		Avraham	Sarah			428
MEILIKER		M		Avraham	Sarah			428
MEILIKER	David	M	married				And children	428
MEILIKER		F	married			David	And children	428
MEILIKER	Yehoshua	M						428
MEILIKER	Yitzhak	M	married			Frayda		428
MEILIKER	Frayda	F	married			Yitzhak		428
MEILIKER	Yisrael	M						428
MEILIKER	Chana	F						428
MEILIKER	Pesach	M						428
MEILIKER	Yosef	M						428
MILMAN	Aharon	M	married			Risel	And child	428
MILMAN	Risel	F	married			Aharon	And child	428
MILMAN	Chaim	M	married			Esther		428
MILMAN	Esther	F	married			Chaim		428
MILMAN	Avraham	M						428
MILMAN	Liza	F						428
MILMAN	Shmuel	M	married			Tova		428
MILMAN	Tova	F	married			Shmuel		428
MILMAN	Chaya Sarah	F						428
MILMAN	Golda	F						428
MEILER	Mordecai	M						428
MEILER	Feirl	F						428
MILLER	Etel	F					Her husband was a Shochet	428
MILLER	Elia	M	married			Pesia		428
MILLER	Pesia	F	married			Elia		428

MILLER	Batya	F					428
MILLER	Yoel	M					428
MILLER	Bluma	F					428
MILLER	Ita	F					428
MILLER	Moshe	M	married		Chaika		428
MILLER	Chaika	F	married		Moshe		428
MILLER	Yehuda	M					428
MILLER	Beika	F					428
MILLER	Yisrael	M				And child	429
MILLER		F		Yisrael			429
MEILER	Yitzhak	M	married		Sheindel		429
MEILER	Sheindel	F	married		Yitzhak		429
MEILER	Ya'akov	M					429
MEILER		F					429
MINTZ	Natan	M	married			The family name (MAZHORITZ) appears after the listing of his name. And 4 children	429
MINTZ		F	married		Natan	And 4 children	429
MINTZ	Munya	M	married			And 2 children	429
MINTZ		F	married		Munya	And 2 children	429
MIROCHNIK	Chantzi	F					429
MIROCHNIK		F		Chantzi			429
MIROCHNIK	Eliyahu	M	married			And 2 children	429
MIROCHNIK		F	married		Eliyahu	And 2 children	429
MELENOW	Gnesia	F					429
MELENOW	Shimshon	M	married		Sarah	And 2 children	429
MELENOW	Sarah	F	married		Shimshon	And 2 children	429
MELAMED	Yechiel	M	married		Frayda		429
MELAMED	Frayda	F	married		Yechiel		429
MELAMED	Shlomo	M					429
MELAMED	Arieh	M					429

MELAMED	Isser	M	married		Bela	He is the brother of Yitzhak	429
MELAMED	Bela	F	married		Isser		429
MELAMED	Leib	M					429
MELAMED	Zvi	M					429
MELAMED	Tova	F	married			And husband & 4 children	429
MELAMED	Pinchas	M	married		Elka		429
MELAMED	Elka	F	married		Pinchas		429
MELAMED	Yitzhak	M	married		Rivkah Yenti		429
MELAMED	Rivkah Yenti	F	married		Yitzhak		429
MARGALIT	Yosef	M	married		Miriam		429
MARGALIT	Miriam	F	married		Yosef		429
MARGALIT	Chana	F					429
MARGALIT	Bora						429
MARGALIT	Ya'akov	M					429
MARGALIT	Shmuel	M	married		Zisel		429
MARGALIT	Zisel	F	married		Shmuel		429
MARGALIT	Charna	F					429
MARGALIT	Meir	M					429
MARDER	Chaika	F					429
MARDER	Hentzia	F					429
MARDER	Moshe	M				On the list it states that he was a soldier who was killed in battle during the war	429
NUDEL	Yerachmiel	M	married			And 4 children	429
NUDEL		F	married		Yerachmiel	And 4 children	429
SEGAL	Yehudit	F			Shalom		429
SEGAL	Natan	M	married			And 4 children	429
SEGAL		F	married		Natan	And 4 children	429
SEGAL	Chana	F		Natan			429

Surname	First Name	Sex	Status	Father	Spouse	Notes	Page
SEGAL	Moshe	M		Natan		On the list it states that he was a soldier who was killed in battle during the war; the family information is based on a Page of Testimony	429
STOLER	Yitzhak	M	married		Fruma	The word (Frantchoiz) appears after his name on the list	429
STOLER	Fruma	F	married		Yitzhak		429
STRIK	Leizer	M					429
SAMBIRER	Ya'akov	M	married		Henka		429
SAMBIRER	Henka	F	married		Ya'akov		429
SAMBIRER	Eliyahu	M					429
SAMBIRER	Eliezer	M					429
SANDOWITZ	Aharon	M	married		Babli		429
SANDOWITZ	Babli	F	married		Aharon		429
SPIRT	Yosef Ozer	M	married		Rachel		429
SPIRT	Rachel	F	married		Yosef Ozer		429
SPIRT	Pinchas	M					430
SPEKTOR	Leibush	M	married			On the list it states that he was the son-in-law of Chana the Kropnitzki	430
SPEKTOR		F	married	Chana	Leibush		430
SPEKTOR	David	M		Leibush			430
SPEKTOR		F		Leibush			430
POLACK	Shmuel	M	married		Reizi		430
POLACK	Reizi	F	married		Shmuel		430
POLACK	Sheindel	F					430
POLACK	Yehoshua	M					430
POLACK	Yitzhak	M					430
STEIN	Rivkah	F	married			Maiden name WEINSTEIN	430

STEIN		M	married		Rivkah		430
FOGEL	Moshe	M	married		Chaika		430
FOGEL	Chaika	F	married		Moshe		430
FOGEL		M		Moshe			430
FOGEL		F		Moshe			430
PUTERMAN	Motel	M	married				430
PUTERMAN		F	married		Motel		430
PUTERMAN	Pesia	F					430
PUTERMAN	Avraham Avremel	M	married	Sofer	Feiga	On the list after his name in parenthesis it states (Avremel the 'schreiber' - author)	430
PUTERMAN	Feiga	F	married		Avraham Avremel		430
PUTERMAN		F		Avraham Avremel	Feiga			430
FOX	Natan	M	married				430
FOX		F	married		Natan		430
FOX		M		Natan			430
FOX	Zev	M	married		Yenta		430
FOX	Yenta	F	married		Zev		430
FOX	Esther	F					430
FORMAN	Shmuel	M	married		Faiye		430
FORMAN	Faiye	F	married		Shmuel		430
FORMAN	Yerucham	M	married				430
FORMAN		F	married		Yerucham		430
FORMAN		M		Yerucham			430
FORMAN		M		Yerucham			430
FORMAN	Meir	M	married		Feiga	And another relative	430
FORMAN	Feiga	F	married		Meir	On the list it states 'their sister and her son Mendeli - it is not clear if she is the sister of Meir FORMAN or of his	430

					wife Feiga. And another relative	
	Mendele	M				430
FORMAN	Yisrael	M			On the list it states that he was killed in the War	430
FORMAN	Moshe	M	married	Menucah		430
FORMAN	Menucah	F	married	Moshe		430
FORMAN	Moshe	M	married	Frieda		430
FORMAN	Frieda	F	married	Moshe		430
FORMAN	Gittel	F				430
FORMAN	Michael	M	married		And 5 children	430
FORMAN		F	married	Michael		430
FORMAN	Moshe	M	married			430
FORMAN		F	married	Moshe		430
FORMAN	Yitzhak	M				430
FORMAN	Yehoshua	M				430
FORMAN	David Hersh	M	married			430
FORMAN		F	married	David Hersh		430
PACHT	Dov	M	married			430
PACHT		F	married	Dov		430
PACHT	Zelik	M				430
PACHT	Tzipora	F				430
PLETZEL	Moshe	M	married			430
PLETZEL		F	married	Moshe		430
FINGERHUT	Zev	M	married			430
FINGERHUT		F	married	Zev		430
FINGERHUT	Mordecai Leibish	M	married			430
FINGERHUT		F	married	Mordecai Leibish		430
FEUERSTEIN	Bezalel	M	married	Sarah		430

FEUERSTEIN	Sarah	F	married		Bezalel		430
FEUERSTEIN	Yisrael	M					430
FEUERSTEIN	Binyamin	M					430
FEUERSTEIN	Perl	F					430
FEUERSTEIN	Bluma	F					430
FEUERSTEIN	Moshe	M				On the list it states that he was killed in the War	430
FISHMAN		M				On the list it states that there were 8 members to the family; the name appears as FISHMAN MAISKOVITZ. And whole family	430
PLETZEL	Beirel	M				On the list it states that he was a hunchback	430
PASTERNAK	David	M	married			And child	431
PASTERNAK		F	married		David		431
PEARLMUTTER	Zev	M	married			And children	431
PEARLMUTTER		F	married		Zev	And children	431
PARNAS	Yitzhak	M	married				431
PARNAS		F	married		Yitzhak		431
PARNAS	Bela	F	married			And husband	431
PARNAS	Zalman	M	married		Itka		431
PARNAS	Itka	F	married		Zalman		431
PARNAS		M		Zalman			431
PARNAS		F		Zalman			431
PARNAS	Meir	M	married			And children	431
PARNAS		F	married		Meir		431
	Reiza	F	married			On the list after the family listing of Meir PARNAS his sister, Reiza, her husband and their children are listed	431

		M	married		Reiza	And children	431
PRESSMAN (BILANTZIK)	Bracha	F				The name (BILANTZIK) appears in parenthesis after the name PRESSMAN; the list states 'a number of children' names & number not given	431
PRESSMAN (BILANTZIK)	Nachum	M	married			The name (BILANTZIK) appears in parenthesis after the name PRESSMAN; the list states 'a number of children' names & number not given	431
PRESSMAN (BILANTZIK)		F	married		Nachum	And children	431
TZOREF	Etti Chayes	F		Chaya		On the list it states 'the Aunt of Yehezkel SCHMUKLER;	431
TZOREF	Moshe	M	married			The family name (MAZHORITZ) appears after the listing of his name. And children	431
TZOREF		F	married		Moshe	And children	431
KAGAN	Feivel	M	married		Feiga		431
KAGAN	Feiga	F	married		Feivel		431
KAGAN	Shmuel	M	married				431
KAGAN		F	married		Shmuel		431
KAGAN	Batya	F					431
KAGAN	Zeida	M					431
KAGAN		F		Zeida			431
KWAITEL	Akiva	M	married		Chana	And 2 children	431
KWAITEL	Chana	F	married		Akiva		431
KOLTON		F			Yosil		431
KOLCHINSKY	Frayda	F					431
KOLCHINSKY	Odiya						431
KOPITZ	Abba	M	married		Reizel	And child	431

Surname	Given	Sex	Status			Spouse	Notes	Page
KOPITZ	Reizel	F	married			Abba	Maiden name BRILANT. And a child	431
KOPITZ	Ayzik	M	married			Klara		431
KOPITZ	Klara	F	married			Ayzik	On the list it states the daughter of BINBLATT the pharmacist	431
KOPITZ	David	M	married			Ita	And 4 children	431
KOPITZ	Ita	F	married			David	And 4 children	431
KOPITZ	Yisrael	M	married					431
KOPITZ		F	married			Yisrael		431
KOPITZ	Moshe	M	married			Feiril		431
KOPITZ	Feiril	F	married			Moshe		431
KOPITZ	Pinchas	M						431
KOPITZ	Mordecai	M						431
KOPITZ	Shmulik	M	married			Gittel		431
KOPITZ	Gittel	F	married			Shmulik		431
KAUFMAN	Kehat	M	married				And 4 children	431
KAUFMAN		F	married			Kehat		431
KOIFMAN	Rachel	F						431
KOIFMAN	Devorah	F						431
KOIFMAN	Shlomo	M						431
KOIFMAN	Uziel	M						431
	Koppel	M	married				On the list it states Koppel from Gribova. And his wife & daughter	431
KUPERWASSER	Yisrael Avraham	M	married			Frayda		431
KUPERWASSER	Frayda	F	married			Yisrael Avraham		431
KUPERWASSER	Shimon	M						431
COOPERMAN	Shlomo	M						432
COOPERMAN	Reizi	F						432
KORNBERG	Muni	M	married			Slova		432

Surname	Given name	Sex	Status	Father	Mother	Spouse	Notes	Page
KORNBERG	Slova	F	married			Muni	Maiden name BRIMMER	432
KIGEL	Gedalyahu	M	married			Yenti		432
KIGEL	Yenti	F	married			Gedalyahu		432
KIGEL	Bavla	F						432
KIGEL	Sheindela	F						432
KIGEL	David	M	married			Shprintzi		432
KIGEL	Shprintzi	F	married			David		432
KIGEL	Leizer	M						432
KIGEL	Roizi	F						432
KIGEL	Asher Leib	M						432
KIGEL	Michael	M	married			Leah		432
KIGEL	Leah	F	married			Michael		432
KIGEL		F		Michael	Leah			432
		F	married		Leah		Maiden name KIGEL	432
		M	married					432
KIGEL	Zvi	M	married			Miriam		432
KIGEL	Miriam	F	married			Zvi		432
KIGEL	Shlomo	M						432
KIGEL	Simcha	M						432
KIGEL	Moshe	M						432
KIGEL	Reizi	F						432
	Hershel	M						432
	Tziril	F	married				And husband	432
KIGEL	Saratzi	F						432
KIGEL	Yenta	F						432
		F			Yenta		Maiden name KIGEL	432
	Yosef	M						432
KIPERMAN	Shlomo	M	married			Reizi	And children	432
KIPERMAN	Reizi	F	married			Shlomo		432
KIRZNER	Moshe	M	married					432
KIRZNER		F	married			Moshe		432

KIRZNER	Bavtzia	F						432
KIRSHON	Zalman	M	married					432
KIRSHON		F	married		Zalman			432
KLEINMAN	Yosef	M	married		Miriam			432
KLEINMAN	Miriam	F	married		Yosef			432
KLEINMAN	Dov	M						432
KLEINMAN	Yitzhak	M	married					432
KLEINMAN		F	married		Yitzhak			432
KLEINMAN		F		Yitzhak				432
KLEINMAN		F		Yitzhak				432
KANDZIOR	Eliezer	M						432
KANDZIOR		F		Eliezer				432
KANDZIOR		F		Eliezer				432
KANDZIOR	Michael Chirik	M	married		Chava	On the list the name (CHIRIK) appears in parenthesis after his name. And children		432
KANDZIOR	Chava	F	married		Michael	And children		432
KANFER	Baruch	M	married		Feiga			432
KANFER	Feiga	F	married		Baruch			432
KANFER	Zeida	M		Baruch	Feiga			432
KANFER		M		Baruch	Feiga			432
KASEL	Shlomo	M	married					432
KASEL		F	married		Shlomo			432
KASEL	Beirel	M						432
KESSLER	Meshulam	M						432
KESSLER	Shlomo	M						432
KESSLER	Zvi	M				And his family		432
KAPLAN	Yosef	M	married					432
KAPLAN		F	married		Yosef			432
KATZAP	Ozer	M	married		Eidel			432
KATZAP	Eidel	F	married		Ozer			432
KROLER	Ya'akov	M	married		Batya	She is the sister of Mendel KISHKRONIK		432

KROLER	Batya	F	married			Ya'akov	He is the brother of Yocheved LAMSIDER nee KAUFMAN	432
KROLER		F		Ya'akov				432
KROLER		F		Ya'akov				432
	Chana	F					The daughter of Chana di Krupnitzky - she lived in the same house with the PACHT family. And her daughter	432
KARMINITZKY	Abba	M	married					432
KARMINITZKY		F	married			Abba		432
KARMINITZKY	Mordecai	M						432
KARMINITZKY	Feirl	F						432
KARMINITZKY	Sarah	F						432
KARMINITZKY	Tonia	F						432
KARMINITZKY	Dov	M						432
KARMINITZKY	Nachman	M						432
KARMER	Meir	M	married					433
KARMER		F	married			Meir		433
KARMER		M		Meir				433
KARMER	Yitzhak	M	married					433
KARMER		F	married			Yitzhak		433
KARMER	Michael	M	married					433
KARMER		F	married			Michael		433
KARNER	Eliyahu	M	married					433
KARNER		F	married			Eliyahu		433
KARNER	Beirel	M	married				And children	433
KARNER		F	married			Beirel		433
KARNER	Yitzhak	M	married					433
KARNER		F	married			Yitzhak		433
KARNER	Avraham	M					On the list it states that he was a soldier who was killed in battle during the war	433

KARNER	Moshe	M	married				433
KARNER		F	married		Moshe		433
KARNER	Mordecai	M	married		Leah	And 3 children	433
KARNER	Leah	F	married		Mordecai	And 3 children	433
KARPMAN	Rachel	F					433
KARPMAN	Esther	F					433
KARPMAN	Moshe	M					433
KARPMAN	Simcha	M					433
KARPER	Avraham	M	married				433
KARPER		F	married		Avraham		433
KARPER		F		Avraham			433
KARPER		F		Avraham			433
KARPER	Ben Zion	M					433
KARPER		F			Hirsh	And 2 children	433
KARPER	Ben Zion	M	married				433
KARPER		F	married		Ben Zion		433
KARPER		F		Ben Zion			433
KARPER	Chaim Pinchas Pinchaz	M	married	Tova		On the list the name (Pinchaz) appears in parenthesis after his name. And 3 children	433
KARPER		F	married		Chaim Pinchas Pinchaz		433
KARPER	Tova	F					433
KARPER	Michael	M	married				433
KARPER		F	married		Michael		433
KARPER		F		Michael			433
KARPER	Matityahu Matus	M	married			The name (Matus) appears after the listing of his name	433
KARPER		F	married		Matityahu Matus		433
KARPER	Yenta	F	married			And husband	433
KARPER	Nachum	M	married		Reizi		433

KARPER	Reizi	F	married		Nachum		433
KARPER	Mordecai	M					433
KARPER		F	Mordecai				433
RABIN	Aharon	M				On the list it states that he was the last Rabbi of Lanowce	433
RABIN	Yisraelikil	M	married	Ahrili		The name (R' Ahrili's) appears in parenthesis after his name on the list indication that he was the son of Rabbi Aharon RABIN. And children	433
RABIN		F	married		Yisraelikil		433
RABIN	Uziel	M					433
RABIN	Dina	F					433
RABIN	Zunya	F					433
RABIN	Yishayahu (Shaika)	M	married			The name Shaika in parenthesis is after his personal name on the list	433
RABIN		F	married		Yishayahu		433
RABIN	Ruth	F					433
RABINOWITCH	Yosef	M					433
RADER	Michel	M	married		Gita	On the family name (MAISKOVITZ) appears after his name	433
RADER	Gita	F	married		Michel		433
RADER	Bilah	F					433
RADER	Chana	F					433
RADER	Breindel	F					433
RADER	Yosi	M					433
RADER	Leib	M	married		Devorah	On the family name (MAISKOVITZ) appears after his name	433
RADER	Devorah	F	married		Leib		433
ROSENBERG	Avraham	M	married				433

ROSENBERG		F	married			Avraham		433
ROSENBERG	Arieh	M						433
ROSENBERG	Chana	F						433
ROSENBERG	Eliezer	M						433
ROSENBERG	Henya	F	married				And husband	433
ROSENBERG	Chaim	M						434
ROSENBERG	Charna	F						434
ROSENBERG	Sarah Yenti	F						434
ROSENBERG	Chaika	F				Moshe		434
ROSENBERG		F		Moshe	Chaika			434
ROSENTAL	Azriel	M	married				On the list the name (ZEIDCHIS) appears in parenthesis after his name	434
ROSENTAL		F	married			Azriel		434
ROSENTAL	Feirl	F						434
ROSENTAL	Leizi	M						434
ROSENTAL	Chava	F						434
ROSENTAL	Zisel	F						434
ROSENTAL	Rachel	F						434
ROCHTZIS	Meshulam	M	married			Etel	And 8 children	434
ROCHTZIS	Etel	F	married			Meshulam	And 8 children	434
ROICH	Leib	M	married			Etia	On the list it states that they had 4 additional children whose names are not known.	434
ROICH	Etia	F	married			Leib	On the list it states that they had 4 additional children whose names are not known	434
ROICH	Sheindel	F		Leib	Etia			434
ROICH	Bezalel	M		Leib	Etia			434
ROICH	Chaim	M		Leib	Etia			434
REZNIK	Chaim Simcha	M	married			Bela		434

REZNIK	Bela	F	married			Chaim Simcha		434
REZNIK	Yitzhak	M						434
REICHMAN	Uzilik	M	married		Feiga	Tanya	On the list it states that his mother's name was Feiga	434
REICHMAN	Tanya	F	married			Uzilik		434
REICHMAN	Yosef	M		Uzilik	Tanya			434
REICHMAN		F		Uzilik	Tanya			434
REICHMAN	Feiga	F					She is the mother of Uzilik REICHMAN	434
SHWETZ	Yitzhak Yehuda	M	married			Fruma	And 3 children	434
SHWETZ	Fruma	F	married			Yitzhak Yehuda	And 3 children	434
SHWETZ	Mordecai	M		Yitzhak	Fruma			434
SHWETZ	Shlomo	M		Yitzhak	Fruma			434
SHUSTER	David	M	married					434
SHUSTER		F	married			David		434
SHUSTER	Fruma	F						434
STEINBERG	Moshe	M					On the list after his name in parenthesis it states in Yiddish 'der krimer'. And his family	434
SCHECHTER	Malka	F					On the list the name (BRIMMER) appears after her name	434
SCHECHTER		M			Malka			434
SHAMOISH	Zvi	M	married			Miriam		434
SHAMOISH	Miriam	F	married			Zvi		434
SHAMOISH		F		Zvi	Miriam			434
SHAMUCH	Yoel	M					After his name in the listing it states in parenthesis (Napadovker), possibly indicating that he came from the town of Napadov. And his family	434

Surname	Given Name	Sex	Status		Spouse	Notes	Page
SHAMUCH	Pinchas	M				And his family	434
SHAMUCH	Shmuel	M				And his family	434
SHMUKLER	Eliezer	M	married			And children	434
SHMUKLER		F	married		Eliezer		434
SHMUKLER	Moshe	M				On the family name (MAISKOVITZ) appears after his name	434
SHMUKLER	Yehudit	F					434
SHMUKLER	Chaya	F					434
SHMUKLER	Atzi						434
GAYLIKHEN	Bela	F	married		Avraham	Maiden name KIGEL	434
GAYLIKHEN	Avraham	M	married		Bela		434
SHMUKLER	Shlomo	M					434
SHMUKLER	Yisrael	M					434
SHMUKLER	Natan	M					434
SHMUKLER	Leizer	M	married		Esther		434
SHMUKLER	Esther	F	married		Leizer		434
SHMUKLER	Shlomo	M	married		Batya		434
SHMUKLER	Batya	F	married		Shlomo	On the list the family name (MAISKOVITZ) appears in parenthesis after their name	434
SCHNEIDMAN	Akiva	M	married		Malia		434
SCHNEIDMAN	Malia	F	married		Akiva		434
SCHNEIDMAN	Yehoshua	M					434
SCHNEIDMAN	Reiza	F					434
SCHNEIDER	Ayzik	M	married			On the list the name (Motzik) in parenthesis appears after his personal name	434
SCHNEIDER		F	married		Ayzik		434
SCHNEIDER		F		Ayzik			434
SCHNEIDER	Eliyahu	M	married		Yenta		434
SCHNEIDER	Yenta	F	married		Eliyahu		434

SCHNEIDER	Manya	F					434
SCHNEIDER	Feigele	F					434
SCHNEIDER	Hertzia	M	married		Chana		435
SCHNEIDER	Chana	F	married		Hertzia		435
SCHNEIDER	Chaim	M					435
SCHNEIDER	Chaya	F	married			On the list it states 'Koppel from Gribova'. And husband	435
SCHNEIDER		F		Yozip			435
SPEIZMAN	Mordecai Motel	M				On the list after his name it states (Rabbi Reb Motel)	435
SPEIZMAN	Etia	F					435
SHPIELER	Muni	M	married		Manya	On the list the personal name (Muni) appears in parenthesis next to his family name	435
SHPIELER	Manya	F	married		Muni	The family name (KATZ) appears in parenthesis after her name	435
SHPIELER	Mordecai	M	married		Molly		435
SHPIELER	Molly	F	married		Mordecai		435
SHPIELER	Meir Meitzi	M				The name (Meitzi) appears in parenthesis after his listing	435
SHPIELER	Fanya	F					435
SHATZUGAL	Shimshon	M	married			And his family	435
SHATZUGAL		F	married		Shimshon		435
SAKURNIK	Yisrael	M	married		Frieda		435
SAKURNIK	Frieda	F	married	Baruch	Yisrael	On the list after her name it states in parenthesis (Baruch Partzi's) probably indicating that she was the daughter of Baruch	435
	Chava	F					435

Last Name	First Name	Sex	Comments	Related	Notes	House
		M			And family	435
	Sarel	F			On the list the family name (MAISKOVITZ) appears in parenthesis after their name. And her brother	435
RINKIWITZER	Hurtzi	M			And his family	435
	Hitiya	F		Chaya	On the list in parenthesis after her name is states in Yiddish (di Bubba) 'the grandmother'	435
KRUPDERNIK	Chaim Yisrael	M	married			435
KRUPDERNIK		F	married	Chaim Yisrael		435

[Pages 436-440]

List of Homeowners of Houses Shown on Lanovits City Sketch

Prepared by Joseph Voss and Sol Sylvan

This is a list of the town as it was occupied just before the German occupation in 1941. In the last column are the numbers of the houses on the Yizkor Book map (the last photo in "Photo captions from the Lanovtsy Yizkor book" at bottom of the table of contents) that was hand drawn by the "survivors" in 1969.

Last Name	First Name	Nickname	Comments	House Number
Akerman	Mordekhai		tenant	120
Addess	Roni & Dizi		tenants	110
Adler	Baruch Daniel			110
Adler	Hayim Shlomo			111
Adler	Sander		tenant	187
Adler	Esther	Mentsch		111
Bachtel	Shmuel			189
Baruch	Motiyah		tenant	56
Beinblatt			Pharmacist	120
Berg	Bella			96

Berg	Yitzhak			96
Berman	Eti			162
Berman	Hayim	Rishkowitz		162
Berman	Yeshayahu			162
Berenstein	Golda			127,128,137
Bezhnitz	Shmuel		tenant	71
Bezlinsky	Esther	Lifekhe		98
Blumenfeld	Avraham		tenant	41
Blumenfeld	Zekharyah		Shokhet	163
Breitelman	Moshe		Son-in-law	48
Brilant	Asher			61
Brimmer	Bunim			20
Britweh	Yankel			146
Brodsky	Zalman			77
Bronstein	Lieber			130
Buchstein	Golda			51
Buchstein	Pessach			62
Buchstein	Yehudah		tenant	51
Buchstein	Yitzhak		tenant	51
Buchstein	Shmuel		tenant	51
Chisda	Michel		Blacksmith	19
Chisda	Michel's		Blacksmith shop	197
Delougetch	Shmuel		tenant	17
Eisenberg	Dr. Lotek			59
Eliyah	Itzik			8
Erlich	Moshe			113
Farber	Anik		tenant	137
Feuerstein	Betzalel			203
Fingerhut	Mordekhai Leibush			188
Fingerhut	Velvil			188
Fogel	Asher			18

Fogel	Moshe			179
Fuchs	Netta		tenant	143
Fuchs	Velvil		tenant	152
Furman	David Hirsh			169
Furman	Frieda	Shekhnis		88
Furman	Gitel	Shekhnis		88
Furman	Israel			88
Furman	Me'ir			144
Furman	Michel	Krumer	[Cripple]	95
Furman	Moshe		Warehouse	87
Furman	Moshe	Blinder	[Blind] Residence	88
Furman	Moshe	Shekhnis		88
Furman	Moshe	Weisser	[Blond]	99
Furman	Sarah			144
Furman	Shmuel			153
Furman	Yerukham			144
Futerman	Avramil		tenant	165
Gehrman	Hayim	Lachwitzer		71
Gehrman	Daughter		Daughter & son-in-law	71
Geilikhen	Avraham			10
Gelda	Hersh Mendel		tenant	139
Geldener	Michal			131
Gelkil	Beirel		tenant	91
Geller	Avraham Hersh			84
Geller	Eizik	Michlis		86
Gershom	Moshe		tenant	61
Gershom	Uzi'el		tenant	30
Gershom	Ya'acov		Warehouse	29
Gershom	Ya'acov		Residence	30
Gerstein	Alik			83
Gerstein	Elyakum			107

Gerstein	Pessiah		tenant	19
Ginzburg	Reva	Yosel Mash'hes	tenant	201
Gitelman	Leizer	Greener	[Lumberman]	139
Gitelman	A'haron		tenant	155
Gitelman	Avraham		tenant	155
Gitelman	Yerakhmiel			164
Glinik	Leah			184
Glinik	Leah's		Son-in-law	184
Glinik	Shim'om			136
Glozshtein	Yosef		tenant	42
Gluzman	Froyim		tenant	82
Gluzman	Ya'acov			6
Gluzstein	Seema		tenant	148
Godman	Moshe	Koziles	[Hospital worker]	24
Gofman	Yosef	Vashti		35
Gokhman	Yankel	Matzos	Residence	93
Gokhman	Yankel		Grain Mill Operator	94
Goldberg	Doodi		tenant	93
Goldenberg	Bayya			109
Goldenberg	Mirel	Kazatzker	[Lively person]	101
Goldzaker	Yona			5
Goldzaker	Rabbi			108
Goldzaker	Sima		Daughter & son-in-law	108
Gon	Yakel		tenant	113
Greenberg	Avrahamchik		tenant	54
Greenblatt	Ozer			191
Greenblatt	Yidel	Kiskivitser		191
Grinshpan	Avraham Hirsh			72
Grobnick	Yona	Blacksmith from Vyshnivitz		102

Gruber	Breindel			114
Gruffen	Avraham			159
Gruffen	Sonia			26A
Guberman	Mendel			67
Guberman	Mordekhai		Store	43
Guberman	Mordekhai		Residence	44
Gurwitz	Beinik			145
Gurwitz	Bentzy	Khodiyah	tenant	50
Gurwitz	Bienik		tenant	55
Gurwitz	Itzik Hirsh			14
Gurwitz	Moshe	Rinkivitser		26
Hazan	Devorah		tenant	159
Hazan	Yitzhak		from Vizhenrudek	112
Israel	Hayim			79
Itzkowitz	Fishel		tenant	71
Kagan	David			182
Kagan	Feivel			3
Kagan	Hershel		Sheinberg House	58
Kanfer	Barukh			55
Kanzior	Michel		tenant	21
Kanziyor	Elazar			48
Karfman	Rapha'el			37
Karper	Aron	Aronchi		53
Karper	Avraham		tenant	162
Karper	Benya	Der Toiber	[Deaf]	73
Karper	Benzion		tenant	73
Karper	Hayim Pinchas		tenant	53
Karper	Matos			52
Karper	Michel	Karpusis	tenant	109
Karper	Nachum		tenant	79
Katz	Avraham		from Shumsk	85

Katz	Bentzi			202
Katz	Bernzy & Gershon			106
Katz	Leizer			100
Katz	Moshe	Merimes		126
Katz	Yankel	Sarah Shayes		186
Katz	Yanko & Elka			16
Katz	Yisrael			12
Katz	Yisrael	Hunchback		15
Katz	Yisrael	Barukh Peretz		124
Kerner	Eeda	Zabarah		89
Kerner	Eliyah			91
Kerner	Mordekhai			90
Kerner	Moshe		tenant	89
Kessler	Meshulam	Kotler		167
Kessler	Shlomo			142
Khaikis	Butzi		tenant	68
Khaikis	Hershky	Loshik	tenant	68
Khaikis	Itzi			68
Khukis	Freel		tenant	68
Kigel	Hershel		tenant	37
Kigel	Michel	Shachnes	tenant	56
Kigel	Raisa		tenant	101
Kigel	Shertzi			31
Kigel	Tzirel		tenant	101
Kigel			Warehouse	36
Kigel	Gedalya	Wassertraeger	[Water carrier]	157
Kirschner	Moshe		tenant	26
Kirshon	Zalman			56
Kleinman	Yossi		tenant	19
Klemchik	Leizer		tenant	27
Koifman	Kahat			151

Koifman	Rakhel			201
Kwaitel	Akivah		tenant	42
Kolchinsky	Frieda			45
Kopitz	Abbah		tenant	61
Kopitz	David			180
Kopitz	Moshe			177
Kopitz	Piniyah			176
Kornfeld	No name given		Son-in-law of Brimmer [20]	114
Kozil	Offah			17
Koziles	Meikah		tenant	17
Kreimer	Itzik			147
Kreimer	Michal			147
Kreimer	Myron		tenant	49
Kreimer	Shim'on			147
Kremnezky	Mordekhai			4
Kroler	Yasha			173
Krupnitzky	Mrs.	Die Krupnitzky	[Miller] tenant	28
Kupferwasser	Yisrael Avraham		tenant	147
Kugel	David	Shertzis		78
Kupferman	Shlomo			190
Lagenberg	Shalom		tenant	37
Landau	David Hirsh		tenant	166
Landau	Re'uven			166
Landau	Yosef			160
Landau	Yoyseef		tenant	42
Landau	Zelig			160
Lander	Me'ir			81
Lander	Zalman			149
Lander	Zalman		Carpenter Shop	150
Leider	Moshe		tenant	157

Leider	Yakol Froym		tenant	31
Leizinder	Mendel		tenant	142
Lerner	Elkah		tenant	62
Libergal	Moshe		tenant	50
Liwne	Hayim Yisrael		tenant	157
Lopatin	Me'ir		tenant	198
Mad	Yankel		tenant	84
Mail	Elazar			152
Mailer	Moshe	Schwartzer		97
Marder	Yosef			21
Mardshikes	Aron			50
Margalis	Yosel			70
Margalit	Shmuel		tenant	61
Margalit	Yankel		tenant	192
Maharshak	Aharon		tenant	61
Mazur	Miriam		tenant	84
Medwed	Hersh			198
Medwed	Itzi	Hershmelis		165
Medwed	Manya			198
Medwed	Mayer	Bunders	tenant	52
Medwed	Yosef	Bunder		165
Mehlman	Shmuel & Tonya		tenant	33
Mehlman	Zvi	Starosta	[Village Head]	33
Meiler	Yenkil	Rovtshik		185
Meiliker	Avraham			9
Meiliker	David			25
Meiliker	Itzik	Hatzarud	[The Hoarse one]	199
Meiliker	Yehoshuah			155
Melamed	Pinkhas		tenant	38
Melamed	Yizkhak			23
Melenow	Shimshon			1

Melenow	Gensia			76
Miller	Eliyah		Shokhet	46
Miller	Ethel	Shokhtekeh	[Shokhet's wife]	102
Miller	Mordekhai		tenant	157
Milman	A'haron		tenant	75
Mirochnik	Eliyah			195
Mirochnik	Hantziah	Noz	[Nose]	174
Moshlin	Zvi		tenant	82
Nudel	Yerachmiel		tenant	98
Pacht	Beiril			28
Paltsil	Yankel			38
Parnas	Itzik		tenant	129
Parnas	Michal			129
Parnas	Yitzhak		tenant	105
Parnas	Zalman			66
	Zeilik		Parnas' Son-in-law	129
Pasternak	David			200
Poliak	Shmuel			60
Pressman	Nakhum	Bulenchik		22
Rabin	Rabbi A'hareli			64
Rabin	Uzi'el			57
Rabinowitch	Yossel			143
Rakhtsis	Meshulam			7
Reichman	Bentzi			54
Reichman	Uzi'el		tenant	54
Reznik	Hayim Simkha			178
Riklis	Khaya			161
Rosenberg	Avraham	Materkah		27
Rosenberg	Hayim			13
Rosental	Azri'el	Zeidiks		49
Roykh	Leib	Tzelkis		34

Sambirer	Yankel		tenant	16
Schneider	Eliyah			42
Schneider	Hertzi		Blacksmith	187
Schneider	Hertzi's		Blacksmith shop	193
Schneider	Itzik	Motzik		192
Schweiz	Fruma			172
Segal	Nathan		tenant	77
Seslavsky	Shmuel			156
Shandrowitzt	A'haron		tenant	47
Shchugel	Leib			123
Shkornik	Yisrael			125
Shmuelikhes	Henya			41
Shmukler	Leizer		tenant	191
Shneideman	Akivah	Bluz	tenant	185
Shpiler	Motiyah			119
Shpirt	Yosef Ozer		teacher-tenant	77
Shumsker	Eedel			82
Shuster	David	Davidzi	tenant	164
Spektor	Leibush		tenant	80
Speizman	Reb Motel		teacher-tenant	76
Steinberg	Moshe			63
Stoler	Yosef Frantsoys		[Frenchman] tenant	38
Strik	Leizer			47
Tepper	Moshe		tenant	40
Tepper	Yosef			40
Terlo	Hershel			69
Tichman	Hanoh Re'uven			117
Twerman	Yossel	Tzon	[Shepherd]	116
Wayziah	Khiyah		tenant	32
Werkhman	Miriam			32
Weiner	A'haron		tenant	47

Weiner	David		tenant	47
Weiner	Shmuel			39
Weiner	Zusiya		tenant	39
Weiner	Nakhum			105
Weiner	Yankel		tenant	76
Warman	Beirish		tenant	2
Warzman	Yo'el			2
Washin	Ephrayim		tenant	80
Washin	Hannah			80
Washin	Michel		tenant	80
Weesing	Mordekhai			158
Weesing	Rakhel Leah			158
Weinstein	Benny			141
Weiss	Avraham		tenant	30
Weiss	Zelig		tenant	153
Weiss	Zvi		tenant	75
Wiesman	Shalom		Warehouse	74
Wiesman	Shalom		Residence	75
Weitzman	Yisrael	Pinitch		154
Weitzman	Yerachmiel		tenant	89
Witelstein	Avraham	Vovky	tenant	200
Witelstein	Yeshayahu			115
Witelstein	Yisrael	Betshkis		186
Witelstein	Leib			122
Wietzman	Shlomo			11
Wohl	Paysee			19A
Yishpa	Benyamin			92
Zaltzman	Tsiporah		tenant	66
Zaslawski	Dov			194
Zaslawski	Sarah Rivka			194
Zaslawski	Shmuel			194

Zeid	Eeta			148
Zelner	Moni		tenant	62
Zheliannik	Shlomo			196
Zhelznik	Yankel	Felzely		183

Public Buildings list

Prepared by Joseph Voss and Sol Sylvan

Building's Function	House Number
Goldener's Synagogue	59
A'hareli's Synagogue	65
Main Synagogue	103
Hospital	118
Kostzal [Catholic Church]	121
New Cemetery	132
Mass Grave & Memorial	133
Pravoslavic Cemetery	134
Catholic Cemetery	135
Town Hall	138
Soda Factory	140
Showers	171
Cloister	175
Shraga's Flour Mill	181

NAME INDEX

A

Abraham the teacher, 13
Abramow, 50
Abulofiah, 139
Adamchuk, 67
Addess, 311
Adler, 121, 273, 311
Aharonowitz, 64
Aharulis, 39
Akerman, 42, 274, 311
Aleksandrov, 253
Alexander, 27, 226, 227
Alexander "the blind one", 239
Alexander II, 27, 226
Alexandow, 143, 244, 251
Alharizi, 136, 137
Alters, the owner of a fabric store, 21
Andrusha, 43, 44
Andrushka, 44, 47
Ansky, 147, 249, 250, 252
Ash, 147, 251
Astour, 143, 145, 147
Atchi, 79
Auerbuch, 4, 5, 6
Avital, 10, 127, 259
Azriel, 55, 260

B

Ba'al Shem Tov, 140, 151
Bachtel, 33, 95, 99, 117, 311
Bakar, 131
Bakhur, 139
Balaban, 207
Bar [or Ber], 187
Baratz, 120
Barg, 223
Bari, 276
Baruch, 311
Bashow, 98
Batko, 17
Bazlinsky, 274, 275
Bechtel, 275
Beinblatt, 311
Beker, 49, 51, 150, 232, 275
Belew (or Beluw), 145
Benny, the deaf, 65
Berchik, 38, 79, 120
Berenstein, 99, 119, 240, 257, 276, 312
Berezh, 56
Berg, 99, 275, 311, 312
Berl, 21, 66
Berman, 22, 27, 30, 55, 56, 107, 120, 121, 122, 123, 124, 127, 157, 166, 226, 276, 312
Bernzil, 122, 123
Bezhnitz, 312
Bezlinsky, 312
Bialik, 147, 148, 202, 246, 250, 251, 252
Bilantzik, 300
Binblatt, 301
Blank, 55, 132, 275
Bleimblatt, 275
Blinder, 313
Blumenfeld, 275, 312
Bolek, 88
Borg, 216
Borkowitzer, 292
Borochow, 148, 251, 252
Borowsky, 8
Boshke, the "*felsher*" [country doctor], 239
Bozhenitz, 274
Brandes, 247
Bratz, 276
Breitelman, 312
Brenin, 147
Brick, 21
Brilant, 56, 89, 110, 215, 219, 276, 301, 312
Brimmer, 42, 45, 55, 66, 92, 95, 99, 100, 101, 104, 111, 114, 118, 119, 132, 219, 222, 235, 276, 278, 281, 282, 283, 302, 308, 312, 317
Brinen, 252
Britweh, 312
Brodsky, 42, 50, 52, 67, 275, 276, 282, 312
Bronstein, 38, 79, 275, 312

Buchstein, 21, 22, 33, 45, 55, 106, 107, 108, 112, 119, 120, 124, 132, 154, 161, 162, 166, 240, 274, 283, 312
Bukh, 252
Burstein, 39, 49, 123
Butenko, 238

C

Casimir, 9
Chaikes, 50, 287
Chalamish, 287
Chalibowsky, 8
Chaskalson, 287
Chazan, 287
Chirik, 303
Chisda, 132, 287, 289, 312
Chmielnicki, 208
Cooperman, 301
Czerny, 47

D

Damchuk, 94
Danan, 146
Dawidson, 241
Delougetch, 312
Descartes, 248
Didik, 65
Diduch, 239
Diek, 147
Dimodina, 139
Dinezon, 147, 251
Dlugatz, 282
Dubnow, 251
Dusi, 29, 229

E

Efroim, 219
Ehrlich, 274
Einstein, 258
Eisenberg, 312
Eisenstat, 80, 82
Eliyah, 312
Emden, 136, 138, 208
Engels, 249
Erich, 146

Erlich, 312
Etty, 215
Eybeschutz, 136, 138, 208

F

Farber, 60, 63, 79, 312
Feierberg, 246
Feiga, the Bath Attendant, Feiga Die Baderin, 163
Feigeles, 174
Feigess, 60, 61, 62, 63, 64
Fellig, 220
Fenin, 240
Feuerstein, 298, 299, 312
Fialkow, 201
Fichman, 251
Fiks, 257
Fingerhut, 298, 312
Fisher, 270, 271
Fisherman, 63
Fishman, 146, 167, 267, 299
Fishman Maiskovitz, 299
Fitterman, 56, 60, 63
Fleishman, 201, 202
Flemchik, 92
Fogel, 39, 80, 82, 99, 297, 312, 313
Foiker, 97
Forman, 50, 126, 276, 297, 298
Fox, 297
Friedlander, 147
Frishman, 147, 251
Froman, 39
Fuchs, 200, 239, 313
Furman, 13, 93, 94, 99, 313
Futerman, 123, 313

G

Galperin, 163
Gaon, 139, 140
Gayler, 279
Gaylikhen, 279, 309
Gedaliah, the water carrier, 178
Gehrman, 313
Geilikhen, 313
Gelda, 313

Geldener, 152, 172, 313
Gelkil, 313
Geller, 40, 280, 313
Geltner, 215
Gershom, 220, 281, 313
Gerstein, 281, 292, 313, 314
Ginzburg, 56, 79, 86, 147, 236, 246, 250, 279, 314
Giovannielli, 246
Gitelman, 65, 83, 98, 99, 100, 101, 103, 120, 235, 278, 279, 314
Gladner, 83
Glakil, 280
Glakser, 209
Glazer, 6, 109, 110, 176, 187, 189, 195, 197, 202, 203
Glick, 125
Glinik, 37, 80, 99, 111, 112, 280, 314
Glowerman, 146
Glozshtein, 314
Gluzman, 119, 279, 282, 314
Gluzstein, 65, 192, 279, 280, 281, 291, 314
Gnesin, 147, 252
Gochman, 277
Gochman [the matzoh baker], 40
Godamsky, 238, 239, 240
Godman, 314
Gofman, 277, 314
Gokhman, 314
Goldberg, 27, 72, 80, 82, 86, 277, 314
Goldenberg, 194, 226, 232, 314
Goldener, 50, 322
Goldfagen, 122
Goldin, 279
Goldman, 111, 277
Goldner, 44
Goldstein, 60
Goldzaker, 72, 277, 278, 314
Golender, 40
Gon, 314
Gonn, 277
Gonser, 63
Gordin, 122
Gorman, 281
Gorodetsky, 252
Grawitz, 42, 48, 119

Greenberg, 146, 280, 314
Greenberg-Kagan, 122
Greenblat, 215
Greenblatt, 280, 314
Greenspan, 281
Grinshpan, 314
Grisham, 71
Grobnick, 314
Gruber, 86, 280, 315
Gruffen, 280, 315
Guberman, 34, 93, 218, 221, 222, 276, 315
Gurewitch, 6, 111, 119, 176, 189, 217, 222, 241, 278
Gurwitz, 45, 209, 315

H

Haam, 245, 250, 251
Habrod, 174
Hadar, 198
Haikeles, 40
Haikin, 146
Halevi, 140, 245
Halperin, 9, 20, 201
Haran, 190
Harin, 164
Harkavy, 9
Haromi, 245
Harwan, 147
Hasek, 164
Havis, 55
Hayas, 173
Hayim-Yisrael, the *krupedernik* [barley miller], 17
Hazan, 99, 163, 315
Helban, 55
Heller, 6
Henich, 19
Hertsi the blacksmith, 20
Herutz [or Herotz, 52
Herzl, 21, 22, 55, 111, 114
Hessen, 245
Hettner, 247
Hilpern, 208
Hindes, 98
Hirschbein, 147, 252
Holender, 25

Horodetzky, 147
Horowitz, 147, 252, 282
Horutz, 238, 239

I

Ibn Gvirol, 137, 139, 148
Ibn-Ezra, 137
Ideles, 174
Isaacs, 274
Israel, 315
Isserles, 139
Itzkowitz, 274, 315

K

K'na'any, 138
Kagan, 45, 89, 99, 100, 233, 300, 315
Kalim, 48
Kandzior, 303
Kanfer, 303, 315
Kanzior, 315
Kanziyor, 315
Kaplan, 238, 303
Karalenka, 246
Karepman, 50
Karfman, 315
Karmer, 304
Karminitzky, 304
Karner, 304, 305
Karper, 42, 99, 305, 306, 315
Karpman, 305
Karshenboim, 216
Kasel, 303
Katilansky, 154, 155, 159, 160
Katnelson, 9
Katz, 38, 80, 81, 83, 99, 106, 107, 131, 147, 215, 224, 225, 235, 240, 264, 288, 289, 290, 310, 315, 316
Katzap, 303
Katznelson, 193, 250
Kaufman, 218, 221, 301, 304
Kavkes, 257
Kawkes, 255
Kazatseker, 123
Kazimierz Jagiellonczyk, 207
Kendziurs, 66

Kendzur, 97
Kenfizyur, 99
Kerner, 47, 81, 316
Kerper, 65, 241
Kesil, 219
Kesselman, 34
Kessler, 303, 316
Khaikis, 316
Khilo, 240
Khirik, 95
Khrushchev, 96
Khukis, 316
Kibes, 224
Kigel, 278, 279, 284, 302, 309, 316
Kiperman, 302
Kirschner, 39, 316
Kirshon, 6, 109, 112, 113, 127, 197, 198, 209, 303, 316
Kirzner, 302, 303
Kishka, 80
Kishkeh, 42
Kishkronik, 291, 303
Kiskiwitzer, 49, 167, 169, 215, 267, 269
Kitikisher, 120
Kiwes, 219
Klausner, 147, 250
Kleinman, 38, 86, 303, 316
Klemchik, 53, 316
Klim, 70, 71
Kloizner, 251
Kofets, 49, 55, 99, 111
Kofitz, 174
Koifman, 301, 316, 317
Kolchinsky, 300, 317
Kolton, 300
Kominasky, 8
Kook, 202
Kopitz, 45, 120, 300, 301, 317
Korczaczikh, 238
Korin, 118
Kornberg, 301, 302
Kornfeld, 317
Korolki, 81, 239
Kosakowski, 257
Kosciuszko, 208, 237
Kowel, 117

Kowner, 147, 252
Kozil, 317
Koziles, 314, 317
Kozminska, 4
Krafman, 45
Krashkash, 139
Krawchuk, 80
Kreimer, 317
Kremnezky, 317
Kreper, 47, 50, 83, 234
Krepman, 42, 44, 50
Kroler, 303, 304, 317
Krumer, 313
Krupdernik, 311
Krupnitzky, 72, 304, 317
Kugel, 317
Kuperwasser, 301
Kupferman, 317
Kupferwasser, 317
Kupka, 23
Kurchak, 120
Kusiles, 234
Kuzazker, 85, 86
Kuziel, 115, 119, 215
Kuziles, 113
Kuztseker, 72
Kwaitel, 10, 55, 127, 259, 280, 300, 317

L

Ladiniuk, 112, 118, 216
Laftin, 291
Lagenberg, 317
Lamsider, 291, 304
Landau, 54, 246, 317
Lander, 291, 317
Langberg, 291
Laniwitz, 5
Lashek, 50
Legsiuk, 99
Leibes, 83
Leibish, 174, 221
Leider, 219, 290, 291, 317, 318
Leiser, the Jewish shoemaker, 14
Leizer "The Greener", 164
Leizer der Griener, 224
Leizinder, 318

Lenin, 244, 247, 249
Lerner, 148, 291, 318
Lewinson, 145, 245, 251
Lewitsky, 240
Libergal, 99, 290, 318
Lilienblum, 147, 245
Linsky, 147
Lipe, 240
Lipekh, 219
Lipes, 99
Litwak, 218
Liverant, 240
Liwerant, 163
Liwne, 318
Lopatin, 290, 318
Lutsky, 47
Lutwack, 41, 51, 80
Lutzky, 47
Luzer, 215, 216

M

Mad, 318
Madd, 291, 292
Madwed, 292
Magid, 147
Maharshak, 132, 158, 221, 260, 292, 318
Mahler, 111
Mail, 95, 101, 318
Mailer, 318
Maimonides, 139, 140
Maiskovitz, 306, 309, 311
Mall, 293
Mamot, 64
Mani, 82
Manoses, 287
Mantuk, 47
Marczich, 217
Marder, 95, 100, 101, 102, 103, 104, 235, 295, 318
Mardeshicha, 176
Mardshikes, 318
Margaliot, 240
Margalis, 318
Margalit, 38, 45, 92, 131, 295, 318
Marinkowitz, 83
Marishkewitz, 276

Martin, 143
Marx, 95, 244, 248, 249
Mashiles, 24
Mates, 42, 235
Matwei, 208
Mazhoritz, 286, 294, 300
Mazor, 280
Mazowiecki, 262
Mazur, 318
Medwed, 318
Medwedew, 98
Mehlman, 47, 71, 318
Meil, 97, 235, 262, 263, 292
Meiler, 293, 294, 318
Meiliker, 293, 318
Meilman, 219
Melamed, 39, 49, 55, 73, 77, 80, 82, 84, 127, 179, 217, 224, 234, 236, 240, 294, 295, 318
Melenow, 56, 294, 318, 319
Mendel, the village headman, 16
Mendelson, 136, 139, 245
Mentach, 52
Meriniker, 18
Merinkowitz, 99
Merker, 14
Metusis, 43
Michel the blacksmith, 16, 38, 83, 95, 99
Michlis, 22, 99, 120, 165, 313
Miller, 30, 31, 55, 116, 119, 293, 294, 317, 319
Milman, 52, 235, 293, 319
Mintz, 294
Mirkovich, 147
Mirochnik, 198, 218, 222, 290, 291, 292, 294, 319
Mogilnick, 63
Moishehes, 13
Moldowan, 58
Molkho, 137
Mordche, 256
Mordechai, 216
Morwitz, 9
Moshlin, 292, 319

N

Nartowski, 257
Nashkas, 145
Nathan, 83
Natnes, 99
Nechtelman, 184
Nevukhim, 136, 139
Nicholas III, 23
Niger, 147, 250, 252
Nigeren, 246
Nisanow, 144
Nosson, 235, 239, 240, 259
Nudel, 295, 319
Nuskiss, 33

O

Ofeh, 273, 274
Ogurek, 215
Olishewsky, 175
Opatoshu, 147, 148, 248, 249, 250, 252
Opatowsky, 161
Orbuch, 106
Orlowitz, 9
Ozer, 19, 20, 49, 148, 159, 160, 296, 320

P

Pacht, 33, 66, 83, 97, 99, 298, 304, 319
Paltsil, 319
Pankiewicz, 226
Parnas, 44, 99, 240, 291, 299, 319
Partzi, 310
Partzis, 284
Pasalsky, 90
Pasmanik, 245
Pasternak, 299, 319
Paweli, 67
Pawlichki, 187
Pawlushe, 239
Pearlmutter, 299
Pepin, 247
Perchis, 18
Peretz, 122, 146, 147, 148, 172, 245, 246, 250, 251, 252, 289
Peter the Great, 174
Petrus, 95
Piłsudski, 56, 226
Pines, 40, 61
Pinsky, 146

Pinto, 62, 64
Pioterkowsky, 9
Plazel, 82, 95
Pletsele, 93
Pletsiles, 99
Pletzel, 298, 299
Plezlis, 83
Plotkin, 144
Polack, 296
Poliak, 219, 319
Pomerantz, 63
Poplowski, 267
Poplowsky, 167
Preminger, 112
Pressman, 300, 319
Pressman (Bilantzik), 300
Prilutzki, 244, 248
Primas, 238
Puterman, 297

R

Rabin, 1, 4, 23, 31, 33, 39, 47, 49, 52, 73, 74, 82, 120, 123, 129, 134, 151, 152, 153, 156, 158, 161, 162, 171, 174, 181, 184, 189, 190, 192, 203, 207, 211, 216, 240, 244, 257, 260, 261, 264, 306, 319
Rabinowitch, 23, 306, 319
Racheles, the tailor, 16
Rader, 306
Rakhtsis, 319
Ramanoff, 227
Ran, 189
Rapaport, 252
Rashish, 113
Re'uveni, 99
Rebizines, 30
Reichman, 22, 39, 80, 82, 93, 112, 219, 240, 308, 319
Reisin, 249, 252
Reizen, 147
Reznik, 99, 307, 308, 319
Riba, 216
Richter, 41, 42, 49, 67, 239
Riklis, 319
Rimer, 178, 179, 180
Rinkiwitzer, 311

Rishkowitz, 312
Rochtzis, 307
Rofeh, 218
Roich, 307
Roichman, 12, 18, 123, 184, 185, 193
Romanoff, 6
Rosenberg, 37, 42, 69, 70, 71, 100, 101, 118, 232, 306, 307, 319
Rosental, 6, 111, 113, 209, 307, 319
Roykh, 319
Rynkowiczer, 222

S

Sabaris, 67
Sakurnik, 310
Sambirer, 47, 296, 320
Sander, 55
Sandowitz, 296
Sankiewicz, 5
Schechter, 308
Scheinberg, 34
Schmukler, 300
Schneider, 40, 99, 100, 101, 104, 119, 309, 310, 320
Schneidman, 309
Schneur, 251
Schuster, 123
Schweiger, 144
Schweiz, 320
Segal, 47, 69, 72, 83, 98, 99, 100, 101, 235, 295, 296, 320
Selig, the tailor, 13
Seslavsky, 320
Sfarim, 24, 55, 111, 127, 147, 244
Shabtai Zvi, 136, 140, 208
Shabtchenko, 63
Shachnes, 53, 82
Shalom Aleichem, 121, 122, 146, 147, 148, 233, 245, 246, 248, 250, 251, 252
Shamash, 139
Shamoish, 203, 204, 308
Shamuch, 308, 309
Shandrowitzt, 320
Shapira, 111
Shatzugal, 310
Shchugel, 320

Shekhnis, 313
Sherer, 247
Shewtz, 97
Shiefer, 146
Shifman, 117
Shipper, 207
Shkornik, 320
Shmarak, 222
Shmiel, 55
Shmil, 89
Shmokh, 80, 81, 82, 90
Shmueles, 112, 179
Shmuelikhes, 320
Shmukler, 167, 266, 309, 320
Shne'our, 147
Shneideman, 320
Shneider, 12
Shpieler, 31, 38, 111, 121, 310
Shpiler, 129, 130, 131, 320
Shpirt, 159, 160, 320
Shpizman, 209
Shraga, 93, 322
Shrulis, 7
Shtepshagel, 152
Shulman, 145, 146, 147
Shumilow, 98
Shumsker, 15, 23, 320
Shuster, 81, 308, 320
Shwetz, 308
Shziagel, 223
Shzuleg, 99
Simcha, the tailor, 12
Simyonow, 98
Siret, 26
Skliarski, 249
Slutsky, 60
Sobol, 239
Solimersky, 8
Solomon, 82
Somolatski, 52
Somolitsky, 238
Sotsky, 39
Speizman, 6, 23, 39, 49, 148, 150, 193, 310, 320
Spektor, 246, 250, 252, 296, 320
Spiel, 139
Spinoza, 136, 140, 248

Spirt, 296
Spitzer, 32
Starick, 165, 166
Starosty, 218, 219, 220
Stasik, 218
Stein, 32, 191, 296, 297
Steinberg, 50, 308, 320
Stein-Kwaitel, 190
Stockman, 60, 61
Stoler, 296, 320
Strik, 296, 320
Sylvan, 1

T

Taberman, 287
Taitel, 63, 82, 84, 88, 236, 287
Tamari, 236
Tarlo, 288
Teicher, 53, 54
Teichman, 47, 50, 198, 199, 214, 221, 288
Tepper, 39, 167, 185, 216, 217, 223, 267, 288, 320
Terlo, 60, 63, 82, 320
Todt, 118
Tomzhik, 217
Trelo, 123
Trunk, 207
Twerman, 50, 320
Tzop, 220, 221
Tzoref, 300

U

Uzieles, 89

V

von Buelow, 174, 176

W

Wadas, 42
Wagner, 59
Walaizi, 193
Wall, 282
Warach, 106, 210, 224
Warchman, 285
Warman, 321

Warshawsky, 148, 252
Wartzman, 285
Warzman, 321
Washin, 282, 321
Wasilewskaya, 237
Wayziah, 320
Weesing, 321
Weiner, 38, 51, 89, 95, 132, 234, 236, 240, 283, 284, 285, 320, 321
Weinreich, 146
Weinshel, 155, 283
Weinstein, 237, 260, 283, 296, 321
Weirach, 264, 265, 270
Weisenberg, 250, 252
Weisman, 43, 189, 257, 258, 259
Weiss, 42, 44, 95, 98, 111, 283, 321
Weisser, 313
Weissing, 278, 283
Weitzman, 14, 42, 50, 177, 179, 180, 234, 284, 321
Weitzman-Folker, 111
Werkhman, 320
Wertheim, 151
Wiesman, 52, 71, 132, 222, 283, 321
Wietzman, 321
Wiger, 125
Winchewsky, 250, 251, 252
Wingerow, 247
Winshewsky, 147, 148
Witelstein, 50, 95, 282, 283, 321
Wittman, 65
Wodos, 240
Wohl, 111, 219, 321
Wolbesky, 8
Wolf, 277
Wolf Koifsitz, 32
Wolf-Koifsitz, 190
Wolowicki, 207
Woznikevich, 218

Y

Yalowicki, 4, 5, 8, 9, 207, 208
Yalowitcki, 207
Yankel the cantor, 20
Yasha the barber, 99
Yashchuk, 66
Yehuda Halevi, 137
Yekultiel, 63
Yeshiweye, 245
Yishpa, 19, 113, 187, 288, 321
Yishpa-Gilboa, 50
Yochevet, 152
Yokelson, 163

Z

Zabarer, a horse dealer, 20
Zabares, 99
Zaborsky, 223
Zafes, 45
Zak, 265, 266, 277, 287
Zaltzman, 286, 321
Zalznik, 285, 286
Zamoiski, 27, 226
Zap, 38
Zaslawski, 286, 287, 321
Zbarah, 139
Zeid, 285, 322
Zeidchis, 307
Zeiger, 285
Zeitlin, 250, 252
Zeitun, 147
Zelkes, 50
Zelner, 286, 322
Zhak, 99
Zheliannik, 322
Zhelznik, 322
Zinberg, 7, 8, 25, 26, 80, 133, 134, 135, 136, 137, 138, 139, 140, 141, 142, 143, 145, 146, 147, 148, 152, 180, 243, 244, 245, 246, 247, 248, 249, 250, 251, 252, 253
Zingel, 22, 108, 112, 113, 123, 195, 201
Zinz, 162
Zoberman, 61
Zuber, 99, 239, 240
Zuber, the *felsher* [country doctor], 239

www.ingramcontent.com/pod-product-compliance
Lightning Source LLC
Chambersburg PA
CBHW082004150426
42814CB00005BA/225